经典的回声·ECHO OF CLASSICS

长生殿
THE PALACE OF ETERNAL YOUTH

（清）洪昇 著

杨宪益　戴乃迭　译

By Hong Sheng
Translated by
Yang Xianyi and Gladys Yang

外文出版社
FOREIGN LANGUAGES PRESS

图书在版编目（CIP）数据

长生殿/（清）洪昇著；杨宪益，戴乃迭英译.
—北京：外文出版社，2001．8
（经典的回声）
ISBN 7-119-02888-X

I. 长… II.① 洪…② 杨…③ 戴… III. 英语—对照读物，
传奇剧（戏曲）—汉、英 IV. H319.4:I

中国版本图书馆 CIP 数据核字（2001）第 042717 号

外文出版社网址：
 http://www.flp.com.cn
外文出版社电子信箱：
 info@flp.com.cn
 sales@flp.com.cn

经典的回声（汉英对照）

长生殿

作　　者　（清）洪　昇
译　　者　杨宪益　戴乃迭
责任编辑　余冰清
封面设计　席恒青
印刷监制　蒋育勤
出版发行　外文出版社
社　　址　北京市百万庄大街 24 号　　　　邮政编码　100037
电　　话　（010）68320579（总编室）
　　　　　（010）68329514／68327211（推广发行部）
印　　刷　北京蓝空印刷厂
经　　销　新华书店／外文书店
开　　本　大 32 开　　　　　　　　字　　数　300 千字
印　　数　5001—8000 册　　　　　　印　　张　17
版　　次　2006 年 2 月第 1 版第 2 次印刷
装　　别　平装
书　　号　ISBN 7-119-02888-X／I·694
定　　价　18.00 元

版权所有　侵权必究

出 版 前 言

本社专事外文图书的编辑出版,几十年来用英文翻译出版了大量的中国文学作品和文化典籍,上自先秦,下迄现当代,力求全面而准确地反映中国文学及中国文化的基本面貌和灿烂成就。这些英译图书均取自相关领域著名的、权威的作品,英译则出自国内外译界名家。每本图书的编选、翻译过程均极其审慎严肃,精雕细琢,中文作品及相应的英译版本均堪称经典。

我们意识到,这些英译精品,不单有对外译介的意义,而且对国内英文学习者、爱好者及英译工作者,也是极有价值的读本。为此,我们对这些英译精品做了认真的遴选,编排成汉英对照的形式,陆续推出,以飨读者。

外文出版社

Publisher's Note

Foreign Languages Press is dedicated to the editing, translating and publishing of books in foreign languages. Over the past several decades it has published, in English, a great number of China's classics and records as well as literary works from the Qin down to modern times, in the aim to fully display the best part of the Chinese culture and its achievements. These books in the original are famous and authoritative in their respective fields, and their English translations are masterworks produced by notable translators both at home and abroad. Each book is carefully compiled and translated with minute precision. Consequently, the English versions as well as their Chinese originals may both be rated as classics.

It is generally considered that these English translations are not only significant for introducing China to the outside world but also useful reading materials for domestic English learners and translators. For this reason, we have carefully selected some of these books, and will publish them successively in Chinese-English bilingual form.

Foreign Languages Press

目　　录
CONTENTS

传概　　　　　　　　　　　　　　　　　　　2

第一出　　定情　　　　　　　　　　　　　　6

第二出　　贿权　　　　　　　　　　　　　　18

第三出　　春睡　　　　　　　　　　　　　　28

第四出　　禊游　　　　　　　　　　　　　　38

第五出　　傍讶　　　　　　　　　　　　　　52

第六出　　幸恩　　　　　　　　　　　　　　56

第七出　　献发　　　　　　　　　　　　　　64

第八出　　复召　　　　　　　　　　　　　　76

第九出　　疑谶　　　　　　　　　　　　　　88

第十出　　闻乐　　　　　　　　　　　　　　100

第十一出　制谱　　　　　　　　　　　　　　110

第十二出　权哄　　　　　　　　　　　　　　120

第十三出　偷曲　　　　　　　　　　　　　　128

第十四出　进果　　　　　　　　　　　　　　138

第十五出　舞盘　　　　　　　　　　　　　　150

第十六出　合围　　　　　　　　　　　　　　162

第十七出　夜怨　　　　　　　　　　　　　　170

Prologue   3

Scene 1   The Pledge   7

Scene 2   The Bribe   19

Scene 3   The Spring Siesta   29

Scene 4   The Spring Festival   39

Scene 5   The Mystery   53

Scene 6   The Sisters Gossip   57

Scene 7   A Lock of Hair   65

Scene 8   The Recall   77

Scene 9   The Writing on the Wall   89

Scene 10   Dream Music   101

Scene 11   Writing the Music   111

Scene 12   A Dispute Among the Mighty   121

Scene 13   Stealing the Music   129

Scene 14   The Lichee Fruit   139

Scene 15   The Disk Dance   151

Scene 16   The Hunt   163

Scene 17   A Night of Grief   171

第十八出　　絮阁　　　　　　　　　　　　　180

第十九出　　侦报　　　　　　　　　　　　　198

第二十出　　窥浴　　　　　　　　　　　　　206

第二十一出　密誓　　　　　　　　　　　　　216

第二十二出　陷关　　　　　　　　　　　　　230

第二十三出　惊变　　　　　　　　　　　　　234

第二十四出　埋玉　　　　　　　　　　　　　244

第二十五出　献饭　　　　　　　　　　　　　260

第二十六出　冥追　　　　　　　　　　　　　270

第二十七出　骂贼　　　　　　　　　　　　　282

第二十八出　闻铃　　　　　　　　　　　　　294

第二十九出　情悔　　　　　　　　　　　　　300

第三十出　　剿寇　　　　　　　　　　　　　308

第三十一出　哭像　　　　　　　　　　　　　314

第三十二出　神诉　　　　　　　　　　　　　328

第三十三出　刺逆　　　　　　　　　　　　　338

第三十四出　收京　　　　　　　　　　　　　348

第三十五出　看袜　　　　　　　　　　　　　358

第三十六出　尸解　　　　　　　　　　　　　366

Scene 18   A Visit to the Pavilion   181

Scene 19   The Report   199

Scene 20   The Bath   207

Scene 21   The Secret Vow   217

Scene 22   Storming the Pass   231

Scene 23   The Alarm   235

Scene 24   Death at the Post Station   245

Scene 25   The Gift of Food   261

Scene 26   The Spirit Follows   271

Scene 27   The Patriot and the Rebel   283

Scene 28   Hearing the Bells   295

Scene 29   Lady Yang's Spirit Repents   301

Scene 30   Suppressing the Rebellion   309

Scene 31   Mourning Before the Image   315

Scene 32   The God's Report   329

Scene 33   Assassination of the Rebel   339

Scene 34   Recovering the Capital   349

Scene 35   Lady Yang's Stocking   359

Scene 36   The Resurrection   367

第三十七出　弹词　382

第三十八出　私祭　402

第三十九出　仙忆　414

第四十出　见月　420

第四十一出　驿备　426

第四十二出　改葬　434

第四十三出　丛合　446

第四十四出　雨梦　454

第四十五出　觅魂　466

第四十六出　补恨　490

第四十七出　寄情　498

第四十八出　得信　506

第四十九出　重圆　514

Scene 37   The Rhapsody   383

Scene 38   Sacrifice at the Nunnery   403

Scene 39   A Fairy Visits   415

Scene 40   Looking at the Moon   421

Scene 41   Preparations at the Station   427

Scene 42   The Reburial   435

Scene 43   The Gods Pity the Lovers   447

Scene 44   A Rainy Night   455

Scene 45   The Search for Lady Yang's Spirit   467

Scene 46   Making Amends   491

Scene 47   A Message of Love   499

Scene 48   The Message Is Received   507

Scene 49   The Lovers' Reunion   515

长 生 殿

THE PALACE OF ETERNAL YOUTH

传概

【南吕引子】【满江红】(末上)今古情场，问谁个真心到底？但果有精诚不散，终成连理。万里何愁南共北，两心那论生和死。笑人间儿女怅缘悭，无情耳。感金石，回天地。昭白日，垂青史。看臣忠子孝，总由情至。先圣不曾删郑、卫，吾侪取义翻宫、徵。借太真外传谱新词，情而已。

【中吕慢词】【沁园春】天宝明皇，玉环妃子，宿缘正当。自华清赐浴，初承恩泽。长生乞巧，永订盟香。妙舞新成，清歌未了，鼙鼓喧闹起范阳。马嵬驿、六军不发，断送红妆。西川巡幸堪伤，奈地下人间两渺茫。幸游魂悔罪，已登仙籍。回銮改葬，只剩香

Prologue

Since ancient times how few lovers
Have really remained constant to the end;
But those who were true have come together at last,
Even though thousands of miles apart,
Even though torn from each other by death. And all
Who curse their unhappy fate are simply those
Lacking in love. True love moves heaven and earth,
Metal and stone, shines like the sun and lights
The pages of old histories: loyal subjects
And filial sons are all of them true lovers;
Even Confucius did not delete the love poems
When he compiled the Songs so we shall now
Take music and the tale of Lady Yang
To offer a new play in praise of love!

The Emperor Ming Huang and Lady Yang
Were destined to be lovers. She was granted
The honour of a bath in Huaqing pool,
Then prayed in the Palace of Eternal Youth
For happiness, and there they pledged to love
For ever. She composed a dance divine,
But scarcely had the music died away
When drums and bugles sounded an alarm,
And the imperial troops would go no further
Unless her life were forfeit. Westward then
The emperor fled—alas! the pity of it—
She in the world of ghosts, he still on earth;
But because she repented her sins she became an immortal,
And when men searched for her body nothing was found
But her fragrant pouch. The Weaving Maid in heaven

3

囊。证合天孙,情传羽客,钿盒金钗重寄
将。月宫会、霓裳遗事,流播词场。

　　唐明皇欢好霓裳燕,
　　杨贵妃魂断渔阳变。
　　鸿都客引会广寒宫,
　　织女星盟证长生殿。

Had witnessed their vow; the lady's love was conveyed
To the emperor through a necromancer who brought back
The golden hairpin and the jewel box
Given to pledge their love; and at last they met
In the palace of the moon. This is the story
Which handed down through ages has become
A favourite theme of poets.

第一出　定情

【大石引子】【东风第一枝】(生扮唐明皇引二内侍上)端冕中天，垂衣南面，山河一统皇唐。层霄雨露回春，深宫草木齐芳。升平早奏，韶华好，行乐何妨。愿此生终老温柔，白云不羡仙乡。

　　"韶华人禁闱，宫树发春晖。天喜时相合，人和事不违。九歌扬政要，六舞散朝衣。别赏阳台乐，前旬暮雨飞。"朕乃大唐天宝皇帝是也。起自潜邸，入缵皇图。任人不二，委姚、宋于朝堂；从谏如流，列张、韩于省闼。且喜塞外风清万里，民间粟贱三钱。真个太平致治，庶几贞观之年；刑措成风，不灭汉文之世。近来机务余闲，寄情声色。昨见宫女杨玉环，德性温和，丰姿秀丽。卜兹吉日，册为贵妃。已曾传旨，在华清池赐浴，命永新、念奴伏侍更衣。即着高力士引来朝见，想必就到也。

【玉楼春】(丑扮高力士，二宫女执扇，引旦扮杨

6

SCENE 1
The Pledge

(*The emperor enters with two eunuchs.*)
EMPEROR:

> *Since I became Tang emperor I have ruled*
> *This mighty realm, conferring royal favours*
> *Like the gentle rain in spring.*
> *Flowers in the palace are blooming and peace prevails,*
> *Then why should I not spend my days in pleasure?*
> *For then I need not envy*
> *The gods above the clouds.*
> *Now spring has come to the forbidden palace,*
> *And trees are blossoming in a season of joy;*
> *The affairs of men go well,*
> *And our good government has been celebrated*
> *By loyal subjects with music and with dance.*
> *But I mean to take my pleasure in women too,*
> *For I have found a lady fair as a goddess.*

I am the Tang emperor. Since coming to the throne I have appointed able ministers to govern my empire. All is quiet along the frontier, my people have had good harvests, and peace reigns throughout the world as in the Golden Age of old. I have spent my leisure lately enjoying music and women. I have noticed that one of the palace maids named Yang Yuhuan is gentle and beautiful, and choosing this auspicious day I am making her my concubine. I have ordered her to be given a bath in Huaqing Pool, and told the maids Yongxin and Niannu to wait on her. My eunuch Gao Lishi shoumd be bringing her here soon.

(*The eunuch* Gao *comes in with two maids holding fans, who are leading Lady Yang.*)

7

贵妃上）恩波自喜从天降，浴罢妆成趋彩
仗。（宫女）六宫未见一时愁，齐立金阶偷
眼望。

　　（到介，丑进见生跪介）奴婢高力士见驾。
册封贵妃杨氏，已到殿门候旨。（生）宣进
来。（丑出介）万岁爷有旨，宣贵妃杨娘娘
上殿。（旦进，拜介）臣妾贵妃杨玉环见驾，
愿吾皇万岁！（内侍）平身。（臣）臣妾寒门
陋质，充选掖庭，忽闻宠命之加，不胜陨越
之惧。（生）妃子世胄名家，德容兼备。取
供内职，深惬朕心。（旦）万岁。（丑）平身。
（旦起介，生）传旨排宴。（丑传介）（内奏乐。
旦送生酒，宫女送旦酒。生正坐，旦傍坐介）

【大石过曲】【念奴娇序】（生）寰区万里，遍
求窈窕，谁堪领袖嫔嫱？佳丽今朝、天付
与，端的绝世无双。思想，擅宠瑶宫，褒封
玉册，三千粉黛总甘让。（合）惟愿取恩情

LADY:

> *How happy I am at this stroke of fortune!*
> *I have bathed! and am joining the royal retinue.*

MAIDS:

> *The other neglected court ladies*
> *Are enviously watching her*
> *From the steps of the inner palace.*

(They walk forward, and the eunuch kneels before the emperor.)

GAO: Your slave Gao Lishi reports that the new imperial concubine, Lady Yang, is at the palace gate awaiting your pleasure, sire.

EMPEROR: Send her in.

GAO(*Turning back*): His Majesty orders Lady Yang to approach.

LADY(*Advancing and kneeling before the emperor*): Your slave Yang Yuhuan is here. Long live the emperor!

EUNUCH: You may rise.

LADY: Though poor and plain, I was fortunate enough to be chosen a palace maid; but I am afraid I can never prove worthy of this high honour.

EMPEROR: You come of an illustrious family, and are as beautiful as you are virtuous. I am happy to have you serving in the palace.

LADY (*Curtseying*): Long live the emperor!

GAO: You may rise.

(She gets up.)

EMPEROR: Let the feast begin.

(As Gao passes on the order, music is heard offstage. Lady Yang offers wine to the emperor, and the maids hand a goblet to her. The emperor takes his seat in the centre of the stage, and she sits beside him.)

EMPEROR:

> *I have searched my realm for lovely girls,*
> *But who is loveliest of them all?*
> *Today the gods have given me*
> *One truly matcbless; she shall be*
> *My favourite; with a lady's rank*
> *She shall outshine the rest.*

9

美满,地久天长。

【前腔】【换头】(旦)蒙奖。沉吟半晌,怕庸姿下体,不堪陪从椒房。受宠承恩,一霎里身判人间天上。须仿、冯婕当熊,班姬辞辇,永持彤管侍君傍。(合)惟愿取恩情美满,地久天长。

【前腔】【换头】(宫女)欢赏,借问从此宫中,阿谁第一?似赵家飞燕在昭阳,宠爱处,应是一身承当。休让,金屋装成,玉楼歌彻,千秋万岁捧霞觞。(合)惟愿取恩情美满,地久天长。

【前腔】【换头】(内侍)瞻仰,日绕龙鳞,云移雉尾,天颜有喜对新妆。频进酒,合殿春风飘香。堪赏,圆月摇金,余霞散绮,五云多处易昏黄。(合)惟愿取恩情美满,地久天长。

(丑)月上了。启万岁爷撤宴。(生)朕与妃子同步阶前,玩月一回。(内作乐,生携旦前立,众退后,齐立介)

ALL:

> *May love reign as long as the earth endures!*

LADY:

> *I am overwhelmed by your praise,*
> *For I cannot deserve such an honour.*
> *Raised to the skies by your sudden favour,*
> *I can only imitate good queens of old,*
> *Waiting faithfully on my lord,*
> *And serving humbly at his side.*

ALL:

> *May love reign as long! as the earth endures!*

MAIDS:

> *She will be the most happy from now on,*
> *Like the Lady Swallow of Han;*
> *All the emperor's love will be hers,*
> *In a chamber of gold to live,*
> *In a tower of jade to sing,*
> *For ever and ever to hand him a brimming goblet of wine.*

ALL:

> *May love reign as long as the earth endures!*

EUNUCHS:

> *The sun shines upon dragon scales carved on the pillars,*
> *And the pheasant feathers move like coloured clouds;*
> *The emperor smiles as he looks at his new lady;*
> *Cup after cup is drunk, the spring breeze blows,*
> *The full moon gleams like silver, evening clouds*
> *Make an embroidered tapestry, while night*
> *At this auspicious hour falls easily.*

ALL:

> *May love reign as long as the earth endures!*

GAO: May it please Your Majesty, the moon has risen.

> (*The table is cleared.*)

EMPEROR: I shall watch the moon from the courtyard with Lady Yang.

> (*Music is heard offstage, while the emperor leads* Lady Yang

11

【中吕过曲】【古轮台】(生)下金堂，笼灯就月细端相，庭花不及娇模样。轻偎低傍，这鬓影衣光，掩映出丰姿千状。(低笑，向旦介)此夕欢娱，风清月朗，笑他梦雨暗高唐。(旦)追游宴赏，幸从今得侍君王。瑶阶小立，春生天语，香萦仙仗，玉露冷沾裳。还凝望，重重金殿宿鸳鸯。

(生)掌灯往西宫去。(众应介，内侍、宫女各执灯引生、旦行介)(合)

【前腔】【换头】辉煌，簇拥银烛影千行。回看处珠箔斜开，银河微亮。复道、回廊，到处有香尘飘飏。夜色如何？月高仙掌。今宵占断好风光，红遮翠障，锦云中一对鸾凰。"琼花""玉树"，"春江夜月"，声声齐唱，月影过宫墙。褰罗幌，好扶残醉入兰房。

(丑)启万岁爷，到西宫了。(生)内侍

forward. The others remain in the background.)

EMPEROR:

> I leave the gilded hall
> To gaze at her more raptly under the moon.
> Even the flowers seem faded
> Compared with her hair, her dress,
> And her numberless charms. (*Laughs gently.*)
> So happy am I tonight,
> With the breeze and the brilliant moon,
> I no longer envy the king
> Who was loved by the nymph in his dreams.

LADY:

> How happy I am to be with the emperor,
> Following him in his pleasure and his feasts!
> I stand on the marble steps while he speaks so kindly,
> And fragrance floats from his train. My dress is moist
> With chilly dew, but still I stand here. Birds
> Are already nesting in the palace eaves.

EMPEROR: Attendants! Lanterns! Light the way to the west palace.
(*Gao Lishi shouts assent. The eunuchs and maids carry lanterns to light the way.*)

ALL:

> Now the blazing torches cast a thousand shadows,
> Past the screen inlaid with pearls gleams the Milky Way;
> Through corridors and terraces a perfumed breeze is blowing,
> And high above the great bronze statue rides the moon.
> Now is the night of all nights! The phoenix couple
> Under canopies crimson and green seem to float on clouds;
> Now every tree is jade, every flower is jasper;
> Every moment is the best of this clear spring night;
> As the bright moon sinks behind the palace wall,
> Let the silken curtain be lifted;
> And, intoxicated with love,
> Let them enter their orchid-sweet bower.

GAO: May it please Your Majesty, we have reached the west palace.

13

回避。(丑)春风开紫殿,(内侍)天乐下珠楼。(同下)

【余文】(生)花摇烛,月映窗,把良夜欢情细讲。(合)莫问他别院离宫玉漏长。

　　(宫女与生、旦更衣,暗下,生、旦坐介,生)银烛回光散绮罗,(旦)御香深处奉恩多。(生)六宫此夜含颦望,(合)明日争传"得宝歌"。(生)朕与妃子偕老之盟,今夕伊始。(袖出钗、盒介)特携得金钗、钿盒在此,与卿定情。

【越调近词】【绵搭絮】(生)这金钗、钿盒,百宝翠花钻。我紧护怀中,珍重奇擎有万般。今夜把这钗呵,与你助云盘,斜插双鸾;这盒呵,早晚深藏锦袖,密裹香纨。愿似他并翅交飞,牢扣同心结合欢。(付旦介,旦接钗、盒谢介)

EMPEROR: Attendants, leave us!

GAO:

> *A spring breeze has blown open the purple curtains.*

EUNUCHS:

> *And heavenly music flows from the pearl-decked pavilion.*

(Gao *and the other eunuchs retire.*)

EMPEROR:

> *Moonlight streams through the casement, and the shadows*
> *Of flowers flicker in the candlelight.*
>
> *A glorious night for love—let us forget*
>
> *How slow time drags in the other palaces.*

(*The maids bring fresh, informal clothes to the emperor and* Lady Yang, *then retire. The emperor and* Lady Yang *sit down.*)

EMPEROR:

> *The candles shed soft light on your silken garments.*

LADY:

> *I am greatly favoured by the royal scent.*

EMPEROR:

> *Tonight other beauties may frown,*

TOGETHER:

> *But tomorrow all will tell of the new found jewel.*

EMPEROR: This evening our love begins. (*Takes from his sleeve an ornamental pin for her hair and a jewel box.*) I have brought you this gold pin and this jewel box to pledge our love. Let us love each other as long as we live.

> *Studded with jewels, set with emeralds,*
> *These treasures were close to my heart.*
> *Tonight I give you this phoenix pin for your hair,*
> *And this box, wrapped in a fragrant scarf,*
> *To put in your silken sleeve.*
> *And may we two become*
> *Like the phoenixes on the pin, always flying together;*
> *Like the love-knot on the box—two hearts as one.*

15

【前腔】【换头】谢金钗钿盒赐予奉君欢。只恐寒姿，消不得天家雨露团。（作背看介）恰偷观，凤翥龙蟠，爱杀这双头旖旎，两扇团圞。惟愿取情似坚金，钗不单分盒永完。

（生）胧明春月照花枝，元稹

（旦）始是新承恩泽时。白居易

（生）长倚玉人心自醉，雍陶

（合）年年岁岁乐于斯。赵彦昭

(Gives them to Lady Yang, *who curtseys.)*

LADY:

    I thank Your Majesty for this royal gift,

    But fear my poor looks can make small return

    For such great kindness. (Looks at the gifts.)

    I steal a look at these carvings of dragon and phoenix;

    How I love these twin heads and the curved lids fastened
      together!

    May our love be as close and as firm,

    May the phoenixes never be parted;

    May the box never be divided!

                            (*Exeunt.*)

第二出　贿权

【正宫引子】【破阵子】(净扮安禄山箭衣、毡帽上)失意空悲头角,伤心更陷罗宜。异志十分难屈伏,悍气千寻怎蔽遮?权时宁耐些。

"腹垂过膝力千钧,足智多谋胆绝伦。谁道孽龙甘蟊屈,翻江搅海便惊人。"自家安禄山,营州柳城人也。俺母亲阿史德,求子轧荦山中,归家生俺,因名禄山。那时光满帐房,鸟兽尽都鸣窜。后随母改嫁安延偃,遂冒姓安氏。在节度使张守珪帐下投军。他道我生有异相,养为义子。授我讨击使之职,去征讨奚契丹。一时恃勇轻进,杀得大败逃回。幸得张节度宽恩不杀,解京请旨。昨日到京,吉凶未保。且喜有个结义兄弟,唤作张千,原是杨丞相府中干办。昨已买嘱解官,暂时松放。寻他通个关节,把礼物收去了。着我今日到彼候覆,不免前去走遭。(行介)唉,俺安禄山,也是个好汉,难道便这般结果了么?想起来好恨也!

18

SCENE 2
The Bribe

(*Enter* An Lushan *wearing a military costume and felt hat.*)
AN:

My luck has been bad, my ambition thwarted,
And now I have fallen into a trap.
But still I aspire as high as ever,
My soaring ambition will not be subdued;
Only I must be patient and bide my time.
Big is my belly and great my strength,
I have masterly tactics and boundless courage.
How long will a fiery dragon lie still?
When I stir up the ocean, then let people tremble!

I am An Lushan of Liucheng. My mother prayed to the Yaluoshan
Mountain to give her a son; so when I was born she called me
Lushan. At my birth our tent was flooded with light, and all beasts
and birds fled in terror. Then my mother married a second
husband, An Yanyan, and An became my surname. I enlisted under
Military Governor Zhang Shougui, who struck by my uncommon
appearance adopted me, appointed me a lieutenant and sent me to
fight the tribesmen. Boasting of my courage I advanced recklessly,
only to be badly defeated and forced to fly. Now Governor Zhang
has not had me executed, but has sent me to the capital for
punishment. I only arrived yesterday, and do not yet know my fate.
Fortunately I have a sworn brother named Zhang Qian who is a
steward in Prime Minister Yang's office. Having bribed the escort
to break my fetters, I have sought out my sworn brother and
through him sent presents to the prime minister. Now I am going to
learn the outcome. (*Walks round the stage.*)Can this be the end of
a brave fellow like me? Damnation!

I had intended, like the unruly dragon,

【正宫过曲】【锦缠道】莽龙蛇、本待将河翻海决，反做了失水瓮中鳖，恨樊笼霎时困了豪杰。早知道失军机要遭斧钺，倒不如丧沙场免受缧绁，蓦地裏脚双跌。全凭仗金投暮夜，把一身离阱穴。算有意天生吾也，不争待半路枉摧折。

来此已是相府门首，且待张兄弟出来。(丑扮张千上)"君王舅子三公位，宰相家人七品官。"(见介)安大哥来了。丞相爷已将礼物全收，着你进府相见。(净揖介)多谢兄弟周旋。(丑)丞相爷尚未出堂，且到班房少待。全凭内阁调元手，(净)救取边关失利人。(同下)

【仙吕引子】【鹊桥仙】(副净扮杨国忠引只从上)荣夸帝里，恩连戚畹，兄妹都承天眷。中书独坐揽朝权，看炙手威风赫烜。

"国政归吾掌握中，三台八座极尊崇。

To flood the dykes and wreak great devastation;
But, out of my element, a captured turtle,
Brave as I am, I'm trapped!
Had I known that defeat meant I must lose my head,
I would sooner have died in battle
Than suffer the indignity of chains!
Now let me proceed with haste!
Relying on bribes given at dead of night,
I hope to make good my escape.
Did not Heaven will my birth?
Why allow myself, then, to be killed in mid-career?

I see this is the prime minister's court, where I am to wait for Zhang.

(*Enter* Zhang Qian.)

ZHANG:

As the emperor's relative, Yang has become a duke;
And I as his steward am as good as a magistrate!

(*He greets* An.) So you have come. His Grace has accepted your gifts, and will give you an audience.

AN(*Bowing*): I must thank you for your help.

ZHANG: His Grace has not yet entered the court. Let us wait in my office.

AN:

It is all in the hands of the minister.
May he save the poor fellow defeated at the frontier!
(*Exeunt.*)

(*The prime minister,* Yang Guozhong, *enters with his retinue.*)

YANG:

Related by marriage to the imperial house,
My cousins and I are His Majesty's favourites;
As prime minister I have absolute power at court.
Let all beware! For whoever tries to encroach
On my blazing splendour faces sure disaster!
Now the government is mine to control,
My position is most exalted;

21

退朝日晏归私第，无数官僚拜下风"。下官杨国忠，乃西宫贵妃之兄也。官居右相，秩晋司空。分日月之光华，掌风雷之号令。（冷笑介）穷奢极欲，无非行乐及时；纳贿招权，真个回天有力。左右回避。（从应下）（副净）适才张千禀说，有个边将安禄山，为因临阵失机，解京正法。特献礼物到府，要求免死发落。我想胜败乃兵家常事，临阵偶然失利，情有可原。（笑介）就将他免死，也是为朝廷爱惜人才。已曾分付令他进见，再作道理。（丑暗上见介）张千禀事：安禄山在外伺候。（副净）着他进来。（丑）领钧旨。（虚下，引净青衣、小帽上，丑）这里来。（净膝行进见介）犯弁安禄山，叩见丞相爷。（副净）起来。（净）犯弁是应死囚徒，理当跪禀。（副净）你的来意，张千已讲过了。且把犯罪情由，细说一番。（净）丞相爷听禀：犯弁遵奉军令，去征讨奚契丹呵，（副净）起来讲。（净起介）

【仙吕过曲】【解三酲】恃勇锐冲锋出战，指征途所向无前。不提防番兵夜来围合转，临白刃，剩空拳。（副净）后来怎生得脱？

22

When I leave the court in the evening,
The officers and courtiers bow before me.

I am Yang Guozhong, a cousin of Lady Yang. As prime minister I share the sovereign's glory and control his thunderbolt. (*He laughs sardonically.*) I live a life of luxury, for I believe a man should enjoy himself while he can. I accept bribes, for I have the power to shape the decisions of the emperor. Attendants, leave me!

(*His retinue goes out.*)

A short time ago Zhang Qian reported to me that a frontier lieutenant, An Lushan, who lost his troops in battle, has been brought to the capital for court martial. But he has sent me presents, begging that his life be spared. I suppose there is always an element of luck in war, and to be defeated occasionally is excusable. (*Laughs.*) If I spare him, I shall be saving a useful officer for the state! I have already sent for him, and shall make up my mind when I see him.

(Zhang *enters*)

ZHANG: Your Grace, An Lushan is waiting outside.

YANG: Bring him in.

ZHANG: I will, Your Grace. (*He goes out, then leads in* An Lushan *who is now wearing a blue coat and cap.*) This way.

(An *advances on his knees.*)

AN: The wretched An Lushan salutes Your Grace.

YANG: Rise.

AN: I dare not, since I deserve to be sentenced to death.

YANG: Zhang Qian has reported to me your purpose in coming here. Give me your own account of your offence.

AN: Your Grace, I was ordered to attack the tribesmen....

YANG: Rise and speak.

(An *rises.*)

AN:

Relying on strength and boldness, I charged with my men,
And soon overran all the tribesmen who stood in our path.
But then I was careless. At night they surrounded our camp,
And we fought close quarters, pitting our naked hands

(净)那时犯弁杀条血路,奔出重围。单枪匹马身幸免,只指望鉴录微功折罪愆。谁想今日呵,当刑宪!(叩首介)望高抬贵手,曲赐矜怜。

【前腔】【换头】(副净起介)论失律丧师关钜典,我虽总朝纲敢擅专?况刑书已定难更变,恐无力可回天。(净跪哭介)丞相爷若肯救援,犯弁就得生了。(副净笑介)便道我言从计听微有权,这就里机关不易言。(净叩头介)全仗丞相爷做主!(副净)也罢。待我明日进朝,相机而行便了。乘其便,便好开罗撤网,保汝生全。

(净叩头介)蒙丞相爷大恩,容犯弁犬马图报。就此告辞。(副净)张千引他出去。(丑应,同净出介)"眼望捷旌旗,耳听好消息。"(同下)(副净想介)我想安禄山乃边方

Against the enemy's swords!

YANG: How did you escape?

AN: I fought my way out.

Fortunate to escape alone with my life,
On the strength of past services I hoped to be pardoned;
But now I find myself facing a court martial.

(*Kowtows.*)

Thus I have come to Your Grace, to beg for mercy!

(*The minister rises from his seat.*)

YANG:

To lose an army is a serious matter;
Though I have power at court, how can I show such leniency?
And I fear, when sentence has once been passed,
I have no authority to alter the verdict.

(*On his knees again, An sheds tears.*)

AN: Your Grace can save me!

YANG (*Laughs*): Even if I have a little influence, this is a difficult matter.

AN (*Kowtowing*): My life is in your hands!

YANG: Very well. Tomorrow when I go to court—

I shall see what can be done
To release you from the net,
And to save your life.

AN(*Kowtowing*): I owe Your Grace such gratitude that I can only repay you by serving as your horse or your dog.

Most humbly I take my leave!

YANG: Zhang Qian, show him out.

ZHANG:

Let us look for the messenger's flag,
And wait for good news.

(Zhang *leads* An *out.*)

YANG (*Reflectively*): This An Lushan is a junior officer at the frontier, who has never distinguished himself. If I try to save him, the emperor will suspect something. (*Laughs*) Ah, I have it! The other day Governor Zhang stated in his memorial to the throne that

25

末弁，从未著有劳绩。今日犯了死罪，我若
特地救他，必动圣上之疑。（笑介）哦，有
了。前日张节度疏内，曾说他通晓六番言
语，精熟诸般武艺，可当边将之任。我就授
意兵部，以此为辞，奏请圣上，召他御前试
验。于中乘机取旨，却不是好。

　　　　专权意气本豪雄，卢照邻
　　　　万态千端一瞬中。吴融
　　　　多积黄金买刑戮，李咸用
　　　　不妨私荐也成公。杜荀鹤

An's knowledge of barbarian languages and military skill qualified him for the post of a frontier general. I shall drop a hint to the War Ministry to propose to the emperor that An be summoned to court to be tested by His Majesty. That will give me the opening I need. Yes, that is it!

(*Exit.*)

第三出　春睡

【越调引子】【祝英台近】(旦引老旦扮永新、贴旦扮念奴上)梦回初,春透了,人倦懒梳裹。欲傍妆台,羞被粉脂涴。(老旦、贴旦)趁他迟日房栊,好风帘幕,且消受薰香闲坐。

永新、念奴叩头。(旦)起来。(海棠春)流莺窗外啼声巧,睡未足,把人惊觉。(老)翠被晓寒轻,(贴)宝篆沉烟袅。(旦)宿醒未醒宫娥报,(老、贴)道别院笙歌会早。(旦)试问海棠花,(合)昨夜开多少?(旦)奴家杨氏,弘农人也。父亲元琰,官为蜀中司户。早失怙恃,养在叔父之家。生有玉环在于左臂,上隐"太真"二字。因名玉环,小字太真。性格温柔,姿容艳丽。漫揩罗袂,泪滴红冰;薄试霞绡,汗流香玉。荷蒙圣眷,拔自宫嫔。位列贵妃,礼同皇后。有

SCENE 3
The Spring Siesta

(*Enter* Lady Yang *attended by her maids* Yongxin *and* Niannu.)

LADY:

> *Waking from sleep in early spring I feel*
> *Too tired to dress; before the glass I linger,*
> *Too weary to put on my rouge and powder.*

MAIDS:

> *While the warm sun shines on the eaves*
> *And a soft breeze moves the curtains,*
> *Why not sit awhile enjoying the spicy incense?*

(*Curtseying.*) Your slaves ask if Your Ladyship slept well?

LADY: Rise.

> *As orioles sing outside the window,*
> *I rouse myself reluctantly from sleep.*

YONGXIN:

> *The peacock bed is chilly in the morning cool,*

NIANNU:

> *Incense smoke rises from bronze incense burners;*

LADY:

> *And I wonder if the cherry trees*

TOGETHER:

> *Have blossomed during the night?*

LADY: I am Lady Yang, born in Hongnong District. My father Yang Yuanyan held a government post in Chengdu; but my parents died when I was young, and I was brought up in my uncle's house. I was born wearing a jade bracelet with the name Taizhen on it; so Yuhuan and Taizhen became my names. Gentle and beautiful I won favour with the emperor who raised me from the rank of a palace maid to that of an imperial concubine with all the prerogatives of a queen. My cousin Yang Guozhong is prime

兄国忠,拜为右相,三姊尽封夫人,一门荣宠极矣。昨宵侍寝西宫,(低介)未免云娇雨怯。今日晌午时分,才得起来。(老、贴)镜奁齐备,请娘娘理妆。(旦行介)绮疏晓日珠帘映,红粉春妆宝镜催。

【越调过曲】【祝英台】(坐对镜介)把鬓轻撩,鬟细整,临镜眼频睃。(老)请娘娘贴上这花钿。(旦)贴了翠钿,(贴)再点上这胭脂。(旦)注了红脂,(老)请娘娘画眉。(旦画眉介)着意再描双蛾。(旦立起介)延俄,慢支持杨柳腰身,(贴)呀,娘娘花儿也忘戴了。(代旦插花介)好添上樱桃花朵。(老、贴作看旦介)看了这粉容嫩,只怕风儿弹破。(老、贴)请娘娘更衣。(与旦更衣介)

【前腔】【换头】飘堕,麝兰香,金绣影,更了杏衫罗。(旦步介)(老、贴看介)你看小颤步

minister, and my three sisters have been made duchesses; so my whole family has been greatly honoured. Last night I was with the emperor in the west palace; today I feel a pleasant lassitude in my limbs, and have only just risen from my couch.

MAIDS: All is ready for Your Ladyship's toilet.

LADY:

> *The morning sunlight shines through the pearl-decked*
> *   curtain,*
> *And the bright mirror awaits me.*

(*Walks to the mirror.*)

> *As I comb and dress my hair,*
> *My eyes keep straying to the mirror.*

YONGXIN: Here is an emerald hairpin, my lady.

LADY:

> *Yes, I will put it on.*

NIANNU: And here is the rouge, my lady.

LADY:

> *The rouge is soon smoothed on!*

YONGXIN: Pencil your eyebrows, my lady.

LADY:

> *Two fine, arched eyebrows I trace with care,*

(*Rises.*)

> *Then linger here,*
> *Almost too weary to rise.*

NIANNU: Ah! You have forgotten this flower, my lady.

(*She pins on the flower for her.*)

> *Here I add some cherry blossom!*

(*The two maids look at* Lady Yang.)

> *Her skin is so smooth,*
> *One fears a breeze may harm it!*

MAIDS: Let us change your clothes, my lady. (*They help her into another dress.*)

> *What a perfume comes from her gold-embroidered dress,*
> *When the apricot-coloured silk is taken off!*

(Lady Yang *takes a few steps while her maids watch her.*)

31

摇,轻荡湘裙,(旦兜鞋介)低蹴半弯凌波,停妥。(旦顾影介)(老、贴)袅临风百种娇娆。(旦回身临镜介)(老、贴)还对镜千般婀娜。(旦作倦态,欠伸介)(老、贴扶介)娘娘,恁恹恹,何妨重就衾窝。

(旦)也罢,身子困倦,且自略睡片时。永新、念奴,与我放下帐儿。正是:"无端春色薰人困,才起梳头又欲眠。"(睡介)(老、贴放帐介)(老)万岁爷此时不进宫来,敢是到梅娘娘那边去么?(贴)姐姐,你还不知道,梅娘娘已迁置上阳楼东了!(老)哦,有这等事!(贴)永新姐姐,这几日万岁爷嵩爱杨娘娘,不时来往西宫,连内侍也不教随驾了。我与你须要小心伺候。

(生行上)

【前腔】【换头】欣可,后宫新得娇娃,一日几摩挲!(生作进,老、贴见介)万岁爷驾到。娘娘刚才睡哩。(生)不要惊他。(作揭帐介)试把绡帐慢开,龙脑微闻,一片美人香和。瞧科,爱他红玉一团,压着鸳衾侧卧。(老、

32

Her jewels quiver, and her skirts swirl softly.
(Lady Yang *puts on her slippers.*)
Her feet are light enough to walk on water.
(Lady Yang *looks down at herself.*)
Her grace is matchless in the gentle breeze.
(Lady Yang *looks in the mirror.*)
A thousand charms are mirrored in her glass.
(Lady Yang *yawns sleepily, and the maids support her.*)
Still tired? Why not sleep some more, my lady?

LADY: Yes, I will. I am still tired, and think I'll rest a little longer. Draw the bed curtains for me.
Spring is a drowsy time;
Just combing my hair has made me sleepy again.
(Lady Yang *sleeps, and the maids put down the curtains.*)

YONGXIN: Can the emperor have gone to see Lady Plum Blossom, that he hasn't yet come?

NIANNU: Don't you know? Lady Plum Blossom has moved to the east wing of Shangyang Pavilion.

YONGXIN: Surely not!

NIANNU: Yes, truly. The emperor is so devoted to Lady Yang that he spends all his time in the west palace. He doesn't even bring his attendants. We must wait on them well.
(Enter the emperor.)

EMPEROR:
I take such delight in my fair new mistress,
I caress her again and again every day.
(*As the emperor approaches, the maids curtsey to him.*)

MAIDS: Long live the emperor! Our lady has just gone to sleep.

EMPEROR: Don't wake her. (*He raises the curtains.*)
As I part the silken curtains,
The aroma of ambergris mingles
With a beautiful woman's warm fragrance.
(*He looks at her.*)
Like rose jade she is lying
On the cover embroidered with love birds.

贴背介)这温存,怎不占了风流高座!

【前腔】【换头】(旦作惊醒低介)谁个? 蓦然揭起鸳帏,星眼倦还授。(坐起,摩眼、撩鬓介)(生)早则浅淡粉容,消褪唇朱,掠削鬓儿欹妣。(老、贴作扶旦起,旦作开眼复闭,立起又坐倒介)(生)怜他,侍儿扶起腰肢,娇怯怯难存难坐。(老、贴扶旦坐介)(生扶住介)恁朦腾,且索消详停和。

(旦)万岁! (生)春昼晴和,正好及时游赏,为何当午睡眠? (旦低介)夜来承宠,雨露恩浓,不觉花枝力弱。强起梳头,却又朦胧睡去。因此失迎圣驾。(生笑介)这等说,倒是寡人唐突了。(旦娇羞不语介)(生)妃子,看你神思困倦,且同到前殿去,消遣片时。(旦)领旨。(生、旦同行,老、贴随行介)(生)"落日留王母,(旦)微风倚少儿。(老、贴合)宫中行乐秘,少有外人知。"(生、旦转坐介)(丑上)"昼漏稀闻高阁报,天颜有喜近

MAIDS (*Aside*):
> *With such gallantry it is no wonder*
> *That he has become the king of lovers.*

LADY: (*Waking, in a low voice*):
> *Who is it that so suddenly parts the curtains?*
> *My eyes are not yet open and, drowsy, I rub them.*

(*She sits up, rubbing her eyes and ruffling her hair.*)

EMPEROR:
> *The powder on her face is half rubbed off;*
> *Her rouge too is almost gone, and her hair's in disorder.*

(*The maids help her up. She opens her eyes, then closes them again as she sits down once more.*)

EMPEROR:
> *How moving it is to see her held up by her maids,*
> *So frail she seems neither able to stand nor sit.*

(*The maids support her as she sits, and the emperor assists them.*)

> *She is dreaming still, but presently she will awaken.*

LADY: Long live the emperor!

EMPEROR: On this sunny spring morning, it would be pleasant to stroll outside. Why do you sleep at noon?

LADY (*Speaking low*): Last night I was favoured by Your Majesty. You honoured me so much that today I am weary, and when I started to dress I fell asleep again. That is why I failed to welcome Your Maiesty just now.

EMPEROR (*Laughing*): So the fault is mine, is it?

(*Lady Yang blushes and remains silent.*)

EMPEROR: My love, you still look drowsy. Let us go to the front pavilion to pass a pleasant hour.

LADY: As Your Majesty wishes.

(*They walk forward, followed by the two maids. As they sit down, the eunuch Gao enters.*)

GAO:
> *The palace clepsydra announces the hour;*
> *And I, as a eunuch, know that our sovereign is happy.*

臣知。"启万岁爷：国舅杨丞相，遵旨试验安禄山，在宫门外回奏。(生)宣奏来。(丑宣介)杨丞相有宣。(副净上)"天下表章经院过，宫中笑语隔墙闻。"(拜见介)臣杨国忠见驾。愿吾皇万岁，娘娘千岁！(丑)平身。(副)臣启陛下：蒙委试验安禄山，果系人才壮健，弓马熟娴，特此覆旨。(生)朕昨见张守珪奏称："禄山通晓六番言语，精熟诸般武艺，可当边将之任。今失机当斩，是以委卿验之。既然所奏不诬，卿可传旨禄山，赦其前罪。明日早朝引见，授职在京，以观后效。(副)领旨。(下)(丑)启万岁爷：沉香亭牡丹盛开，请万岁爷同娘娘赏玩。(生)今日对妃子，赏名花。高力士，可宣翰林李白，到沉香亭上，立草新词供奉。(丑)领旨。(下)(生)妃子，和你赏花去来。

倚槛繁花带露开，　罗虬

(旦)相将游戏绕池台。　孟浩然

(生)新歌一曲令人艳，　万楚

(合)只待相如奉诏来。　李商隐

Long live the emperor! On Your Majesty's orders the prime minister has given An Lushan a test, and is now waiting outside the palace to make his report.

EMPEROR: Let him come in.

GAO: His Majesty orders the prime minister to approach.

(Prime Minister Yang *enters.*)

YANG:

> *All reports from the empire pass through my office,*
> *And close at hand, I hear all the palace gossip.*

(*He bows to the emperor.*)

YANG: Long live the emperor! Long live Lady Yang!

GAO: You may rise.

YANG: I have tested An Lushan, Your Majesty, and beg to report that I find him a stout fellow who is skilled in both archery and horsemanship.

EMPEROR: Yesterday General Zhang informed me that this An Lushan knew all the barbarian tongues and all the arts of war, and that he would make a good frontier general, but that he had been defeated in war and was to be court-martialed. That is why I sent you to test him. Since you find him an able man, you may tell him that his mistakes are pardoned, and order him to appear in court tomorrow morning. I shall appoint him to a post in the capital, and see how he conducts himself.

YANG: It shall be done, sire. (*He goes out.*)

GAO: The peonies are in full bloom, sire, at Aloes Pavilion. Would Your Majesty and Her Ladyship care to see them?

EMPEROR: Very good. With such a lady and such rare flowers, you must send Li Bai to the pavilion to compose a new poem for me.

GAO: I will send him at once, sire!

EMPEROR: My love, let us go to see the flowers.

(***Exeunt.***)

第四出　禊游

【双调引子】【贺圣朝】(丑上)崇班内殿称尊,天颜亲奉朝昏。金貂玉带蟒袍新,出入荷殊恩。

咱家高力士是也,官拜骠骑将军。职掌六宫之中,权压百僚之上。迎机导窾,摸揣圣情;曲意小心,荷承天宠。今乃三月三日,万岁爷与贵妃娘娘游幸曲江,命咱召杨丞相并秦、韩、虢三国夫人,一同随驾。不免前去传旨与他。"传声报戚里,今日幸长杨。"(下)

【前腔】(净冠带引从上)一从请托权门,天家雨露重新。累臣今喜作亲臣,壮怀会当伸。

俺安禄山,自蒙圣恩复官之后,十分宠眷。所喜俺生的一个大肚皮,直垂过膝。一日圣上见了,笑问此中何有?俺就对说,惟有一片赤心。天颜大喜,自此愈加

SCENE 4
The Spring Festival

(*The eunuch* Gao *enters.*)
GAO:

> *Exalted in the inner court among the courtiers,*
> *I wait upon the emperor day and night;*
> *In gold and sables, jade and embroidered robes,*
> *In and out of the palace I am specially favoured.*

I, Gao Lishi, General of the Imperial Cavalry, comtrol all the inner palaces and enjoy greater power than any minister. I seize every opportunity to please the emperor and anticipate his wishes, and thanks to my discretion and eagerness to please I have become a great favourite.

Today is the third day of the third moon and the emperor, who is going to visit the River Bend with Lady Yang, has ordered me to instruct the prime minister and the three duchesses to accompany them. I am going now to carry out my instructions.

> *I go to inform all the lady's relatives*
> *That His Majesty requires their presence today.* (*Exit.*)

(*Enter* An Lushan *in official dress, accompanied by attendants.*)
AN:

> *Since I paid court to a powerful minister*
> *I am reinstated in the emperor's favour.*
> *Once a prisoner, I am now a favourite;*
> *It is time that I began to pursue my ambitions.*

Since I regained office through the mercy of the emperor, I have been held in great favour. It is lucky that I was born with such a big belly, reaching nearly to my knees. His Majesty asked me, laughing, what was in it; and I answered "Only my loyal heart!" The emperor was pleased with my reply; and since then he has become fonder of me and more convinced of my loyalty,

39

亲信，许俺不日封王。岂不是非常之遇！左右回避。（从应下）（净）今乃三月三日，皇上与贵妃游幸曲江，三国夫人随驾。倾城士女，无不往观。俺不免换了便服，单骑前往，游玩一番。（作更衣、上马行介）出得门来，你看香尘满路，车马如云，好不热闹也。正是："当路游丝萦醉客，隔花啼鸟唤行人。"（下）（副净、外扮王孙，末扮公子；各丽服，同行上）（合）

【仙吕入双调】【夜行船序】春色撩人，爱花风如扇，柳烟成阵。行过处，辨不出紫陌红尘。（见介）请了。（副净外）今日修禊之辰，我每同往曲江游玩。（末、小生）便是，那边簇拥着一队车儿，敢是三国夫人来了。我每快些前去。（行介）纷纭，绣幕雕轩，珠绕翠围，争妍夺俊。氤氲，兰麝逐风来，衣彩佩光遥认。

　　（同下）（老旦绣衣扮韩国，贴白衣扮虢国，杂绯衣扮秦国，引院子、梅香各乘车行上）（合）

【前腔】【换头】安顿，罗绮如云，斗妖娆，各

40

promising me that soon I shall be made a prince. This is unlooked-for fortune! Attendants! Leave me!

(*His attendants go out.*)

Today is the spring festival, when the emperor and Lady Yang are visiting the River Bend and the three duchesses will be following in their train. All the citizens of the capital are going to watch; and I mean to change into civilian dress and ride there alone to enjoy the spectacle. (*He changes his dress and mounts his horse.*) Now I have passed the city gate. See! Even the roadside dust smells sweet! The carriages and horses like fleeting clouds make a brave show!

The catkins on the road bewilder the drunkards,
And birds call out from the flowers to the passers-by.
　　(*Exit.*)

(*Enter two young lords, magnificently dressed.*)

TOGETHER:

Spring is enchanting! Its blossoms and willows
Shade the dusty road as we pass.

(*They greet each other.*)

FIRST LORD: It is the spring festival today. Shall we go to the River Bend to see the sights?

SECOND LORD: Yes, let's go. Look at that procession of carriages! The three duchesses must be there. Let's hurry over to have a look.

TOGETHER (*Walking*):

In splendid carriages with embroidered curtains,
Blazing with jewels, each outshines the other.
The breeze is sweet with scent of musk and orchids;
Their gems and brilliant gowns make a brave display!
　　(*Exeunt.*)

(*The* Duchess of Han, *the* Duchess of Guo *and the* Duchess of Qin *enter, each in a carriage, accompanied by an attendant and the maid* Meixiang.)

TOGETHER:

Our silken gowns are bright as clouds,

41

逞黛娥蝉鬓。蒙天宠,特敕共探江春。(老旦)奴家韩国夫人,(贴)奴家虢国夫人,(杂)奴家秦国夫人,(合)奉旨召游曲江。院子把车儿趱行前去。(院)晓得(行介)(合)朱轮,碾破芳堤,遗珥坠簪,落花相衬。荣分,戚里从宸游,几队宫妆前进。(同下)

【黑蟆序】【换头】(净策马上,目视三国下介)妙啊,回瞬,绝代丰神,猛令咱一见,半晌销魂。恨车中马上,杳难亲近。俺安禄山,前往曲江,恰好遇着三国夫人,一个个天姿国色。唉,唐天子,唐天子!你有了一位贵妃,又添上这几个阿姨,好不风流也!评论,群花归一人,方知天子尊。且赶上前去,饱看一回。望前尘,馋眼迷奚,不免挥策频频。

(作鞭马前奔,杂扮从人上,拦介)咄,丞相爷在此,什么人这等乱撞!(副净骑马上)为

42

We vie with each other in beauty,
With painted graceful eyebrows
And hair like cicada's wing.
It has pleased the emperor that we should come
To enjoy the spring by the river.

HAN: I am the Duchess of Han.

GUO; I am the Duchess of Guo.

QIN: I am the Duchess of Qin.

TOGETHER: By the emperor's command we are summoned to visit the River Bend together. Attendant! Drive on!

ATTENDANT: As you say, my ladies.

(The carriages move forward.)

TOGETHER:

Red wheels crush the flower-strewn turf,
Trinkets are dropped among fallen petals.
We are honoured to ride in the emperor's train,
And sweep forward in robes of state. (Exeunt.)

(An Lushan rides up and gazes after the duchesses.)

AN: Ah, what beauty!

As they glance back their unmatched loveliness
Leaves me dumbfounded. How I long to gallop
Up to their carriages for a closer view!

On the road to the River Bend I have caught a glimpse of the three duchesses, each of them a peerless beauty. Ah, Son of Heaven, emperor of Tang! You have not only Lady Yang, but her sisters too! You are the most fortunate of men!

All the flowers of the court are his alone—
Is it not grand to be an emperor!
Let me spur on, to feast my eyes on them.
Greedily scanning the carriages ahead,
I whip my horse to gallop on.

(He whips his horse and gallops forward; but attendants bar his way.)

ATTENDANTS: Halt, there! The prime minister is here. Who dares try to charge past?

43

何喧嚷？（净、副净作打照面,净回马急下）（从）小的方才见一人,骑马乱撞过来,向前拦阻。（副净笑介）那去的是安禄山。怎么见了下官,就疾忙躲避了。（作沉吟介）三位夫人的车儿在那里？（从）就在前面。（副净）呀,安禄山那厮怎敢这般无礼!

【前腔】【换头】堪恨,藐视皇亲,傍香车行处,无礼厮混。陡冲冲怒起,心下难忍。叫左右,紧紧跟随着车儿行走,把闲人打开。（众应行介）（副净）忙奔,把金鞭辟路尘,将雕鞍逐画轮。（合）语行人,慎莫来前,怕惹丞相生嗔。（同下）

【锦衣香】（净扮村妇,丑扮丑女,老旦扮卖花娘子,小生扮舍人,行上）（合）妆扮新,添淹润；身段村,乔丰韵,更堪怜芳草沾裾,野花堆髻。（见介）（净）列位都是去游曲江的么？（众）正是。今日皇帝、娘娘,都在那里,我每同去看一看。（丑）听得皇帝把娘娘爱的似宝贝一般,不知比奴家容貌如何？（老旦

(*The prime minister rides in.*)

YANG: What is all this commotion?

(*The prime minister and* An Lushan *look at each other; then* An Lushan *turns hastily and makes off.*)

ATTENDANTS: Just now we saw this man galloping wildly forward, so we stopped him.

YANG (*Laughs*): It is only that fellow An Lushan. But why did he run away from me like that? (*Thinks.*) Where are the carriages of the three ladies?

ATTENDANTS: Just in front.

YANG: So? How dare he, the scoundrel!

How dare he show such contempt for the emperor
As to ride by the duchesses' carriages!
I cannot contain my rage at his presumption!

Attendants! Escort the carriages closely, and drive away all passers-by.

(*The attendants assent.*)

Go forward! Clear the road with your gilded whips,
Your proud mounts following the painted carriages.

ATTENDANTS:

Let passers-by beware! Let none come near,
Lest you offend His Grace the prime minister! (*Exeunt.*)

(*Enter a countrywoman, a plain girl, a flower-girl and a country gentleman.*)

ALL:

In new clothes we, with our country manners,
Imitate the elegant.
Grass clings to our garments,
And we heap petals on our hair.

(*They greet each other.*)

COUNTRYWOMAN: Are all of you going to the River Bend?

THE REST: Yes. Today the emperor and Lady Yang are there. We are going to see royalty.

PLAIN GIRL: They say the emperor dotes on Lady Yang as if she were a jewel. I wonder how her looks compare with mine?

笑介)（小生作看丑介）（丑）你怎么只管看我？
（小生）我看大姐的脸上，倒有几件宝贝。
（净）什么宝贝？（小生）你看眼嵌猫睛石，
额雕玛瑙纹，蜜蜡装牙齿，珊瑚镶嘴唇。
（净笑介）（丑将扇打小生介）小油嘴，偏你没
有宝贝。（小生）你说来。（丑）你后庭像银
矿，掘过几多人！（净笑介）休得取笑。闻
得三国夫人的车儿过去，一路上有东西遗
下，我每赶上寻看。（丑）如此快走。（行
介）（丑作娇态与小生诨介）（合）和风徐起荡晴
云，钿车一过，草木皆春。（小生）且在这草
里寻一寻，可有什么？（老旦）我先去了。
向朱门绣阁，卖花声叫的殷勤。（叫卖花下）
（众作寻、各拾介）（丑问净介）你拾的什么？
（净）是一枝簪子。（丑看介）是金的，上面一
粒绯红的宝石。好造化！（净问丑介）你呢？
（丑）一只凤鞋套儿。（净）好好，你就穿了
何如？（丑作伸脚比介）啐，一个脚指头也着
不下。鞋尖上这粒真珠，摘下来罢。（作摘
珠、丢鞋介）（小生）待我袖了去。（丑）你倒会

(*The flower-girl laughs, and the country gentleman looks the plain girl over.*)

PLAIN GIRL: Why do you look at me like that?

COUNTRY GENTLEMAN: Your face has its share of jewels too.

COUNTRYWOMAN: What jewels?

COUNTRY GENTLEMAN: Your eyes are cat's eye stone, her forehead has the agate's lines, her teeth are amber and her lips pink coral.

(*The countrywoman laughs, and the plain girl beats the country gentleman with her fan.*)

COUNTRYWOMAN: Enough of that. I've heard that whenever the three duchesses pass, all sorts of things are dropped on the road. Let's see what we can find.

PLAIN GIRL: Let's hurry.

(*They walk on, the plain girl teasing the country gentleman.*)

ALL:
In the gentle breeze bright clouds float past;
As the carriage goes by, spring comes to the woods.

COUNTRY GENTLEMAN: Let us see if we can find anything in the grass here.

FLOWER-GIRL: I will leave you now.
I shall call at the rich men's gates
To sell my flowers.

(*She goes out, crying "Flowers to sell!" The others search in the grass, and each picks something up.*)

PLAIN GIRL (*To the countrywoman*): What have you got there?

COUNTRYWOMAN: A hairpin.

PLAIN GIRL (*Examining it*): It's made of gold, with a ruby on it. What luck!

COUNTRYWOMAN: And what have you?

PLAIN GIRL: An embroidered slipper.

COUNTRYWOMAN: Well, put it on.

PLAIN GIRL (*Trying it*): Confound it! I can't even get my toe in. I'll keep the pearl on it though.

(*Taking off the pearl, she throws the slipper on the ground.*)

作揽收拾！你拾的东西，也拿出来瞧瞧。
（小生）一幅鲛绡帕儿，裹着个金盒子。（净
接作开看介）咦，黑黑的黄黄的薄片儿，闻着
又有些香，莫不是耍药么？（小生笑介）是香
茶。（丑）待我尝一尝。（净争吃，各吐介）呸，
稀苦的，吃他怎么！（小生作收介）罢了，大
家再往前去。（行介）（合）蜂蝶闲相趁，柳
迎花引，望龙楼倒泻，曲江将近。

　　（小生、净先下，丑吊场叫介）你们等我一
等。阿呀，尿急了，且在这里打个沙窝儿
去。（下）（老旦、贴、杂引院子、梅香行上）
【浆水令】扑衣香，花香乱熏；杂莺声，笑声
细闻。看杨花雪落覆白蘋，双双青鸟，衔堕
红巾。春光好，过二分，迟迟丽日催车进。
（院）禀夫人，到曲江了。（老旦）丞相爷在
那里？（院）万岁爷在望春宫，丞相爷先到
那边去了。（老旦、杂、贴作下车介）你看果然
好风景也！环曲岸，环曲岸，红酣绿匀。临

COUNTRY GENTLEMN: I'll have that.

PLAIN GIRL: You would. Show me what you've got.

COUNTRY GENTLEMAN: A gold box wrapped in a silk handkerchief.

COUNTRYWOMAN (*Taking the box and opening it*): Oh, here is something brown, in thin slices with rather a sweet smell—could it be some love potion?

COUNTRY GENTLEMAN (*Laughs*): No, this is scented tea.

PLAIN GIRL: Let me try it. (*She and the countrywoman taste some, but spit it out.*) Pah! It's bitter! How can people eat this?

COUNTRY GENTLEMAN (*Taking back the box*): All right. Let's go on.

(*They walk on.*)

ALL:
> Butterflies and bees are busy flying
> In and out of the willow trees and the flowers.
> The River Bend and Dragon Tower are near!

(*The countrywoman and country gentleman walk off.*)

PLAIN GIRL: Wait for me! (*Exit.*)

(*Enter the three duchesses with their attendant and maid.*)

DUCHESSES:
> Mingled with our perfume is the flowers' fragrance,
> Interspersed with orioles' cries laughter can be heard.
> Willow seeds are drifting like snow across the duckweed;
> And mating birds in couples come to carry off red petals,
> This is the height of spring; through the long sunny day
> We are driving ahead.

ATTENDANT: May it please Your Ladyships, we have arrived at the River Bend.

HAN: Where is the prime minister?

ATTENDANT; His Grace has gone to Wangchun Palace, where His Majesty is now.

(*The duchesses alight from the carriages.*)

DUCHESSES: It is really beautiful here.
> At the River Bend, at the River Bend,

曲水,临曲水,柳细蒲新。

(丑引小内侍、控马上)"敕传玉勒桃花马,骑坐金泥蛱蝶裙。"(见介)皇上口敕:韩、秦二国夫人,赐宴别殿。虢国夫人,即命乘马入宫,陪杨娘娘饮宴。(老旦、杂、贴跪介)万岁!(起介)(丑向贴介)就请夫人上马。(贴)

【尾声】内家官,催何紧。姐姐妹妹,偏背了春风独近。(老旦、杂)不枉你淡扫蛾眉朝至尊。

(贴乘马,丑引下)(杂)你看裴家姐姐,竟自扬鞭去了。(老旦)且自由他。(梅香)请夫人别殿里上宴。

红桃碧柳禊堂春, 沈佺期
(老旦)一种佳游事也均。张谔
(杂)愿奉圣情欢不极,武平一
(合)向风偏笑艳阳人。杜牧

> *Red blooms are flushed as with wine amid lush green*
> *   leaves.*
> *By the water's edge, by the water's edge,*
> *Are slender willow tendrils and sweet young flags.*

(*The eunuch* Gao *rides up with an attendant.*)

GAO:

> *I seek the lady in butterfly-patterned skirt,*
> *To ask her to ride on a horse with a fine jade bit.*

(*Greets them.*) By His Majesty's orders, the Duchess of Han and the Duchess of Qin will be feasted in the second pavilion, while the Duchess of Guo is to ride to Wangchun Palace to feast with Lady Yang.

DUCHESSES (*Kneeling*): Long live the emperor! (*They rise.*)

GAO (*To the* Duchess of Guo): Will you be mounted, my lady?

GUO:

> *The palace officer urges me to hasten;*
> *And I am singled out from both my sisters*
> *To enjoy this favour alone!*

HAN and QIN:

> *It is thanks to your natural charm,*
> *For you can appear before the emperor*
> *With your face unpainted.*

(*The* Duchess of Guo *rides off, preceded by* Gao.)

QIN: See how she flicks her whip as she rides off!

HAN: Let her go.

ATTENDANT: Will you come to the pavilion for the feast, my ladies?

(*Exeunt.*)

第五出　傍讶

【中吕过曲】【缕缕金】(丑上)欢游罢,驾归来。西宫因个甚,恼君怀? 敢为春筵畔,风流尴尬。怎一场乐事陡成乖? 教人好疑怪,教人好疑怪。

前日万岁爷同杨娘娘游幸曲江,欢天喜地。不想昨日娘娘忽然先自回宫,万岁爷今日才回,圣情十分不悦。未知何故? 远远望见永新姐来了,咱试问他。(老旦上)

【前腔】宫帏事,费安排。云翻和雨覆,蓦地闹阳台。(丑见介)永新姐,来得恰好。我问你,万岁爷为何不到杨娘娘宫中去?(老)唉,公公,你还不知么! 两下参商后,装幺作态。(丑)为着甚来?(老)只为并头莲傍有一枝开。(丑)是那一枝呢?(老笑介)公公,你聪明人自参解,聪明人自参解。

(丑笑介)咱那里得知! 永新姐,你可

SCENE 5
The Mystery

(Gao *enters.*)

GAO:

> *His Majesty has come back from his pleasure trip;*
> *But how can Lady Yang have offended him?*
> *What can have happened that day at the spring feast?*
> *And how can a pleasure trip have caused displeasure?*
> *This is strange, very strange.*

The day before yesterday the emperor went with Lady Yang to the River Bend and they were perfectly happy; but yesterday Lady Yang came back alone, while His Majesty only returned today, looking very angry, I wonder what the reason is? Here comes Yongxin. I will ask her.

(*Enter* Yongxin.)

YONGXIN:

> *All's out of joint in the inner palace;*
> *A storm has blown up—the lovers have quarrelled!*

GAO (*Greets her*): You have come just at the right time.
I want to ask you why His Majesty has stopped going to Lady Yang's chamber.

YONGXIN: Ah, don't you know?

> *After their quarrel neither will give way.*

GAO: What did they quarrel about?

YONGXIN

> *It was all because of a fair rival!*

GAO: Who do you mean?

YONGXIN:

> *You are clever enough to guess!*

GAO (*Laughs*): How should I know? Tell me.

说与我听。(老)若说此事,原是我娘娘自己惹下的。(丑)为何?(老)只为娘娘把那虢国夫人呵,

【剔银灯】常则向君前喝采,妆梳淡,天然无赛。那日在望春宫,教万岁召他侍宴。三杯之后,便暗中筑座连环寨,哄结上同心罗带。(丑拍手笑介)阿呀,咱也疑心有此。却为何烦恼哩?(老)后来娘娘恐怕夺了恩宠,因此上嫌猜。恩情顿乖,热打对鸳鸯散开。

　　(丑)原来虢国夫人,在望春宫有了言语,才回去的。(老)便是。那虢国夫人去时,我娘娘不曾留得。万岁爷好生不快,今日竟不进西宫去了。娘娘在那里只是哭哩。(丑)咱想杨娘娘呵,

【前腔】娇痴性,天生忒利害。前时逼得个梅娘娘,直迁置楼东无奈。如今这虢国夫人,是自家的妹子,须知道连枝同气情非外,怎这点儿也难分爱。(老)这且休提。只是往常,万岁爷与娘娘行坐不离,如今两下不相见面,怎生是好?(丑)吾侪,如何布摆,且和你从旁看来。

(内)有旨宣高公公。(丑)来了。

　　狎宴临春日正迟,韩偓
　(老旦)宠深还恐宠先衰。罗虬
　　(丑)外头笑语中猜忌,陆龟蒙
　(老旦)若问傍人那得知! 崔颢

YONGXIN: Well, it was Lady Yang who started the trouble.

GAO: How?

YONGXIN:

> *She was always praising the Duchess of Guo to His Majesty,*
> *Saying how simply she dresses*
> *And claiming that no one can equal*
> *Her artless beauty!*

That day in Wangchun Palace she asked the emperor to send for the duchess. Then after cups of wine

> *She drew the emperor and her sister together,*
> *Ane tied them in a love-knot.*

GAO (*Claps his hands and laughs*): I suspected as much! But then why should she be angry?

YONGXIN: Then she was afraid that the duchess might take her place in the emperor's affections.

> *She intervened,*
> *And the love birds were estranged.*

GAO: Then, I suppose, the duchess was offended and left?

YONGXIN: Yes. When the duchess took her leave, Lady Yang did not press her to stay, and the emperor was very angry. He has not been near her today, and my lady is crying bitterly.

GAO: I think that Lady Yang carries matters too far. The other day she insisted that Lady Plum Bloossom move to the east pavilion; and this duchess, after all, is her own sister.

> *They are like two branches of one tree;*
> *Then why refuse to share the emperor's love?*

YONGXIN: Never mind that. In the past the emperor never left Lady Yang's side, but now he is staying away from her. What can we do?

GAO:

> *What can we do? Why, I and you*
> *Can only watch from the side.*

(*A voice offstage summons* Gao.) Coming!

(***Exeunt.***)

第六出　幸恩

【商调引子】【绕池游】(贴上)瑶池陪从,何意承新宠!怪青鸾把人和哄。寻思万种,这其间无端噘动,奈谣诼蛾眉未容。

"玉燕轻盈弄雪辉,杏梁偷宿影双依。赵家姊妹多相妒,莫向昭阳殿里飞。"奴家杨氏,幼适裴门。琴断朱弦,不幸文君早寡;香含青琐,肯容韩掾轻偷?以妹玉环之宠,叨膺虢国之封。虽居富贵,不爱铅华。敢夸绝世佳人,自许朝天素面。不想前日驾幸曲江,敕陪游赏。诸姊妹俱赐宴于外,独召奴家,到望春宫侍宴。遂蒙天眷,勉尔承恩。圣意虽浓,人言可畏。昨日要奴同进大内,再四辞归。仔细想来,好傥幸人也。

【商调过曲】【字字锦】恩从天上浓,缘向生前种。金笼花下开,巧赚娟娟凤。烛花红,只见弄盏传杯。传杯处,蓦自里话儿唧哝。匆匆,不容宛转,把人央入帐中。思量帐中,帐中欢如梦。绸缪处,两心同。绸缪

56

SCENE 6
The Sisters Gossip

(*Enter the* Duchess of Guo.)
GUO:

> *Serving the emperor in his pleasure palace,*
> *I won his favour; but too soon my hopes*
> *Were dashed, and now ten thousand doubts beset me;*
> *For my jealous sister has slandered me,*
> *And will tolerate no rival.*
> *A snow-white swallow flies to her love in the beams;*
> *But my sister is jealous; I may not enter the palace.*

I am a daughter of Yang who married into the Pei family; but my husband died early. My sister used her influence to have me made Duchess of Guo; but in spite of my high rank I care nothing for finery, and confident in my natural beauty I dare go into the emperor's presence without powdering my face. When His Majesty visited the River Bend the other day, we were told to follow in his train; but while my two sisters were feasted in the pavilion outside, I was summoned into the palace to attend the emperor. Then I won his favour, and was made to stay. But though the emperor is very fond of me, I am afraid slanderers may speak against me; so yesterday when His Majesty asked me to accompany him to the palace, I declined persistently and came back. Still, I am a fortunate woman!

> *This was a heaven-sent favour!*
> *Surely Fate had destined us to love.*
> *I was trapped like a phoenix in a golden cage,*
> *While wine flowed under the torches,*
> *And the emperor whispered in my ear;*
> *I could not protest before I was borne to his bed.*
> *It was all like a dream, our two hearts beating as one;*

处,两心暗同。奈朝来背地,有人在那里,人在那里,妆模作样,言言语语,讥讥讽讽。咱这里羞羞涩涩,惊惊恐恐,直恁被他抟弄。

【不是路】(末扮院子、副净扮梅香暗上)(老旦引外扮院子,丑扮梅香上)吹透春风,戚畹花开别样秾。前日裴家妹子独承恩幸。我约柳家妹子,同去打觑一番。不料他气的病了,因此独自前去。(外)禀夫人到虢府了。(老旦)通报去。(外报介)(末传介)韩国夫人到。(贴)道有请。(副净请介)(外、末暗下)(贴出,迎老旦进介)(贴)姊姊请。(副净、丑诨下)(老旦)妹妹喜也。(贴)有何喜来?(老旦)邀殊宠,一枝已傍日边红。(贴作羞介)姊姊,说那里话!我进离宫,也不过杯酒相陪奉,湛露君恩内外同。(老旦笑介)虽则一般赐宴,外边怎及里边。休调哄,九重春色偏知重,有谁能共?(贴)有何难共?

(老旦)我且问你,看见玉环妹妹,在宫

Yet there in the morning my sister came to mock me,
And in shame, confusion and fear
I had to accept her taunts.

(*Enter the* Duchess of Han *with girl attendants.*)

HAN:

If the spring breeze blows on all flowers alike,
Why should one blossom outdo the rest?

The other day the Duchess of Guo was favoured by the emperor, and today I asked my other sister, the Duchess of Qin, to come with me to see her. But the Duchess of Qin is sick with envy, so I must pay this visit alone.

ATTENDANTS: We have reached the duchess' house, my lady.

HAN: Go in and announce my arrival.

(*An attendant goes in to announce her, and the* Duchess of Guo *comes out.*)

GUO: Welcome, sister.

(*The attendants retire.*)

HAN: I have come to congratulate you, darling.

GUO: To congratulate me on what?

HAN:

I see a flower blooming in the sun's caresses!

GUO: (*Blushing*): What do you mean?

I went to the pleasure palace
To wait upon the emperor during the feast.
As for His Majesty's favours,
We have an equal share in them.

HAN (*Laughing*): We all partook of a feast in our honour; but what we had outside was not what you had inside the palace!

Do not pretend now!
Who can share that special honour?

GUO:

What was so special about it?

HAN: Never mind. Let me ask you, how is our younger sister?

光景如何？

【满园春】(贴)春江上，景融融。催侍宴，望春宫。那玉环妹妹呵，新来倚贵添尊重。(老旦)不知皇上与他怎生恩爱？(贴)春宵里，春宵里，比目儿和同。谁知得雨云踪？(老旦)难道一些不觉？(贴)只见玉环妹妹的性儿，越发骄纵了些。细窥他个中，漫参他意中，使惯娇憨。惯使娇憨，寻瘢索绽，一谜儿自逞心胸。

【前腔】【换头】(老旦)他自小性儿是这般的，妹妹，你还该劝他才是。(贴)那个耐烦劝他？(老旦)他情性多骄纵，恃天生百样玲珑，姊妹行且休傍作诵。况他近日呵，昭阳内，昭阳内，一人独占三千宠，问阿谁能与竞雌雄？(贴)谁与他争！只是他如此性儿，恐怕君心不测！(老旦起，背介)细听裴家妹子之言，必有缘故。细窥他个中，漫参他意中，使恁骄嗔。恁使骄嗔，藏头露尾，敢别有一段心胸！

(末上)"意外闻严旨，堂前报贵人。"(见介)禀夫人，不好了。贵妃娘娘忤旨，圣上大怒，命高公公送归丞相府中了。(老旦惊介)有这等事！(贴)我说这般心性，定然惹下事来。(老旦)虽然如此，我与你姊妹之情，且是关系大家荣辱，须索前去看他才是！(贴)正是，就请同行。(老旦)

GUO:

> *Spring was beautiful by the river,*
> *And I waited upon the emperor in the palace.*
> *As for our sister—she is in high favour.*

HAN: How much does His Majesty love her?

GUO:

> *How should I know how they pass these spring nights?*

HAN: Didn't you get any inkling?

GUO: My only impression is that she has become even more quick-tempered than before.

> *She always finds fault with others,*
> *And insists on having her way!*

HAN: That has always been the case. You should talk to her about it, sister.

GUO: I've no patience with her!

HAN:

> *She is proud of her gifts and accomplishments;*
> *But as sisters we should not just gossip behind her back;*
> *For of all the court ladies, which one can remotely compare*
> *With her in the favour she finds in the emperor's eyes?*

GUO: I have not been competing with her. I am only afraid her behaviour may make him change his mind about her.

HAN (*Aside*): She seems to be hinting at something.

> *Why is she so angry and bitter?*
> *What is she hiding?*

(*An attendant enters.*)

ATTENDANT: An unfortunate thing has happened, my ladies. Lady Yang has offended the emperor, and Gao Lishi. has been ordered to take her back to the prime minister's house.

HAN (*Alarmed*): Can it be true?

GUO: I said her temper would get her into trouble!

HAN: Even so, we are sisters, and this may affect us too. I think we should go to see her.

GUO: You are right. Let us go together.

61

【尾声】忽闻严谴心惊恐,(贴)整香车同探
吉凶。姊姊,那玉环妹妹,可不被梅妃笑杀
也!(合)倒不如冷淡梅花仍开紫禁中!

    (贴)传闻阙下降丝纶,刘长卿
    (老旦)出得朱门入戟门。贾岛
      (贴)何必君恩能独久,乔知之
    (老旦)可怜荣落在朝昏。李商隐

HAN:
This sudden bad news has set me trembling!
GUO:
Let us call the carriage, sister
And go to hear what she has to say.
Won't Lady Plum Blossom think it amusing?
TOGETHER:
It is better to be a lonely plum blossom,
For she, after all, still blooms witin the palace.

(***Exeunt.***)

第七出　献发

（副净急上）"天有不测风云，人有旦夕祸福。"下官杨国忠，自从妹子册立贵妃，权势日盛。不想今早忽传贵妃忤旨，被谪出宫，命高内监单车送到门来。未知何故？好生惊骇！且到门前迎接去。（暂下）

【仙吕过曲】【望吾乡】（丑引旦乘车上）无定君心，恩光那处寻？蛾眉忽地遭撅窖，思量就里知他怎？弃掷何偏甚！长门隔，永巷深。回首处，愁难禁。

（副净上，跪接介）臣杨国忠迎接娘娘。（丑）丞相，快请娘娘进府，咱家还有话说。（副）院子，分付丫环每，迎接娘娘到后堂去。（丫环上，扶旦下车，拥下）（副净揖丑介）老公公请坐，不知此事因何而起？（丑）娘娘呵，

【一封书】君王宠最深，冠椒房专侍寝。昨日呵，无端忤圣心，骤然间商与参。丞相不

64

SCENE 7
A Lock of Hair

(*The prime minister enters hurriedly.*)

YANG: Fortune is as changeable as the weather! Since my cousin was made an imperial concubine, our power has grown daily. Who could tell that this morning news would come that she has offended the emperor and been dismissed from the palace, and that the eunuch Gao is bringing her home in a single carriage. This is a terrible blow! I must go to the gate to meet them. (*Exit.*)

(*Enter* Lady Yang *in a carriage accompanied by* Gao.)

LADY:
Our sovereign's heart is fickle,
Where is his former favour?
Banished from court so suddenly—
How could he be so cruel?
Far, far removed from the emperor now,
As I look back I cannot restrain my grief.

YANG (*Greets her*): Your Ladyship!

GAO: When you have shown Her Ladyship in, Your Grace, I would like a word with you.

YANG: Attendants, order the maids to take Her Ladyship to the back hall.

. (*Maids enter, help* Lady Yang *out of the carriage and lead her off.*)

YANG (*Greets Gao*): Be seated, my lord. How did this happen?

GAO:
Of all the imperial concubines
Lady Yang was His Majesty's favourite;
But yesterday she offended the Son of Heaven,
And suddenly they were estranged.
If I may speak bluntly, Your Grace,

65

要怪咱家多口,娘娘呵,生性娇痴多习惯,未免嫌疑生抱衾。(副净)如今谪遣出来,怎生是好?(丑)丞相且到朝门谢罪,相机而行。(副净)老公公,全仗你进规箴,悟当今。(丑)这个自然。(合)管重取宫花入上林。

(丑)就此告别。(副净)下官同行。(向内介)分付丫环,好生伺候娘娘。(内应介)(副净)"乌鸦与喜鹊同行,吉凶事全然未保。"(同丑下)

【中吕引子】【行香子】(旦引梅香上)乍出宫门,未定惊魂,渍愁妆满面啼痕。其间心事,多少难论。但惜芳容,怜薄命,忆深恩。

"君恩如水付东流,得宠忧移失宠愁。莫向樽前奏'花落',凉风只在殿西头。"我杨玉环,自入宫闱,过蒙宠眷。只道君心可托,百岁为欢。谁想妾命不犹,一朝逢怒。遂致促驾宫车,放归私第。金门一出,如隔九天。(泪介)天那,禁中明月,永无照影之期;苑外飞花,已绝上枝之望。抚躬自悼,掩袂徒嗟。好生伤感人也!

> *Her Ladyship is inclined to be self-willed*
> *And unduly jealous of the other ladies.*

YANG: But what can be done now that she is banished?

GAO: You, sir, had better to court to apologise for her, and see how this can be remedied.

YANG: I shall depend on you, my lord,
> *To put in a word to influence the emperor.*

GAO: You can count on me.

TOGETHER:
> *The palace flower must bloom again*
> *In her proper place at court.*

GAO: I will take my leave now.

YANG: I am coming with you. (*He calls to his attendant.*) Tell the maids to look after Her Ladyship well. (*An attendant's assent can be heard offstage.*)
> *Like the crow that travels with the magpie,*
> *I do not know to what fate I fly.* (*They leave.*)

(*Enter* Lady Yang *with a maid.*)

LADY:
> *Fresh from the palace and filled with alarm,*
> *Tears have marred my face; but how can I express*
> *The thoughts of my heart? I feel only great grief*
> *At my beauty rejected and my unhappy fate*
> *Which has caused me to forfeit the emperor's favour.*
> *His favour is gone, like water flowing seaward!*
> *Do not say that flowers must fall and the wind grow*
>   *chill!*

When I went to the palace, I was such a favourite that I thought the emperor's heart would never change. But I was unlucky enough to offend His Majesty, and he called for a carriage to send me home. Out of the palace, I feel as far from him as earth from heaven. (*She sheds tears.*)
> *The moon in the palace shall see my shadow no more;*
> *Like a fallen flower that can never return to the bough,*
> *I weep in self pity. Unhappy that I am,*

【中吕过曲】【榴花泣】【石榴花】罗衣拂拭，犹是御香熏。向何处谢前恩？想春游春从晓和昏，(泣颜回)岂知有断雨残云。我含娇带嗔，往常间他百样相依顺，不提防为着横枝，陡然把连理轻分。

丫环，此间可有那里望见宫中？(梅)前面御书楼上，西北望去，便是宫墙了。(旦)你随我楼上去来。(梅)晓得。(旦登楼介)"西宫渺不见，肠断一登楼。"(梅指介)娘娘，这一带黄设设的玻璃瓦，不是九重宫殿么？(旦作泪介)

【前腔】凭高洒泪，遥望九重阍，咫尺里隔红云。叹昨宵还是凤帏人，冀回心重与温存。天乎太忍，未白头先使君恩尽。(梅指介)呀，远远望见一个公公，骑马而来，敢是召娘娘哩！(旦叹介)料非他丹凤衔书，多又恐乌鸦传信。

(旦下楼介)(丑上)"暗将怀旧意，报与失欢人。"(见介)高力士叩见娘娘。(旦)高

As I wipe my tears on my sleeve
I can still smell the imperial scent.
How can I thank the emperor
For all his former love?
I shared his pleasures both day and night;
How could I then foretell this separation?
In the past he gave in to my every whim; but now
For the sake of a sister flower I am torn from the bough.

Tell me, girl, where can I see the palace from here?

MAID: From the pavilion in front, if you look northwest, Your Ladyship will see the palace wall.

LADY: Come with me to the pavilion.

MAID: Yes, my lady. (*They ascend the pavilion.*)

LADY:

I cannot see the palace in the distance.
My heart is broken as I climb the stairs.

MAID (*Pointing*): Do you see those yellow glazed tiles over there, my lady? Isn't that the palace?

LADY (*In tears*):

Shedding tears I gaze at the towering palace,
So near and yet severed from me by the mist.
Last night I still lay there hoping that he would relent
And come back to me. Heaven is cruel. Though I am still
    young,
He loves me no more.

MAID (*Pointing*): There in the distance I can see a eunuch on horseback. He may be coming to call you back, my lady.

LADY (*Sighs*):

This cannot be a phoenix bringing good tidings;
I fear it is only an ill-omened crow.

(*As she descends the steps*, Gao *enters.*)

GAO:

I have come in secret to tell the lovelorn maid
That he still pines for her.

(*Greets her.*) Your servant, madam.

力士，你来怎么？（丑）奴婢恰才覆旨，万岁爷细问娘娘回府光景，似有悔心。现今独坐宫中，长吁短叹。一定是思想娘娘，因此特来报知。（旦）唉，那里还想着我！（丑）奴婢愚不谏贤，娘娘未可太执意了。倘有什么东西，付与奴婢，乘间进上，或者感动圣心，也未可知。（旦）高力士，你教我进什么东西去好？（想介）

【喜渔灯犯】【喜渔灯】思将何物传情悃，可感动君？我想一身之外，皆君所赐，算只有愁泪千行，作珍珠乱滚；又难穿成金缕，把雕盘进。哦，有了，【剔银灯】这一缕青丝香润，曾共君枕上并头相偎衬，曾对君镜里撩云。丫环，取镜台金剪过来。（梅应取上介）（旦解发介）哎，头发，头发！【渔家傲】可惜你伴我芳年，剪去心儿未忍。只为欲表我衷肠，（作剪发介）剪去心儿自悯。（作执发起，哭介）头发，头发！【喜渔灯】全仗你寄我殷勤。（拜介）我那圣上呵，奴身、止鬈鬈发数根，这便是我的残丝断魂。

（起介）高力士，你将去与我转奏圣上。（哭介）说妾罪该万死，此生此世，不能再睹天颜！谨献此发，以表依恋。（丑跪接发搭肩上介）娘娘请免愁烦，奴婢就此去了。“好凭缕缕青丝发，重结双双白首缘。”

LADY: What brings you here again, my lord?

GAO: Just now when I reported your return home to His Majesty, he asked me all that had happened here, as if he regretted what had taken place. He is sitting alone, sighing, and he must be longing for you; so I came to report this to Your Ladyship.

LADY: Ah no, how could he be thinking of me?

GAO: Forgive me if I advise you, madam, not to be too stubborn. Have you nothing which you could give me to take to His Majesty? You never know, but it might move his heart.

LADY: What can I send to the emperor, my lord? (*Thinks.*)

> *With what can I send my love to move his heart?*
> *All that I have are gifts from the emperor.*
> *I have only my flowing tears, which drop like pearls;*
> *But I cannot string them together to send as a gift.*
> *Ah, yes! I have it! This lock of glossy hair*
> *Once lay near his head on the pillow, and I used to comb it*
> *While looking at him in the mirror.*

Girl, bring me the mirror and the golden scissors from my dressing table. (*The maid brings the scissors, while* Lady Yang *lets down her hair.*)

> *I am sorry to have to cut you off,*
> *That have been with me all my youth;*
> *But to show my faithful heart* (*She clips her hair,*)
> *Cut I must, though it makes me grieve.*

(*Holding the lock of hair, she weeps.*) Ah, hair,

> *I depend on you to show my love.* (*Curtseys.*)
> *Your Majesty, this lock*
> *Conveys my love and grief!*

Take it, my lord, and tell the emperor, (*Weeping.*) that I know I deserve a thousand deaths; and as I shall never look upon his serene countenance again in this life, I present him with this lock of hair as a token of my love.

GAO (*Takes the lock of hair and places it on his shoulder*):

Take heart, my lady. I shall leave you now. May this lock of silken hair once more unite the lovers! (*Exit.*)

71

（下）（旦坐哭介）（老旦、贴上）

【榴花灯犯】【剔银灯】听说是贵妃妹忤君，【石榴花】听说是返家门，【普天乐】听说是失势兄忧悯，听说是中官至，未审何云？（进介）贵妃娘娘那里？（梅）韩、虢二国夫人到了。（旦作哭不语介）（老旦、贴见介）（老旦）贵妃请免愁烦。（同哭介）（贴）前日在望春宫，皇上十分欢喜，为何忽有此变？【渔家傲】我只道万岁千秋欢无尽，【尾犯序】我只道任伊行笑謦，【石榴花】我只道纵差池，谁和你评论！（老旦）裴家妹子，【锦缠道】休只管闲言絮陈。贵妃，你逢薄怒其中有甚根因？（旦作不理介）（贴）贵妃，你莫怪我说，【剔银灯】自来宠多生嫌衅，可知道秋叶君恩？恁为人，怎趋承至尊？（老旦合）【雁过声】姊妹每情切来相问，为什么耳畔哝哝，总似不闻！（旦）

【尾声】秋风团扇原吾分，多谢连枝特过存。总有万语千言，只在心上忖。

（竟下）（贴）姊姊，你看这个样子，如何

(Lady Yang *sits weeping. The* Duchess of Han *and the* Duchess of Guo *enter.*)

DUCHESSES:

We hear that our sister has angered our lord,
We hear she has had to come home;
We hear that our cousin is sadly disturbed;
We hear the chief eunuch has come.

(*They walk in.*)Where is Her Ladyship?

MAID: The Duchess of Han and the Duchess of Guo are here.

(Laky Yang *weeps and says nothing.*)

HAN: Don't distress yourself so. (*She weeps with her.*)

GUO: That day in the pleasure palace His Majesty was in high good humour. How could this have happened?

I thought your happiness would know no end;
I thought you could laugh or sulk just as you pleased;
I thought that however badly you behaved,
The emperor would never take offence.

HAN:

Don't say any more, sister.
Tell us, Lady Yang, what happened?

GUO:

Excuse me for speaking frankly, sister,
But too much favour can only lead to trouble.
You must know that the emperor's love is like autumn leaves,
And you should learn to please His Majesty.

DUCHESSES:

We have come to show concern, because as sisters
We sympathize with you. Then why pretend
Not to hear us?

LADY:

It is my fate to be discarded like a fan in autumn;
I am grateful that my sisters should show such concern;
But though preyed on by a thousand griefs and cares,
I shall try to keep my sorrows to myself. (*Exit.*)

GUO: Well, sister! See how she treats us!

73

使得？（老旦）正是，我每特来看他，他心上
有事，竟自进房去了。妹子，你再到望春宫
时，休要学他。（贴羞介）啐！

　　　今朝忽见下天门，张籍
　（老旦）相对那能不怆神。廖匡图
　（贴）冷眼静看真好笑，徐夤
　（老旦）中含芒刺欲伤人。陆龟蒙

HAN: Yes, indeed. We came specially to see her, but she flies off in a passion. Next time *you* go to the pleasure palace, sister, be sure you don't behave like that!

(*The* Duchess of Guo *blushes and pretends to be angry.*)

(*Exeunt.*)

第八出　复召

【南吕引子】【虞美人】(生上)无端惹起闲烦恼,有话将谁告? 此情已自费支持,怪杀鹦哥不住向人提。

　　"辇路生春草,上林花满枝。凭高何限意,无复侍臣知。"寡人昨因杨妃娇妒,心中不忿,一时失计,将他遣出。谁想佳人难得,自他去后,触目总是生憎,对景无非惹恨。那杨国忠入朝谢罪,寡人也无颜见他。(叹介)咳,欲待召取回宫,却又难于出口,若是不召他来,教朕怎生消遣,好刮划不下也!

【南吕过曲】【十样锦】【绣带儿】春风静,宫帘半启,难消日影迟迟。听好鸟犹作欢声,睹新花似斗容辉。追悔,【宜春令】悔杀咱一划儿粗疏,不解他十分的娇殢,枉负了怜香惜玉,那些情致。(副净扮内监上)"脍下

SCENE 8
The Recall

(*The emperor enters.*)
EMPEROR:

> *I am suddenly plunged in despair;*
> *But to whom can I bare my heart?*
> *It is hard enough to endure such misery,*
> *Yet, to make it worse, the parrot keeps calling her name.*
> *Grass grows on the road where carriages pass,*
> *And flowers are blossoming upon the boughs.*
> *I gaze afar with bitter longing,*
> *But none of my subjects knows my heart.*

Yesterday when Lady Yang was jealous I was displeased, and in a fit of anger I sent her away. But there is no one to take her place; and since she left, all that I see disgusts me and everything arouses feelings of regret. When the prime minister came just now to apologise, I was embarrassed to see him. (*Sighs.*) I want to recall her, yet am ashamed to give the order. But if she is not recalled I shall never know happiness again. This is a hard decision.

> *The wind has dropped,*
> *The curtains are half drawn,*
> *Yet time hangs heavily,*
> *Though birds are singing for joy*
> *And spring flowers are ablaze with colour now.*
> *Remorse gnaws at my heart*
> *When I think how rashly I behaved,*
> *With no regard for her sensitive feelings,*
> *Or for our love for each other.*

(*A eunuch comes in and kneels before the emperor.*)

77

玉盘红缕细，酒开金瓮绿醅浓。"（跪见介）请万岁爷上膳。（生不应介）（副净又请介）（生恼介）咄，谁着你请来！（副净）万岁爷自清晨不曾进膳，后宫传催排膳伺候。（生）咄，什么后宫！叫内侍。（二内侍应上）（生）揣这厮去打一百，发入净军所去。（内侍）领旨。（同揣副净下）（生）哎，朕在此想念妃子，却被这厮来搅乱一番。好烦恼也！【降黄龙换头】思伊，纵有天上琼浆，海外珍馐，知他什般滋味！除非可意立向跟前，方慰调饥。（净扮内监上）"尊前绮席陈歌舞，花外红楼列管弦。"（见跪介）请万岁爷沉香亭上饮宴，听赏梨园新乐。（生）咄，说什沉香亭，好打！（净叩头介）非干奴婢之事，是太子诸王，说万岁爷心绪不快，特请消遣。（生）咄，我心绪有何不快！叫内侍。（内侍应上）（生）揣这厮去打一百，发入惜薪司当火者去。（内侍）领旨。（同揣净下）（生）内侍过来。（内侍应上）（生）着你二人看守宫门，不许一人擅入，违者重打。（内侍）领旨。

EUNUCH:

> *Finely sliced meat on a plate of jade,*
> *Pale green wine in a golden jug.*

May it please Your Majesty, dinner is served.

(*The emperor does not answer, and the eunuch repeats his message.*)

EMPEROR (*Angrily*): Curse you! Who told you to come?

EUNUCH: Your Majesty has eaten nothing since early morning, and the ladies told us to prepare a meal.

EMPEROR: What ladies? Confound you! Attendants! (*Two attendants enter.*) Take him away! Give him a hundred lashes and send him to be a sweeper.

ATTENDANTS: As Yonr Majesty commands! (*They take the eunuch away.*)

EMPEROR: Ah! I was thinking of Lady Yang when this infuriating fool disturbed me.

> *How I long for her! Even if I had ambrosia*
> *And heavenly elixirs, I should find them tasteless*
> *Without the presence of the one I love.*

(*Another eunuch enters and kneels before the emperor.*)

EUNUCH:

> *With lutes and pipes beside the flowers,*
> *Dancing and singing will entertain the feast.*

Will it please Your Majesty to come to feast at Aloes Pavilion, and hear the new music composed by the imperial musicians?

EMPEROR: Aloes Pavilion now! I shall have you beaten!

EUNUCH: It is not your slave's fault. The princes feared Your Majesty was unhappy, and wanted to drive away your cares.

EMPEROR: How dare they call me unhappy! Attendants! (*The attendants enter.*) Take this fellow and give him a hundred lashes, then send him to be a scullion.

ATTENDANTS: It shall be done! (*They take the eunuch away.*)

EMPEROR: Attendants! (*More attendants enter.*) Two of you stand at my door and allow no one to come in. If you disobey, I shall have you thrashed within an inch of your lives.

（作立前场介）（生）唉，朕此时有甚心情，还去听歌饮酒。【醉太平】想亭际、凭阑仍是玉阑干，问新妆有谁同倚？就有新声呵，知音人逝，他鹍弦绝响，我玉笛羞吹。（丑肩搭发上）【浣溪纱】离别悲，相思意，两下里抹媚谁知！我从旁参透个中机，要打合鸾凰在一处飞。（见内侍介）万岁爷在那里？（内侍）独自坐在宫中。（丑欲入，内侍拦介）（丑）你怎么拦阻咱家？（内侍）万岁爷十分着恼，把进膳的连打了两个，特着我每看守宫门，不许一人擅入。（丑）原来如此，咱家且候着。（生）朕委无聊赖，且到宫门外闲步片时。（行介）看一带瑶阶依然芳草齐，不见蹴裙裾珠履追随。（丑望介）万岁爷出来了，咱且闪在门外，觑个机会。（虚下、即上听介）（生）寡人在此思念妃子，不知妃子又怎生思念寡人哩！早间问高力士，他说妃子出去，泪眼不干，教朕寸心如割。这半日间，无从再知消息。高力士这厮，也竟不

ATTENDANTS: As Your Majesty commands! (*They step to the front of the stage and stand there.*)

EMPEROR:

> *What heart have I now to drink or enjoy new music?*
> *There stands the pavilion still,*
> *But where is she who used to lean with me there*
> *On the marble balustrade?*
> *New music is played,*
> *But with whom can I now enjoy it?*
> *Now the sound of her lute is silenced,*
> *I shall play no more on my flute.*

(Gao *enters with* Lady Yang's *hair on his shoulder.*)

GAO:

> *The parted lovers are longing for each other,*
> *And I, a bystander, have watched for a chance*
> *To bring the two love birds together.*

(*He greets the attendants.*) Where is His Majesty?

ATTENDANTS: His Majesty is sitting alone.

(Gao *starts to go in, but they stop him.*)

GAO: Why do you stop me?

ATTENDANTS: His Majesty is very angry. He has had two eunuchs punished, and has forbidden us to admit anyone.

GAO: Very well, I shall wait outside.

EMPEROR: I am thoroughly sick at heart. I shall take a stroll. (*He paces up and down.*)

> *Spring grass has grown up to the marble steps,*
> *But where are the silken skirt and pearl-decked shoes*
> *That used to follow behind me?*

GAO: Here comes the emperor. I shall hide myself by the door until I have a chance to approach him. (*He goes out, then enters again and listens.*)

EMPEROR: As I long for her here, I wonder whether she is thinking of me? This morning Gao Lishi told me that she had been weeping ever since she left the palace. It breaks my heart to hear it! That was several hours ago; but there has been no more news, and that

81

到朕跟前,好生可恶!(丑见介)奴婢在这里。(生)(作看丑介)(生)高力士,你肩上搭的什么东西?(丑)是杨娘娘的头发。(生笑介)什么头发?(丑)娘娘说道:"自恨愚昧,上忤圣心,罪应万死。今生今世,不能够再睹天颜,特剪下这头发,着奴婢献上万岁爷,以表依恋之意。(献发介)(生执发看,哭介)哎哟,我那妃子呵!【啄木儿】记前宵枕边闻香气,到今朝剪却和愁寄。觑青丝肠断魂迷。想寡人与妃子,恩情中断,就似这头发也。一霎里落金刀长辞云髻。(丑)万岁爷!【鲍老催】请休惨凄,奴婢想杨娘娘既蒙恩幸,万岁爷何惜宫中片席之地,乃使沦落外边!春风肯教天上回,名花便从苑外移。(生作想介)只是寡人已经放出,怎好召还?(丑)有罪放出,悔过召还,正是圣主如天之度。(生点头介)(丑)况今早单车送出,才是黎明,此时天色已暮,开了安庆坊,从太华宅而入,外人谁得知之。(叩头介)乞鉴原,赐迎归。无淹滞,稳情取一笑愁城自解围。(生)高力士,就着你迎取贵妃回宫便了。(丑)领旨。(下)(生)咳,妃

scoundrel Gao Lishi has been keeping out of my way.

GAO (*Bows*): Long live the emperor!

EMPEROR(*Looks at* Gao): What have you there on your shoulder?

GAO: Her Ladyship's hair.

EMPEROR (*Smiles*): What hair?

GAO: Lady Yang swears that she repents the folly which made her offend Your Majesty, and that she deserves a thousand deaths. Because she will never be able to look upon your face again, she has cut off this lock of hair and asked your slave to present it to Your Majesty as a token of her love. (*Presents the hair.*)

EMPEROR (*Holding the hair, looks at it and sheds tears*): Ah, my darling!

> *This hair perfumed my pillow two nights ago,*
> *But today it is shorn and given as a token of grief.*
> *My heart is torn by this symbol of separation*
> *Of our love so suddenly cut by the golden scissors of fate.*

GAO: Your Majesty, do not grieve. Since Lady Yang is your favourite, why begrudge a small space for her in the palace and make her remain outside?

> *Should spring return with the breeze,*
> *Then this beautiful flower*
> *Could be brought back again to the palace.*

EMPEROR (*Reflectively*): But I have already dismissed her. How am I to recall her?

GAO: To dismiss her because of her fault and recall her because she has repented would show the divine mercy of the Son of Heaven. (*The emperor nods.*)

GAO: Besides, it was barely dawn when she was sent out in a single carriage; and now it is dusk. If we open the gate of Anqing Quarter and let her in from there, who will know of it? (*Kowtows.*)

> *Your slave begs that she be called at once;*
> *For her laughter can dispel the emperor's grief.*

EMPEROR: Very well, I order you to bring Her Ladyship back.

子来时,教寡人怎生相见也!【下小楼】喜得玉人归矣,又愁他惯娇嗔,背面啼,那时将何言语饰前非!罢,罢,这原是寡人不是,拼把百般亲媚,酬他半日分离。(丑同内侍、宫女纱灯引旦上)【双声子】香车曳,香车曳,穿过了宫槐翠。纱笼对,纱笼对,掩映着宫花丽。(内侍、宫女下)(丑进报介)杨娘娘到了。(生)快宣进来。(丑)领旨。杨娘娘有宣。(旦进见介)臣妾杨氏见驾,死罪,死罪!(俯伏介)(生)平身。(丑暗下)(旦跪泣介)臣妾无状,上干天谴。今得重睹圣颜,死亦瞑目。(生同泣介)妃子何出此言?(旦)【玉漏迟序】念臣妾如山罪累,荷皇恩如天容庇。今自艾,愿承鱼贯,敢妒蛾眉?

　　(生扶旦起介)寡人一时错见,从前的话,不必再提了。(旦泣起介)万岁!(生携旦手与旦拭泪介)

GAO: I will go at once, sire. (*Exit.*)

EMPEROR: Ah, how am I going to face her?

> *I delight in my lady's return, and yet I fear*
> *That she may be angry and turn her face away;*
> *For if she weeps how can I excuse my fault?*
> *I was greatly to blame; but now I must comfort her,*
> *And make amends for this half day's separation.*

(Gao *comes in with attendants and maids holding lanterns and leading in* Lady Yang.)

GAO:

> *The fragrant carriage drives past the verdant ash trees,*
> *And lanterns shine in pairs on the palace flowers.*

(*The atendants and maids withdraw.*)

GAO (*Advancing*): Her Ladyship is here.

EMPEROR: Bring her in quickly.

GAO: At once, Your Majesty. (*To* Lady Yang.) His Majesty orders Lady Yang to enter.

LADY: Your slave deserves death for her offence. (*She curtseys.*)

EMPEROR: You may rise.

(Gao *withdraws.*)

LADY(*Kneels, weeping*): I have acted wrongly and offended Your Majesty. But now that I behold your serene countenance, I shall die content.

EMPEROR: Do not say that, my love. (*He sheds tears.*)

LADY:

> *My guilt weighs on me as heavy as a mountain;*
> *Yet Your Majesty is as merciful as Heaven.*
> *But now I have repented,*
> *And in future I shall keep my proper place,*
> *And never more reveal my jealousy.*

(*The emperor raises her up.*)

EMPEROR: The fault was mine. Let us not speak of it any more.

LADY (*Rising and weeping*): Long live the emperor! (*The emperor takes her hand and wipes her tears.*)

【尾声】从今识破愁滋味，这恩情更添十倍。妃子，我且把这一日相思诉与伊！

（宫娥上）西宫宴备，请万岁爷、娘娘上宴。

（生）陶出真情酒满尊，　李中
（旦）此心从此更何言。　罗隐
（生）别离不惯无穷忆，　苏颋
（旦）重入椒房拭泪痕。　柳公权

EMPEROR:
> *A taste of sorrow has increased our love tenfold.*
> *I shall tell you now how I longed for you all day.*
> (*A maid enters.*)

MAID: A feast is ready in the west palace, Your Majesty, Your Ladyship.

(***Exeunt.***)

第九出　疑讖

（外扮郭子仪将巾、佩剑上）壮怀磊落有谁知，一剑防身且自随。整顿乾坤济时了，那回方表是男儿。"自家姓郭名子仪，本贯华州郑县人氏。学成韬略，腹满经纶。更思量做一个顶天立地的男儿，干一桩定国安邦的事业。今以武举出身，到京调选。正值杨国忠窃弄威权，安禄山滥膺宠眷。把一个朝纲，看看弄得不成模样了。似俺郭子仪未得一官半职，不知何时，才得替朝廷出力也呵！

【商调集贤宾】论男儿壮怀须自吐，肯空向杞天呼？笑他每似堂间处燕，有谁曾屋上瞻乌！不提防枏虎樊熊，任纵横社鼠城狐。几回家听鸡鸣，起身独夜舞。想古来多少乘除，显得个勋名垂宇宙，不争便姓字老樵渔！

且到长安市上，买醉一回。（行科）

SCENE 9
The Writing on the Wall

(*Enter* Guo Ziyi *wearing a military costume and sword.*)

GUO ZIYI:

Who can appreciate my high ideals?
Wearing a sword in self-defence,
I wait for the time to set the world aright;
Then I shall show myself a realman,

I am Guo Ziyi, a native of Zhengxian. I have mastered all military arts and devised various strategies, in the hope that some day I may become a mighty hero and help to bring peace to the empire. Now, having passed the military examination, I have come to the capital to await my appointment. I find that Prime Minister Yang is taking all power into his own hands, and An Lushan is the emperor's favourite. The government is going to rack and ruin, while a man of my calibre still lacks an official post. Heaven knows how much longer I must wait to serve my country.

A hero should carve out his way,
Not simply rail at fate;
The men of today are thoughtless as the swallows
That nest beneath the eaves,
Not knowing that crows have swarmed upon the roof;
They do not guard against the bear and tiger,
They suffer rats and foxes to run riot;
But I, at cockcrow, rise to steel myself.
Since ancient times, how often
Have rebels tried to seize the throne;
I mean to make my name shine in the world;
I will not live my life out
As a mere fisherman or woodcutter.

I will walk to the market now.

【逍遥乐】向天街徐步,暂遣牢骚,聊宽逆旅。俺则见来往纷如,闹昏昏似醉汉难扶,那里有独醒行吟楚大夫!俺郭子仪呵,待觅个同心伴侣,怅钓鱼人去,射虎人遥,屠狗人无。

　　(下)(丑扮酒保上)"我家酒铺十分高,罚誓无赊挂酒标。只要有钱凭你饮,无钱滴水也难消。"小子是这长安市上,新丰馆大酒楼,一个小二哥的便是。俺这酒楼,在东、西两市中间,往来十分热闹。凡是京城内外,王孙公子,官员市户,军民百姓,没一个不到俺楼上来吃三杯。也有吃寡酒的,吃案酒的,买酒去的,包酒来的,打发个不了。道犹未了,又一个吃酒的来也。(外行上)

【上京马】遥望见绿杨斜靠画楼隅,滴溜溜一片青帘风外舞,怎得个燕市酒人来共沽!(唤科)酒家有么?(丑迎科)客官,请楼上坐。(外作上楼科)是好一座酒楼也。敞轩窗日朗风疏。见四周遭粉壁上,都画着醉仙图。

　　(丑)客官自饮,还是待客?(外)独饮

90

As I stroll in the street to master my depression,
A stranger here, I watch the jostling crowds;
They are all like drunkards; where is Qu Yuan the poet
Who alone stayed sober to sing in a land of drunkards?
I long to find a companion after my heart,
But the men I could admire are dead and gone:
The leader who was a fisherman,
The general who shot the tiger,
And the warrior who worked first as a butcher. (*Exit.*)
(*Enter a waiter.*)

WAITER:

Our tavern is so superior, I swear,
That all our wine sells out in no time.
You may drink all you please if you have money,
But you'll not even get water if you've none.

I serve in Xinfeng Restaurant in Chang'an. Our inn stands just
between the east and the west markets, where many people pass.
Citizens of the capital and travellers from beyond, lords and
officers, merchants, soldiers and common folk all come to our
tavern to drink. Some buy only wine, others have a meal with it;
some take the wine home, others order feasts here. We are kept
hard at it. See, while I am talking, here comes another customer.
(Guo Ziyi *enters.*)

GUO ZIYI:

I see a green willow in the distance
Inclining towards a colourful pavilion,
And a blue trade sign flying in the breeze.
I wish I had a friend to drink with me.
(*Calls out.*) Do you serve wine?

WAITER (*Greeting him*) : Come upstairs, sir.

GUO ZIYI: This is a fine tavern.

Sun shines through the open windows, and the breeze
Blows in; while the walls are painted with drunken fairies.

WAITER: Are you drinking alone, sir, or will you wait for other
guests?

91

三杯,有好酒呵取来。(丑)有好酒。(取酒上科)酒在此。(内叫科)小二哥,这里来。(丑应忙下)(外饮酒科)

【梧叶儿】俺非是爱酒的闲陶令,也不学使酒的莽灌夫,一谜价痛饮兴豪粗。撑着这醒眼儿谁偢睬?问醉乡深可容得吾?听街市恁喧呼,偏冷落高阳酒徒。

(作起看科)(老旦扮内监,副净、末、净扮官,各吉服,杂捧金币、牵羊担酒随行上,绕场下)(丑捧酒上)客官,热酒在此。(外)酒保,我问你咱,这楼前那些官员,是往何处去来?(丑)客官,你一面吃酒,我一面告诉你波。只为国舅杨丞相,并韩国、虢国、秦国三位夫人,万岁爷各赐造新第。在这宣阳里中,四家府门相连,俱照大内一般造法。这一家造来,要胜似那一家的;那一家造来,又要赛过这一家的。若见那家造得华丽,这家便拆毁了,重新再造。定要与那家一样,方才住手。一座厅堂,足费上千万贯钱钞。今日完工,因此合朝大小官员,都备了羊酒礼物,前往各家称贺,打从这里过去。(外惊科)哦,有这等事!(丑)待我再去看热酒来波。(下)(外叹科)呀,外戚宠盛,到这个地位,如何是了也!

GUO ZIYI: I will have a few cups by myself. Bring the best you have.

WAITER: We have only the best here, sir. (*Brings the wine.*) Here you are, sir.

(*Someone calls from offstage: "Is the waiter there?" The waiter goes out, and* Guo Ziyi *begins to drink.*)

GUO ZIYI:

> I am no wine-loving poet,
> No rough, hard-drinking soldier;
> When I drink I look soberly round,
> Feeling this country of drunkards no place for me;
> There is too much noise and bustle in the streets,
> But I stay here alone.

(*He gets up to look out to the window. Richly dressed eunuchs and officials pass with attendants carrying gold, silk, sheep and wine. The waiter brings in more wine.*)

WAITER: Here is some freshly heated wine, sir.

GUO ZIYI: Tell me, my friend, where are those officials outside going to?

WAITER: I'll tell you as you drink. The emperor has ordered new mansions in Xuanyang Quarter to be given to Prime Minister Yang Guozhong and the three duchesses, his cousins. The four mansions will be next to each other, and each will be built like an imperial palace. Nowadays every family wants to outshine every other. When one family sees their neighbour's house is better than theirs, they pull theirs down and rebuild, until they have one exactly the same. This way, one single hall may cost millions. Today the new buildings are finished, so all the government officials are going there to offer congratulations and take presents of sheep and wine. They all pass this way.

GUO ZIYI (*Shocked*): Is it possible?

WAITER: Excuse me, sir. I shall go to warm up some more wine for you. (*Exit.*)

GUO ZIYI (*Sighs*): If the favourite concubine's relatives are indulging in such display, what will it lead to?

【醋葫芦】怪私家恁僭窃，竞豪奢夸土木。一班儿公卿甘作折腰趋，争向权门如市附。再没有一个人呵，把兴情向九重分诉。可知他朱甍碧瓦，总是血膏涂！

（起科）心中一时忿懑，不觉酒涌上来，且向四壁闲看一回。（作看科）这壁厢细字数行，有人题的诗句。我试觑波。（作看念科）"燕市人皆去，函关马不归。若逢山下鬼，环上击罗衣。"呀，这诗是好奇怪也！

【幺篇】我这里停睛一直看，从头儿逐句读。细端详，诗意少祯符。且看是什么人题的？（又看念科）李遐周题。（作想科）李遐周，这名字好生识熟！哦，是了，我闻得有个术士李遐周，能知过去未来，必定就是他了。多则是就里难言藏谶语，猜诗谜杜家何处？早难道醉来墙上信笔乱鸦涂！

（内作喧闹科）（外唤科）酒保那里？（丑上）客官，做什么？（外）楼下为何又这般喧闹？（丑）客官，你靠着这窗儿，往下看去就是。（外看科）（净王服、骑马、头踏职事前导引

Now private citizens usurp
The emperor's prerogatives,
Rival each other's luxury
And boast of their fine palaces;
While courtiers and ministers
Have learned a new servility,
Flocking to fawn on the mighty
As country folk flock to a fair.
Yet none dare telll the emperor
That these vermilion roofs and brilliant tiles
Are stained with the people's blood!

(*He rises from his seat.*) Disgust has made the wine go to my head. Let me look around. (*Looks at the wall.*) Here are a few lines of poetry, closely written. Let me read it. (*Reads.*)

When the northern town is deserted,
And no horses return from the Pass,
He comes to the ghost beneath the hill,
And there hangs a silken dress on the ring.

What a strange poem!

When I read it carefully line by line
And ponder the meaning well,
I find it has a sinister significance.

I wonder who the author is. (*Reads*) Li Xiazhou. (*Thinks.*) The name sounds familiar. Ah, yes, I have heard that there is a fortune-teller named Li Xiazhou who is good at foretelling the future. This must be the man.

No doubt it predicts disaster in veiled terms;
But who can explain the riddle?
Or can it be the scribbling of some drunkard?

(*A noise is heard offstage,*)

GUO ZIYI (*Calling*): Waiter!

WAITER: Yes, sir?

GUO ZIYI: What is the meaning of that hubbub outside?

WAITER: Well, sir, just take a look out of the window.

(Guo Ziyi *looks out and sees* An Lushan *riding past, wearing a*

95

上,绕场行下科)(外)那是何人?(丑笑指科)
客官,你不见他那个大肚皮么?这人姓安
名禄山。万岁爷十分宠爱他,把御座的金
鸡步障,都赐与他坐过,今日又封他做东平
郡王。方才谢恩出朝,赐归东华门外新第,
打从这里经过。(外惊怒科)呀,这、这就是
安禄山么?有何功劳,遽封王爵?唉,我看
这厮面有反相,乱天下者,必此人也!

【金菊香】见了这野心杂种牧羊的奴,料蜂
目豺声定是狡徒。怎把个野狼引来屋里
居?怕不将题壁诗符?更和那私门贵戚,
一例逞妖狐。

　　(丑)客官,为甚事这般着恼来?(外)
【柳叶儿】哎,不由人冷飕飕冲冠发竖,热烘
烘气夯胸脯,咭当当把腰间宝剑频频觑。
(丑)客官,请息怒,再与我消一壶波。(外)
呀,便教俺倾千盏,饮尽了百壶,怎把这重
沉沉一个愁担儿消除!

　　(作起身科)不吃酒了,收了这酒钱去
者。(丑作收科)别人来"三杯和万事",这客
官"一气惹千愁"。(下)(外作下楼、转行科)
我且回到寓中去波。

【浪来里】见着那一桩桩伤心的时事逻,凑
着那一句句感时的诗谶伏,怕天心人意两

prince's costume and preceded by retainers.)

GUO ZIYI: Who is that?

WAITER (*Laughing as he points at* An): Don't you see that big belly, sir? That is An Lushan, a great favourite with the emperor. His Majesty has even allowed him to recline on a couch under the golden cock canopy. Today he was made Prince of Dongping, and he is on his way back from the court to his new palace outside Donghua Gate.

GUO ZIYI (*Looks shocked and angry*): So this is An Lushan? What has he done to be made a prince so quickly? He has the face of a rebel; he will certainly bring ruin to the empire.

> *I see an ambitious cur, a bastard, a paltry shepherd,*
> *With bulging eyes like a bee, and the voice of a jackal;*
> *This must be a cunning rogue. But how is it this wolf*
> *Has been brought to live in the house?*
> *The lines on the wall will come true*
> *When he and the relatives of Lady Yang*
> *Play knavish tricks.*

WAITER: Why do you look so gloomy, sir?

GUO ZIYI:

> *Ah! My hair stands on end and blazing fury*
> *Flames in my heart. My eyes turn to my sword.*

WAITER: Don't look so depresed, sir. Let me get you another pot of wine.

GUO ZIYI:

> *A thousand cups, a hundred pots of wine,*
> *Could never wash away my heavy gloom.*

(*He stands up.*)I have drunk enough. Here is your money.

(*The waiter takes the money.*)

WAITER: Other men after three cups are at peace with the whole world; but this gentleman has a thousand sorrow. (*Exit.*)

GUO ZIYI (*Walking down the stairs and along the road*) : I shall go back to my room.

> *These shocking sights and that mysterious poem*
> *Suggest that Heaven's will is unfathomable.*

97

难摸,好教俺费沉吟,趷踏地将眉对蹙。看满地斜阳欲暮,到萧条客馆,兀自意踌蹰。

(作到寓进坐科)(副净扮家将上)(见科)禀爷,朝报到来。(外看科)"兵部一本:为除授官员事。奉圣旨,郭子仪授为天德军使。钦此。"原来旨意已下,索早收拾行李,即日上任去者。(副净应科)(外)俺郭子仪虽则官卑职小,便可从此报效朝廷也呵!

【高过随调煞】赤紧似尺水中展鬣鳞,枳棘中拂毛羽。且喜夺云霄有分上天衢,直待的把乾坤重整顿,将百千秋第一等勋业图。纵有妖氛孽蛊,少不得肩担日月,手把大唐扶。

马蹄空踏几年尘,　胡宿

长是豪家据要津,　司空图

卑散自应霄汉隔,　王建

不知忧国是何人?　吕温

As I pace along, knitting my brows in thought,
The sun sets, and I reach my lonely room,
A prey to doubt.

(*He enters his room and sits down. An attendant cones in.*)

ATTENDANT: Master, the bulletin has come.

GUO ZIYI (*Reading the bulletin*): "The Ministry of War announces that by imperial decree Guo Ziyi is appointed military commissioner for Tiande." So the decree has come! I had better pack my things and go at once to my post. Though it is a small post, at least I shall now be able to serve the state.

In only a foot of water, a fish can dart;
Hedged in by brambles, a bird can preen its wings;
At last I have a chance to scale the sky,
To set the world in order and achieve
Deeds that will live for ever. Though dark forces
Are set on devilry, upon my shoulder
I'll prop the sun and moon, and with my hand
Support the tottering throne.

(*Exit.*)

第十出　闻乐

【南吕引子】【步蟾宫】(老旦扮嫦娥,引仙女上)清光独把良宵占,经万古纤尘不染。散瑶空风露洒银蟾,一派仙音微飐。

"药捣长生离劫尘,清妍面目本来真。云中细看天香落,仍倚苍苍桂一轮。"吾乃嫦娥是也,本属太阴之主,浪传后羿之妻。七宝团圆,周三万六千年内;一轮皎洁,满一千二百里中。玉兔、金蟾,产结长明至宝;白榆、丹桂,种成万古奇葩。向有"霓裳羽衣"仙乐一部,久秘月宫,未传人世。今下界唐天子,知音好乐。他妃子杨玉环,前身原是蓬莱玉妃,曾经到此。不免召他梦魂,重听此曲。使其醒来记忆,谱入管弦。竟将天上仙音,留作人间佳话。却不是好!寒簧过来。(贴)有。(老旦)你可到唐宫之内,引杨玉环梦魂到此听曲。曲终之后,仍旧送回。(贴)领旨。(老旦)"好凭一枕游

SCENE 10
Dream Music

(*Enter Chang'e, the goddess of the moon, with her fairy maid Hanhuang.*)

CHANG'E:

> *Throughout the ages my unsullied rays*
> *Alone have brightened the most lovely night;*
> *Dew from the azure wets my silver orb,*
> *And down the breeze drift fairy melodies.*
> *Far from the dusty world of men,*
> *I show my true form clear and beautiful;*
> *Sweet petals fall from the clouds,*
> *And I lean against the luxuriant cassia tree.*

I am Chang'e, mistress of the moon. Within this precious globe I have passed thirty-six thousand years, and my bright light is shed over a thousand leagues. Here are the jade hare and silver toad, rare and luminous, and the white elm and red cassia which bloom for all eternity. I have a melody, too, called the Dance of the Rainbow and Feathery Garments, long kept in the moon and unknown to men. Now the Tang emperor on the earth below is fond of music, and his concubine Yang Yuhuan was a fairy maid on the fairy mountain, who used to visit me during her last life. I will summon her spirit to hear this tune again, so that when she awakes she can transcribe it, carrying the music of heaven to mortals on earth. Come, Hanhuang!

HANHUANG: Ready, my lady!

CHANG'E: Go to the Tang palace and bring the sleeping girl's spirit to hear our music. When the dance has been played, you may send her back.

HANHUANG: I go, my lady.

CHANG'E: Through this fairy dream we shall secretly teach the girl

仙梦,暗授千秋法曲音。"(引丑下)(贴)奉着娘娘之命,不免出了月宫,到唐宫中走一遭也。(行介)

【南吕过曲】【梁州序犯】【本调】明河斜映,繁星微闪。俯将尘世遥觇,只见空濛香雾。早离却玉府清严,一任珮摇风影,衣动霞光,小步红云垫。待将天上乐授宫襜,密召芳魂入彩蟾。来此已是唐宫之内。【贺新郎】你看鱼钥闭,龙帏掩,那杨妃呵,似海棠睡足增娇艳。【本序尾】轻唤起,拥冰簟。

（唤介）杨娘娘起来。（旦扮梦中魂上）

【渔灯儿】恰才的追凉后雨困云淹,畅好是酣眠处粉腻黄黏。（贴）娘娘有请。（旦）呀,深宫之内,檐下何人叫唤? 悄没个宫娥报,轻来画檐。（贴）娘娘快请。（旦作倦态欠身介）我娇怯怯朦胧身欠,慢腾腾待自起开帘。

（作出见贴介）呀,原来是一个宫人!
（贴）

【前腔】俺不是隶长门,帚奉曾嫌;（旦)不是宫人,敢是别院的美人?（贴）俺不是列昭容,御座曾瞻。（旦）这等你是何人?（贴）

102

our immortal dance. (Chang'e *leaves.*)

HANHUANG: I must leave the moon now, at my mistress'
command, to go to the imperial Tang palace.

The Milky Way sparkles where a myriad stars twinkle,
And I gaze at the dusty world through a misty void;
Leaving the splendid heavens, my jade pendants quiver,
My gown reflecting brightness as I tread on rosy clouds.
To teach the palace maid our heavenly music,
I must call her sleeping spirit to the moon.

Here is the Tang palace.

The gate is locked, the curtains drawn,
And, beautiful as cherry blossom,
Lady Yang lies fast asleep;
Then quickly let me call her from her bed.

Get up, Lady Yang!

(Lady Yang's *spirit enters.*)

LADY:

Just now the rain ceased, but wet clouds
Hung low in the sky and the air was cool;
So I slept deep.

HANHUANG: Your Ladyship!

LADY: Who is that calling from the palace gate?

How is it that a guest comes unannounced?

HANHUANG: Come quickly, my lady! This way!

LADY(*Yawns*):

Still drowsy with sleep, I rise
And slowly draw back the curtains.

(*She sees* Hanhuang.) Oh, it is a palace maid.

HANHUANG:

I am no palace maid.

LADY: Do you come, then, from one of the other courtyards?

HANHUANG:

I am no concubine either.

LADY: Who are you then?

HANHUANG: I am a fairy maid of the moon, and my name is

103

儿家月中侍儿,名唤寒簧,则俺的名在瑶宫月殿金。(旦惊介)原来是月中仙子,何因到此?(贴)恰才奉姮娥口敕亲传点,请娘娘到桂宫中花下消炎。

(旦)哦,有这等事!(贴)娘娘不必迟疑。儿家引导,就请同行。(引旦行介)(合)【锦渔灯】指碧落,足下云生冉冉;步青霄,听耳中风弄纤纤。乍凝眸,星斗垂垂似可拈,早望见烂辉辉宫殿影在镜中潜。

(旦)呀,时当仲夏,为何这般寒冷?(贴)此即太阴月府,人间所传广寒宫者是也。就请进去。(旦喜介)想我浊质凡姿,今夕得到月府,好侥幸也。(作进看介)【锦上花】清游胜,满意饮。(想介)这些景物都似曾见过来!环玉砌,绕碧檐,依稀风景漫猜嫌。那壁桂花开的恁早!(贴)此乃月中丹桂,四时常茂,花叶俱香。(旦看介)果然好花也。看不足,喜更添。金英缀,翠

Hanhuang.

My name is on the list of fairies in the moon.

LADY (*Startled*): Oh! So you are a fairy from the moon! How did you come here?

HANHUANG:

Just now my mistress, the goddess of the moon,
Ordered me to invite you to come with me
And enjoy our cassia blossoms.

LADY: Can it be true?

HANHUANG: Don't hesitate, my lady; but let me lead the way. Come with me!

(*She leads her along.*)

TOGETHER:

We fly towards the azure sky,
While clouds float past beneath our feet,
And the wind whispers softly into our ears;
Then we gaze at the stars,
So near we could reach out a hand to pluck them.
We see the glorious palace of the moon
Like a reflection in a rounded mirror.

LADY: This is mid-summer—how is it that I feel so cold?

HANHUANG; Pepole call the moon the Palace of Boundless Cold. You may enter now.

LADY(*Overjoyed*): Tonight I, an ordinary mortal, have come to the moon! How fortunate I am! (*She enters the moon and looks round.*)

After that blissful journey I feel enchanted.

(*Thinks.*)

I seem to have seen this before.
The marble steps here and the emerald eaves
Look strangely familiar.

How could the cassia bloom so early?

HANHUANG: The cassia in the moon blooms all the year round, and both its flowers and leaves are fragrant.

LADY: It is really beautiful!

叶兼。氤氲芳气透衣缣,人在桂阴潜。

（内作乐介）（旦）你看一群仙女,素衣红裳,从桂树下奏乐而来,好不美听。（贴）此乃"霓裳羽衣"之曲也。（杂扮仙女四人、六人或八人,白衣、红裙、锦云肩、璎珞、飘带,各奏乐,唱,绕场行上介）、（旦贴旁立看介）（众）

【锦中拍】携天乐花丛斗拈,拂霓裳露沾。迥隔断红尘荏苒,直写出瑶台清艳。纵吹弹舌尖、玉纤,韵添;惊不醒人间梦魇,停不驻天宫漏签。一枕游仙,曲终闻盐,付知音重翻检。

（同下）（旦）妙哉此乐。清高宛转,感我心魂,真非人间所有也!

【锦后拍】缥缈中簇仙姿宛曾觇。听彻清音意厌厌,数琳琅琬琰;数琳琅琬琰,一字字偷将凤鞋轻点,按宫商揦记指儿尖。晕羞脸,枉自许舞娇歌艳,比着这钧天雅奏多是歉。

One never tires of looking,
For its charm grows as one gazes;
The blossoms seem of gold, the leaves of emerald,
And its heavy fragrance perfumes the clothes
Of all within its shade.
(*Music is heard offstage.*) Look! There is a group of fairies in white tunics and red skirts coming this way, playing music. How sweet the melody!

HANHUANG: This is the Dance of the Rainbow and Feathery Garments.

(*Fairies in white tunics and red skirts, with cloud-like belts and tassels, come in singing and playing music.* Lady Yang *and* Hanhuang *stand watching.*)

FAIRIES:

Among the flowers we play our heavenly music,
Our rainbow dresses touched with dew, far from the world of
    men;
Our music well expresses the moon's translucent beauty;
But though we sing, and play the flute and cymbals,
We shall not waken mortals from their slumbers,
Nor halt the fleeting hours in the moon.
We play the whole dance for her as she dreams,
That she may write it down when she awakes.
(*The fairies troop off.*)

LADY:

Marvellous music, so clear and melodious,
That moves my heart strangely!
This certainly is not a tune of the earth.
As the fairies thronged through the mist,
Their features seemed familiar;
And I listened intently to mark each note,
Following the rhythm with my fingers
And the beat with the tip of one foot.
I blush to remember my pride in my singing and dancing,

请问仙子，愿求月主一见。（贴）要见月主还早。天色渐明，请娘娘回宫罢。

【尾声】你攀蟾有路应相念，（旦）好记取新声无欠，（贴）只误了你把枕上君王半夜儿闪。

（旦下）（贴）杨妃已回唐宫，我索向月主娘娘覆旨则个。

碧瓦桐轩月殿开，曹唐
还将明月送君回。丁仙芝
钧天虽许人间听，李商隐
却被人间更漏催。黄滔

Which now seem so worthless compared with this heavenly music.

Tell me, fairy maid, may I see the mistress of the moon?

HANHUANG: The time for that has not yet come. It is nearly dawn, and Your Ladyship should return to your palace. But do not forget your trip to the moon!

LADY:

I can promise to remember this new melody.

HANHUANG:

We are sorry to have kept you from your emperor's side.

(Lady Yang *leaves*.)

HANHUANG: Now Lady Yang has returned to the Tang palace, I shall report my success to my mistress of the moon.

(*Exit*.)

第十一出　制谱

【仙吕过曲】【醉罗歌】【醉扶归】(老旦上)西宫才奉传呼罢,安排水榭要清佳。慢掷晶帘散朝霞,玉钩却映初阳挂。奴家永新是也。与念奴妹子同在西宫,承应贵妃杨娘娘。我娘娘再入宫闱,万岁爷更加恩幸。真乃"三千宠爱在一身,六宫粉黛无颜色"。今早娘娘分付,收拾荷亭,要制曲谱。念奴妹子在那里伏侍晓妆,奴家先到此间,不免将文房四宝,摆设起来。【皂罗袍】你看笔床初拂,光分素劄;砚池新注,香浮墨华——绿阴深处多幽雅。【排歌尾】竹风引,荷露洒,对波纹帘影弄参差。

　　呀,兰麝香飘,珮环风定,娘娘早则到也。(旦引贴上)

【正宫引子】【新荷叶】幽梦清宵度月华,听"霓裳羽衣"歌罢。醒来音节记无差,拟翻新谱消长夏。

SCENE 11
Writing the Music

(*The maid* Yongxin *enters.*)
YONGXIN:

I am carrying out the orders of Lady Yang,
To make the lakeside pavilion clean and pleasant;
As I roll up the crystal curtain the red clouds scatter,
And the morning sun shines in on the jasper clasp.

I, Yongxin, serve with Niannu in the west palace, where we wait
on Lady Yang. Since she came back to the palace the emperor has
shown her greater favour than ever, until his love for all his palace
ladies seems centred on one. None of the others can compare with
her. This morning Her Ladyship ordered me to prepare Lotus
Pavilion so that she compose some music here. Niannu is helping
her to dress, and I have come on ahead to set out the brushes and
ink.

The newly dusted brush-stand and paper are shining.
And the inkstone is filled with fragrant, fresh-ground ink;
In this green shade and chaste seclusion
The breezes whisper through the bamboo grove,
Dew drips from lotus leaves,
And the curtains' reflection quivers on the lake.

I can smell musk and hear the tinkle of jade pendants—
Her Ladyship is coming.

(Lady Yang *enters with* Niannu.)
LADY:

I dreamed last night that I visited the moon,
Where I saw the Rainbow and Feathery Garment Dance.
When I woke I still heard the music distinctly,
And I mean to write the melody down
To beguile this long summer day.

111

"斗画长眉翠淡浓,远山移入镜当中。晓窗日射胭脂颊,一朵红酥旋欲融。"我杨玉环自从截发感君之后,荷宠弥深。只有梅妃"惊鸿"一舞,圣上时常夸奖。思欲另制一曲,掩出其上。正在推敲,昨夜忽然梦入月宫。见桂树之下,仙女数人,素衣红裳,奏乐甚美。醒来追忆,音节宛然。因此分付永新,收拾荷亭,只待细配宫商,谱成新曲。(老旦)启娘娘:纸、墨、笔、砚,已安排齐备了。(旦)你与念奴一同在此伺候。(老旦、贴应,作打扇、添香介)(旦作制谱介)

【正宫过曲】【刷子带芙蓉】【刷子序】荷气满窗纱,鸾笺慢伸,犀管轻拿,待谱他月里清音,细吐我心上灵芽。这声调虽出月宫,其间转移过度,细微曲折之处,须索自加细审。安插,一字字要调停如法,一段段须融和入化。这几声尚欠调匀,拍**怎下?(内作莺啼,旦执笔听介)呀,妙阿!(作改介)【玉芙蓉】听宫莺数声,恰好应红牙。

(搁笔介)谱已制完,永新,是什么时候了?(老旦)晌午了。(旦)万岁爷可曾退

I have drawn my slender eyebrows,
Fair as the distant hills;
And the morning sun shines in
On rouged cheeks like a tender rose.

Since I cut off a lock of hair and moved the emperor's heart, he loves me more than ever; but he often praises that Frightened Swan Dance written by Lady Plum Blossom; so I have always wanted to compose a better tune. I was thinking of this last night, when I fell asleep and dreamed that I went to the moon and watched from under the cassia tree while fairies in white tunics and red skirts played some enchanting music. When I woke, the melody still seemed to be ringing in my ears, and I ordered Yongxin to clear Lotus Pavilion so that I could write the music for a new dance.

YONGXIN: All you need for writing is ready, my lady.

LADY: You and Niannu may stay here.

(Yongxin *and* Niannu *wave fan and burn incense, while* Lady Yang *writes.*)

LADY:

The scent of lotus fills the gauze-screened window;
I straighten the paper and take a brush to transcribe
The music of the moon and give expression
To my inspired thoughts.
Though I know the melody of this heavenly dance,
All the details must be carefully considered;
The words must be fitting, and the stanzas follow
In proper sequence.

These notes are not in harmony.

This rhythm—

(*An oriole sings, and* Lady Yang *listens.*) The very thing!
(*She corrects the score.*)

The trilling of the oriole was just what I needed.

(*She puts down her brush.*) Now the music is ready. What time is it, Yongxin?

YONGXIN: It is just noon.

LADY: Has His Majesty returned from the court yet?

113

朝？（老旦）尚未。（旦）永新，且随我更衣去来。念奴在此伺候，万岁爷到时，即忙通报。（贴）领旨。（旦）"好凭晚镜增蛾翠，漫试香纱换蝶衣。"（引老旦随下）（生行上）

【渔灯映芙蓉】【山渔灯】散千宫，朝初罢。拟对玉人，长昼闲话。寡人方才回宫，听说妃子在荷亭上，因此一径前来。依流水待觅胡麻，把银塘路踏。（作到介）（贴见介）呀，万岁爷到了。（生）念奴，你娘娘在何处闲欢耍？怎堆香几，有笔砚交加？（贴）娘娘在此制谱，方才更衣去了。（生）妃子，妃子！美人韵事，被你都占尽也。但不知制甚曲谱，待寡人看来。（作坐翻看介）消详，从头觑咱。妙哉，只这锦字荧荧银钩小，更度羽换宫没半米差。好奇怪，这谱连寡人也不知道。细按音节，不是人间所有，似从天下，果曲高和寡。妃子，不要说你婷婷绝世，只这一点灵心，有谁及得你来？【玉芙蓉】恁聪明，也堪压倒上阳花。

YONGXIN: Not yet.

LADY: Come with me, Yongxin, to help me change my dress. You wait here, Niannu, so that you can tell me as soon as His Majesty comes.

NIANNU: Very good, my lady.

LADY:

> *I shall repaint my eyebrows for the evening,*
> *And change into a fragrant butterfly gown.*

(Lady Yang *goes out with* Yongxin. *The emperor enters.*)

EMPEROR:

> *Having dismissed my ministers,*
> *I come from the court to see my beauty*
> *To while away this long, long day;*
> *At the palace I heard she had gone to Lotus Pavilion,*
> *So I follow the flowing stream to my paradise.*

NIANNU (*Curtseys*): Long live the emperor!

EMPEROR:

> *Where is your mistress, Niannu?*
> *What is this stationery*
> *Here on her fragrant desk?*

NIANNU: Her Ladyship has been composing music here, and has just gone to change her dress.

EMPEROR: My darling has all the accomplishments that grace a lovely woman. What music has she been composing? Let me have a look. (*He sits down to read the score.*)

> *As I read the score I marvel*
> *At the beauty of her delicate notation;*
> *And there is not the faintest dissonance*
> *In her transposal of scales.*

Strange! I have never heard this tune before. The melody has an unearthly quality, as if it came from heaven. It is indeed rare music. My darling is not only unmatched in beauty, but the genius she shows here has never been surpassed.

> *With intelligence alone she can outshine*
> *All the beauties in the palace.*

115

【普天赏芙蓉】【普天乐】(旦换妆,引老旦上)换轻妆,多幽雅;试生绡,添潇洒。(见生介)臣妾见驾。(生扶介)妃子坐了。(坐介)(生)妃子,看你晚妆新试,妩媚益增。似迎风袅袅杨枝,宛凌波濯濯莲花。芳兰一朵斜把云鬟压,越显得庞儿风流煞。(旦)陛下今日退朝,因何恁晚?(生)只为灵武太守员缺,地方紧要,与廷臣议了半日,难得其人。朕特擢郭子仪,补授此缺,因此退朝迟了。(旦)妾候陛下不至,独坐荷亭,爱风来一弄明纱,闲学谱新声奏雅。【玉芙蓉】怕输他舞"惊鸿",曲终满座有光华。

(生)寡人适见此谱,真乃千古奇音,"惊鸿"何足道也!(旦)妾凭臆见,草草创成。其中错误,还望陛下更定。(生)再同妃子,细细点勘一番。(老旦、贴暗下)(生、旦并坐翻谱介)

【朱奴折芙蓉】【朱奴儿】倚长袖香肩并亚;翻新谱玉纤同把。(生)妃子,似你绝调佳人世真寡,要觅破绽并无毫发。再问妃子,

116

(Lady Yang *enters in a different dress, attended by* Yongxin.)

LADY:

> *I have changed into a lighter, more graceful dress,*
> *And the silk tunic adds to its charm.*

(*She curtseys.*) Long live the emperor!

EMPEROR (*Helps her to rise*): Take a seat. (*She sits.*) This new style of dress makes you look more charming than ever.

> *You are like a willow in the breeze,*
> *A lotus glimmering in the lake;*
> *With that orchid in your hair,*
> *Your face is doubly enchanting.*

LADY: Why has Your Majesty returned from court so late today?

EMPEROR: Because it was necessary to appoint a new governor for Lingwu Province, and that is an important post. I discussed the matter with my ministers the whole morning without being able to find a suitable man; and finally promoted Guo Ziyi to the post. That is what delayed me.

LADY: As I was waiting alone for Your Majesty in Lotus Pavilion—

> *Enjoying the breeze from the window,*
> *I tried to write a new tune;*
> *But it falls far short of the Frightened Swan,*
> *For that outshines all others.*

EMPEROR: I have just seen it, and it is quite unique. How can that Swan Dance compare with this?

LADY: I wrote it hastily, without much thought; I hope Your Majesty will correct its mistakes.

EMPEROR: I shall go through it carefully with you.

(*The maids go out, and the emperor and* Lady Yang *sit down together to read the music.*)

EMPEROR:

> *I touch your long silk sleeve and your sweet shoulder*
> *As we sit together,*
> *And together our fingers go through the pages.*
> *Never has such a tune gladdened the world of men;*
> *I cannot find one flaw.*

117

此谱何名？（旦）妾于昨夜梦入月宫，见一群仙女奏乐，尽着霓裳羽衣。意欲取此四字，以名此曲。（生）好个"霓裳羽衣"！非虚假，果合伴天香桂花。【玉芙蓉】（作看旦介）觑仙姿，想前身原是月中娃。

此谱即当宣付梨园，但恐俗手伶工，未谙其妙。朕欲令永新、念奴，先抄图谱，妃子亲自指授。然后传与李龟年等，教习梨园子弟，却不是好。（旦）领旨。（生携旦起介）天已薄暮，进宫去来。

【尾声】晚风吹，新月挂，（旦）正一缕凉生凤榻。（生）妃子，你看这池上鸳鸯，早双眠并蒂花。

　　（生）芙蓉不及美人妆，王昌龄
　　（旦）杨柳风多水殿凉，刘长卿
　（老旦）花下偶然歌一曲，曹唐
　　（合）传呼法部按"霓裳"。王建

Tell me, what is the name of this piece?

LADY: Last night I dreamed that I was in the moon and saw a group of fairy musicians, dressed in rainbow-coloured and feathery garments; so I want to call it the Rainbow and Feathery Garment Dance.

EMPEROR: Good!

It is certainly heavenly music
To match the cassia flowers in the moon.

(*Looks at her.*)

And your unearthly beauty makes me think
You must once have been a fairy of the moon.

We must give this tune to the conservatory. But I am afraid ordinary musicians will not fully appreciate its excellence. I would like Yongxin and Niannu to copy this script and learn it from you, after which they can tell my orchestra leader, Li Guinian, how to teach it to his musicians. What do you say to this?

LADY: Yes, Your Majesty.

EMPEROR (*Helping* Lady Yang *to rise*): It is growing late; let us return to the palace.

An evening breeze is blowing,
The crescent moon has risen.

LADY:

The imperial couch will soon be growing cool.

EMPEROR:

And see, my sweet, where the lotus on the lake
Has lulled to rest the loving duck and drake.

(***Exeunt.***)

第十二出　权哄

【双调引子】【秋蕊香】（副净引丑从上）狼子野心难料，看跋扈渐肆咆哮，挟势辜恩更堪恼，索假忠言入告。

下官杨国忠。外凭右相之尊，内恃贵妃之宠。满朝文武，谁不趋承！独有安禄山这厮，外面假作痴愚，肚里暗藏狡许。不知圣上因甚爱他，加封王爵！他竟忘了下官救命之恩，每每遇事欺凌，出言挺撞。好生可恨！前日曾奏圣上，说他狼子野心，面有反相，恐防日后酿祸，怎奈未见听从。今日进朝，须索相机再奏，必要黜退了他，方快吾意。来此已是朝门，左右回避。（从下）（内喝道介）（副净）呀，那边呵殿之声，且看是谁？（净引丑从上）

【玉井莲后】宠固君心，暗中包藏计狡。

左右回避。（从下）（净见副净介）请了。（副净笑介）哦，原来是安禄山！（净）老杨，

120

SCENE 12
A Dispute Among the Mighty

(*Enter the prime minister with attendants.*)
YANG:

> Who can judge the ambition of the wolf cub
> That starts to snarl and glories in its power,
> Forgetting the gratitude it owes?
> My duty is to warn the emperor.

Now all the ministers and generals in the government bow before me because I am prime minister and cousin of the emperor's favourite—all but that fellow An Lushan, who pretends to be naive but is really plotting mischief. Why should His Majesty have grown so fond of him, and made him a prince? He forgets that I saved his life, and often opposes me and behaves insolently. Curse him! The other day I warned His Majesty that An is an ambitious wolf cub with treason written clearly on his face, and that steps should be taken to prevent his making trouble in the future; but the emperor did not listen to me. Today at court I shall find an opportunity to warn His Majesty again. Nothing short of having An dismissed will satisfy me. Here is the gate to the court. Attendants! Leave me!

(*The attendants retire. Shouts are heard offstage: "Clear the way!"*)

There is someone coming. I will see who it is.

(An Lushan *enters with attendants.*)

AN:

> Strongly entrenched in the emperor's favour,
> I hide my secret design.

Attendants, leave me! (*His attendants withdraw, and he greets the prime minister.*) Good day, my lord.

YANG (*Laughs*): So it is An Lushan.

你叫我怎么？（副净）这是九重禁地，你怎敢在此大声呵殿？（净作势介）老杨，你看我："脱下御衣亲赐着，进来龙马每教骑。常承密旨趋朝数，独奏边机出殿迟。"我做郡王的，便呵殿这么一声，也不妨，比似你右相还早哩！（副净冷笑介）好，好个"不妨"！安禄山，我且问你，这般大模大样是几时起的？（净）下官从来如此。（副净）安禄山，你也还该自去想一想！（净）想什么？（副净）你只想当日来见我的时节，可是这个模样么？（净）彼一时，此一时，说他怎的。（副净）唉，安禄山，

【仙吕入双调过曲】【风入松】你本是刀头活鬼罪难逃，那时节长跪阶前哀告。我封章入奏机关巧，才把你身躯全保。（净）赦罪复官，出自圣恩，与你何涉？（副净）好，倒说得干净！只太把良心昧了。恩和义，付与水萍飘。

（净）唉，杨国忠，你可晓得，

【前腔】世间荣落偶相遭？休夸着势压群僚。你道我失机之罪，可也记得南诏的事

AN: Well, old man, and what have you to say to me?

YANG: This is the imperial palace—how dare your attendants raise this uproar?

AN (*Insolently*): See here, Old Yang—

The robes I wear were given me by the emperor,
The horses I ride are from the imperial stable;
I am summoned for private discussions on frontier affairs,
And dismissed from the palace long after all others have left.

Since I am a prince and enjoy His Majesty's confidence, there can be no objection if my attendants call out to clear the way for me. That is nothing, of course, compared with your dignity as a minister.

YANG (*Laughs coldly*): So there can be no objection, eh? Let me ask you, An Lushan, since when have you become so high and mighty?

AN: I have always been like this.

YANG: Think back a little.

AN: To what?

YANG: To the time when you first came to see me. Were you like this then?

AN: That was different. Why harp on the past?

YANG: Why, An Lushan? Because

As good as dead, with no hope of reprieve,
You knelt at my feet to plead.
It was thanks to my cunning intervention
That the prisoner's life was spared.

AN: His Majesty in his mercy pardoned me and restored me to my post. What had you to do with it?

YANG: Well said, indeed!

You sin against your conscience!
Favour and kindness to you are like floating duckweed!

AN: As you know, Yang Guozhong—

Fame and disgrace depend upon fortune;
Then why should you boast of your pre-eminence?

You mentioned my failure; but do you remember the attack on

么？胡卢提掩败将功冒，怪浮云蔽遮天表。
（副净）圣明在上，谁敢朦蔽？这不是谤君
么！（净）还说不朦蔽，你卖爵鬻官多少？
贪财货，竭脂膏。（副净）住了，你道卖官鬻
爵，只问你的富贵，是那里来的？（冷笑介）
（净）也非止这一桩。若论你恃戚里，施奸
狡；误国罪，有千条。（副净）休得把诬蔑
语，凭虚造。（扯净介）我与你同去面当朝！

（净）谁怕你来，同去，同去！（作同扭进
朝俯伏介）（副净）臣杨国忠谨奏：

【前腔】【本调】禄山异志腹藏刀，外作痴愚
容貌，奸同石勒倚东门啸。他不拜储君，公
然桀傲，这无礼难容圣朝。望吾皇立赐罢
斥，除凶恶，早绝祸根苗。

（净伏介）臣安禄山谨奏：

【前腔】念微臣谬荷主恩高，遂使嫌生权要，
愚蒙触忤知难保。（泣介）陛下呵，怕孤立
终落他圈套。微臣呵，寸心赤，只有吾皇鉴

Nanzhao?

You hid the truth, and claimed that your defeat
Was a victory. Deceitful ministers
Like the drifting clouds obscuere their sovereign's splendour.

YANG: Who would dare deceive our sovereign? This is treason!

AN: Have you never deceived him?

How many posts and official ranks have you sold?
You have squeezed the people dry in your greed for wealth.

YANG: Hold your tongue! You talk about the sale of official posts.
How did you get *your* wealth if not through me? (*He laughs*
cynically.)

AN: Nor is that all, by any means.

You rely on your cousin's influence and your craft;
You are guilty of thousands of crimes against the state.

YANG:

Stop this baseless slander! (Yang *seizes* An.)
And come with me to the emperor!

AN: Who is afraid of you? Let us go!

(*Each gripping the other, they enter the royal presence and*
bow.)

YANG: May it please Your Majesty—

An Lushan hides a dagger in his heart;
Posing as a fool, he is at heart a traitor;
Often he gives vent to his treacherous ambition;
He once actually insulted the crown prince at court!

I beg Your Majesty to mete out justice immediately.

Such insolence is not to be endured.
This evil must be struck down while yet there is time.

AN: Your Majesty—

Such royal favour has been shown to me,
This man, great as he is, is jealous.
And, simple as I am, where can I fly,
Now that I have aroused his enmity?

(*Pretends to shed tears.*)

I fear I shall fall his victim soon;

125

昭。容出镇,犬马效微劳。(内)圣旨道来:杨国忠、安禄山互相讦奏,将相不和,难以同朝共理。特命安禄山为范阳节度使,克期赴镇。谢恩。(净、副净)万岁!(起介)(净向副净拱手介)老丞相,下官今日去了,你再休怪我大模大样。朝门内,一任你张牙爪,我去开幕府,自逍遥。(副净冷笑介)(净欲下,复转向副净介)还有一句话儿,今日下官出镇,想也仗回天力相提调。(举手介)请了,我且将冷眼,看伊曹。

　　(下)(副净看净下介)呀,有这等事!
【前腔】【本调】一腔块垒怎生消,我待把他威风抹倒;谁知反分节钺添荣耀,这话靶教人嘲笑。咳,但愿禄山此去,做出事来,方信我忠言最早!圣上、圣上,到此际可也悔今朝!

去邪当断勿狐疑, 周昙
祸稔萧墙竟不知; 储嗣宗
壮气未平空咄咄, 徐铉
甘言狡计奈娇痴! 郑嵎

126

Only the emperor knows my loyalty;
I beg permission to leave the capitl,
To serve at the frontier in some humble post.

VOICE OFF: His Majesty decrees that since Yang Guozhong and An Lushan accuse each other and will not work together, they must not both serve in the capital. The emperor herewith appoints An Luahan military governor of Fanyang, and orders him to proceed at once to his post.

AN and YANG: Long live the emperor! (*They rise.*)

AN (*Bows to* Yang): I am going now, old man. You will not be troubled any more by my insolence.

In the court you shall do as you please; and so shall I,
When I go to govern my principality.

(*The prime minister laughs bitterly. An starts to go, then turns back again.*)

One last word—

I suppose I should thank you, too, for this new appointment!
(*He salutes by bringing both hands together.*)

Goodbye! (*Aside.*)I Shall be watching him with interest! (*Exit.*)

YANG (*Watching him go*): This is a bad business, confound it!

I wanted to overthrow him;
But promoted instead he has troops at his command.
How can I vent my anger?
I shall be laughed at over this!

I only hope that An Lushan does revolt. Then—

The emperor will see that I warned him rightly,
And may regret the decision made today.

(*Exit.*)

第十三出　偷曲

【仙吕过曲】【八声甘州】(老旦、贴携谱上)(老旦)霓裳谱定,(贴合)向绮窗深处,秘本翻誊。香喉玉口,亲将绝调教成。(老旦)奴家永新,(贴)奴家念奴。(老旦)自从娘娘制就"霓裳"新谱,我二人亲蒙教授。今驾幸华清宫,即日要奏此曲。命我二人,在朝元阁上,传谱与李龟年,连夜教演梨园子弟。(贴)散序俱已传习,今日该传拍序了。(老旦)你看月明如水,正好演奏。我和你携了曲谱,先到阁中便了。(行介)(合)凉蟾正当高阁升,帘卷薰风映水晶。高清,恰称广寒宫仙乐声声。(下)

【道宫近词】【鱼儿赚】(末苍髯,扮李龟年上)乐部旧闻名,班首新推独老成。早暮趋承,上直更番入内廷。自家李龟年是也。向作伶官,蒙万岁爷点为梨园班首。今有贵妃

128

SCENE 13
Stealing the Music

(*Enter* Yongxin *and* Niannu *carrying the musical score.*)

YONGXIN:

At last the Dance of the Rainbow Garments is ready.

NIANNU:

By the gauze-screened window we copied the score,
And she with her silvery voice has taught us the tune.

YONGXIN: Her Ledyship composed this music and has taught it to us. Today the emperor is coming to Huaqing Palace to watch this dance, and he has ordered us to instruct the orchestra leader Li Guinian in Chaoyuan Pavilion, so that he can train his orchestra day and night.

NIANNU: They have learned the overture, and today we must teach them the first movement.

YONGXIN: Look, the moonlight is as limpid as water; it is just the hour for music. Let us take the score to the pavilion. (*They walk forward.*)

TOGETHER:

The cool moon rises over the high roof,
The warm breeze blows through the curtain,
And the moonlight is crystal clear;
This is a fitting night to play the fairy music of the
moon. (*Exeunt.*)

(*Enter the grey-bearded orchestra leader* Li Guinian.)

LI:

Well known to musicians as the old orchestra leader,
The whole day long I serve the emperor,
Who summons me often into the inner palace.

I am Li Guinian, formerly a court musician, until the emperor made me leader of the orchestra. Now Lady Yang's new music has been

娘娘"霓裳"新曲,奉旨令永新、念奴传谱出来,在朝元阁上教演,立等供奉。只得连夜趱习,不免唤齐众兄弟每同去。兄弟每那里?(副净扮马仙期上)仙期方响鬼神惊,(外扮雷海青上)铁拨争推雷海青。(净白须扮贺怀智上)贺老琵琶擅场屋,(丑扮黄幡绰上)黄家幡绰板尤精。(同见末介)李师父拜揖。(末)请了。列位呵,君王命,霓裳催演不教停。那永新、念奴呵,两娉婷,把红牙小谱携端正,早向朝元待月明。(众)如此,我每就去便了。(末)请同行。(同行介)趁迟迟宫漏夜凉生,把新腔敲订,新腔敲订。(同下)

【仙吕过曲】【解三酲犯】(小生巾服扮李谟)

【解三酲】逞风魔少年逸兴,借曲中妙理陶情。传闻今夜蓬莱境,翻妙谱,奏新声。小生李谟是也,本贯江南,遨游京国。自小谙通音律,久以铁笛擅名。近闻宫中新制一

copied by Yongxin and Niannu who are teaching it to us at Chaoyuan Pavilion. It is to be performed soon; so we have to rehearse day and night. I must call my musicians now. Hallo, there! Where are you all?

(*Enter* Ma Xianqi, *the stone-chime player.*)

MA:

My stone-chime startles even the gods on high!

(*Enter* Lei Haiqing, *the lute-player.*)

LEI:

No one can handle the plectrum better than I.

(*Enter* He Huaizhi, *a white-bearded lute-player.*)

HE:

My performance on the lute outshines the rest.

(*Enter* Huang Fanchuo, *the castanet-player.*)

HUANG:

But I believe my castanets are best!

ALL (*Greeting their leader*): Good evening, sir.

LI: Greetings.

The emperor orders us to rehearse the new music
Until we master it; and Her Ladyship's maids
Are waiting with the score in the moonlit pavilion.

ALL: Let us go, then.

LI: Right. (*They walk forward together.*)

ALL:

As the palace water-clock sounds and the night grows cool,
Let us learn to play the new melody aright. (*Exeunt.*)

(*The scholar Li Mo enters.*)

LI MO:

The eagerness of youth has drawn me on
To hear sweet music;
In the palace grounds
New melodies will be rehearsed tonight.

I am Li Mo, a native of Jiangnan, and I live in the capital; I studied music in my youth, and am noted for my performance on the iron flute. I hear that a new Rainbow Dance has just been

131

曲,名曰"霓裳羽衣"。乐工李龟年等,每夜在朝元阁中演习。小生慕此新声,无从得其秘谱。打听的那阁子,恰好临着宫墙,声闻于外。不免袖了铁笛,来到骊山,趁此月明如画,窃听一回。一路行来,果然好景致也。(行介)林收暮霭天气清,山入寒空月彩横。真佳景,【八声甘州】宛身从画里游行。

(场上设红帷作墙,墙内搭一阁介)(小生)说话之间,早来到宫墙下了。

【道宫调近词】【应时明近】只见五云中,宫阙影,窈窕玲珑映月明。光辉看不定,光辉看不定。想潜通御气,处处仙楼,阑干畔有玉人闲凭。

闻那朝元阁,在禁苑西首,我且绕着红墙,迤逦行去。(行介)

【前腔】花阴下,御路平,紧傍红墙款款行。(望介)只这垂杨影里,一座高楼露出墙头,想就是了。凝眸重细省,凝眸重细省,只见画帘缥缈,文窗掩映。(指介)兀的不是上有红灯!

(老旦、贴在墙内上阁介)(末众在内云)今日该演拍序,大家先将散序,从头演习一番。(小生)你看上面灯光隐隐,似有人声,一定是这里了。我且潜听一回。(作潜立听介)

【双赤子】悄悄冥冥,墙阴窃听。(内作乐介)(小生作袖出笛介)不免取出笛来,倚声和之。就将音节,细细记明便了。听到月高初更

132

composed in the palace, which Li's musicians are practising every night at Chaoyuan Pavilion; but though I want to hear it, I have not been able to get hold of the score. However, I have learned that the pavilion is just by the palace wall, so that the music can be heard outside. As I take my flute to Lishan to listen to the music in the bright moonlight, I enjoy the beautiful scenery along the road.

The evening mist in the forest has dispersed,
And the hills stand out against the spangled sky
Flooded with moonlight. In so sublime a scene,
I feel that I have wandered into a painting.

(*In the background there is a wall with a pavilion behind it.*)
I seem to have reached the palace wall already.

Against the clouds the palace stands out in relief,
Delicately silhouetted in the moonlight;
Pavilion after pavilion dazzles the eye,
Where lovely girls must be leaning against the railings.

I have heard that Chaoyuan Pavilion lies at the west end.
I will make my way there along the wall. (*He walks on.*)

Under the flowering trees the road is smooth,
As I walk forward skirting the crimson wall. (*He looks round.*)

I see a tall pavilion shaded by willows on the other side of the wall—that must be the place.

If I strain my eyes,
I can see painted curtains and latticed windows,
With red lanterns glowing inside.

(*The maids enter the pavilion on the other side of the wall,*)

LI (*From the other side of the wall*): Before we learn the first movement, let us rehearse the overture once more.

LI MO: Lanterns are lit, and I seem to hear voices. This must be the place. Now let me listen carefully. (*Listens.*)

I am listening secretly by the wall.

(*Music sounds and* Li Mo *takes out his flute.*) I shall accompany the music on my flute; that is the best way to remember the notes.

As the moon rises high, stringed instruments

后,果然弦索齐鸣。恰喜禁垣,夜深人静,玲珑齐应。这数声恍然心领,那数声恍然心领。

(内细十番,小生吹笛和介)(乐止,老旦、贴在内阁上唱后曲,小生吹笛合介)(老旦、贴)

【画眉儿】骊珠散迸,入拍初惊。云翻袂影,飘然回雪舞风轻。飘然回雪舞风轻,约略烟蛾态不胜。(小生接唱)这数声恍然心领,那数声恍然心领。

(内细十番如前,老旦、贴内唱,小生笛合介)(老旦、贴)

【前腔】珠辉翠映,凤翥鸾停。玉山蓬顶,上元挥袂引双成。上元挥袂引双成,尊绿回肩招许琼。(小生接唱)这数声恍然心领,那数声恍然心领。

(内又如前十番,老旦、贴内唱,小生笛合介)(老旦、贴)

【前腔】音繁调骋,丝竹纵横。翔云忽定,慢收舞袖弄轻盈。慢收舞袖弄轻盈,飞上瑶天歌一声。(小生接唱)这数声恍然心领,那数声恍然心领。

Begin to play on this forbidden ground;
The night is still,
But now castanets and chimes
Join in the lovely melody.
Yes, I have marked this music!

(Li Mo *plays his flute to accompany the music inside. When the music stops, the maids sing a chorus and* Li Mo *plays his flute again.*)

MAIDS:

Like scattered pearls the clear notes fall,
Like floating clouds our long skirts swirl,
Lightly as whirling snow we dance,
Softly and modestly.

LI MO:

Yes, I have marked this too!

(*Music sounds again and the maids sing again, while* Li Mo *plays his flute.*)

MAIDS:

Splendid with emeralds and pearls,
Like phoenixes that soar and then alight,
There on the crest of the enchanted hill
The fairies turn and wave their sleeves
To beckon each other on.

LI MO:

Yes, I have marked this too!

(*Music sounds again and then the maids sing again, while* Li Mo *plays his flute.*)

MAIDS:

Melodies swift and intricate are woven
From the stringed instruments;
Like floating clouds alighting,
Slowly we drop our sleeves and cease our dancing;
But our song still echoes in the moonlit sky.

LI MO:

Yes, I have marked this too!

（内又十番一通，老旦、贴暗下）（小生）妙哉曲也。真个如敲秋竹，似戛春冰，分明一派仙音，信非人世所有。被我都从笛中偷得，好侥幸也！

【鹅鸭满渡船】霓裳天上声，墙外行人听。音节明，宫商正，风内高低应。偷从笛里，写出无余剩。呀，阁上寂然无声，想是不奏了。人散曲终红楼静，半墙残月摇花影。

你看河斜月落，斗转参横，不免回去罢。（袖笛转行介）

【尾声】却回身，寻归径。只听得玉河流水韵幽清，犹似霓裳袅袅声。

　　　　倚天楼殿月分明，杜牧

　　　　歌转高云夜更清。赵嘏

　　　　偷得新翻数般曲，元稹

　　　　酒楼吹笛有新声。张祜

(*Music sounds again, and the maids go out.*)

LI MO: Wonderful! It is like the whispering of an autumn breeze in the bamboos or the swirling of water in spring. This is surely divine music, not of the world of men; yet I have caught it all with my flute. How fortunate I am.

I heard the heavenly music from behind the wall,
And captured its clear cadence with my flute;
Now from the hushed pavilion the musicians
Have gone, the singing is ended, the palace still,
While in the moonlight the shadows of flowers tremble.

The moon is going down and the Dipper's handle has turned. It is time to go back. (*He turns back.*)

As I take my homeward path, the rippling stream,
Gentle and clear, seems to echo the Rainbow Dance.

(***Exit.***)

第十四出　进果

【过曲】【柳穿鱼】(末扮使臣持竿、挑荔枝篮，作鞭马急上)一身万里跨征鞍，为进离支受艰难。上命遣差不由己，算来名利怎如闲！巴得个、到长安，只图贵妃看一看。

自家西州道使臣，为因贵妃杨娘娘，爱吃鲜荔枝，奉敕涪州，年年进贡。天气又热，路途又远，只得不惮辛勤，飞马前去。

(作鞭马重唱"巴得个"三句跑下)

【撼动山】(副净扮使臣持荔枝篮、鞭马急上)海南荔子味尤甘，杨娘娘偏喜啖。采时连叶包，缄封贮小竹篮。献来晓夜不停骖，一路里怕耽，望一站也么奔一站！

自家海南道使臣。只为杨娘娘爱吃鲜荔枝，俺海南所产，胜似涪州，因此敕与涪州并进。但是俺海南的路儿更远，这荔枝过了七日，香味便减，只得飞驰赶去。(鞭

SCENE 14
The Lichee Fruit

(*The first envoy rides in, carrying a basket of lichee fruit suspended from a pole.*)

FIRST ENVOY:

A thousand miles in the saddle,
And a hard, rough journey,
Just to deliver this lichee fruit.
Orders from above must be obeyed;
So it is better to live a life of leisur
Than look for fame or fortune.
I only hope, when I reach Chang'an,
That my fruit will be given to Lady Yang.

I am the envoy from Sichuan. As Lady Yang is partial to lichee fruit, the emperor has ordered Fuzhou District to send lichee as tribute every year. With the heat and the great distance to the capital, a man has to put up with a lot of hardships if he is to make a speedy journey. (*He gallops off.*)

(*The second envoy rides in, carrying a basket of lichee fruit.*)

SECOND ENVOY:

The lichee of the south is sweetest,
And Lady Yang likes it well;
When the fruit is picked it is wrapped in leaves,
Packed in a basket and sent on swiftly
From one posting station to another,
With no time to rest on the road.

I am the envoy of Guangzhou. Lady Yang likes fresh lichee fruit, and the lichee grown in Guangzhou is even better than that of Fuzhou; so we are ordered to send it too; only our district is even further from the capital. Seven days after it is picked, the lichee

139

马重唱"一路里"二句跑下）

【十棒鼓】（外扮老田夫上）田家耕种多辛苦，
愁旱又愁雨。一年靠这几茎苗，收来半要
偿官赋，可怜能得几粒到肚！每日盼成熟，
求天拜神助。

　　老汉是金城县东乡一个庄家。一家八
口，单靠着这几亩薄田过活。早间听说进
鲜荔枝的使臣，一路上捎着径道行走，不知
踏坏了人家多少禾苗！因此，老汉特到田
中看守。（望介）那边两个算命的来了。
（小生扮算命瞎子手持竹板，净扮女瞎子弹弦子，
同行上）

【蛾郎儿】住褒城，走咸京，细看流年与五
星。生和死，断分明，一张铁口尽闻名。瞎
先生，真灵圣，叫一声，赛神仙，来算命。

（净）老的，我走了几程，今日脚疼，委实走
不动。不是算命，倒在这里挣命了。（小
生）妈妈，那边有人说话，待我问他。（叫
介）借问前面客官，这里是什么地方了？
（外）这是金城东乡，与渭城西乡交界。（小
生斜揖介）多谢客官指引。（内铃响，外望介）

140

loses flavour; so I have to hurry. (*He gallops off.*)

(*An old peasant enters.*)

PEASANT:

> *The peasant's lot is hard,*
> *With worry about drought and rain;*
> *Only this little grain each year,*
> *Yet after harvest half of it goes for taxes,*
> *And what is left is not enough to eat;*
> *So every day we pray to Heaven*
> *To let it ripen soon.*

I am a peasant of the eastern village of Jincheng District. I have eight mouths to feed, but only these few acres of land; and this morning I heard the envoys who are delivering lichee fruit galloping across the fields to shorten their road. Who knows how many crops they have trampled underfoot! So I have come to guard my crops. (*He looks round.*) Two fortune-tellers are coming this way.

(*A blind man with a clapper and a blind woman with a stringed instrument come in.*)

TOGETHER:

> *We travel east and west,*
> *Reading men's horoscopes or from the stars*
> *Foretelling life and death;*
> *And our prophecies are known to all,*
> *For blind though we may be we are inspired.*
> *Is there anyone here who wants his fortune told?*

BLIND WOMAN: We have travelled a long way today, husband, and my feet are aching. I can't go any further. It's our death we shall be foretelling soon, not other people's fortunes.

BLIND MAN: There is someone here, wife. Let me ask him where we are. (*He calls out.*)Pray, sir, what district is this?

PEASANT: This is the east village of Jincheng, next to the west village of Weicheng.

BLIND MAN (*Bowing*):Thank you, sir.

(*Horses' bells are heard.*)

呀，一队骑马的来了。（叫介）马上长官，往大路上走，不要踏了田苗！（小生一面对净语介）妈妈，且喜到京不远，我每叫向前去，雇个毛驴子与你骑。（重唱"瞎先生"三句走介）（末鞭马重唱前"巴得个"三句急上，冲倒小生、净下）（副净鞭马重唱前"一路里"二句急上，踏死小生下）（外跌脚向鬼门哭介）天啊，你看一片田禾，都被那厮踏烂，眼见的没用了。休说一家性命难存，现今官粮紧急，将何办纳！好苦也！（净一面作爬介）哎呀，踏坏人了，老的啊，你在那里？（作摸着小生介）呀，这是老的。怎么不做声，敢是踏昏了？（又摸介）哎呀，头上湿渌渌的。（又摸闻手介）不好了，踏出脑浆来了！（哭叫介）我那天呵，地方救命。（外转身作看介）原来一个算命先生，踏死在此。（净起斜福介）只求地方，叫那跑马的人来偿命。（外）哎，那跑马的呵，乃是进贡鲜荔枝与杨娘娘的。一路上来，不知踏坏了多少人，不敢要他偿命。何况你这一个瞎子！（净）如此怎了！（哭介）我那老的呵，我原算你的命，是要倒路死的。只这个尸首，如今怎么断送！（外）也罢，你那里去叫地方，就是老汉同你抬去埋了罢。（净）如此多谢，我就跟着你做一家儿，可不是好！（同抬小生）（哭，诨下）（丑扮驿卒上）

PEASANT (*Looking round*): Oh, horsemen are coming! (*He calls out.*) Keep to the highway, gentlemen, and don't trample on the grain!

BLIND MAN: It is not far to the capital, wife; I will go ahead to hire a donkey for you. (*He walks on. The first envoy rides up and knocks down the blind couple, then gallops off. Immediately after, the second envoy rides up and tramples the blind man to death, then gallops off.*)

PEASANT (*Stamping and wailing*): Heaven help us! All the grain has been trampled and destroyed—we shall have nothing to eat, and the tax-collectors are pressing us hard. How can we pay them? (*The blind woman is crawling on the ground.*)

BLIND WOMAN: They trampled us underfoot, the scoundrels! Where are you, husband? (*She feels the blind man.*) Here is my husband; but why is he so quiet? Has he fainted? (*She passes her hands over him.*) Oh, his head is wet! ... Oh! His brains have been crushed! (*Cries.*) Heaven take pity on us!

PEASANT (*Looking round*): So the blind fortuneteller has been killed too.

BLIND WOMAN (*Getting up*): I must beg the authorities here to make that rider pay for my man's life.

PEASANT: Those horsemen are sending lichee fruit as tribute for Lady Yang. Heaven knows how many people they have trampled to death; but who dares to ask for compensation? And what chance has a blind woman?

BLIND WOMAN: What's to be done, then? (*Cries.*) Oh, my husband, I knew that your fate was to die on the road; but how am I to get you buried?

PEASANT: How can *you* find the local authorities? I had better help you to bury him.

BLIND WOMAN: Oh thank you kindly. If I could only stay here with you!

(*Weeping, they carry the corpse off. A groom from the posting station enters.*)

143

【小引】驿官逃,驿官逃,马死单单剩马瞭。驿子有一人,钱粮没半分。拼受打和骂,将身去招架,将身去招架!

自家渭城驿中,一个驿子便是。只为杨娘娘爱吃鲜荔枝,六月初一是娘娘的生日,涪州、海南两处进贡使臣,俱要赶到。路由本驿经过,怎奈驿中钱粮没有分文,瘦马刚存一匹。本官怕打,不知逃往那里去了,区区就便权知此驿。只是使臣到来,如何应付?且自由他!(末飞马上)

【急急令】黄尘影内日衔山,赶赶赶,近长安。(下马介)驿子,快换马来。(丑接马、末放果篮、整衣介)(副净飞马上)一身汗雨四肢瘫,趱趱趱,换行鞍。

(下马介)驿子,快换马来。(丑接马,副净放果篮,与末见介)请了,长官也是进荔枝的?(末)正是。(副净)驿子,下程酒饭在那里?(丑)不曾备得。(末)也罢,我每不吃饭了,快带马来。(丑)两位爷在上,本驿只剩有一匹马,但凭那一位爷骑去就是。

GROOM:

> *The station master has fled,*
> *And all the horses are dead;*
> *I am the only groom that's left.*
> *I don't get paid, yet I am cursed and whipped,*
> *And made to take all the blame.*

I am a groom at Weicheng posting station. Lady Yang is fond of eating lichee fruit and the first of the sixth moon is her birthday; so the envoys sending tribute of fruit from Fuzhou and Guangzhou must reach the capital by that day; and they will be passing here. But there is no more money in our station and only one lean nag left, while the station master has made off to avoid being beaten, leaving me in charge. What am I going to say to the envoys when they come? Well, it can't be helped.

(*The first envoy gallops up.*)

FIRST ENVOY:

> *The sun sinks in clouds of dust behind the hills;*
> *But I gallop on and on in haste to Chang'an.*

(*He alights.*) Station master! Give me a new horse quickly.

(*The groom takes his reins, while the envoy puts down his basket and dusts his clothes.*)

(*The second envoy gallops up.*)

SECOND ENVOY:

> *Aching in every limb and drenched with sweat,*
> *I race to change my horse.*

(*He alights.*) Station master! Give me a new horse at once. (*The groom takes his reins, while the second envoy put down his fruit basket and greets the first envoy.*) Good day, sir. Are you sending fruit too?

FIRST ENVOY: I am.

SECOND ENVOY: Where is our meal, groom?

GROOM: It isn't ready.

FIRST ENVOY: Never mind, we won't eat now; just bring the horses out quickly.

GROOM: I am sorry, gentlemen, but there is only one horse left in

145

（副净）哎，偌大一个渭城驿，怎么只有一匹马！快唤你那狗官来，问他驿马那里去了？（丑）若说起驿马，连年都被进荔枝的爷每骑死了。驿官没法，如今走了。（副净）既是驿官走了，只问你要。（丑指介）这棚内不是一匹马么？（末）驿子，我先到，且与我先骑了去。（副净）我海南的来路更远，还让我先骑。（末作向内介）

【恁麻郎】我只先换马，不和你斗口。（副净扯介）休恃强，惹着我动手。（末取荔枝在手介）你敢把我这荔枝乱丢！（副净取荔枝向末介）你敢把我这竹笼碎扭！（丑劝介）请罢休，免气吼，不如把这匹瘦马同骑一路走！（副净放荔枝打丑介）哎，胡说！

【前腔】我只打你这泼腌臜死囚！（末放荔枝打丑介）我也打你这放刁顽贼头！（副净）克官马，嘴儿太油。（末）误上用，胆儿似斗。

our station; you can decide yourselves which of you shall have it.

SECOND ENVOY : What! Such a big station, and only one horse? Call your rogue of a station master out, and I'll ask him what he's done with the horses!

GROOM: These last few years our horses have been ridden to death by envoys sending the tribute fruit. The station master was at his wit's end, so he ran away.

SECOND ENVOY: If the station master is not here, we can demand the horses from you.

GROOM (*Pointing to the stable*): There is the horse.

FIRST ENVOY: I got here first; let me have it.

SECOND ENVOY: I come from Guangzhou, which is farther away; you should let me have it.

FIRST ENVOY (*Turing to the stable*):
  I have no time to argue with you;
  I am going to change my horse.

SECOND ENVOY (*Pulling him back*):
  Don't stubborn, or you'll feel my fist.

FIRST ENVOY: Don't you dare touch my lichee fruit!
  (*He picks up his basket.*)

SECOND ENVOY: Don't you dare touch my basket!
  (*He picks up his basket.*)

GROOM (*Pleading*):
  Steady on, gentlemen!
  Suppose you both ride the lean horse?

SECOND ENVOY (*Putting down his basket and starting to beat the groom*):
  You dolt! I'm going to beat you well, you rascal!

FIRST ENVOY: (*Putting down his basket and starting to beat the groom too*):
  I'm going to beat you too, you trickster!

SECOND ENVOY:
  You glib-tongued stealer of government horses, you!

FIRST ENVOY:
  You bold thief, holding up business of state!

（同打介）（合）鞭乱抽，拳痛殴，打得你难捱，那马自有！

【前腔】（丑叩头介）向地上连连叩头，望台下轻轻放手。（末、副净）若要饶你，快换马来。（丑）马一匹驿中现有，（末、副净）再要一匹。（丑）第二匹实难补凑。（末、副净）没有只是打！（丑）且慢纽，请听剖，我只得脱下衣裳与你权当酒！

（脱衣介）（末）谁要你这衣裳！（副净作看衣、披在身上介）也罢，赶路要紧。我原骑了那马，前站换去。（取果上马，重唱前"一路里"二句跑下）（末）快换马来我骑。（丑）马在此。（末取果上马，重唱前"巴得个"三句跑下）（丑吊场）咳，杨娘娘，杨娘娘，只为这几个荔枝呵！

铁关金锁彻明开，崔液
黄纸初飞敕字回。元稹
驿骑鞭声砉流电，李郢
无人知是荔枝来。杜牧

(*They beat him.*)

ENVOYS:

> *Under the strokes of our whips and fists,*
> *You may think better of it, and produce the horses!*

GROOM (*Kowtowing*):

> *Again and again I kowtow,*
> *And beg your honours to let me go!*

ENVOYS: If you want us to let you off, quickly bring the horses!

GROOM:

> *There is one horse in the stable.*

ENVOYS: We need another.

GROOM:

> *But I can't get you another.*

ENVOYS: Then we shall have to beat you again.

GROOM:

> *Just a moment, gentlemen!*
> *Please take my jacket to buy wine.*

(*He takes off his jacket.*)

FIRST ENVOY: Who wants your clothes?

(*The second envoy examines the coat, and puts it on.*)

SECOND ENVOY: All right, I must hurry. I shall change my horse at the next station. (*Picking up his fruit basket, he mounts his horse and rides off.*)

FIRST ENVOY: Quickly bring me the new horse.

GROOM: Here you are, sir.

(*The first envoy picks up his basket, mounts the horse and rides off.*)

GROOM: Oh, Lady Yang, Lady Yang! This is all because of your lichee fruit!

(***Exit.***)

第十五出　舞盘

【仙吕引子】【奉时春】（生引二内侍、丑随上）
山静风微昼漏长，映殿角火云千丈。紫气
东来，瑶池西望，翩翩青鸟庭前降。

朕同妃子避暑骊山。今当六月朔日，
乃是妃子诞辰。特设宴在长生殿中，与他
称庆，并奏"霓裳"新曲。高力士传旨后宫，
宣娘娘上殿。（丑）领旨。（向内传介）（内厅
"领旨"介）（旦盛妆、引老旦、贴上）

【唐多令】日影耀椒房，花枝弄绮窗。门悬
小帨赭罗黄，绣得文鸾成一对，高傍着五云
翔。

（见介）臣妾杨氏见驾。愿陛下万岁，
万万岁！（生）与妃子同之。（旦坐介）（生）
紫云深处婺光明，（旦）带露灵桃倚日荣。

SCENE 15
The Disk Dance

(*Enter the emperor, accompanied by two attendants and the eunuch* Gao Lishi.)

EMPEROR:

> *Breezes play in the quiet mountains*
> *While the sun moves slowly,*
> *Flaming on the sultry clouds*
> *Banked high above the palace;*
> *From the east rises a purple mist,*
> *And fairy blue birds out of paradise*
> *Alight in our court.*

I am spending the summer with Lady Yang in Lishan, and today, the first of the sixth moon, is her birthday; so I have ordered a feast for her in the Palace of Eternal Youth, and the new Dance of the Rainbow Garments will be performed. Gao Lishi, pass on the order to the inner palace requesting Her Ladyship to come.

GAO: Yes, sire. (*He gives the order, and* Lady Yang *enters, gorgeously dressed and accompanied by her two maids.*)

LADY:

> *The sun shines into the scented chamber,*
> *And flowers rustle against the gauze-screened windows;*
> *Over the door hangs a curtain of yellow silk.*
> *Embroidered with phoenixes soaring above bright clouds.*

(*She curtseys.*) Long live the emperor! May Your Majesty live ten thousand years!

EMPEROR: Long life to my love!

(Lady Yang *sits down.*)

EMPEROR:

> *Deep in the purple clouds shines the Lady Star.*

(老旦、贴)岁岁花前人不老,(丑合)长生殿里庆长生。(生)今日妃子初度,寡人特设长生之宴,同为竟日之欢。(旦)薄命生辰,荷蒙天宠。愿为陛下进千秋万岁之觞。(丑)酒到。(旦拜,献生酒,生答赐,旦跪饮,叩头呼"万岁",坐介)(生)

【高平过曲】【八仙会蓬海】【八声甘州】风薰日朗,看一叶阶蓂摇动炎光。华筵初启,南山遥映霞觞。【玩仙灯】(合)果合欢,桃生千岁;花并蒂,莲开十丈。【月上海棠】宜欢赏,恰好殿号长生,境齐蓬阆。

（小生扮内监,捧表上)"手捧金花红榜子,齐来宝殿祝千秋。"(见介)启万岁爷、娘娘,国舅杨丞相,同韩、虢、秦三国夫人,献上寿礼贺笺,在外朝贺。(丑取笺送生看介)(生)生受他每。丞相免行礼,回朝办事。

LADY:

I am like the peach tree bathed in splendid sunlight.

MAIDS:

May old age never come to the happy pair.

TOGETHER:

May they even be young in the Palace of Eternal Youth!

EMPEROR: I have prepared a feast, because it is your birthday, to wish you eternal youth. And we shall spend this day in pleasure.

LADY: I am overwhelmed by your royal favour, and would like to drink to your eternal life.

GAO: The wine is served.

(Lady Yang *curtseys and offers wine to the emperor, who then passes her the cup. She drinks kneeling to express her thanks.*)

EMPEROR:

Warm breeze and blazing sun—

The leaves in the courtyard tremble

In burning light.

A magnificent feast is spread,

And we raise to our lips the bright and brimming goblet.

TOGETHER:

We take pleasure here, where the peach trees bloom

For a thousand years and huge lotus flowers open in
    pairs.

Well is the palace named "Eternal Youth,"

For here one knows the joys of paradise.

(*A eunuch enters with a scroll.*)

EUNUCH:

Bearing a crimson scroll with gold design,

They come to the palace to offer congratulations.

I beg to report to Your Majesty and Your Ladyship that the prime minister and the three duchesses have come to offer congratulations, bringing a congratulatory address and gifts. (*He presents the scroll to the emperor.*)

EMPEROR: Give them our thanks. The prime minister need not stand on ceremony, but should return to his office to attend to

三国夫人，候朕同娘娘回宫筵宴。（小生）
领旨。（下）（净扮内监捧荔枝、黄袱盖上）"正
逢瑶圃千秋宴，进到炎州十八娘。"（见介）
启万岁爷，涪州、海南贡进鲜荔枝在此。
（生）取上来。（丑接荔枝去袱、送上介）（生）妃
子，朕因你爱食此果，特勒地方飞驰进贡。
今日寿宴初开，佳果适至，当为妃子再进一
觞。（旦）万岁！（生）宫娥每，进酒。（老贴
进酒介）（旦）

【杯底庆长生】【倾杯序】【换头】盈筐，佳果
香，幸黄封远勒来川广。爱他浓染红绡，薄
裹晶丸，入手清芬，沁齿甘凉。【长生导引】
（合）便火枣交梨应让，只合来万岁台前，千
秋筵上，伴瑶池阿母进琼浆。

　　高力士，传旨李龟年，押梨园子弟上殿
承应。（丑）领旨。（向内传介）（末引外、净、副
净、丑各锦衣、花帽，应"领旨"上）"红牙待拍筝
排柱，催着红罗上舞筵，换戴柘枝新帽子，
随班和到御阶前。"（见介）乐工李龟年，押
领梨园子弟，叩见万岁爷、娘娘。（生）李龟
年，"霓裳"散序昨已奏过，"羽衣"第二叠可

154

affairs of state. The three duchesses may wait to feast with us later in the palace.

EUNUCH: The emperor's orders shall be obeyed. (*Exit.*)

(*Another eunuch enters carrying lichee fruit covered with yellow silk.*)

SECOND EUNUCH:

> *At the birthday feast of the gods*
> *We present the southern fruit.*

May it please Your Majesty, the lichee fruit from Fuzhou and Guangzhou has arrived.

EMPEROR: Bring it here.

(Gao Lishi *receives the fruit, and removes the cover.*)

My love, knowing your fondness for this fruit, I ordered the local authorities to send it here posthaste; and now it has arrived in time for your feast. For this I shall drink to you.

LADY: Long live the emperor!

EMPEROR: Maids, fill the cups.

(*The two maids fill their cups.*)

> *I see two baskets of fragrant fruit*
> *From far-off Sichuan and Guangzhou;*
> *Like crystal globes in crimson satin wrapped,*
> *Cool, fragrant fruit, surpassing in its sweetness*
> *Both dates and pears, and fit fare for a goddess*
> *With elixirs at the feast of eternal youth.*

Now, Gao Lishi, order Li Guinian and his musicians to play to us.

GAO: As you command! (*Gives the order, and* Li Guinian *enters with the other musicians, all of them wearing silk livery and bright caps.*)

MUSICIANS:

> *With lutes and harps, in crimson silk,*
> *We enter in high hats to halt by the steps.*

Li Guinian and his musicians salute Your Majesty snd Your Ladyship.

EMPEROR: Yesterday you played us the overture; have you rehearsed the first movement for today?

曾演熟?（末）演熟了。（生）用心去奏。
（末）领旨。（起介）（暗下）（旦）妾启陛下，此
曲散序六奏，止有歇拍而无流拍。中序六
奏，有流拍而无促拍，其时未有舞态。

【八仙会蓬海】【换头】只是悠扬，声情俊爽。
要停住彩云，飞绕虹梁。至羽衣三叠，名曰
饰奏。一声一字，都将舞态含藏。其间有
慢声，有缠声，有衰声，应清圆，骊珠一串；
有入破，有摊破，有出破，合袅娜齆觬千状；
还有花犯，有道和，有傍拍，有间拍，有催
拍，有偷拍，多音响，皆与慢舞相生，缓歌交
畅。

（生）妃子所言，曲尽歌舞之蕴。（旦）
妾制有翠盘一面，请试舞其中，以博天颜一
笑。（生）妃子妙舞，寡人从未得见。永新、
念奴，可同郑观音、谢阿蛮伏侍娘娘，上翠
盘来者。（老、贴）领旨。（旦起福介）告退更
衣。"整顿衣裳重结束，一身飞上翠盘中。"
（引老、贴下）（生）高力士，传旨李龟年，领梨
园子弟按谱奏乐。朕亲以羯鼓节之。（丑）
领旨。（向内传介）（生起更衣，末、众在场内作
乐介）（场上设翠盘，旦花冠、白绣袍、璎珞、锦云
肩、翠袖、大红舞裙，老、贴同净，副净扮郑观音、谢
阿蛮，各舞衣、白袍，痕迹执五彩霓旌、孔雀云扇，

LI: May it please Your Majesty, we have.

EMPEROR: See that you play it well.

LI: We will, Your Majesty. (*Exit* Li *with his musicians.*)

LADY: May I venture to point out that both the overture and the first movement contain six bars which are not accompanied by dancing.

> *They open with a flourish,*
> *To arrest the rosy clouds*
> *And make the echoes linger in the rafters;*
> *But in the second movement*
> *Each note, each word, conforms*
> *To a new motion in the dance.*
> *So, like a string of pearls,*
> *The enchanting music and the dance evolve*
> *Each from the other.*

EMPEROR: You have explained the dance very well.

LADY: I have had a green disk made, and I would like to dance on it for Your Majesty's amusement.

EMPEROR: I have never seen you dance—that must be an entrancing sight. Yongxin and Niannu, Zheng Guanyin and Xie Aman, accompany Her Ladyship as she dances on the disk.

MAIDS: Yes, sire.

LADY:

> *Let me change into a dancing costume,*
> *Then swiftly take my place on the emerald disk.*

(Lady Yang *withdraws to change her costume, accom-panied by the maids.*)

EMPEROR: Gao Lishi, order Li Guinian and his musicians to play the music according to the score, while I beat the rhythm on the drum.

GAO: Yes, Your Majesty.

(*As he gives the order, the emperor retires to change his clothes. The musicians begin to play, and a green disk is placed on the stage.* Lady Yang *comes back wearing an embroidered headdress, embroidered white tunic with green sleeves, a cape with coloured cloud designs, and a red dancing skirt. The four maids, who are*

157

密遮旦簇上翠盘介）（乐止，旌扇徐开，旦立盘中舞，老、贴、净、副唱，丑跪捧鼓，生上坐击鼓，众在场内打细十番合介）

【羽衣第二叠】【画眉序】罗绮合花光，一朵红云自空漾。【皂罗袍】看霓旌四绕，乱落天香。【醉太平】安详，徐开扇影露明妆。【白练序】浑一似天仙，月中飞降。（合）轻飏，彩袖张，向翡翠盘中显伎长。【应时明近】飘然来又往，宛迎风菡萏，【双赤子】翩翩叶上。举袂向空如欲去，乍回身侧度无方。（急舞介）盘旋跌宕，花枝招飐柳枝扬，凤影高骞鸾影翔。【拗芝麻】体态娇难状，天风吹起，众乐缤纷响。【小桃红】冰弦玉柱声嘹亮，鸾笙象管音飘荡，【花乐栏】恰合着羯鼓低昂。按新腔，度新腔，【怕春归】褰金裙，齐作留仙想。（生住鼓，丑携去介）【古轮台】舞住敛霞裳，（朝上拜介）重低额，山呼万

*also wearing embroidered white tunics, carry peacock fans and
banners with coloured cloud designs with which they hide* Lady
Yang *from view when she has stepped on the disk. As the music
stops, the fans slowly part to disclose* Lady Yang *standing in the
centre of the disk. The maids start to sing,* Gao Lishi *kneels to
hold the drum, and the emperor sits down in the middle of the
stage and beats the drum while the other musicians play their own
instruments.*)

ALL:

    With lustrous silk and brilliant flowers
    A rosy cloud seems floating in the air;
    Rainbow-bright banners wave and fragrant petals
    Are showered from the sky;
    The parted fans reveal a heavenly beauty
    Descending from the moon. Her bright sleeves flutter
    As she displays her skill on the emerald disk,
    And sways there like a lotus in the wind,
    With leaves that quiver; till her sleeves float high
    As if to soar away, swaying from side to side
    With matchless grace. (The music quickens.)
    Whirling, rising and falling like flowering sprays,
    Like a quivering willow or phoenix flying on high,
    Her grace and fascination defy description;
    The wind springs up and heavenly music sounds,
    Like the crackling of ice or clanging tinkle of jade;
    Flutes, pipe-organs and lutes have shattered the silence,
    The drum beats out the time for the tune,
    And gilded skirts whirl,
    As in the famous dance of Lady Swallow.

(*The emperor stops playing the drum, which* Gao Lishi *carries
off.*)

    The dance is over,
    The cloud-like garments are still.

(Lady Yang *curtseys to the emperor.*)

    And she bows low

岁拜君王。

（老、贴、净、副扶旦下盘介）（净、副暗下）（生起，前携旦介）妙哉，舞也！逸态横生，浓姿百出。宛若翻风回雪，恍如飞燕游龙，真独擅千秋矣。宫娥每，看酒来，待朕与妃子把杯。（老、贴奉酒，生擎杯介）

【千秋舞霓裳】【千秋岁】把金觞，含笑微微向，请一点点檀口轻尝。（付旦介）休得留残，休得留残，酬谢你舞怯腰肢劳攘。（旦接杯谢介）万岁！【舞霓裳】亲颁玉醴恩波广，惟惭庸劣怎承当！（生看旦介）俺仔细看他模样，只这持杯处，有万种风流殢人肠。

（生）朕有鸳鸯万金锦十疋，丽水紫磨金步摇一事，聊作缠头。（出香囊介）还有自佩瑞龙脑八宝锦香囊一枚，解来助卿舞珮。（旦接香囊谢介）万岁。（生携旦行介）

【尾声】（生）霓裳妙舞千秋赏，合助千秋祝未央。（旦）微幸杀亲沐君恩透体香。

（生）长生秘殿倚青苍。吴融
（旦）玉醴还分献寿觞。张说
（生）饮罢更怜双袖舞，韩翃
（旦）满身新带五云香。曹唐。

160

To wish the emperor eternal life.

(Yongxin *and* Niannu *help* Lady Yang *down from the disk, while the two other maids retire. The emperor steps forward to take* Lady Yang's *hands.*)

EMPEROR: That was an exquisite dance, which proved that there is no end to your charms. It was like whirling snow or a swallow in flight, surpassing anything that has been for many centuries. Maids, bring the wine! Let me offer you a cup.

(*The maids bring the wine, and the emperor holds the cup.*)

Smiling I hold the golden goblet,
And hope your sweet lips will but taste the wine.

(*He gives it to her.*)

In thanks for your dance,
I ask you to drain this cup.

(Lady Yang *receives the cup and curtseys.*)

LADY: Long live the emperor!

The emperor himself holds out the cup,
Making me blush with shame to have danced so ill.

EMPEROR (*Gazing at her*):

The way that she holds the cup
Is utterly alluring.

I shall give you ten silk rolls with birds embroidered in gold, and a gold tiara as fee for this fairy dance. (*Takes out a scented pouch.*) And I give you this jewelled pouch containing ambergris, which I wear myself, to wear when you are dancing.

LADY (*Takes the pouch and curtseys*): Long live the emperor!

EMPEROR (*Taking* Lady Yang *by the hand to leave*):

Just as this Rainbow Dance will be immortal,
To you I wish eternal youth for ever.

LADY:

How fortunate I am, to be bathed
In the emperor's own perfume!

(*Exeunt.*)

161

第十六出　合围

（外末、副净、小生扮四番将上）（外）三尺镔刀耀雪光，（末）腰间明月角弓张。（副净）葡萄酒醉胭脂血，（小生）貂帽花添锦绣装。（外）俺范阳镇东路将官何千年是也。（末）俺范阳镇西路将官崔乾祐是也。（副净）俺范阳镇南路将官高秀岩是也。（小生）俺范阳镇北路将官史思明是也。（各弯腰见科）请了，昨奉王爷将令，传集我等，只得齐至帐前伺候。道犹未了，王爷升帐也。

（内鼓吹、掌号科）（净戎装引番姬、番卒上）

【越调紫花拨四】统貔貅雄镇边关，双眸觑破番和汉，掌儿中握定江山，先把这四周围爪牙迭办。

我安禄山夙怀大志，久蓄异谋。只因一向在朝，受封东平王爵，宠幸无双，富贵已极，咱的心愿倒也罢了。叵耐杨国忠那厮，与咱不合，出镇范阳。且喜跳出樊笼，

SCENE 16
The Hunt

(*Enter four Tartar geneals* Ho Qiannian, Cui Qianhu, Gao Xiuyan *and* Shi Siming.)

HO:

My three-foot sword glitters white as snow!

CUI:

At my waist I gird a crescent bow!

GAO:

I love to drink the red juice of the vine!

SHI:

Embroidered suit and sable cap are mine!

HO: I am Ho Qiannian, general of the eastern front of Fanyang.

CUI: I am Cui Qianhu, general of the western front of Fanyang.

GAO: I am Gao Xiuyan, general of the southern front of Fanyang.

SHI: I am Shi Siming, general of the northern front of Fanyang.

ALL (*Greeting each other*): Well met, gentlemen. Yesterday the prince ordered us to muster, and we are going to his camp for orders. Here is His Highness now.

(*Trumpets sound and* An Lushan *enters, in military dress and accompanied by Tartar attendants and maids.*)

AN:

My mighty army holds the frontier pass,
Controlling both barbarians and Chinese;
Now the whole kingdom lies within my grasp,
But first my teeth and talons I must whet.

I have long nursed a great ambition; but while I remained at court as the Prince of Dongping and a prime favourite of the emperor, I was fairly satisfied with my wealth and position. Then that fellow Yang Guozhong fell out with me, with the result that I was appointed governor of Fanyang. I am pleased to have flown out of

163

正好暗图大事。俺家所辖,原有三十二路
将官,番汉并用,性情各别,难以任为腹心。
因此奏请一概俱用番将。如今大小将领,
皆咱部落。(笑科)任意所为,都无顾忌了。
昨日传集他每俱赴帐前,这咱敢待齐也。
(众进见科)三十二路将官参见。(净)诸将
少礼。(众)请问王爷,传集某等,不知有何
钧令?(净)众将官,目今秋高马壮,正好演
习武艺。特召你等,同往沙地,大合围场,
较猎一番。多少是好!(众)谨遵将令。
(净)就此跨马前去。(同众作上马科)(净)

【胡拨四犯】紫缰轻挽,(合)双手把紫缰轻
挽,骗上马,将盔缨低按。(行科)闪旗影云
殿,没揣的动龙蛇,一直的通霄汉。按奇门
布下了九连环,觑定了这小中原在眼,消不
得俺众路强蕃。(众四面立,净指科)这一员
身材标悍,那一员结束牢拴,这一员莽兀喇
拳毛高鼻,那一员恶支沙雕目胡颜,这一员
会急进格邦的弓开月满,那一员会滴溜扑
碌的锤落星寒,这一员会咭吒克擦的枪风
闪烁,那一员会悉力飒剌的剑雨澎滩,端的

the cage and to be able to prepare to execute my great design.
Formerly I had thirty-two generals under me, half of them Chinese
and half Tartars, but they were always at odds, and I could not
rely on them; so I requested to have Tartar generals only under
me, and now all my subordinates are my own tribesmen.
(*Laughs*) I shall be able to do as I like. Yesterday I summoned
them to come to my camp. They should be here by now.
(*The generals bow to him.*)

GENERALS: Your thirty-two generals salute Your Highness.

AN: I greet my warriors.

GENERALS: May we ask why Your Highness has called us here?

AN: It is fine autumn weather, and the horses are in good fettle—the
time has come to practise our military arts; so I have summoned
you to hunt on the sandy plain, where we should have good sport.

GENERALS: Yes, Your Highness.

AN: To saddle then! (*They mount their horses.*)

ALL:

> Lightly holding the purple reins,
> We leap to the saddle, our tasselled helmets low,

(*They ride forward.*)

> Our banners fluttering like crimson clouds,
> Writhing like snakes and dragons in the air,
> Deploying in nine rings we laugh to scorn
> This petty empire. Can the Hans withstand
> The mighty Tartars?

(*They group themselves around* An Lushan, *who points at one
after another.*)

AN:

> Here is a bold, fierce warrior,
> And here one built like a giant;
> Here one with curly hair and a prominent nose,
> One with an eagle eye and cruel beard,
> One who can stretch his bow like the full moon,
> And one who can whirl his mace till it gleams like a star,
> One whose keen spear cuts through the air like wind,

165

是人如猛虎离山涧,显英雄天可汗!(众行科)(合)振军威,扑通通鼓鸣,惊魂破胆;排阵势,韵悠悠角声,人疾马闲。抵多少雷轰电转,可正是海沸也那河翻。折末的铜作壁,铁作垒,有什么攻不破、攻不破也雄关!(净)这里地阔沙平,就此摆开围场,射猎一回者。(净同番姬立高处,众排围射猎下)(净)摆围场这间、这间,四下里来挤趱、挤趱。马蹄儿泼剌剌旋风赳,不住的把弓来紧弯,弦来急攀。一回呵滚沙场兔鹿儿无头赶,都难动弹,就地里踠跧。(众射鸟兽上)(净)把鹰、犬放过去者。(众应,放鹰、犬科,跑下)(净)呀呀呀,疾忙里一壁厢把翅摩霄的玉爪腾空散,一壁厢把足驾雾的金獒逐路拦,霎时间兽积、兽积如山。(众上献猎物科)禀王爷,众将献杀。(净)打的鸟兽,散给众军。就此高坡上,把人马歇息片时。大家炙肉暖酒,番姬每歌的歌,舞的舞,洒落一

And one who hurls his darts as thick as rain.
They are like some savage tigers
Leaving their mountain lair to show their prowess.
Then am I not indeed the all-powerful khan,
The king of kings?
(*They ride on.*)

ALL:

As we display our might, the roar of the drums
Strikes fear into all who hear;
The bugles sound to form the ranks for battle,
And soldiers gallop swift as a flash of lightning,
Hoof-beats like thunder surging like the sea.
What walls or strongholds wrought in bronze or iron
Can stand against us? Or what mighty pass
Can we not hurtle through?

AN: The sandy plain is wide and flat. Let us begin our hunt.
(An Lushan *stands with a Tartar maid on high ground while his general ride off to hunt.*)

AN:

The hunt is on. From all sides riders gallop,
And like a whirlwind flash the horses' hooves;
The bows twang ceaselessly, till stags and hares
Tremble because they find no hiding-place,
And cower in abject fear.

(*Generals ride in, shooting at the game.*)

AN: Unleash the hounds and hawks. (*The hounds and hawks are loosed.*)

The taloned birds soar swiftly to the sky,
The tawny hounds close in from every side;
Soon the dead quarry piles up mountain-high.

(*Generals present the game to* An Lushan.)

GENERALS: We present the bag to our prince.

AN: Give this game to the troops, and let the men and horses rest on this slope while we roast the meat and warm the wine, and the girls sing and dance for our pleasure.

回者。(众)得令。(同席地坐,番姬送净酒,众作拔刀割肉,提背壶斟酒,大饮啖科)(番姬弹琵琶、浑不是),众打太平鼓板(合)斟起这酪浆儿,满满的浮金盏,满满的浮金盏。更把那连毛带血肉生餐,笑拥着番姬双颊丹,把琵琶忒楞楞弹也麽弹,唱新声"菩萨蛮"。(净起科)吃了一会,酒醉肉饱。天色已晚,诸将各回汛地。须要整顿兵器,练习车马,听候将令便了。(众应科)得令。(作同上马吹海螺,侧帽、摆手绕场疾行科)听罢了令,疾翻身跃登锦鞍,侧着帽、摆手轻偨。各自里回还,镇守定疆藩。摆搁些旗竿,装摺着轮辕,听候传番,施逞凶顽。天降摧残,地起波澜。把渔阳凝盼,一飞羽箭,争赴兵坛,专等你个抱赤心的将军、将军来调拣。

(众下)(净)你看诸路番将,一个个人强马壮,眼见得(俺)的羽翼已成。(笑科)唐天子,唐天子,你怎当得也!

【煞尾】没照会,先去了那掣肘汉家官;有机谋,暗添上这助臂番儿汉。等不的宴华清"霓裳"法曲终,早看俺闹鼓鼙渔阳骁将反。

六州番落从戎鞍。薛逢
战马闲嘶汉地宽。刘禹锡
倏忽抟风生羽翼。骆宾王
山川龙战血漫漫。胡曾

GENERALS: It shall be done.

(*The girls play their lutes and guitars, and the men sound tambourines and castanets.*)

ALL:

> *We fill our golden goblets to the brim*
> *With mares' millk, and devour the meat half raw;*
> *With laughter we embrace our rosy girls,*
> *Strumming our lutes and singing Tartar songs.*

AN (*Rising*): We have eaten our fill and the day is growing late. Return to your own garrisons, and keep your weapons and horses in readiness for further orders.

GENERALS: We shall do so, sire. (*They mount their horses, blowing their horns, and with caps tilted to one side wave their hands and ride quickly round.*)

> *At the word of command we leap to embroidered saddles,*
> *With headgear askew we swing triumphant arms;*
> *Back at our posts our banners and carts are awaiting*
> *The summons to fight. When Heaven decrees Han's ruin*
> *And the earth is in tumult, then we shall look to our lord,*
> *Rushing to arms when the sign is given for battle,*
> *To answer the call of the prince, our high-hearted commander.*

(*Exeunt.*)

AN: Now that my Tartar generals are mighty and well-equipped, I am fully fledged. (*Laughs.*) Ah, Tang emperor, Tang emptror, how are you going to withstand me?

> *Without arousing his suspicion,*
> *I have rid myself of those troublesome Chinese generals,*
> *And in accordance with my plan*
> *Increased the number of my tribal chiefs.*
> *While in his pleasure palace the emperor feasts*
> *And music is played, a sudden alarm will be heard,*
> *And my brave lads will begin the revolt.*

(*Exit.*)

第十七出　夜怨

【正宫引子】【破阵子】【破阵子头】(旦上)宠极难拼轻舍，欢浓分外生怜。【齐天乐】比目游双，鸳鸯眠并，未许恩移情变。【破阵子尾】只恐行云随风引，争奈闲花竞日妍，终朝心暗牵。

　　【清平乐】"卷帘不语，谁识愁千缕。生怕韶光无定主，暗里乱催春去。心中刚自疑猜，那堪踪迹全乖。凤辇却归何处？凄凉日暮空阶。"奴家杨玉环，久邀圣眷，爱结君心。叵耐梅精江采频，意不相下。恰好触忤圣上，将他迁置楼东。但恐采频巧计回天，皇上旧情未断，因此常自堤防。唉，江采频，江采频，非是我容你不得，只怕我忍了你，你就容不得我也！今早圣上出朝，日色已暮，不见回宫，连着永新、念奴打听去了。此时情绪，好难消遣也！

【仙吕入双调】【风云会四朝元】【四朝元头】烧残香串，深宫欲暮天。把文窗频启，翠箔

170

SCENE 17
A Night of Grief

(Lady Yang *enters.*)
LADY:

Though favoured above all others,
I cannot endure a moment's separation,
So at the height of joy I still feel sad;
For, like the birds that fly in pairs,
I cannot bear to think that he may change;
And yet I fear the cloud
May be enticed away by some soft breeze;
All flowers court the favour of the sun;
So all day long my heart is ill at ease.
I roll up the curtain in silence, my grief unknown,
And fear that all too soon the spring will be gone,
My heart is heavy; the emperor has not come;
Though the sun is setting, my courtyard is empty still.

I have long been the emperor's favourite; but Jiang Caipin—Lady Plum Blossom—still hopes to supplant me. Luckily she offended His Majesty and was moved to the east pavilion; but I am afraid she may hit on some trick to get round him, and that he still has some feeling for his old love. So I cannot help worrying. Ah, Jiang Caipin, it is not that I cannot tolerate you; but I fear, if I do, you will not tolerate me. It is already dark, yet the emperor has not come back here since he left the court. I have sent Yongxin and Niannu to find out what has happened. It is very hard to while away the time.

The incense is burning low and the palace grows dark,
Yet still I keep opening the latticed window
And moving aside the curtain above the door,
Tiring my eyes with watching. On other days,

高卷,眼儿几望穿。但常时此际,但常时此际,【会河阳】定早驾到西宫,执手齐肩。【四朝元】花映房栊,春生颜面,【驻云飞】百种耽欢恋。嗏,今夕问何缘,【一江风】芳草黄昏,不见承回辇?(内作鹦哥叫"圣驾来也"介)(旦作惊看介)呀,圣上来了!(作看介)咦,原来是鹦哥弄巧言,把愁人故相骗。【四朝元尾】只落得徘徊伫立,思思想想,画栏凭遍。

(老旦上)"闻道君王前殿宿,内家各自撤红灯。"(见介)启娘娘:万岁爷已宿在翠华西阁了。(旦呆介)有这等事!(泣介)【前腔】君情何浅,不知人望悬!正晚妆慵卸,暗烛羞剪,待君来同笑言。向琼筵启处,向琼筵启处,醉月觞飞,梦雨床连。共命无分,同心无舛,怎蓦把人疏远!(老旦)万岁爷今夜偶不进宫,料非有意疏远,娘娘请勿伤怀!(旦)嗏,若不是情迁,便宿离宫,阿监何妨遣。我想圣上呵,从来未独眠,鸳衾厌孤展,怎得今宵枕畔,清清冷冷,竟无人荐!

He would have been with me by now and, holding my hand
In the flower-brightened chamber, beaming with joy,
Would have shown his love in a hundred ways. But tonight,
Though the sun is setting behind the verdant plain,
Still the emperor's carriage has not come.

(*Offstage a parrot cries: "The emperor is here!" Lady Yang starts and looks round.*)

Has His Majesty come? (*She catches sight of the bird.*)
Ah, no.

It is only the parrot which has learnt these words
To mock me in my sadness. I stand in doubt,
Lost in thought as I lean upon the railing.

(Yongxin *enters.*)

YONGXIN:

We hear that our sovereign is in the front palace tonight;
The other court ladies need wait for him no longer.

Your Ladyship, His Majesty is sleeping in the Emerald Pavilion.

(Lady Yang *is silent for a moment.*)

LADY: Can it be true? (*She weeps.*)

How heartless he is, not to care that I am waiting!
I have not taken off my evening gown
Nor trimmed the guttering candle,
But was waiting for my lord
That we might laugh and have sweet talk together,
Then feast and drink to the moon,
And, wearied, go at last to bed together.
Yet see how he forsakes me!

YONGXIN: I am sure it is quite by chance that His Majesty hasn't come, my lady. It can't be deliberate. Don't be sad, Your Ladyship.

LADY:

If he loved me still, he could send a eunuch
To tell me that he would be sleeping outside.
But the emperor never passes a night alone;
Can it be there is no one to lie by his side tonight?

173

（贴上）"雪隐鸳鸯飞始见，柳藏鹦鹉语方知。"（见介）娘娘，奴婢打听翠阁的事来了。（旦）怎么说？（贴）娘娘听启，奴婢方才呵，【月临江】"悄向翠华西阁，守将时近黄昏，忽闻密旨遣黄门。"（旦）遣他何处去呢？（贴）"飞鞭乘戏马，灭烛召红裙。"（旦急问介）召那一个？（贴）"贬置楼东怨女，梅亭旧日妃嫔。"（旦惊介）呀，这是梅精了。他来也不曾？（贴）"须臾簇拥那佳人，暗中归翠阁。"（老旦问介）此话果真否？（贴）"消息探来真。"（旦）唉，天那，原来果是梅精复邀宠幸了。（做不语闷坐、掩泪介）（老旦、贴）娘娘请免愁烦。（旦）

【前腔】闻言惊颤，伤心痛怎言。（泪介）把从前密意，旧日恩眷，都付与泪花儿弹向天。记欢情始定，记欢情始定，原似钗股成双，盒扇团圆。不道君心，霎时更变，总是奴当谴，嗏，也索把罪名宣。怎教冻蕊寒葩，暗识东风面。可知道身虽在这边，心终

(Niannu *enters.*)

> *When the egret is hidden by snow,*
> *One sees it only when it begins to fly.*
> *When the parrot is hidden behind a willow,*
> *One detects it only when it begins to speak.*

NIANNU: Your Ladyship, I have found out the truth about the Emerald Pavilion.

LADY: What is it?

NIANNU: Just now I went quietly through the dusk to the Emerald Pavilion, my lady; and I heard His Majesty order a eunuch—

LADY: Yes?

NIANNU: To ride as fast as he could through the darkness to fetch—

LADY: Fetch whom?

NIANNU: The lady who fell from favour and was moved to the east pavilion.

LADY (*Startled*): Ah! So it is Lady Plum Blossom! And did she go?

NIANNU: In less than no time the eunuch came back with the lady, and they went in the dark to the Emerald Pavilion.

YONGXIN: Are you certain of what you are saying?

NIANNU: Quite certain.

LADY: Ah, Heaven! It is Lady Plum Blossom after all! She is in favour again. (*She sits silently down and weeps.*)

MAIDS: Don't be distressed, Your Ladyship.

LADY:

> *I tremble at this news,*
> *And cannot utter the grief I feel.*
> *The former love and favour have turned to tears.*
> *When we first pledged our love,*
> *We vowed to be true as the phoenixes on the pin,*
> *As the two halves of the jewel case;*
> *But now his heart has changed.*
> *If I have done wrong, then he should tell me my fault.*
> *How can the warm spring marry the frozen plum*
>   *flower?*

175

系别院。一味虚情假意,瞒瞒昧昧,只欺奴善。

（贴）娘娘还不知道,奴婢听得小黄门说,昨日万岁爷在华萼楼上,私封珍珠一斛去赐他,他不肯受。回献一诗,有"长门自是无梳洗,何必珍珠慰寂寥"之句,所以致有今夜的事。（旦）哦,原来如此,我那里知道!

【前腔】他向楼东写怨,把珍珠暗里传。直恁的两情难割,不由我寸心中如剪。也非咱心太褊,只笑君王见错;笑君王见错,把一个罪废残妆,认是金屋婵娟。可知我守拙鸾凰,斗不上争春莺燕!（老旦）万岁爷既不忘情于他,娘娘何不迎合上意,力劝召回。万岁爷必然欢喜,料他也不敢忘恩。（旦）唉,此语休提。他自会把红线缠。嗏,何必我重牵。只怕没头兴的媒人,反惹他憎贱。你二人随我到翠阁去来。（贴）娘娘去怎的?（旦）我到那里,看他如何逞媚妍,如何卖机变,取次把君情鼓动,颠颠倒倒,暗中迷恋。

（贴）奴婢想今夜翠阁之事,原怕娘娘知道。此时夜将三鼓,万岁爷必已安寝。娘娘猝然走去,恐有未便。不如且请安眠,

All the time he was here his heart had fled to another.
He is false, and has deceived me.

NIANNU: I heard, my lady, from a eunuch, that yesterday the emperor secretly sent a pack of pearls to her from Blooming Flower Pavilion; but she wouldn't accept them, and sent them back with a poem saying that

Since her dismissal she has not decked her hair,
And pearls cannot console her in her grief.

That accounts for what happened tonight.

LADY: So that is it! How could I know?

He wrote of his grief to her in the east pavilion,
And sent her the pearls in secret.
Now they will not be parted again,
And jealousy gnaws at my heart;
For nobody can call me narrow-minded,
But my lord has been misled.
Why should he return to a lady he once rejected?
And how can I—a simple, innocent girl—
Compete with these swallows which flit from place to place?

YONGXIN: Since the emperor is still fond of her, why don't you fall in with his wishes, my lady, and plead for her return? Then His Majesty will be pleased, and show that he is grateful.

LADY: Ah, no.

He can bind her himself in a love-knot;
He does not need me as a go-between;
And if I were to do that,
The emperor would only despise me more.

Come with me, both of you , to the Emerald Pavilion.

NIANNU: Why do you want to go there, my lady?

LADY:

I'll see what magic she uses, what spell she casts
To charm our lord and fascinate him so!

NIANNU: The emperor didn't want you to know of tonight's happenings, my lady. And it is nearly midnight now: His Majesty will be asleep. If Your Ladyship goes there suddenly, it may

177

到明日再作理会。(旦作不语,掩泪叹介)唉,

罢罢,只今夜教我如何得睡也!

【尾声】他欢娱只怕催银箭,我这里寂寥深

院,只索背着灯儿和衣将空被卷。

紫禁迢迢宫漏鸣,　戴叔伦

碧天如水夜云生。　温庭筠

泪痕不与君恩断,　刘皂

斜倚薰笼坐到明。　白居易

embarrass him. You had better rest, and deal with the matter tomorrow.

(Lady Yang *falls silent, sheds tears and sighs.*)

LADY: Very well. But what sleep can I get tonight?

Time flies too fast for him, as he takes his pleasure,
Leaving me here to lie in a lonely bed.

(*Exeunt.*)

第十八出　絮阁

（丑上）"自闭昭阳春复秋，罗衣湿尽泪还流。一种蛾眉明月夜，南宫歌舞北宫愁。"咱家高力士，向年奉使闽粤，选得江妃进御，万岁爷十分宠幸。为她性爱梅花，赐号梅妃，宫中都称为梅娘娘。自从杨娘娘入侍之后，宠爱日夺，万岁爷竟将他迁置上阳宫东楼。昨夜忽然托疾，宿于翠华西阁，遣小黄门密召到来。戒饬宫人，不得传与杨娘娘知道。命咱在阁前看守，不许闲人擅进。此时天色黎明，恐要送梅娘娘回去，只索在此伺侯咱。（虚）（旦行上）

【北黄钟】【醉花阴】一夜无眠乱愁搅，未拔白潜踪来到。往常见红日影弄花梢，软哈哈春睡难消，犹自压绣衾倒。今日呵，可甚的凤枕急忙抛，单则为那篝儿撇不掉。

（丑一面暗上望科）呀，远远来的，正是杨

SCENE 18

A Visit to the Pavilion

(Gao Lishi *enters.*)

GAO:

> *Spring and autumn have passed*
> *Since she was confined in disgrace;*
> *Yet, her dress wet with tears, she still weeps on.*
> *The same moon shines on the two pavilions;*
> *But the south palace rings with song and dance,*
> *While in the north palace is nothing but grief.*

Many years ago I brought Jiang Caipin back with me from a trip to the south, and she took the emperor's fancy. Because she liked plum blossom she was given the title Lady Plum Blossom, which is what we all call her. But after Lady Yang's arrival she fell from favour, and His Majesty had her removed to the east pavilion of Shangyang Palace. Last night, however, on pretext of sickness, the emperor slept in the Emerald Pavilion and sent a eunuch secretly to summon Lady Plum Blossom. The maids have been told not to let Lady Yang know of this, and I have been ordered to stand guard outside the pavilion and not allow anyone in. Now it is dawn, I dare say Lady Plum Blossom will soon be sent back. I had better wait round the corner. (*Exit.*)

(*Enter* Lady Yang.)

LADY:

> *Sleepless all night with grief,*
> *I tiptoe here before the dawn.*
> *In the past, when the rising sun caressed the flowers,*
> *I would cling drowsily to my soft bed;*
> *But today I impatiently tossed away my pillow,*
> *Made restless by a strange uneasiness.*

(Gao Lishi *comes in again, and sees her.*)

娘娘,莫非走漏了消息么?现今梅娘娘还在阁里,如何是好?(旦到科)(丑忙见科)奴婢高力士,叩见娘娘。(旦)万岁爷在那里?(丑)在阁中。(旦)还有何人在内?(丑)没有。(旦冷笑科)你开了阁门,待我进去看者。(丑慌科)娘娘且请暂坐。(旦坐科)(丑)奴婢启上娘娘,万岁爷昨日呵,

【南画眉序】只为政勤劳,偶尔违和厌烦扰。(旦)即是圣体违和,怎生在此驻宿?(丑)爱清幽西阁,暂息昏朝。(旦)在里面做什么?(丑)偃龙床静养神疲。(旦)你在此何事?(丑)守玉户不容人到。(旦怒科)高力士,你待不容我进去么?(丑慌叩头科)娘娘息怒,只因亲奉君王命,量奴婢敢行违拗!

【北喜迁莺】(旦怒科)哎,休得把虚脾来掉,嘴喳喳弄鬼妆幺。(丑)奴婢怎敢?(旦)焦

182

GAO: Ah, here comes Lady Yang. Can the news have leaked out? Lady Plum Blossom is still in the pavilion—what shall I do?

(Lady Yang *approaches, and* Gao *bows.*) Your slave, my lady.

LADY: Where is His Majesty?

GAO: In the pavilion.

LADY: And who is with him?

GAO: No one.

LADY (*Laughing coldly*): Open the door and let me see for myself.

GAO (*In panic*): Please take a seat, Your Ladyship. (Lady Yang *sits down.*) I beg to inform you, my lady—

> *Weighed down with affairs of state,*
> *The emperor slept here last night for the sake of quiet.*

LADY: If His Majesty did not feel well, why should he stay here?

GAO:

> *Longing for quietness, he chose to spend*
> *The night in the Emerald Pavilion.*

LADY: What is he doing there?

GAO:

> *Reclining on the imperial couch,*
> *He is resting his weary head.*

LADY: And what are *you* doing here?

GAO:

> *I am guarding the door,*
> *So that no one may go in.*

LADY (*Angrily*): You mean you are here to keep me out, Gao Lishi?

GAO: (*Kowtowing in confusion*):

> *Please don't be angry, my lady.*
> *I am only carrying out the emperor's orders.*
> *How dare I disobey him?*

LADY(*Angrily*):

> *How long will you keep up this farce?*
> *You smooth-tongued villain!*

也波焦，急的咱满心越恼。我晓得你今日
呵，别有个人儿挂眼梢，倚着他宠势高，明
欺我失恩人时衰运倒。（起科）也罢，我只
得自把门敲。

（丑）娘娘请坐，待奴婢叫开门来。（做
高叫科）杨娘娘来了，开了阁门者。（旦坐
科）（生披衣引内侍上，听科）

【南画眉序】何事语声高，蓦忽将人梦惊觉。
（丑又叫科）杨娘娘在此，快些开门。（内侍）
启万岁爷，杨娘娘到了。（生作呆科）呀，这
春光漏泄，怎地开交？（内侍）这门还是开
也不开？（生）慢着。（背科）且教梅妃在夹
幕中，暂躲片时罢。（急下）（内侍笑科）哎，
万岁爷，万岁爷，笑黄金屋怎样藏娇，怕葡
萄架霎时推倒。（生上作伏桌科）内侍，我着
床傍枕伴推睡，你索把兽环开了。

（内侍）领旨。（作开门科）（旦直入，见生
科）妾闻陛下圣体违和，特来问安。（生）寡
人偶然不快，未及进宫。何劳妃子清晨到
此。（旦）陛下致疾之由，妾倒猜着几分了。

GAO: How dare I deceive you, my lady?

LADY:

Desperation will drive me quite distracted!
I know you fix your hopes on that other lady,
Insulting me openly now I am out of luck.

(*She rises.*) Very well!

I shall have to knock at the door myself.

GAO: Please take a seat, madam, while I ask them to let you in. (*He calls out.*) Lady Yang is here! Open the door! (*Lady Yang sits down again.*)

(*Enter the emperor, not yet fully dressed, with an attendant.*)

EMPEROR:

Who is calling so loud,
To wake me from my sleep?

GAO: Lady Yang is here! Quickly open the door!

ATTENDANT: If it please Your Majesty, Lady Yang is here.

EMPEROR (*Dazed*):

Ah, what shall we do if she finds out the truth?

ATTENDANT: Shall I open the door or not?

EMPEROR: Wait! (*Aside.*) I had better hide Plum Blossom behind the curtain. (*Exit hastily.*)

ATTENDANT (*Laughing*): Ah, Your Majesty,

Do you think you can hide your sweetheart in your chamber?
I fear your love nest is going to be turned upside down!

(*The emperor comes in again, and rests his head on the desk.*)

EMPEROR:

I will pretend to sleep here;
You may unlock the door.

ATTENDANT: Very good, sire.

(*He opens the door, and* Lady Yang *darts in.*)

LADY: Hearing that you were unwell, Your Majesty, I have come to ask after your health.

EMPEROR: I happened to feel slightly indisposed, so I did not go to the palace. But why should you trouble to come here so early in the morning?

(生笑科)妃子猜着何事来？（旦）

【北出队子】多则是相思萦绕，为着个意中人把心病挑。（生笑科）寡人除了妃子，还有甚意中人？（旦）妾想陛下向来钟爱，无过梅精。何不宣召他来，以慰圣情牵挂。（生惊科）呀，此女久置楼东，岂有复召之理！（旦）只怕悄东君偷泄小梅梢，单只待望着梅来把渴消。（生）寡人那有此意。（旦）既不沙，怎得那一斛珍珠去慰寂寥！

（生）妃子休得多心。寡人昨夜呵，

【南滴溜子】偶只为微疴，暂思静悄。恁兰心蕙性，慢多度料，把人无端奚落。（作欠伸科）我神虚懒应酬，相逢话言少。请暂返香车，图个睡饱。

（旦作看科）呀，这御榻底下，不是一双凤舄么？（生急起，作欲掩科）在那里？（怀中掉出翠钿科）（旦拾看科）呀，又是一朵翠钿！此皆妇人之物，陛下既然独寝，怎得有此？（生作羞科）好奇怪！这是哪里来的？连寡人也不解。（旦）陛下怎么不解？（丑作急

LADY: I think I can guess the reason for Your Majesty's sickness.

EMPEROR (*Laughing*): What is your guess?

LADY:

> *You were longing for someone you love;*
> *So your illness was a malady of the heart.*

EMPEROR: Whom do I love but you? (*Laughs.*)

LADY: As Your Majesty has never loved anyone so much as Lady Plum Blossom, why don't you summon her here to satisfy your longing?

EMPEROR (*Startled*): Plum Blossom? I sent her away long ago to the east pavilion. Why should I recall her?

LADY:

> *I fear that, as spring steals upon the plum tree,*
> *You may long for the fruit to quench your bitter thirst.*

EMPEROR: How could I?

LADY: In that case,

> *Who sent her that pack of pearls to console her?*

EMPEROR: These suspicions are unworthy of you, my love.

> *A trifling ailment made me long for quiet;*
> *It is not kind of you to suspect and mock me*
> *For no good reason.* (*He yawns.*)
> *Still weary, I am disinclined to talk.*
> *I beg you to go back now in your carriage,*
> *To let me sleep my fill.*

LADY (*Looking round*): Isn't that a pair of women's slippers under your bed?

EMPEROR (*Rising hastily to hide them*): Where?

(*As he stands up, an emerald trinket falls from his lap. Lady Yang picks it up and looks at it.*)

LADY: A trinket too! This is a woman's ornament. If you were sleeping alone, where did these things come from?

EMPEROR (*Embarraassed*): Strange indeed! Where could they have come from? I cannot understand it.

LADY: Are you sure?

(*Gao turns in desperation to the attendant.*)

187

态,一面对内侍低科)呀,不好了,见了这翠钿、凤舄,杨娘娘必不干休。你们快送梅娘娘,悄从阁后破壁而出,回到楼东去吧。(内侍)晓得。(从生背后虚下)(旦)

【北刮地风】子这御榻森严宫禁遥,早难道有神女飞度中宵。则问这两般信物何人掉?(作将舄、钿掷地,丑暗拾科)(旦)昨夜谁侍陛下寝来?可怎生般凤友鸾交,到日三竿犹不临朝?外人不知呵,都只说殢君王是我这庸姿劣貌。那知道恋欢娱别有个雨窟云巢!请陛下早出视朝,妾在此候驾回宫者。(生)寡人今日有疾,不能视朝。(旦)虽则是蝶梦余,鸳浪中,春情颠倒,困迷离精神难打熬,怎负他凤墀前鹄立群僚!

(旦作向前背立科)(丑悄上与生耳语科)梅娘娘已去了,万岁爷请出朝罢。(生点头科)妃子劝寡人视朝,只索勉强出去。高力士,你在此送娘娘回宫者。(丑)领旨。(向内科)摆驾。(内应科)(生)"风流惹下风流苦,不是风流总不知。"(下)(旦坐科)高力士,你

188

GAO (*Whispering*): This is bad. Now that she has seen these, there will be no stopping her. Quickly take Lady Plum Blossom back quietly through some gap in the wall to the east pavilion.

ATTENDANT: Very good. (*Exit stealthily.*)

LADY:

> *The emperor's chamber is sacred and secluded;*
> *Can it be that some goddess alighted here last night?*
> *Or was it a woman who let fall these two tokens?*

(*She throws the slippers and trinket to the ground, and* Gao Lishi *picks them up when she is not looking.*)

Who shared the emperor's bed last night?

> *All night the phoenix so enjoyed his mate,*
> *That now, although the sun is high in heaven,*
> *He has not gone to court.*
> *I may be blamed for keeping the emperor;*
> *But I am not charming enough for that.*
> *He has another love nest,*
> *Where he can take his pleasure.*

I beg Your Majesty to go to court. I shall wait here till you come back.

EMPEROR: I am not feeling well today; I shall not go to court.

LADY:

> *Though Your Majesty is drowsy and exhausted*
> *After such bouts of pleasure, is it right*
> *To keep your ministers waiting in the court?*

(*She turns her back on the emperor.*)

GAO (*Quietly advancing to whisper to the emperor*): Lady Plum Blossom has gone. Your Majesty had better go to court.

EMPEROR (*Nods*): Since Lady Yang wishes me to go, I will make the effort. Gao Lishi, stay here to see Her Ladyship back.

GAO: Yes, sire. (*He calls out.*) Prepare the emperor's carriage.

(*An answering shout is heard offstage.*)

EMPEROR:

> *All this trouble arises from love,*
> *And only lovers can understand it.* (*Exit.*)

189

瞒着我做得好事！只问你这翠钿、凤舄,是那一个的？（丑）

【南滴滴金】告娘娘省可闲烦恼。奴婢看万岁爷与娘娘呵,百从千随真是少。今日这翠钿、凤舄,莫说是梅亭旧日恩情好,就是六宫中新窈窕,娘娘呵,也只合佯装不晓,直恁破工夫多计较！不是奴婢擅敢多口,如今满朝臣宰,谁没有个大妻小妾,何况九重,容不得这宵！

【北四门子】（旦）呀,这非是衾裯不许他人抱,道的咱量似斗筲！只怪他明来夜去装圈套,故将人瞒的牢。（丑）万岁爷瞒着娘娘,也不过怕娘娘着恼,非有他意。（旦）把似怕我焦,则休将彼邀。却怎的劣云头,只思别岫飘。将他假做抛,暗又招,转关儿心肠难料。

（作掩泪坐科）（老旦上）清早起来,不见了娘娘,一定在这翠阁中,不免进去咱。

（作进见旦科）呀,娘娘呵,

【南鲍老催】为何泪抛,无言独坐神暗消？

LADY (*Sitting down*) A fine trick you have played behind my back, Gao Lishi. Now tell me who these things belong to.

GAO:

> *Your Ladyship should not worry over trifles.*
> *His Majesty's love for you is unparalleled,*
> *For he tries at all times to please you.*
> *As for these slippers and trinket,*
> *You would do well, my lady, to ignore them,*
> *Even if they belong to some new beauty,*
> *To say nothing of Lady Plum Blossom,*
> *The emperor's former favourite.*
> *Why distress yourself for no reason?*
> *Even the high officials have concubines.*
> *Then will you deny the emperor one night's pleasure?*

LADY:

> *I do not begrudge another's share in his bed—*
> *I am not so narrow—minded;*
> *But I am hurt to find that he deceives me.*

GAO: If the emperor did not want Your Ladyship to know, it is only because he did not want to make you unhappy.

LADY:

> *If he is afraid of hurting me,*
> *Why did he send for her?*
> *Why should the floating cloud*
> *Drift to another valley?*
> *He pretends to forsake her,*
> *Then summons her again;*
> *The emperor's love is not to be relied on.*

(*She sheds tears.*)

(Yongxin *enters.*)

YONGXIN: When I got up this morning, I found Lady Yang had gone. She must have come to this pavilion. I will go in to look for her. (*She enters and curtseys.*)

> *Ah, my lady, why are you sitting here crying,*
> *Eating your heart out in silence?*

（问丑科）高公公，是谁触着他情性娇？（丑低科）不要说起。（作暗出钿、舄与老旦看科）只为见了这两件东西，故此发恼。（老旦笑，低问科）如今那人呢？（丑）早已去了。（老旦）万岁爷呢？（丑）出去御朝了。永新姐，你来得甚好，可劝娘娘回宫去罢。（老旦）晓得了。（回向旦科）娘娘，你慢将眉黛颦，啼痕渗，芳心恼。晨餐未进过清早，怎自将千金玉体轻伤了？请回宫去，寻欢笑。

　　（内）驾到。（旦起立科）（生上）"媚处娇何限，情深妒亦真。且将个中意，慰取眼前人。"寡人图得半夜欢娱，反受十分烦恼。欲待呵叱他一番，又恐他反道我偏爱梅妃，只索忍耐些罢。高力士，杨娘娘在那里？（丑）还在阁中。（老旦、丑暗下）（生作见旦，旦背立不语掩泣科）（生）呀，妃子，为何掩面不语？（旦不应科，生笑科）妃子休要烦恼，朕和你到华萼楼上看花去。（旦）

192

(*To* Gao.) Who has offended her, sir?

GAO (*In a low voice*): It is a long story. (*Stealthily showing her the trinket and slippers.*) She is angry at finding these.

YONGXIN (*Smiling, asks in a low voice*): Where is that lady now?

GAO: She has already gone.

YONGXIN: Where is His Majesty?

GAO: Gone to the court. You have come at the right time. You had better persuade Her Ladyship to go back now.

YONGXIN: Yes. (*She turns to* Lady Yang.)

> *My lady, if you frown and cry*
> *And make yourself too sad to eat,*
> *Will you not harm your health, which is far more precious*
> *Than gold or jade? I beg you to come back*
> *To find some happiness in your own palace.*

(*An attendant outside announces the emperor's return.*)

(*Enter the emperor.*)

EMPEROR:

> *When she looks coy she is charming,*
> *It is love that makes her jealous; then let me console her.*

I have certainly been made to suffer for half a night's pleasure. But if I reproach her, she will say that I love Lady Plum Blossom; so I had better have patience. Gao Lishi, where is Her Ladyship?

GAO: Still inside.

(Yongxin *and* Gao Lishi *go out. The emperor greets* Lady Yang, *but she turns her back on him and wipes her tears without a word.*)

EMPEROR: My love, why do you cover your face and not say a word?

(Lady Yang *does not answer; and the emperor smiles.*)

EMPEROR: Do not grieve like this, my darling. Let us go to Blooming Flower Pavilion to see the flowers.

(*Laughing.*)

LADY (*Sobbing*):

> *Are the flowers as lovely there as in the east pavilion?*
> *Since the plum tree flowers first in the spring,*

【北水仙子】问、问、问、问华萼娇,怕、怕、怕、怕不似楼东花更好。有、有、有、有梅枝儿曾占先春,又、又、又、又何用绿杨牵绕。(生)寡人一点真心,难道妃子还不晓得!(旦)请、请、请、请真心向故交,免、免、免、免人怨为妾情薄。(跪科)妾有下情,望陛下俯听。(生扶科)妃子有话,可起来说。(旦泣科)妾自知无状,谬窃宠恩。若不早自引退,诚恐谣诼日加,祸生不测,有累君德鲜终,益增罪戾。今幸天眷犹存,望赐斥放。陛下善视他人,勿以妾为念也。(泣拜科)拜、拜、拜、拜辞了往日君恩天样高。(出钗、盒科)这钗、盒是陛下定情时所赐,今日将来交还陛下。把、把、把、把深情密意从头缴。(生)这是怎么说?(旦)省、省、省、省可自承旧赐、福难消。

(旦悲咽,生扶起科)妃子何出此言,朕和你两人呵,

【南双声子】情双好,情双好,纵百岁犹嫌少。怎说到,怎说到,平白地分开了。总朕错,总朕错,请莫恼,请莫恼。(笑觑旦科)见了你这颦眉泪眼,越样生娇。

妃子可将钗、盒依旧收好。既是不耐看花,朕和你到西宫闲话去。(旦)陛下诚不弃妾,妾复何言。(袖钗、盒,福生科)

Do you need the clinging willow?

EMPEROR: Don't you know where my true love lies?

LADY:

I beg Your Majesty to be true to your first love;
For then I will not be blamed for your lack of faith.

(*Kneeling.*) I have one favour to ask the emperor.

EMPEROR (*Raising her*): What is it, my darling?

LADY (*Sobbing*): I know that I do not deserve Your Majesty's favour, and that unless I leave the palace soon I may be slandered and ruined; but if any slur is cast on your reputation when that happens, I shall feel doubly wretched. So, while Your Majesty's favour lasts, I beg to be dismissed. Be kind to your new favourite, and do not think of me any more. (*She weeps.*)

Bowing, I say goodbye to your boundless favour.

(*She takes out the hairpin and jewel box.*)

These pledges that you gave me of your faith,
I retrun to you now with my deep, undying love.

EMPEROR: Oh, come now.

LADY:

I willingly admit that I am not worthy
Of such good fortune. (*She sobs.*)

EMPEROR (*Helping her to rise*): How can you speak like this?

We two will love for a hundred years,
And still it will not be enough;
So why should you speak so suddenly of parting?
It is all my fault, and I beg you not to be angry.

(*He smiles at her.*)

Angry and pouting, you are doubly charming.

Keep this jewel box and hairpin. If you do not want to see the flowers, we can go to the west palace for a chat.

LADY: If Your Majesty really wants me to stay, then I have no more to say. (*She puts away the love tokens, and curtseys.*)

I put away the hairpin and the box;
Tonight when we share one bed together
I shall tell you again of all that I felt

【北尾煞】领取钗、盒再收好,度芙蓉帐暖今宵,重把那定情时心事表。

　　(生携旦并下)(丑复上)万岁爷同娘娘进宫去了。咱如今且把这翠钿、凤舄,送还梅娘娘去。

　　　　柳色参差映翠楼, 司马札
　　　　君王玉辇正淹留。钱起
　　　　岂知妃后多娇妒, 段成式
　　　　恼乱东风卒未休。罗隐

When first we pledged our love.
(*They walk off.*)
(*Enter* Gao Lishi.)
GAO: Now that the emperor and Lady Yang have gone back to the palace, I must return the trinket and slippers to Lady Plum Blossom.

(***Exit.***)

第十九出 侦报

（外引末扮中军，四杂执刀棍上）"出守岩疆典钜城，风闻边事实堪惊。不知忧国心多少，白发新添四五茎。"下官郭子仪，叨蒙圣恩，擢拜灵武太守。前在长安，见安禄山面有反相，知其包藏祸心。不想圣上命彼出镇范阳，分明纵虎归山。却又许易番将，一发添其牙爪。下官自天德军升任以来，日夜担忧。此间灵武，乃是股肱重地，防守宜严。已遣精细哨卒，前往范阳采听去了。且待他来，便知分晓。

【双调夜行船】（小生扮探子，执小红旗上）两脚似星驰和电捷，把边情打听些些。急离燕山，早来灵武。（作进见外，一足跪叩科）向黄堂爆雷般唱一声高喏。

（外）探子，你回来了么？（小生）我"肩挑令字小旗红，昼夜奔驰疾似风。探得边关多少事，从头来报主人公。"（外）分付掩

SCENE 19
The Report

(*Enter* Guo Ziyi *with his lieutenant and attendants armed with swords and clubs.*)

GUO ZIYI:

>As I guard the border and garrison a great city,
>News from the frontier is so disquieting
>That concern for the empire makes my hair turn white.

I, Guo Ziyi, have been appointed by His Majesty governor of Lingwu. When I was in the capital I saw that An Lushan looked like a rebel and knew that he was plotting mischief; but then the emperor suddenly sent him to command Fanyang—this is like letting the tiger go back to the mountain. Later the emperor allowed him to substitute Tartar chiefs for the Chinese generals under him, thus adding to his strength. Since my promotion from the Tiande Army district, I have been worrying about this day and night. My province, Lingwu, is of great strategic importance and should be well defended; I have sent my best scout to Fanyang, and shall understand the situation better when he returns.

(*A scout enters holding a small red flag.*)

SCOUT:

>Swift as a shooting star or lightning flash,
>I gathered information at the frontier;
>Returning now from Fanyang to Lingwu,
>I report to the governor in a voice like thunder!

GUO ZIYI: So you are back.

SCOUT:

>The red flag on my shoulder,
>I travelled day and night as swift as wind;
>Now, with much information on the frontier,
>I have returned to report to my commander.

门。(众掩门科下)(外)探子,你探的安禄山
军情怎地,兵势如何? 近前来,细细说与我
听者。(小生)爷爷听启,小哨一到了范阳
镇上呵,

【乔木鱼】见枪刀似雪,密匝匝铁骑连营列。
端的是号令如山把神鬼慑。那知有朝中天
子尊,单逞他将军令阃外阵嗻。

　　(外)那禄山在边关,近日作何勾当?
(小生)

【庆宣和】他自请那番将更来,把那汉将撤,
四下里牙爪排设。每日价跃马弯弓斗驰
猎,把兵威耀也、耀也!

　　(外)还有什么举动波? (小生)

【落梅花】他贼行藏真难料,歹心肠忒肆邪。
诱诸番密相勾结,更私招四方亡命者,巢窟
内尽藏凶孽。

　　(外惊科)呀,有这等事! 难道朝廷之
上,竟无人奏告么? (小生)闻得一月前,京
中有人告称禄山反状,万岁爷暗遣中使,去
到范阳,瞰其动静。那禄山见了中使呵,

【风入松】十分的小心礼貌假妆呆,尽金钱
遍布盖奸邪。把一个中官哄骗的满心悦,
来回奏把逆迹全遮。因此万岁爷愈信不
疑,反把告叛的人,送到禄山军前治罪。一

GUO ZIYI: Close the gate. (*The attendants go out, closing the gate.*) Tell me, scout, what is An Lushan's military strength? How powerful is his army? Step forward now, and tell me in full.

SCOUT: My lord, when I reached Fanyang, I found—

Snow-bright spears and swords,
And a host of army tents and horsemen;
Military curfew is strictly observed,
There is no respect for the central government.
But An Lushan's word is law.

GUO ZIYI: What is An Lushan doing now?

SCOUT:

He has dismissed his Chinese generals
And appointed Tartars in their place.
Putting his own men in all important positions.
Each day they hunt to improve their horsemanship,
And display their military might.

GUO ZIYI: What else?

SCOUT:

Who could suspect such treacherous behaviour?
By underhand and sinister devices
He has rallied the barbarians together
Secretly gathering outlaws and criminals,
Many of whom are hiding in his lair.

GUO ZIYI: Indeed! (*Startled.*) But has no one informed the government of this?

SCOUT: I heard that a month ago someone in the capital accused him of plotting rebellion, and the emperor secretly sent an envoy to Fanyang to watch him; but when An Lushan met the envoy,

He pretended to be a fool,
And behaved politely
Bribing his officers to conceal his guilt.
The envoy was tricked and favourably impressed;
So back at court he cleared An Lushan completely
Of every charge of treason. Now the emperor
Trusts him implicitly and has had the informer

任他横行傲桀，有谁人敢再弄唇舌！

（外叹介）如此怎生是了也！（小生）前日杨丞相又上一本，说禄山叛迹昭然，请皇上亟加诛戮。那禄山见了此本呵，

【拨不断】也不免脚儿跌，口儿嗟，意儿中忐忑心儿里怯。不想圣旨倒说禄山诚实，丞相不必生疑。他一闻此信，便就呵呵大笑，骂这谗臣奈我耶，咬牙根誓将君侧权奸灭，怒轰轰急待把此仇来雪。

（外）呀，他要诛君侧之奸，非反而何？且住，杨相这本怎么不见邸抄？（小生）此是密本，原不发抄。只因杨丞相要激禄山速反，特着塘报抄送去的。（外怒科）唉，外有逆藩，内有奸相，好教人发指也！（小生）小哨还打听的禄山近有献马一事，更利害哩！

【离亭宴歇拍煞】他本待逞豺狼、魆地里思抄窃。巧借着献骓骝、乘势去行强劫。（外）怎么献马？可明白说来者。（小生）他遣何千年赍表，奏称献马三千四，每马一匹，有甲士二人，又有二人御马，一人刍牧，共三五一万五千人，护送入京。一路里兵

Sent to An's camp for punishment.
Thus he can do exactly as he pleases,
And no one dares to breathe a word against him.

GUO ZIYI (*Sighs*): What will this lead to?

SCOUT: Recently the prime minister also presented a memorial to the throne, declaring that An Lushan's treason was plain to see, and asking His Majesty to have him executed. When An Lushan heard of this

He swore and raged, for he feared his end had come;
But the emperor declared that An was loyal
And rebuked the prime minister for his suspicions;
And An, when he heard this, laughed aloud and cried:
"What can slanderers do to me?"
Then through clenched teeth
He vowed to destroy the all-powerful minister,
And now, in his rage, he is burning to take revenge.

GUO ZIYI: So he wants to destroy the prime minister! That means he is ready to rebel. One minute, though—how is it I have never seen this memorial from the prime minister in the bulletin?

SCOUT: It was marked confidential and was not published in the bulletin; but in order to goad An Lushan to revolt, the prime minister had a copy sent to him.

GUO ZIYI (*Angrily*): A rebellious general at the frontier and a treacherous minister at court—I can hardly contain myself for anger!

SCOUT: I have also learned of a scheme of An Lushan's for presenting horses, which is even more dastardly.

Like some fierce wolf he plots to seize the kingdom,
And will make a gift of horses to gain his end.

GUO ZIYI: How? Explain this to me.

SCOUT: He sent his general, He Qiannian, with a memorial to the throne asking to be allowed to present three thousand horses, each to be accompanied by two armed guards, two trainers and one groom; so that there will be fifteen thousand men to take the horses to the capital.

强马劣,闹汹汹怎堤防!乱纷纷难镇压,急攘攘谁拦截。生兵入帝畿,野马临城阙,怕不把长安来闹者!(外惊科)唉,罢了,此计若行,西京危矣。(小生)这本方才进去,尚未取旨。只是禄山呵,他明把至尊欺,狡将奸计使,险备机关设。马蹄儿纵不行,狼性子终难帖。逗的鼙鼓向渔阳动也,爷爷呵,莫待传白羽始安排。小哨呵,准备闪红旗再报捷。

(外)知道了。赏你一坛酒,一腔羊,五十两花银,免一月打差。去罢。(小生叩头科)谢爷。(外)叫左右,开门。(众应上,作开门科)(小生下)(外)中军官。(末应介)(外)传令众军士,明日教场操演,准备酒席犒赏。(末)领钧旨。(先下)

(外)数骑渔阳探使回,　杜牧
　　威雄八阵役风雷。　刘禹锡
　　胸中别有安边计,　曹唐
　　军令分明数举杯。　杜甫

They will raise a great commotion along the way,
With more men than horses; and it will be hard
To check them. But when once these foreign troops
And horses reach Chang'an, they will cause great trouble.

GUO ZIYI (*Startled*): Ah, if he succeeds in this plan, the capital will be in danger.

SCOUT: This memorial has just been sent, and the emperor has not yet granted his request. But it is obvious that

An Lushan is plotting against the throne.
Should this plan fail, ambition will spur him on
To hatch some other plot, until at last
The alarm of war is sounded at Yuyang.
Then do not wait, my lord, for the arrow to fly
Before you take precautions; and I shall be
Ready with my red flag to report your victory.

GUO ZIYI: Very good. I shall reward you with a jar of wine, one sheep and fifty taels of silver, as well as a month's leave. Go now.

SCOUT (*Bowing*): I thank you, my lord.

GUO ZIYI: Tell the attendants to open the gate.

(*The attendants come in to open the gate, and the scout withdraws.*)

GUO ZIYI: Lieutenant!

LIEUTENANT: Here, my lord.

GUO ZIYI: Issue orders for manoeuvres tomorrow, and have a feast prepared for the troops.

LIEUTENANT: Very good, my lord.

(***Exeunt.***)

第二十出　窥浴

【仙吕入双调】【字字双】(丑扮宫女上)自小生来貌天然,花面;宫娥队里我为先,扫殿。忽逢小监在阶前,胡缠;伸手摸他裤儿边,不见。

"我做宫娥第一,标致无人能及。腮边花粉糊涂,嘴上胭脂狼籍。秋波俏似铜铃,弓眉弯得笔直。春纤十个擂槌,玉体浑身糙漆。柳腰松段十围,莲瓣滩船半只。杨娘娘爱我伶俐,选做霓裳部色。只因喉咙太响,歌时嘴边起个霹雳。身子又太狼伉,舞去冲翻了御筵桌席。皇帝见了发恼,打落子弟名籍。登时发到骊山,派到温泉殿中承值。昨日銮舆临幸,同杨娘娘在华清驻跸。传旨要来共浴汤池,只索打扫铺陈收拾。"道犹未了,那边一个宫人来也。

【雁儿舞】(副净扮宫女上)担阁青春,后宫怨

206

SCENE 20
The Bath

(*A maid enters.*)

MAID:

I have always had a natural grace,
Although my face is pockmarked;
I am first among the maids,
For who else can rival my beauty?
My lips and cheeks are smeared with powder and rouge;
My eyes are as fair as bronze bells;
My eyebrows are two straight lines;
My fingers are like ten drum-sticks,
My skin like coarse, thick varnish,
My willowy waist like a tree trunk,
And my tiny feet like two boats.
Liking my wit, Lady Yang made me a dancer;
But my voice when I sing is like thunder,
And when in my last dance I knocked over a table
The angry emperor struck me of the list;
Then I was sent to the warm springs in Lishan,
To work in the pleasure palace.
Yesterday the emperor came here with Lady Yang
To stay by Huaqing Pool,
And they are going to take a bath today.
My task is to sweep the place and get everything ready.
Here comes another maid.

(*Anotherr maid enters.*)

SECOND MAID:

Lonely in the back palace,
Wasting our youth,
Though we beat our breasts and stamp our feet,

女,漫跌脚捶胸,有谁知苦。拼着一世没有丈夫,做一支孤飞雁儿舞。

(见介)(丑)姐姐,你说什么"雁儿"舞!如今万岁爷,有了杨娘娘的"霓裳"舞,连梅娘娘的"惊鸿"舞,也都不爱了。(副净)便是。我原是梅娘娘的宫人。只为我娘娘,自翠阁中忍气回来,一病而亡,如今将我拨到这里。(丑)原来如此,杨娘娘十分妒忌,我每再休想有承幸之日。(副净)罢了。(丑)万岁爷将次到来,我和你且到外厢伺候去。(虚下)(末、小生扮内侍,引生、旦、老旦、贴随行上)

【羽调近词】【四季花】别殿景幽奇:看雕梁畔,珠帘外,雨卷云飞。逶迤,朱阑几曲环画溪,修廊数层接翠微。绕红墙,通玉扉。(末、小生)启万岁爷,到温泉殿了。(生)内侍回避。(末、小生应下)(生)妃子,你看清渠屈注,洄澜皱漪,香泉柔滑宜素肌。朕同妃子试浴去来。(老、贴与生、旦脱去大衣介)(生)妃子,只见你款解云衣,早现出珠辉玉丽,不由我对你、爱你、扶你、觑你、怜你!

Who knows of our sorrow?
Like a wild swan dancing alone,
I am destined never to find a husband.
(*She greets the first maid.*)

MAID: What dancing swan are you talking about? Now the emperor has Lady Yang with her Rainbow Garment Dance, he no longer cares even for Lady Plum Blossom's Swan Dance.

SECONE MAID: That's true. I used to wait on Lady Plum Blossom; but after she came back angry from the Emerald Pavilion, she fell ill and died. So I was sent here.

MAID: Is that why? Lady Yang is so jealous, I don't suppose we shall ever have a chance with the emperor.

SECOND MAID: Never mind.

MAID: His Majesty will be here soon. We had better wait outside. (*Exeunt.*)
(*A palace eunuch leads in the emperor,* Lady Yang *and her two maids.*)

EMPEROR:

The pleasure palace grounds are still and strange,
Carved beams float there like clouds
And pearl screens gleam like rain-drops;
Red railings skirt the stream,
And covered walks wind up the hill,
Leading past the crimson wall to the palace gate.

EUNUCH: May it please Your Majesty, we have reached Warm Spring Pavilion.

EMPEROR: Then leave us. (*The eunuch withdraws.*)
See, love—

The clear spring water ripples in the pool,
So fragrant, soft and soothing to the skin.

Let us bathe here. (*The maids help them take off their outer garments.*)

When you cast off your cloud-like garments,
Your pearl-bright, jade-fine beauty is revealed.
I cannot help but feast my eyes upon you,

209

（生携旦同下）（老旦）念奴姐，你看万岁爷与娘娘恁般恩爱，真令人羡杀也。（贴）便是。（老旦）

【凤钗花络索】【金凤钗】花朝拥，月夜偎，尝尽温柔滋味。【胜如花】（贴合）镇相连似影追形，分不开如刀划水。【醉扶归】千般捆纵百般随，两人合一副肠和胃。【梧叶儿】密意口难提，写不迭鸳鸯帐，绸缪无尽期。（老旦）姐姐，我与你伏侍娘娘多年，虽睹娇容，未窥玉体。今日试从绮疏隙处，偷觑-觑何如？（贴）恰好，（同作向内窥介）【水红花】（合）悄偷窥，亭亭玉体，宛似浮波菡萏，含露弄娇辉。【浣溪纱】轻盈臂腕消香腻，绰约腰身漾碧漪。【望吾乡】（老旦）明霞骨，沁雪肌。【大胜乐】（贴）一痕酥透双蓓蕾，（老旦）半点春藏小麝脐。【傍妆台】（贴）爱杀红巾罅，私处露微微。永新姐，你看万岁爷呵，【解三酲】凝睛睇，【八声甘州】恁孜孜含笑，浑似呆痴。【一封书】（合）休说俺偷眼宫娥魂欲化，则他个见惯的君王

Caressing, cherishing and loving you.

(*The emperor and* Lady Yang *walk out.*)

YONGXIN: Look, Niannu, how fond the emperor and Lady Yang are of each other. Don't you envy them?

NIANNU: Yes, I do.

YONGXIN:

Caressing each other among the flowers by day,
And leaning together under the moonlight at night,
They taste all the joys of love.

NIANNU:

They are always together,
Like a shadow that follows its object;
Nor can they ever be parted,
Like water that's cut with a knife.
In perfect accord, their two hearts beat as one;
And their love defies description by pen or tongue;
In the royal bed they enjoy each other for ever.

YONGXIN: We have waited on Lady Yang for several years now; yet we have never seen her without her clothes on. Shall we peep through the curtain?

NIANNU: Yes, let's. (*They look.*)

BOTH:

We take a stealthy look. Her slender body
Is floating like a lotus on the waves,
In all its limpid beauty; there she moves
Her supple ankles, her smooth, scented arms
And her willowy waist through the translucent water.

YOUGXIN:

Look, how fine-boned she is,
And what a snow-white skin!

NIANNU: Yongxin, look

How the emperor has fixed his eyes on her,
With a smile on his face as if he had taken leave
Of all his senses!

也不自持。【皂罗袍】(老旦)恨不把春泉翻竭,(贴)恨不把玉山洗颓,(老旦)不住的香肩鸣嗫,(贴)不住的纤腰抱围,【黄莺儿】(老旦)俺娘娘无言匿笑含情对。(贴)意怡怡,【月儿高】灵液春风,潋荡恍如醉。【排歌】(老旦)波光暖,日影晖,一双龙戏出平池。【桂枝香】(合)险把个襄王渴倒阳台下,恰便似神女携将暮雨归。

(丑、副净暗上笑介)两位姐姐,看得高兴啊,也等我每看看。(老旦、贴)姐姐,我每伺候娘娘洗浴,有甚高兴。(丑、副净暗上笑介)只怕不是伺候娘娘,还在那里偷看万岁爷哩。(老旦、贴)啐,休得胡说,万岁爷同娘娘出来也。(丑、副净暗下)(生同旦上)

【二犯掉角儿】【掉角儿】出温泉新凉透体,睹玉容愈增光丽。最堪怜残妆乱头,翠痕干晚云生腻。(老旦、贴与生、旦穿衣介)(旦作软态,老旦、贴扶介)(生)妃子,看你似柳含

YONGXIN:

They would like to bathe till the water runs dry!

NIANNU;

To bathe till they're both exhausted.

YONGXIN:

Again and again he kisses her shoulder!

NIANNU:

Again and again he strokes her slender waist.

YONGXIN:

And our lady without a word
Gazes at him with smiling, loving eyes.

NIANNU:

They frolic in the pool and the soft spring breeze,
As if they were drunk with wine.

YOUGXIN:

In the warm water, under the shining sun,
They are like two dragons gamblling at play.

BOTH:

To the emperor, parched with desire.
She is like the nymph who comes with the evening rain.

(*Two other maids come in and laugh.*)

MAIDS: You are having fun. Let us have a look too.

BOTH: We are just waiting on Lady Yang as she takes her bath. What is there to see?

MAIDS: We're afraid you are not just waiting on Lady Yang, but taking a good look at the emperor too.

BOTH: Be quiet! They are coming out.

(*The maids go out, and the emperor and* Lady Yang *enter.*)

EMPEROR:

The warm spring leaves one's body fresh and cool,
And my lady looks more beautiful and radiant,
Her dark hair ruffled like the evening clouds
After a shower.

(Yongxin *and* Niannu *dress them.* Lady Yang *looks tired and the maids support her.*)

213

风,花怯露。软难支,娇无力,倩人扶起。

(二内侍引杂推小车上)请万岁爷娘娘上如意

小车,回华清宫去。(生)将车儿后面随着。

(二内侍)领旨。(生携旦行介)妃子,【排歌】

朕和你肩相并,手共携,不须花底小车催,

【东瓯令】趁扑面好风归。

【尾声】(合)意中人,人中意,则那些无情花

鸟也情痴,一般的解结双头学并栖。

  (生)花气浑如百和香, 杜甫

  (旦)避风新出浴盆汤。 王建

  (生)侍儿扶起娇无力, 白居易

  (旦)笑倚东窗白玉床。 李白

EMPEROR:

> *My love, you look tired out*
> *And hardly able to support yourself—*
> *Like a drooping willow in the wind*
> *Or flowers weighed down by dew.*

(*Two eunuchs enter with a driver and a carriage.*)

EUNUCHS: May it please Your Majesty, the carriage is here to take you back to the palace.

EMPEROR: Let the carriage follow us.

EUNUCHS: Yes, Your Majesty.

EMPEROR (*Helping* Lady Yang *along*):

> *Let us saunter together, hand in hand,*
> *We need no carriage to drive through this balmy breeze;*
> *True lovers see how even the birds and flowers*
> *Are couched in pairs in their downy nests and beds.*

(***Exeunt.***)

第二十一出 密誓

【越调引子】【浪淘沙】(贴扮织女,引二仙女上)云护玉梭儿,巧织机丝。天宫原不着相思,报道今宵逢七夕,忽忆年时。

【鹊桥仙】"纤云弄巧,飞星传信,银汉秋光暗度。金风玉露一相逢,便胜却人间无数。柔肠似水,佳期如梦,遥指鹊桥前路。两情若是久长时,又岂在朝朝暮暮。"吾乃织女是也。蒙上帝玉敕,与牛郎结为天上夫妇。年年七夕,渡河相见。今乃下界天宝十载,七月七夕。你看明河无浪,乌鹊将填,不免暂撤机丝,整妆而待。(内细乐扮乌鹊上,绕场飞介)(前场设一桥,乌鹊飞止桥两边介)(二仙女)鹊桥已驾,请娘娘渡河。(贴起行介)

SCENE 21
The Secret Vow

(*Enter the Heavenly Weaving Maid and two other fairies.*)

WEAVING MAID:

> *With my jade shuttle in the fleecy clouds,*
> *I weave the whole year round.*
> *There can be no love-longing in heaven;*
> *But now that Double Seventh has come*
> *I remember our last reunion.*
> *Light wisps of clouds that interlace,*
> *And shooting stars, convey our messages;*
> *In the Milky Way autumn slips in unheeded,*
> *We meet once a year in the chilly wind and dew,*
> *Yet fare better than mortal lovers for all their meetings.*
> *My heart melts at the thought;*
> *Our tryst is like a dream;*
> *Magpies will form a bridge ahead;*
> *And when love is true,*
> *It makes no difference how seldom lovers meet.*

I am the Heavenly Weaving Maid. With the Heavenly Emperor's permission, I married the Heavenly Cowherd; and every year on the seventh day of the seventh moon, I cross the Milky Way to meet my love. Today on earth it is the seventh day of the seventh moon of the tenth year of the Tianbao period. Now the Milky Way is calm and the magpies are coming to make a bridge. I will stop weaving and dress myself to wait for the appointed hour.

(*Music is heard offstage, and magpies are seen flying around. A bridge is set up, and the magpies support both ends.*)

FAIRIES: The magpie bridge is ready. Your Ladyship may cross the Milk Way.

(*The* Weaving Maid *advances.*)

217

【越调过曲】【山桃红】【下山虎头】俺这里乍抛锦字,暂驾香辐。(合)趁碧落无云滓,新凉暮飔,(作上桥介)端上这桥影参差,俯映着河光净泚。【小桃红】更喜杀新月纤,华露滋,低绕着乌鹊双飞翅也。【下山虎尾】陡觉的银汉秋生别样姿。(做过桥介)(二仙女)启娘娘,已渡过河来了。(贴)星河之下,隐隐望见香烟一簇,摇飏腾空,却是何处?(仙女)是唐天子的贵妃杨玉环,在宫中乞巧哩。(贴)生受他一片诚心,不免同了牛郎,到彼一看。(合)天上留佳会,年年在斯,却笑他人世情缘顷刻时。(齐下)

【商调过曲】【二郎神】(二内侍挑灯,引生上)秋光静,碧沉沉轻烟送暝。雨过梧桐微做冷,银河宛转,纤云点缀双星。(内作笑声,生听介)顺着风儿还细听,欢笑隔花阴树影。内侍,是那里这般笑语?(内侍问介)万岁爷问,那里这般笑语?(内)是杨娘娘到长生殿去乞巧哩。(内侍回介)杨娘娘到长

WEAVING MAID:

> *I toss aside my web and mount my carriage;*
> *The sky is cloudless, the evening breeze is cool.*

(*She reaches the bridge.*)

> *I step upon the bridge, which casts its shadow*
> *Across the stream below; the crescent moon*
> *Is bathed in dew, the magpies circle low,*
> *And the autumn sky was never so fair as now.*

(*She reaches the other side of the bridge.*)

FAIRIES: We have crossed the bridge, my lady.

WEAVING MAID: Far under the Milky Way I see a wisp of smoke. Where does it come from?

FAIRIES: It is Lady Yang, concubine of the Tang emperor, praying in the palace on this Double Seventh for happiness.

WEAVING MAID: Since she is so reverent, I shall go with my husband to watch her.

ALL:

> *Year after year we meet in heaven,*
> *Pitying mortals because their love is transient.* (*Exeunt.*)

(*Enter two eunuchs holding lanterns, followed by the emperor.*)

EMPEROR:

> *The autumn night is still and the sky deep blue,*
> *The light mist scatters with the dusk;*
> *After a shower freshness breathes from the trees;*
> *And fragments of bright cloud*
> *Wreathe the twin stars beside the Milky Way.*

(*Laughter is heard. The emperor listens.*)

> *A light breeze carries the sound of happy laughter*
> *Through the shade of flowers and trees.*

Attendants, who is that laughing and talking there?

EUNUCH (*Calling to someone offstage*): His Majesty asks who is laughing and talking there?

VOICE OFF: Lady Yang is going to the Palace of Eteral Youth to pray for happiness on this Double Seventh!

EUNUCH (*To the emperor*): Lady Yang is going to the Palace of

生殿去乞巧，故此笑语。（生）内侍每不要
传报，待朕悄悄前去。撤红灯，待悄向龙墀
觑个分明。（虚下）

【前腔】【换头】（旦引老旦、贴同二宫女各捧香
盒、纨扇、瓶花、化生金盆上）宫庭，金炉篆霭，
烛光掩映。米大蜘蛛厮抱定，金盘种豆，花
枝招展银瓶。（老旦、贴）已到长生殿中，巧
筵齐备，请娘娘拈香。（作将瓶花、化生盆设
桌上，老旦捧香盒，旦拈香介）妾身杨玉环，虔
爇心香，拜告双星，伏祈鉴佑。愿钗盒情缘
长久订，（拜介）莫使做秋风扇冷。（生潜上
窥介）觑娉婷，只见他拜倒在瑶阶，暗祝声
声。

（老旦、贴作见生介）呀，万岁爷到了。
（旦急转，拜生介）（生扶起介）妃子在此，作何
勾当？（旦）今乃七夕之期，陈设瓜果，特向
天孙乞巧。（生笑介）妃子巧夺天工，何须

Eternal Youth to pray for happiness. That's the reason for the talk and laughter.

EMPEROR: Do not announce me. I will go there quietly.

I will go alone, without the crimson lanterns,
To watch unseen from the courtyard of the palace.
   (*Exeunt.*)

(Lady Yang *come's in. With her are* Yongxin, Niannu *and two other maids who are carrying a box, a fan, a vase of flowers and a golden basin.*)

LADY:

Incense mounts in the courtyard from the golden censer,
Candlelight gleams, and the spider spins its web;
Here is a goleten basin,
And flowers of many hues in a silver vase.

MAIDS: Here we are at the Palace of Eternal Youth, and the offering is ready. Will it please Your Ladyship to offer incense?

(*The maids place the vase of flowers and the golden basin on the table.* Yongxin *takes the box to* Lady Yang, *who picks out several sticks of incense.*)

LADY: I, Yang Yuhuan, reverently burn this incense, the offering of a true heart, as I pray to the twin stars above. Look into my heart, and give me protection!

May our love, pledged by hairpin and jewel box, last for ever!
May I not be cast off like a fan when chill autumn comes!

(*While* Lady Yang *is worshipping, the emperor comes in quietly and stands watching her.*)

EMPEROR:

My love is kneeling on the marleble steps,
There, in seclusion, praying in low tones.

MAIDS (*Seeing the emperor*): Ah! His Majesty is here!

(Lady Yang *turns hastily to kneel to him. The emperor helps her up.*)

EMPEROR: What are you doing here, my love?

LADY: It is the evening of the seventh day of the seventh moon, so I am praying to the Weaving Maid for grace and skill.

221

更乞。(旦)惶愧。(生、旦各坐介)(老旦、贴同
二宫女暗下)(生)妃子,朕想牵牛、织女隔断
银河,一年才会得一度,这相思真非容易
也。

【集贤宾】秋空夜永碧汉清,甫灵驾逢迎,奈
天赐佳期刚半顷,耳边厢容易鸡鸣。云寒
露冷,又趱上经年孤另。(旦)陛下言及双
星别恨,使妾凄然。只可惜人间不知天上
的事。如打听,决为了相思成病。

　　(做泪介)(生)呀,妃子为何掉下泪来?
(旦)妾想牛郎织女,虽则一年一见,却是地
久天长。只恐陛下与妾的恩情,不能够似
他长远。(生)妃子说哪里话!

【黄莺儿】仙偶纵长生,论尘缘也不恁争。
百年好占风流胜,逢时对景,增欢助情,怪
伊底事翻悲哽?(移坐近旦低介)问双星,朝
朝暮暮,争似我和卿!

　　(旦)臣妾受恩深重,今夜有句话儿
……(住介)(生)妃子有话,但说不妨。(旦
对生鸣咽介)妾蒙陛下宠眷,六宫无比。只
怕日久恩疏,不免白头之叹!

EMPEROR (*Laughs*): You are already cleverer than any heavenly weaving maid. What more do you have to ask for?

LADY: You flatter me, sire.

(*The emperor and* Lady Yang *take seats. The maids withdraw.*)

EMPEROR: Look, my love, at the Weaving Maid and the Cowherd. Separated by the Milky Way, they can only meet one night each year. How they must long for each other!

Still is the autumn night, and limpid the blue sky;
The time has come for the heavenly lovers to meet.
But their time is short, for soon the cock will crow,
And, parting in cold clouds and chilly dew,
They must wait another year in loneliness.

LADY: When you speak of the twin stars' grief at parting, sire, you make me sad. It is a pity we mortals do not know what happens in heaven.

They must be lovesick too, if the truth were known.

(*She wipes away tears.*)

EMPEROR: Ah, my darling, why are you shedding tears?

LADY: Though the Weaving Maid and the Cowherd meet only once a year, their love will endure for all eternity. But our love, I am afraid, will not last as long.

EMPEROR: Why should you asy that, my love?

Though the heavenly pair are immortal,
They are scarcely more fortunate than lovers on earth,
For we in our hundred years know more of love's joy.
And so on a night like this we ought to be merry.
I cannot understand why you weep instead.

(*He moves closer to her and whispers.*)

Can the stars take pleasure as we do, day and night?

LADY: Your Majesty has been very kind to me, but there is something I beg to be allowed to say tonight. (*She pauses.*)

EMPEROR: Don't hesitate. What is it?

LADY (*Sobbing*): I am the most favoured now of all Your Majesty's servants in the imperial palaces. But I am afraid that as time passes you will stop loving me, and I shall be forsaken.

【莺簇一金罗】【黄莺儿】提起便心疼,念寒微侍掖庭,更衣傍辇多荣幸。【簇御林】瞬息间,怕花老春无剩,【一封书】宠难凭。(牵生衣泣介)论恩情,【金凤钗】若得一个久长时,死也应;若得一个到头时,死也瞑。

【皂罗袍】抵多少平阳歌舞,恩移爱更;长门孤寂,魂销泪零:断肠枉泣红颜命!

　　(生举袖与旦拭泪介)妃子,休要伤心。朕与你的恩情,岂是等闲可比。

【簇御林】休心虑,免泪零,怕移时,有变更。(执旦手介)做酥儿拌蜜胶粘定,总不离须臾顷。(合)话绵藤,花迷月暗,分不得影和形。

　　(旦)既蒙陛下如此情浓,趁此双星之下,乞赐盟约,以坚终始。(生)朕和你焚香设誓去。(携旦行介)

【琥珀猫儿坠】(合)香肩斜靠,携手下阶行。一片明河当殿横,(旦)罗衣陡觉夜凉生。

The thought of this makes me sad;
It preys on my mind.
Of humble birth, I have been exceedingly honoured,
Able to serve at the emperor's side.
But all too soon your love for me may vanish,
For, when the flower fades and springtime is gone,
I fear the imperial favour will pass to another.
(*She clings to the emperor's robe and weeps.*)
Often I think of Your Majesty's kindness.
If only our love can endure, then death holds no fears!
If only our love can endure, I shall die content!
But how many court ladies have been forsaken at last,
When, left alone in the palace,
With the emperor's love and favour transferred to another,
They can only shed tears to lament their unhappy fate!

EMPEROR (*Wiping her tears*): Don't be so sad, my darling. Ours is no common love.

Take comfort and dry your tears.
You need have no fear that our love will change.
(*He takes her hand.*)
We are so close to each other,
That not for a single moment can we be parted.

TOGETHER:

Our love will be unbroken,
Our love will be everlasting;
For we are like flowers in the moonlight,
Substance and shadow blended completely in one.

LADY: If you love me so much, sire, I beg you to vow under the twin stars to make our love eternal.

EMPEROR: Let us go then to offer incense and make a vow together.

(*They walk together.*)
Shoulder to shoulder and hand in hand,
We walk down the marble steps.
The Milky Way is gleaming above our heads.

225

(生)惟应和你悄语低言,海誓山盟。

　　(生上香揖同旦福介)双星在上,我李隆基与杨玉环,(旦合)情重恩深,愿世世生生,共为夫妇,永不相离。有渝此盟,双星鉴之。(生又揖介)在天愿为比翼鸟,(旦拜介)在地愿为连理枝。(合)天长地久有时尽,此誓绵绵无绝期。(旦拜谢生介)深感陛下情重,今夕之盟,妾死生守之矣。(生携旦介)

【尾声】长生殿里盟私订。(旦)问今夜有谁折证?(生指介)是这银汉桥边,双双牛女星。(同下)

【越调过曲】【山桃红】(小生扮牵牛,云巾、仙衣,同贴引仙女上)只见他誓盟密矢,拜祷孜孜,两下情无二,口同一辞。(小生)天孙,你看唐天子与杨玉环,好不恩爱也!悄相

LADY:

In my silken dress I feel the night grow cool.

EMPEROR:

The time is right to whisper to you of love,
And vow to be true for ever.

(*The emperor offers incense. They both bow to the stars.*)

May the twin stars in heaven be our witness! We, Li Longji, the Tang emperor, and Yang Yuhuan...

TOGETHER: ... love each other so dearly that we wish to be husband and wife in every fresh life and never be parted. May the twin stars witness our vow!

(*The emperor bows again.*)

EMPEROR:

In the sky we will be two love birds flying together.

(Lady Yang *bows again.*)

LADY:

On the earth we will be twin branches on one tree.

TOGETHER:

Though heaven and earth may end,
May this vow last for ever and for ever!

LADY (*Curtseying*): I thank the emperor from the bottom of my heart. I shall remain true to this vow in life and death.

EMPEROR: (*Taking her arm*):

We have made a secret vow in the Palace of Eternal Youth.

LADY:

Are there no witnesses to our vow tonight?

EMPEROR (*Pointing overhead*):

The Weaving Maid and the Cowherd,
Twin stars that shine beside the Milky Way. (*Exeunt.*)

(*Enter the* Cowherd *wearing a cap with cloud designs and fairy garments, accompanied by the* Weaving Maid *and other fairies.*)

TOGETHER:

We saw them make their vow, two with one heart;
They were earnest in their prayers.

COWHERD: See, my lady, how devoted the Tang emperor and

假,倚着香肩,没些缝儿。我与你既缔天上良缘,当作情场管领。况他又向我等设盟,须索与他保护。见了他恋比翼,慕并枝,愿生生世世情真至也,合令他长作人间风月司。(贴)只是他两人劫难将至,免不得生离死别。若果后来不背今盟,决当为之绾合。(小生)天孙言之有理。你看夜色将阑,且回斗牛宫去。(携贴行介)(合)天上留佳会,年年在斯,却笑他人世情缘顷刻时!

何用人间岁月催,罗邺
星桥横过鹊飞回。李商隐
莫言天上稀相见,李郢
没得心情送巧来。罗隐

Lady Yang are to each other.

Hand in hand, they lean together.

We lovers in heaven should watch over lovers on earth; and as they have asked us to witness their secret vow of love, we should protect them.

Since as love birds, as two boughs on a single tree,
They desire to love for ever, in all their lives,
It is right for us to make them
The arbiters of love in the world below.

WEAVING MAID: But a sad fate awaits them, for they will soon be separated by death. Yet if they remain true, we can bring them together again.

COWHERD: You are right. But now the night is nearly done, and we must go back to our palace.

(*They walk forward together.*)

TOGETHER:

Year after year we meet in heaven,
Pitying mortals because their love is transient.

(***Exeunt.***)

第二十二出　陷关

【越调引子】【杏花天】(净领二番将,四军执旗上)狼贪虎视威风大,镇渔阳兵雄将多。待长驱直把殽函破,奏凯日齐声唱歌。

咱家安禄山,自出镇以来,结连塞上诸蕃,招纳天下亡命,精兵百万,大事可举,只因唐天子待我不薄,思量等他身后方才起兵。叵耐杨国忠那厮,屡次说我反形大著,请皇上急加诛戮。天子虽然不听,只是咱在边关,他在朝内,若不早图,终恐遭其暗算。因此假造敕书,说奉密旨,召俺领兵入朝诛戮国忠。乘机打破西京,夺取唐室江山,可不遂了我平生大愿! 今乃黄道吉日,蕃将每,就此起兵前去。(众)得令。(发号行介)(净)

【越调过曲】【豹子令】只为奸臣酿大祸,(众)酿大祸,(净)致令边镇起干戈,(众)起干戈。(合)逢城攻打逢人剁,尸横遍野血

SCENE 22
Storming the Pass

(*Enter* An Lushan *with two Tartar generals and four soldiers carrying flags.*)

AN:

> *Like a ravening wolf or tiger, proud in my strength,*
> *I have garrisoned Yuyang with a mighty force;*
> *Soon we shall march to the west to storm the Pass;*
> *We shall sing aloud in the day of victory!*

Since coming to the frontier, I have entered into a league with the tribes of the north and rallied outlaws and vagabonds from all parts of the empire. With a million picked troops, I am now strong enough to rebel. Because the Tang emperor always treated me well, I intended to revolt only after his death; but that scundrel Yang Guozhong has kept warning the emperor against me, saying that I am disloyal and asking to have me killed. Though his advice has been ignored, he is in the court while I am far away at the frontier; and unless I forestall him sooner or later I shall be destroyed by him. So I have forged a decree in the emperor's name, ordering me to march secretly to the capital with my army to kill the prime minister. I shall take this opportunity to seize the capital and the empire, thus fulfilling my life ambition. Today, my Tartar generals, is an auspicious day. Let us begin our march!

ALL: Your Highness can count on us!

(*Trumpets sound and they begin to march.*)

AN:

> *The evil minister brings ruin on the empire,*
> *Forcing us at the frontier to take up arms.*

ALL:

> *Storming cities and massacring the people,*
> *We will heap the plain with corpses*

231

流河,烧家劫舍抢娇娥。(喊杀下)

【水底鱼】(丑白须扮哥舒老将引二卒上)年纪无多,刚刚八十过。渔阳兵至,认咱这老哥。自家老将哥舒翰是也,把守潼关。不料安禄山造反,杀奔前来,决意闭关死守。争奈监军内侍,立逼出战。势不由己,军士每,与我拼力杀上前去。(卒)得令。(行介)(净领众杀上)(丑迎杀大战介)(净众擒丑绑介)(净)拿这老东西过来。我今饶你老命,快快献关降顺。(丑)事已至此,只得投降。(推丑下)(净)且喜潼关已得,势如破竹,大小三军,就此杀奔西京便了。(众应,呐喊行内)跃马挥戈,精兵百万多。靴尖略动,踏残山与河,踏残山与河。

平旦交锋晚未休,　王道
动天金鼓逼神州。　韩偓
潼关一败番儿喜,　司空图
倒把金鞭上酒楼。　薛逢

And blood will flow in torrents,
As we burn and pillage and rape young girls.
(*Shouting war cries, they march off.*)
(*Enter an old general,* Geshu Han, *with two soldiers.*)
GESHU:

I am a stripling of eighty;
When the rebels come from Yuyang,
They will have me to deal with.

My name is Geshu Han, and I am in charge of the defence of the Pass. Now An Lushan has revolted and is marching against us. My plan was to defend the Pass; but the army inspector from the court insisted that I come out to fight them, and I had to give in to him. Now, men, let us advance and fight hard.

SOLDIERS: We will, sir.

(*They walk forward. An Lushan comes in with his men. They fight, and* Geshu Han *is captured.*)

AN: Bring that old fellow over here. I will spare your life on condition that you surrender the Pass.

GESHU: Things have gone so far, I suppose I shall have to surrender.

(Geahu Han *and his soldiers are pushed off.*)

AN: Now that we have the Pass, we shall carry all before us. Let us sweep down, my men, to the capital!

(*They cheer and march on.*)

ALL:

Galloping forward, brandishing our spears,
A million or more picked men,
We shall trample the empire under our feet!
We shall trample the empire under our feet!

(*Exeunt.*)

第二十三出　惊变

（丑上）"玉楼天半起笙歌,风送宫嫔笑语和。月殿影开闻夜漏,水晶帘卷近秋河。"咱家高力士,奉万岁爷之命,着咱在御花园中安排小宴,要与贵妃娘娘同来游赏,只得在此伺候。（生、旦乘辇,老旦、贴随后,二内侍引,行上）

【北中吕粉蝶儿】天淡云闲,列长空数行新雁。御园中秋色斓斑:柳添黄,蘋减绿,红莲脱瓣。一抹雕阑,喷清香桂花初绽。

（到介）（丑）请万岁爷娘娘下辇。（生、旦下辇介）（丑同内侍暗下）（生）妃子,朕与你散步一回者。（旦）陛下请。（生携旦手介）（旦）

【南泣颜回】携手向花间,暂把幽怀同散。凉生亭下,风荷映水翩翩。爱桐阴静悄,碧沉沉并绕回廊看。恋香巢秋燕依人,睡银

SCENE 23
The Alarm

(*Enter* Gao Lishi.)

GAO:

> *From the marble pavilion come sounds of flutes and singing,*
> *Wind carries the laughter and chat of the palace maids;*
> *In the shade of the moonlit palace the waterclock sounds;*
> *And as screens are drawn back the Milky Way seems near.*

By His Majesty's order I have prepared a small feast in the imperial garden, and presently the emperor and Lady Yang will be coming here. I will wait for them.

(*Enter the emperor and* Lady Yang *in a carriage, followed by* Yongxin, Niannu *and two palace eunuchs.*)

EMPEROR:

> *Clouds drift through the pale blue sky, and wild geese*
> *Fly past in rows; while autumn paints the garden*
> *With many colours: willow leaves turn yellow,*
> *The duckweed grows less green, and the red lotus*
> *Sheds all its petals; but there by the carved railings*
> *The cassia flowers in bloom give a sweet scent.*

GAO: May it please you to alight here, Your Majesty and Your Ladyship.

(*The emperor and* Lady Yang *get out of the carriage.* Gao *and the other eunuchs retire.*)

EMPEROR: Let us take a short stroll, my love.

LADY: Yes, sire.

(*The emperor takes her hand.*)

> *Hand in hand we wander among the flowers,*
> *Past the cool pavilion, and past the wind-blown lotus*
> *Which trembles on the lake. I love the calm*
> *Of these planes which form such deep green avenues.*

235

塘鸳鸯蘸眼。

（生）高力士，将酒过来，朕与娘娘小饮数杯。（丑）宴已排在亭上，请万岁爷娘娘上宴。（旦作把盏，生止住介）妃子坐了。

【北石榴花】不劳你玉纤纤高捧礼仪烦，子待借小饮对眉山。俺与你浅斟低唱互更番，三杯两盏，遣兴消闲。妃子，今日虽是小宴，倒也清雅。回避了御厨中，回避了御厨中烹龙炰凤堆盘案，咿咿哑哑乐声催趱。只几味脆生生，只几味脆生生蔬和果清肴馔，雅称你仙肌玉骨美人餐。

妃子，朕与你清游小饮，那些梨园旧曲，都不耐烦听他。记得那年在沉香亭上赏杜丹，召翰林李白草"清平调"三章，令李龟年度成新谱，其词甚佳。不知妃子还记得么？（旦）妾还记得。（生）妃子可为朕歌之，朕当亲倚玉笛以和。（旦）领旨。（老旦进玉笛，生吹介）（旦按板介）

【南泣颜回】花繁、秾艳想容颜。云想衣裳光璨，新妆谁似，可怜飞燕娇懒。名花国

The swallows are still lingering by their nests,
While the duck and drake sleep in the silver pool.

EMPEROR: Gao Lishi, bring wine! I shall drink a few cups with
Her Ladyship.

GAO: The feast is already spread in the pavilion. Please step over
here.

(Lady Yang *starts to pour the wine, but is stopped by the
emperor.*)

EMPEROR: Sit down, my darling.

There is no need to stand on ceremony
Or present the wine to me with your slender fingers.
But let us drink face to face,
Singing soft melodies by turns,
As we while away the evening together.

Though this is such a simple meal today, it is rather pleasant to get
away for once

From the banquets prepared by the imperial kitchen,
When the tables groan under sumptuous fare,
And the palace musicians play as we eat.
Today crisp vegetables and fresh fruit
Make simple fare which suits a dainty lady.

I am not in the mood to hear any of those old tunes today; but I
remember one year when we were enjoying the peony flowers in
Aloes Pavilion, we summoned Li Bai to write some stanzas for us,
and ordered Li Guinian to set them to music. The poem was a
charming one. Do you still remember it?

LADY: Yes, I do.

EMPEROR: Will you sing it for me, then, while I play an
accompaniment on my jade flute?

LADY: Gladly, Your Majesty.

(Yongxin *brings the jade flute, and the emperor starts playing.*
Lady Yang *rattles the castanets and sings.*)

Her dress is like a brilliant cloud,
A flower in bloom her face;
And none but Lady Swallow can

237

色,笑微微常得君王看。向春风解释春愁,沉香亭同倚阑干。

(生)妙哉,李白锦心,妃子绣口,真双绝矣。宫娥,取巨觞来,朕与妃子对饮。(老旦、贴送酒介)(生)

【北关鹌鹑】畅好是喜孜孜驻拍停歌,喜孜孜驻拍停歌,笑吟吟传杯送盏。妃子干一杯,(作照干介)不须他絮烦烦射覆藏钩,闹纷纷弹丝弄板。(又作照杯介)妃子,再干一杯。(旦)妾不能饮了。(生)宫娥每,跪劝。(老旦、贴)领旨。(跪旦介)娘娘,请上这一杯。(旦勉饮介)(老旦、贴作连劝介)(生)我这里无语持觞仔细看,早子见花一朵上腮间。(旦作醉介)妾真醉矣。(生)一会价软咍咍柳軃花歆,软咍咍柳軃花歆,困腾腾莺娇燕懒。

妃子醉了,宫娥每,扶娘娘上辇进宫去者。(老旦、贴)领旨。(作扶旦起介)(旦作醉态呼介)万岁!(老旦、贴扶旦行)(旦作醉态介)

【南扑灯蛾】态恹恹轻云软四肢,影濛濛空

Compare with her in grace.
The queen of flowers, the matchless girl,
And a happy king between,
Telling the breeze of love's lassitude
On the balustrade they lean.

EMPEROR: Excellent! The poet's genius and your singing are two
wonders. Maids, bring the large cups for us to drink from.
(*The maids pour the wine.*)

She smiles as she ends her song,
And I smile as I offer her wine.

Drink this, my love. (*He drinks a cup with her.*)

We need no drinking games,
No piercing, clamorous musical instruments.

(*He drinks to her again.*) Now, another cup.

LADY: I cannot drink any more.

EMPEROR: Yongxin and Niannu, come and beg your mistress to
drink.

MAIDS: Yes, Your Majesty. (*They kneel before* Lady Yang.) Do
drink another cup, my lady.

(Lady Yang *forces herself to drink, and the maids urge her
again.*)

EMPEROR:

Holding my cup I watch her without a word,
And see the red roses blossoming on her cheeks.

LADY (*Tipsily*): I am really drunk.

EMPEROR:

She is suddenly limp as a drooping willow or flower,
Languorous as a young swallow or oriole in spring.

Her Ladyship is drunk! Yongxin and Niannu! Help Lady Yang to
the carriage.

MAIDS: Yes, Your Majesty. (*They help her up.*)

LADY (*Drunkenly*): Oh, Your Majesty! (*She takes a few steps,
leaning on her maids.*)

I feel as if I were walking on air
And stagger as if I were dazzled;

花乱双眼,娇怯怯柳腰扶难起,困沉沉强抬娇腕,软设设金莲倒褪,乱松松香肩軃云鬟,美甘甘思寻凤枕,步迟迟倩宫娥挽入绣帏间。

（老旦、贴扶旦下）（丑同内侍暗上）（内击鼓介）（生惊介）何处鼓声骤发？（副净急上）"渔阳鼙鼓动地来,惊破霓裳羽衣曲。"（问丑介）万岁爷在那里？（丑）在御花园内。（副净）军情紧急,不免迳入。（进见介）陛下,不好了。安禄山起兵造反,杀过潼关,不日就到长安了。（生大惊介）守关将士何在？（副净）哥舒翰兵败,已降贼了。（生）

【北上小楼】呀,你道失机的哥舒翰……称兵的安禄山,赤紧的离了渔阳,陷了东京,破了潼关。唬得人胆战心摇,唬得人胆战心摇,肠慌腹热,魂飞魄散,早惊破月明花粲。

卿有何策,可退贼兵？（副净）当日臣曾再三启奏,禄山必反,陛下不听,今日果

My willowy waist is limp, for I feel so tired
That to raise my arms is hard;
The ground slips away from under my feet,
And with hair in disorder I long for my bed,
As my maids help me slowly behind the embroidered curtain.
(*The maids escort* Lady Yang *out.*)

(*Enter* Gao *with other eunuchs. Drums are heard in the distance.*)

EMPEROR (*Startled*): From where comes the sound of drums?

(Yang Guozhong, *the prime minister, enters hastily.*)

YANG:

The sound of rebel drums makes the whole earth quake,
Shattering the Rainbow Garment Dance.
(*To* Gao.) Where is the emperor?

GAO: In the imperial garden.

YANG: The situation is serious. I must go straight in.

(*He sees the emperor.*) Your Majesty, I have bad news! An Lushan has revolted with his army and entered the Tongguan Pass. He is marching on the capital.

EMPEROR (*Greatly alarmed*): What of the troops defending the Pass?

YANG: General Geshu Han was defeated and has surrendered to the rebels.

EMPEROR: Ah!

An Lushan has rebelled,
And Geshu Han has surrendered!
The rebels have taken the eastern capital
And broken through the Pass!
This news strikes dread into our hearts
And makes us quake with fear,
Destroying our pleasure in the moonlight
And the beauty of the flowers.

What plans have you to resist the rebels?

YANG: In the past I warned Your Majesty repeatedly that An would rebel, but you would not believe me. Now it has happened as I

应臣言。事起仓卒,怎生抵敌? 不若权时幸蜀,以待天下勤王。(生)依卿所奏。快传旨,诸王百官,即时随驾幸蜀便了。(副净)领旨。(急下)(生)高力士,快些整备军马。传旨令右龙武将军陈元礼,统领羽林军士三千扈驾前行。(丑)领旨。(下)(内侍)请万岁爷回宫。(生转行叹介)唉,正尔欢娱,不想忽有此变,怎生是了也!

【南扑灯蛾】稳稳的宫庭宴安,扰扰的边廷造反。冬冬的鼙鼓喧,腾腾的烽火烟。的溜扑碌臣民儿逃散,黑漫漫乾坤覆翻,碜磕磕社稷摧残,碜磕磕社稷摧残。当不得萧萧飒飒西风送晚,黯黯的一轮落日冷长安。

(向内问介)宫娥每,杨娘娘可曾安寝?(老旦、贴内应介)已睡熟了。(生)不要惊他,且待明早五鼓同行。(泣介)天那,寡人不幸,遭此播迁,累他玉貌花容,驱驰道路。好不痛心也!

【南尾声】在深宫兀自娇慵惯,怎样支吾蜀道难! (哭介)我那妃子呵,愁杀你玉软花柔,要将途路趱。

宫殿参差落照间, 卢纶
渔阳烽火照函关。 吴融
遏云声绝悲风起, 胡曾
何处黄云是陇山。 武元衡

242

predicted. In this emergency we are powerless to resist him. Your Majesty had better go to Chengdu for the time being, and wait there until the generals from the provinces can rally to defend the throne.

EMPEROR: Very well. Give the order at once for all the princes and ministers to prepare to accompany me to Chengdu.

YANG: It shall be done, sire. (*Hurries out.*)

EMPEROR: Gao Lishi, quickly prepare horses, and order Chen Yuanli, Commander of the Imperial Guards, to muster three thousand men to escort us.

GAO: The emperor's orders shall be obeyed. (*Exit.*)

EUNUCH: May it please Your Majesty to return to the palace.

EMPEROR (*Walking forward, sighing*): Ah, what a bolt from the blue! What is to be done?

> *While we were feasting peacefully in the palace,*
> *Rebellion had broken out at the frontier.*
> *Alarms have been sounded and beacon fires are lit;*
> *The people are fleeing in panic,*
> *And the empire faces ruin.*
> *The autumn wind bids farewell to the setting sun,*
> *And Chang'an, my capital, is growing cold.*

(*He calls to the maids offstage.*) Her Lady Yang retired?

MAIDS (*Offstage*): Yes, she is fast asleep.

EMPEROR: Do not wake her. We shall start tomorrow at dawn. (*He weeps.*) Ah, Heaven, how unfortunate I am to be overtaken with such disaster! And how distressing to think of her taking to the road, with her flower-like beauty.

> *In the palace she is used to luxury,*
> *How can she stand the hard journey to Chengdu?*

(*He weeps.*) Ah, my darling—

> *Tenderly reared as a flower, and delicate as jade,*
> *How can you travel that rugged mountain road?*

(*Exit.*)

第二十四出　埋玉

【南吕过曲】【金钱花】（末扮陈元礼引军士上）
拥旄仗钺前驱，前驱，羽林拥卫銮舆，銮舆。
匆匆避贼就征途。人跋涉，路崎岖。知何
日，到成都。

　　下官右龙武将军陈元礼是也。因禄山
造反，破了潼关，圣上避兵幸蜀，命俺统领
禁军扈驾。行了一程，早到马嵬驿了。（内
鼓噪介）（末）众军为何呐喊？（内）禄山造
反，圣驾播迁，都是杨国忠弄权，激成变乱。
若不斩此贼臣，我等死不扈驾。（末）众军
不必鼓噪，暂且安营。待我奏过圣上，自有
定夺。（内应介）（末引军重唱"人跋涉"四句下）
（生同旦骑马，引老旦、贴、丑行上）
【中吕过曲】【粉孩儿】匆匆的弃宫闱珠泪
洒，叹清清冷半张銮驾，望成都直在天一
涯。渐行来渐远京华，五六搭剩水残山，两

SCENE 24
Death at the Post Station

(*Enter* Commander Chen Yuanli *with troops.*)

CHEN:

Marching ahead with pennants and halberds,
The imperial guards protect the emperor.
We travel in haste, to escape from the rebel army,
Along rugged mountain roads.
Will we ever reach Chengdu?

I am Chen Yuanli, Commander of the Imperial Guards. Because An Lushan has rebelled and taken the Pass by storm, the emperor is going to Chengdu to be out of danger; and I have been ordered to accompany His Majesty at the head of the imperial guards. We have travelled some way, and have just reached Mawei Station. (*Shouting is heard offstage.*) What is that shouting?

VOICE OFF: It is all Yang Guozhong's fault that An Lushan has rebelled and the emperor has had to leave the capital. If that treacherous minister is not put to death, we shall not escort His Majesty even if you threaten to kill us!

CHEN: Stop shouting and pitch camp quietly. I shall report to the emperor and ask for his orders.

(*A shout of assent is heard.* Chen *and his soldiers go out.*)

(*Enter the emperor,* Lady Yang, *her two maids and* Gao Lishi.)

EMPEROR:

We left the palace in haste,
To shed lonely tears,
Escorted by only half our equipage.
Our destination far beyond the horizon,
We are leaving the capital further and further behind.
In front lie scattered hills and a lonely stream,
And four or five empty houses with broken tiles.

245

三间空舍崩瓦。

（丑）来此已是马嵬驿了，请万岁爷暂住銮驾。（生、旦下马，作进坐介）（生）寡人不道，误宠逆臣，致此播迁，悔之无及。妃子，只是累你劳顿，如之奈何！（旦）臣妾自应随驾，焉敢辞劳。只愿早早破贼，大驾还都便好。（内又喊介）杨国忠专权误国，今又交通吐蕃，我等誓不与此贼俱生。要杀杨国忠的，快随我等前去。（杂扮四军提刀赶副净上，绕场奔介）（军作杀副净，呐喊下）（生惊介）高力士，外面为何喧嚷？快宣陈元礼进来。（丑）领旨。（宣介）（末上见介）臣陈元礼见驾。（生）众军为何呐喊？（末）臣启陛下：杨国忠专权召乱，又与吐蕃私通。激怒六军，竟将国忠杀死了。（生作惊介）呀，有这等事。（旦作背掩泪介）（生沉吟介）这也罢了，传旨起驾。（末出传旨介）圣旨道来，赦汝等擅杀之罪。作速起行。（内又喊介）国忠虽诛，贵妃尚在。不杀贵妃，誓不扈驾。

GAO: We have arrived at Mawei Station. May it please Your Majesty to alight.

(*The emperor and* Lady Yang *alight, enter the station and sit down.*)

EMPEROR: I made a great mistake in trusting that rebel; but it is too late to regret that now. I am only sorry to have involved you in this trouble, my love.

LADY: I shall follow you, sire, wherever you go, and not shrink from any hardship. I only hope that the rebels will be defeated quickly, so that we can return soon to the capital.

VOICE OFF (*Shouting*): Yang Guozhong got us into this! And now he is secretly scheming with the western tribesmen! We have vowed his death—whoever wants to kill Yang Guozhong come with us!

(Yang Guozhong *runs in, pursued by guards armed with sword. After a scuffle, the prime minster is killed, and with a shout of triumph the soldiers troop off.*)

EMPEROR: (*Startled*): Gao Lishi, what is all that shouting outside? Order Commander Chen to enter at once.

GAO: Yes, Your Majesty. (*He passes on the order, and* Chen Yuanli *enters.*)

CHEH: Long live the emperor!

EMPEROR: Why are the soldiers shouting?

CHEN: Your Majesty, by trying to take all power into his own hands, Yang Guozhong endangered the state. And when the guards discovered that he had been carrying on secret negotiations with the western tribesmen, they were indignant and killed him.

EMPEROR (*Startled*): What?

(Lady Yang *turns her head to wipe away tears.*)

EMPEROR (*After a moment's thought*): Very well. Give orders to resume our journey.

CHEN (*Loudly*): His Majesty pardons the guards for killing the prime minister, and orders you to set out again at once.

SHOUTS OFF: Though the prime minister is dead, his cousin, Lady Yang, is still with the emperor! Until she is killed, we will not go

247

（末见生介）众军道，国忠虽诛，贵妃尚在，不肯起行。望陛下割恩正法。（生作大惊介）哎呀，这话如何说起！（旦慌牵生衣介）（生）将军，

【红芍药】国忠纵有罪当加，现如今已被劫杀。妃子在深宫自随驾，有何干六军疑讶。

（末）圣论极明，只是军心已变，如之奈何！

（生）卿家，作速晓谕他，恁狂言没些高下。

（内又喊介）（末）陛下呵，听军中恁地喧哗，教微臣怎生弹压！

　（旦哭介）陛下呵，

【耍孩儿】事出非常堪惊诧。已痛兄遭戮，奈臣妾又受波查。是前生事已定，薄命应折罚。望吾皇急切抛奴罢，只一句伤心话……

　（生）妃子且自消停。（内又喊介）不杀贵妃，死不扈驾。（末）臣启陛下：贵妃虽则无罪，国忠实其亲兄，今在陛下左右，军心不安。若军心安，则陛下安矣。愿乞三思。

a step further!

CHEN (*To the emperor*): The soldiers say that though Yang Guozhong is dead, as long as Lady Yang remains alive they will not go any further. I beg Your Majesty to execute your favourite.

EMPEROR (*Greatly alarmed*): How can they ask this?

(Lady Yang *fearfully takes hold of the emperor's sleeve.*)

EMPEROR: My lord—

If Yang Guozhong was guilty of treason,
He has already paid with his life;
But his cousin only served in the inner palace;
Of what can the army suspect her?

CHEN: Your Majesty is right. Yet the troops are in an ugly mood—what can we do?

EMPEROR:

Go at once and reason with them.
This is a mad, impertinent demand!
(*Shouts off.*)

CHEN: Listen, Your Majesty—

The troops are in an uproar,
How can I pacify them?

LADY (*Weeping*): Your Majesty—

This has taken me by surprise!
As I grieve for my cousin's death
I find that I, too, am involved.
I must have been fated to suffer!
I beg you, sire, to give me up at once;
Though it breaks my heart, this is my earnest wish.

EMPEROR: Wait, my love.

SHOUTS OFF: We shall not move a step unless Lady Yang is executed!

CHEN: Though Lady Yang is innocent, Your Majesty, she is the prime minister's cousin. As long as she is sat your side the troops will feel insecure; but only when the troops feel secure will your own safety be assured. I hope Your Majesty will consider this carefully.

249

（生沉吟介）

【会河阳】无语沉吟，意如乱麻。（旦牵生衣哭介）痛生生怎地舍官家！（合）可怜一对鸳鸯，风吹浪打，直恁的遭强霸！（内又喊介）（旦哭介）众军逼得我心惊唬，（生作呆想，忽抱旦哭介）贵妃，好教我难禁架！

（众军呐喊上，绕场、围驿下）（丑）万岁爷，外厢军士已把驿亭围了。若再迟延，恐有他变，怎么处？（生）陈元礼，你快去安抚三军，朕自有道理！（末）领旨。（下）（生、旦抱哭介）（旦）

【缕缕金】魂飞飏，泪交加。（生）堂堂天子贵，不及莫愁家。（合哭介）难道把恩和义，霎时抛下！（旦跪介）臣妾受皇上深恩，杀身难报。今事势危急，望赐自尽，以定军心。陛下得安稳至蜀，妾虽死犹生也。算

EMPEROR: (*Thinking*)

> *In silence, I try to reflect;*
> *But my thoughts are a tangled skein.*

LADY: (*Clinging to the emperor's robes and crying*):

> *Unhappy that I am,*
> *How can I leave you?*

TOGETHER:

> *Like an unlucky duck and drake,*
> *Buffeted by the angry waves,*
> *We face appalling danger.*

(*Shouts are heard again.*)

Lady (*Crying*): The soldiers frighten me so!

> *How can I bear this, my darling?*

(*Soldiers burst in, shouting. They walk around, showing that they have besieged the station, then withdraw.*)

GAO: Your Majesty, the troops have besieged the station. If we hesitate, they may become desperate. What is to be done?

EMPEROR: Commander Chen, go quickly to pacify the troops, while I find a way out.

CHEN: Yes, Your Majesty. (*Exit.*)

(*They emperor and* Lady Yang *cling to each other and weep.*)

LADY:

> *My very soul is trembling,*
> *Drenched in tears.*

EMPEROR:

> *Though the emperor is exalted,*
> *He is not as free as a private citizen.*

TOGETHER (*Shedding tears*):

> *How can we ever forget our love?*

LADY (*Kneeling*): Your Majesty has shown me so much favour that even if I kill myself I cannot repay your kindness. Now the situation is desperate, I beg you to allow me to commit suicide to pacify the troops. For then you will arrive at your destination safely, and I shall feel comforted though I die.

> *I can see no other way to quell them;*

251

将来无计解军哗,残生愿甘罢,残生愿甘
罢!

(哭倒生怀介)(生)妃子说那里话! 你
若捐生,朕虽有九重之尊,四海之富,要他
则甚! 宁可国破家亡,决不肯抛舍你也!
【摊破地锦花】任灌哗,我一谜妆聋哑,总是
朕差。现放着一朵娇花,怎忍见风雨摧残,
断送天涯。若是再禁加,拼代你陨黄沙。

(旦)陛下虽则恩深,但事已至此,无路
求生。若再留恋,倘玉石俱焚,益增妾罪。
望陛下舍妾之身,以保宗社。(丑作掩泪,跪
介)娘娘既慷慨捐生,望万岁爷以社稷为
重,勉强割恩罢。(内又喊介)(生顿足哭介)
罢罢,妃子既执意如此,朕也做不得主了。
高力士,只得但、但凭娘娘罢!(作哽咽、掩
面哭下)(旦朝上拜介)万岁!(作哭倒介)(丑向
内介)众军听着,万岁爷已有旨,赐杨娘娘
自尽了。(众内呼介)万岁,万岁,万万岁!
(丑扶旦起介)娘娘,请到后边去。(扶旦行
介)(旦哭介)
【哭相思】百年离别在须臾,一代红颜为君
尽!

(转作到介)(丑)这里有座佛堂在此。
(旦作进介)且住,待我礼拜佛爷。(拜介)佛

Therefore let me be sacrificed.

(*She cries, her head in the emperor's lap.*)

EMPEROR: How can you say that, my love? If you die, what are my throne and empire to me? I would rather lose my empire than abandone you.

Let them clamour and shout;
I shall simply turn a deaf ear.
The fault was mine, and I cannot allow this flower
To be crushed and destroyed by the cruel wind and rain.
If the troops still insist,
I will die for you.

LADY: Though Your Majesty is so kind, things have come to such a pass that there is no other way out. If I hesitate any longer, we may all be destroyed; and then my guilt will be greater. Please give me up, to preserve your empire.

Gao (*Wiping his tears, kneeling*): Since Lady Yang shows such spirit and wishes to sacrifice herself, I beg Your Majesty to think of the empire and force yourself to agree to her request.

(*Shouts off.*)

EMPEROR: (*Stamping his foot and weeping*): So be it then! If she insists, I cannot forbid her. Let Her Ladyship do as she thinks right, Gao Lishi. (*Sobbing, he covers his face and withdraws.*)

LADY (*Bowing*): Long live the emperor!

GAO (*Calling to the men outside*): Listen, men! His Majesty has ordered Lady Yang to commit suicide.

SHOUTS OFF: Long live the emperor!

(Gao Lishi *helps* Lady Yang *to rise.*)

GAO: Please come this way, Your Ladyship. (*He helps her along.*))

LADY (*In tears*):

Now we are going to part for ever,
And I shall die for the emperor.

(*They halt.*)

GAO: Here is a shrine.

LADY: (*Entering the shrine*): Wait! Let me bow to the Buddha.

爷,佛爷! 念杨玉环呵,

【越恁好】罪孽深重,罪孽深重,望我佛度脱咱。(丑拜介)愿娘娘好处生天。(旦起哭介)(丑跪哭介)娘娘,有甚话儿,分付奴婢几句。(旦)高力士,圣上春秋已高,我死之后,只有你是旧人,能体圣意,须索小心奉侍。再为我转奏圣上,今后休要念我了。(丑哭应介)奴婢晓得。(旦)高力士,我还有一言。(作除钗、出盒介)这金钗一对,钿盒一枚,是圣上定情所赐。你可将来与我殉葬,万万不可遗忘。(丑接钗盒介)奴婢晓得。(旦哭介)断肠痛杀,说不尽恨如麻。(末领军拥上)杨妃既奉旨赐死,何得停留,稽迟圣驾。(军呐喊介)(丑向前拦介)众军士不得近前,杨娘娘即刻归天了。(旦)唉,陈元礼,陈元礼,你兵威不向逆寇加,逼奴自杀。(军又喊介)(丑)不好了,军士每拥进来了。(旦看介)唉,罢、罢,这一株梨树,是我杨玉环结果之处了。(作腰间解出白练,拜介)臣妾杨玉环,叩谢圣恩。从今再不得相见了。(丑泣介)(旦作哭缢介)我那圣上啊,我一命儿便

(*She bows.*) Great Buddha!
My sins are many;
Have mercy on my soul!

GAO (*Bowing*): May Her Ladyship enter paradise!

(Lady Yang *rises, weeping.*)

GAO (*Kneels, crying*): Your Ladyship, have you any last commands for me?

LADY: Gao Lishi, the emperor is growing old. When I am dead, you will be the only one who can understand him. You must look after him well, and tell him not to think of me any more.

GAO (*Weeping*): I will, my lady.

LADY: And there is something else. (*She unfastens the hairpin from her hair and takes out the jewel box.*) The emperor gave me this hairpin and jewel box to pledge his love. Bury them with my body—be sure that you don't forget!

GAO (*Taking them*): Yes, my lady.

LADY (*Weeping*):
My heart is broken,
My grief is too great to express.

(Chen Yuanli *hurries in with his troops.*)

CHEN: lady Yang has been ordered to commit suicide. Why is she still here, delaying His Majesty's journey?

(*The troops shout.*)

GAO (*Stopping them*): Keep back! Lady Yang is about to die.

LADY: Ah, Chen Yuanli!
Why do you not press forward against the rebels,
Instead of against me?

(*The soldiers shout angrily again.*)

GAO: Alas! The soldiers are breaking in.

LADY (*Looking round*): Why, then, I shall end my life on this pear tree here. (*She takes off her white silk belt, and curtseys towards the distance.*) Yang Yuhuan thanks the emperor for his past kindness; for we shall never meet again.

(Gao *weeps.*)

LADY (*Weeps and prepares to hang herself*): Your Majesty!

死在黄泉下，一灵儿只傍着黄旗下。

（做缢死下）（末）杨妃已死，众军速退。

（众应同下）（丑哭介）我那娘娘啊！（下）（生

上）"六军不发无奈何，宛转蛾眉马前死。"

（丑持白练上，见生介）启万岁爷，杨娘娘归天

了。（生作呆不应介）（丑又启介）杨娘娘归天

了。自缢的白练在此。（生看大哭介）哎哟，

妃子，妃子，兀的不痛杀寡人也！（倒介）

（丑扶介）（生哭介）

【红绣鞋】当年貌比桃花，桃花，（丑）今朝命

绝梨花，梨花。（出钗盒介）这金钗、钿盒，是

娘娘分付殉葬的。（生看钗盒哭介）这钗和

盒，是祸根芽。长生殿，恁欢洽，马嵬驿，恁

收煞！

（丑）仓卒之间，怎生整备棺椁？（生）

也罢，权将锦褥包裹。须要埋好记明，以待

日后改葬。这钗盒就系娘娘衣上罢。（丑）

领旨。（下）（生哭介）

【尾声】温香艳玉须臾化，今世今生怎见他！

（末上跪介）请陛下起驾。（生顿足恨介）咳，

256

Here I die. But although my body lies in the earth,
My spirit will always follow the imperial pennants.
   (*Dies.*)

CHEN: Lady Yang is dead, men. Withdraw!
   (*The soldiers troop off.*)

GAO (*Crying*): Ah, my lady! (*Exit.*)
   (*The emperor enters.*)

EMPEROR:
   The army will not advance; they have forced my hand;
   And the girl with the graceful eyebrows is doomed to die.
   (Gao *enters and bring the white belt to him.*)

GAO: Your Majesty, Lady Yang is dead. (*The emperor is speechless.*) Lady Yang is dead, sir. Here is the silk belt with which she hanged herself.

EMPEROR (*Looking at the belt, cries bitterly*): Ah, my love, my love! How can I bear this? (*He staggers, and* Gao Lishi *supports him.*)
   She was fairer than the peach blossom,
   Fairer than the peach blossom.

GAO:
   She is dead now under the pear blossom,
   Dead under the pear blossom.
   (*He shows the hairpin and box.*) Her Ladyship ordered that these be buried with her body.

EMPEROR: (*Looks at them and cries*):
   This hairpin and box are the root of all our trouble:
   We knew too much joy in the Palace of Eternal Youth;
   So our love has ended like this at Mawei Station.

GAO: In this emergency, how shall we find a coffin?

EMPEROR: Never mind that. Wrap her up in a silk quilt for the time being, and mark the place well so that we can remove the body later. The hairpin and box can be fastened to her clothes.

GAO: I will do as your Majesty orders. (*Exit.*)

EMPEROR (*In tears*):
   Her warmth and fragrance and beauty are gone;

我便不去西川也值什么!（内呐喊、掌号,众军上）

【仙吕入双调过曲】【朝元令】（丑暗上,引生上马行介）（合）长空雾黏,旌旆寒风飐。长征路淹,队仗黄尘染。谁料君臣,共尝危险。恨贼寇横兴逆焰,烽火相兼,何时得将豺虎歼。遥望蜀山尖,回将凤阙瞻,浮云数点,咫尺把长安遮掩,长安遮掩。

　　　　翠华西拂蜀云飞, 章碣

　　　　天地尘昏九鼎危。吴融

　　　　蝉鬓不随銮驾去, 高骈

　　　　空惊鸳鹭忽相随。钱起

Never more in this life shall I see her again.
(Commander Chen *enters.*)

CHEN: May it please Your Majesty, your horse is ready.

EMPEROR (*Stamping*): What do I care if I never reach Chengdu?
(*Trumpets sound and the guards march in.* Gao Lishi *enters and leads the emperor to his horse.*)

ALL:
Thick mist hangs heavy,
And a cold wind blows our banners;
The way is long and the riders covered with dust;
Both the emperor and his subjects are in danger;
The rebels are looting and burning, and beacon fires
Gleam all along the road.
When will these wild beasts be destroyed
Far, far ahead are the outlines of craggy mountains,
And looking back can see the palace receding,
For as wisps of cloud float over,
Chang'an, the capital, is lost from sight.

(***Exeunt.***)

第二十五出　献饭

【黄钟引子】【西地锦】(生引丑上)懊恨蛾眉
轻丧，一宵千种悲伤。早来慵把金鞭飐，午
余玉粒谁尝。

　　寡人匆匆西幸，昨在马嵬驿中，六军不
发。无计可施，只得把妃子赐死。(泪介)
咳，空做一朝天子，竟成千古忍人。勉强行
一程，已到扶风地面。驻跸凤仪宫内，不免
少息片时。(外扮老人持麦饭上)"炙背可以
见天子，献芹由来知野人。"老汉扶风野老
郭从谨是也。闻知皇上西巡，暂驻凤仪宫
内。老汉煮得一碗麦饭，特来进献，以表一
点敬心。(见丑介)公公，烦乞转奏一声，说
野人郭从谨特来进饭。(丑传介)(生)召他
进来。(外进见介)草莽小臣郭从谨见驾。
(生)你是那里人？(外)念小臣呵，

260

SCENE 25
The Gift of Food

(*The emperor enters with* Gao Lishi.)

EMPEROR:

Remorse at having surrendered my love so lightly
Caused me to pass the whole long night in sorrow;
I set out early, listlessly whipping my horse;
It is long past noon, yet I have not tasted food.

In my flight westwards yesterday, at Mawei Station the troops refused to advance, and the only way to pacify them was to sacrifice Lady Yang. (*He sheds tears.*) Ah, what is the good of being an emperor, if one has to be so cruel? We have pressed forward with difficulty to Fufeng, and are now staying in Fengyi Palace. We shall rest here for a short time.

(*An old peasant comes in carrying a bowl of oatmeal.*)

PEASANT:

A peasant can see the emperor.
A rustic fellow can offer herbs as gifts.

I an a peasant of Fufeng District, and my name is Guo Congjin. Hearing that the emperor has come west and is staying at Fengyi Palace, I have cooked some oatmeal for him as a token of my respect. (*He sees* Gao Lishi.) Please, sir, will you let His Majesty know that the peasant Guo Congjin is here to present oatmeal.

(Gao Lishi *announces him.*)

EMPEROR: Let him come in.

PEASANT (*Greeting the emperor*): Your humble subject Guo Congjin salutes Your Majesty.

EMPEROR: Where are you from?

PEASANT:

I am a native here, Your Majesty.

261

【过曲黄钟】【降黄龙】生长扶风，白首躬耕，共庆时康。听蓦然变起，凤辇游巡，无限惊惶。聊将、一盂麦饭，匍匐向旗门陈上。愿吾君不嫌粗粝，野人供养。

（生）生受你了，高力士取上来。（丑接饭送生介）（生看介）寡人晏处深宫，从不曾尝着此味。

【前腔】【换头】寻常、进御大官，馔玉炊金，食前方丈，珍羞百味，犹兀自嫌他调和无当。（泪介）不想今日，却将此物充饥。凄凉、带麸连麦，这饭儿如何入嗓？（略吃便放介）抵多少滹沱河畔、失路萧王！

（外）陛下，今日之祸，可知为谁而起？（生）你道为着谁来？（外）陛下若赦臣无罪，臣当冒死直言。（生）但说不妨。（外）只为那杨国忠呵，

【前腔】【换头】猖狂，倚恃国亲，纳贿招权，毒流天壤。他与安禄山十年构衅，一旦里兵戈起自渔阳。（生）国忠构衅，禄山谋反，寡人那里知道。（外）那禄山呵，包藏祸心

I tilled the land till my hair turned white,
Happy to live in a time of peace;
Now suddenly we hear of this rebellion
And see Your Majesty is flying west.
I am much afraid; so I come today to present
A bowl of oatmeal, hoping you will not find
Our simple country fare too rough or coarse.

EMPEROR: Thank you. Bring it to me, Gao Lishi.

(Gao *takes the bowl and offers it to the emperor.*)

EMPEROR: (*Looking at it*): Living in luxury in the palace, I have
never tasted anything like this;

When my attendants offered food to me,
Though every dish was some rare delicacy,
I often thought it ill prepared. (*He sheds tears.*)

Who could have thought that today I should satisfy my hunger with
this?

Oats and husks—
How can I swallow this?

(*After eating a little, he puts down the bowl.*)

I am like that prince of old who was defeated
And fled from the enemy by Hutuo River.

PEASANT: Your Majesty, whom do you consider responsible for the
trouble we are in today?

EMPEROR: Who would you say?

PEASANT: I hope you will forgive me if I speak out frankly.

EMPEROR: Don't hesitate. Go on.

PEASANT: It was all Yang Guozhong's fault.

Relying on his relationship with Your Majesty,
He accepted bribes and strengthened his evil power,
Till he corrupted the whole empire;
And he waged a ten years' feud with An Lushan;
This is the reason for the revolt at Yuyang.

EMPEROR: How could I know of Yang Guozhong's quarrel with An
Lushan and the danger of revolt?

PEASANT: An Lushan has been

日久,四海都知逆状。去年有人上书,告禄山逆迹,陛下反赐诛戮。谁肯再甘心铁钺,来奏君王!

(生作恨介)此乃朕之不明,以致于此。

【前腔】【换头】斟量,明目达聪,原是为君的理当察访。朕记得姚崇、宋璟为相的时节,把直言数进,万里民情,如在同堂。不料姚、宋亡后,满朝臣宰,一味贪位取容。郭从谨呵,倒不如伊行,草野怀忠,直指出逆藩奸相。(外)若不是陛下巡幸到此,小臣那里得见天颜。(生泪介)空教我噬脐无及,恨塞饥肠。

(外)陛下暂息龙体,小臣告退。(叹介)"从饶白发千茎雪,难把丹心一寸灰。"

(下)(副净扮使臣、二杂抬彩上)

【太平令】鸟道羊肠,春彩驮来驿路长。连山铃铎频摇响,看日近帝都旁。

自家成都道使臣,奉节度使之命,解送春彩十万疋到京。闻得驾幸扶风,不免就

Planning to revolt for a long time,
And everyone knew of his treason.

But last year, when some one informed against him, Your Majesty had the informer put to death.

And after that who would risk his life to warn you?

EMPEROR (*Regretfully*): Yes, I have been much to blame.

A ruler should be all-seeing, all-knowing.
And should understand conditions in his country.

I remember when Yao Chong and Song Jing were my ministers of state,

They advised me so well that I felt I could see my subjects
All over the country as if they were before me.

But after they died, new ministers simply tried to seize power or curry favour with me.

They were not like you, a loyal citizen,
Who points out traitors frankly and fearlessly.

PEASANT: But if Your Majesty had not come here what chance would I have had of an audience with you?

EMPEROR (*Shedding tears*):

Now vain remorse
Gnaws at my hungry heart.

PEASANT: I will leave you now, Your Majesty, to rest.

(*He sighs.*)

Though my old hairs are turning white as snow,
The embers of my loyal heart still glow. (*Exit.*)

(*Enter an envoy from Chengdu with two attendants carrying rolls of silk.*)

ENVOY:

Along tortuous mountain tracks
I have brought the tribute silk:
The way is long, and the bells on our baggage train
Echo among the hills as we near Chang'an.

I am the envoy from Chengdu, ordered by the military governor to bring one hundred thousand rolls of silk to the capital. I hear that the emperor has come to Fufeng, so I shall present my tribute

此进上。(向丑介)烦乞启奏一声,说成都使臣,贡春彩到此。(丑进奏介)(生)春彩照数收明,打发使臣回去。(二杂抬彩进介)(副净同二杂下)(生)高力士,可召集将士,朕有面谕。(丑)万岁爷宣召龙武军将士听旨。(众扮将士上)"晓起听金鼓,宵眠抱玉鞍。"龙武军将士叩见万岁爷。(生)将士每,听朕道来,

【前腔】变出非常,远避兵戈涉异方。劳伊仓卒随行仗,今日呵,别有个好商量。

(众)不知万岁爷有何论旨?(生)

【黄龙衮】征人忆故乡,征人忆故乡,蜀道如天上。不忍累伊每,把妻儿父母轻撇漾。朕待独与子孙中官,慢慢的捱到蜀中。尔等今日,便可各自还家。省得跋涉程途,饥寒劳攘。高力士,可将使臣进来春彩,分给将士,以为盘费。没军资,分彩币,聊充饷。

(丑应分彩介)(众哭介)万岁爷圣谕及

266

here. (*To* Gao Lishi.) Please inform His Majesty that the envoy from Chengdu bringing the spring tribute of silk is here.

(Gao Lishi *informs the emperor.*)

EMPEROR: Accept the rolls of silk, then send the envoy back. (*The attendavts bring in the silk, and retire again with the envoy.*) Gao Lishi, order the guards to gather; I have something to say to them.

GAO: His Majesty summons the imperial guards to receive his orders!

(*The guards enter.*)

GUARDS:

> *Rising at dawn to the sound of drums,*
> *Sleeping at night by the saddle,*
> *We are the imperial guards*
> *Who await Your Majesty's pleasure.*

EMPEROR: Soldiers, listen to me,

> *In this catastrophe and flight*
> *We have travelled far, and I thank you for your escort;*
> *Today, however, I have a plan to propose.*

GUARDS: What are Your Majesty's orders?

EMPEROR:

> *Travellers long for home, and the road to Chengdu*
> *Is hard as the road to heaven;*
> *I do not want to tear you all away*
> *From your parents, wives and children.*

I propose to go on slowly with the eunuchs and young Princes to Chengdu; but the rest of you may return to your homes.

> *You need not travel further, cold and hungry,*
> *Through every kind of hardship.*

Gao Lishi, distribute the silk brought by the envoy to the guards as their travelling expenses.

> *Since the army has no money,*
> *We shall pay them in silk instead.*

(Gao Lishi *begins to distribute the silk.*)

GUARDS (*Shedding tears*): Hearing Your Majesty's words we are

267

此,臣等寸心如割。自古养军千日,用在一朝。臣等呵,

【前腔】无能灭虎狼,无能灭虎狼,空愧熊罴将。生死愿从行,军声齐恃天威壮。这春彩,臣等断不敢受。请留待他时论功行赏,若有违心,皇天鉴,决不爽。

(生)尔等忠义虽深,朕心实有不忍,还是回去罢。(众)呀,万岁爷,莫不因贵妃娘娘之死,有些疑惑么?(生)非也,

【尾声】他长安父老多悬望,你每回去呵,烦说与翠华无恙。(众)万岁爷休出此言,臣等情愿随驾,誓无二心。(合)只待净扫妖氛,一同返帝乡。

(生)天色已晚,今夜就此权驻,明日早行便了。(众)领旨。

万里飞沙咽鼓鼙, 钱起

(丑)沉沉落日向山低。骆宾王

(生)如今悔恨将何益, 韦庄

(丑)更忍车轮独向西? 周昙

broken-hearted. Soldiers are trained for use in time of crisis,
But we proved useless, and could not destroy the foe;
In our shame, we want to follow you till death,
For the emperor's presence will increase our courage.
As for the silk, we do not dare accept it;
Please keep it for rewards in the day of victory.
Heaven be our witness that we speak from our hearts!

EMPEROR: Loyal as you are, I cannot bear to keep you. You must return home.

GUARDS: Can it be that Your Majesty is offended with us because of Lady Yang's death?

EMPEROR: No, that is not the reason.
But the citizens of Chang'an are concerned for us;
Go back to tell them that I am safe and well.

GUARDS: Your Majesty, don't order us to leave you. We shall follow you without wavering.
And later, when the rebels are swept away,
We shall return to the capital together.

EMPEROR: It is growing late; we will spend the night here, and start early tomorrow.

GUARDS: The emperor's orders shall be obeyed!

(*Exeunt.*)

第二十六出　冥追

【商调过曲】【山坡五更】【山坡羊】(魂旦白练系颈上,服色照前"埋玉"折)恶歆歆一场喽罗,乱匆匆一生结果。荡悠悠一缕断魂,痛察察一条白练香喉锁。【五更转】风光尽,信誓捐,形骸浼。只有痴情一点、一点无摧挫,拚向黄泉,牢牢担荷。

　　我杨玉环随驾西行,刚到马嵬驿内,不料六军变乱,立逼投缳。(泣介)唉,不知圣驾此时到那里了!我一灵渺渺,飞出驿中,不免望着尘头,追随前去。(行介)

【北双调新水令】望銮舆,才离了马嵬坡,咫尺间不能飞过。俺悄魂轻似叶,他征骑疾如梭。刚打个磨陀,翠旗尖又早被树烟锁。(虚下)

【南仙吕入双调】【步步娇】(生引丑、二内侍、四军拥行上)没揣倾城遭凶祸,去住浑无那,行行唤奈何。马上回头,两泪交堕。(丑)启万岁爷,前面就是驻跸之处了。(生叹

SCENE 26
The Spirit Follows

(*Enter* Lady Yang's *spirit. The white belt is fastened round her throat, and she is dressed as at the time of her death.*)

LADY:

Amid confusion and uproar my life was ended,
And here I drift, a wandering spirit,
With my white belt fastened around my throat,
All pleasure is gone, our pledge is at an end,
And my body is no more;
But my love remains unchanged,
And still, in the nether world, I hold to it fast.

I was travelling westwards with the emperor; but when we reached Mawei Station the troops mutinied and forced me to hang myself. (*She sheds tears.*) I do not know where His Majesty is now; but my spirit has flown out from the posting station, and I must follow the emperor's train.

The imperial carriage has just left Mawei Slope,
Yet, near as it is, I cannot overtake it,
For my spirit is light as a leaf, and their steeds are fast;
As I turn the corner the banners are hidden again by trees.

(*Exit.*)

(*Enter the emperor with* Gao Lishi, *two other attendants and four guards.*)

EMPEROR:

Who could have foretold my lady's pitiful end!
What do I care whether we halt or go no!
Lamenting all the way, looking back from my steed,
My tears fall like rain.

GAO: May it please Your Majesty, we have nearly arrrived at the station.

介)唉,我已厌一身多,伤心更说甚今宵卧。

(齐下)

【北折桂令】(旦行上)一停停古道逶迤,俺只索虚趁云行,弱倩风驮。(向内望科)呀,好了,望见大驾,就在前面了也。这不是羽盖飘扬,鸾旌荡漾,翠辇嵯峨!不免疾忙赶上者。(急行科)愿一灵早依御座,便牢牵衮袖黄罗。(内鸣锣作风起科)(旦作惊退科)呀,我望着銮舆,正待赶上,忽然黑风过处,遮断去路,影都不见了。好苦呵,暗濛濛烟障林阿,杳沉沉雾塞山河。闪摇摇不住徘徊,悄冥冥怎样腾挪?

(贴在内叫苦介)(旦)你看那边愁云苦雾之中,有个鬼魂来了,且闪过一边。(虚下)

(贴扮虢国夫人魂上)

【南江儿水】艳冶风前谢,繁华梦里过。风流谁识当初我?玉碎香残荒郊卧,云抛雨断重泉堕。(二鬼卒上)唗,那里去?(贴)奴家虢国夫人。(鬼卒笑介)原来就是你。你

EMPEROR (*Sighing*):

> *I am weary of this meaningless existence;*
> *Do you think I care where we put up tonight?*

(*Exeunt.*)

(Lady Yang's *spirit enters.*)

LADY:

> *The old road winds slowly along,*
> *But I float like a cloud*
> *Borne by the wind.*

(*She looks ahead.*) Good, I see the imperial train just ahead.

> *There are the familiar canopies, phoenix pennants*
> *And towering emerald carriages.*

I will hurry forward. (*She quickens her pace.*)

> *May my spirit soon come to where the emperor sits,*
> *To cling again to his silken sleeve!*

(*A gust of wind rises, and she shrinks back in fear*)

Ah! just as I was nearing the imperial carriage, a dusty wind sprang up and hid the way from my sight. Alas!

> *The woods are dark and dense,*
> *Overhung by a heavy mist;*
> *I wander about and lose my way,*
> *Not knowing what direction to take un this gloom.*

(*A woman is heard crying.*) I see another spirit coming through the mist. I will step aside. (*Exit.*)

(*Enter the ghost of the* Duchess of Guo.)

GUO:

> *My flower-like beauty has withered in the wind,*
> *The pomp and splendour have vanished like a dream;*
> *And who could recognize the once fair duchess*
> *Ruined and forsaken in the wilderness?*
> *My romance is at an end.*
> *And I am doomed to stay in the nether world.*

(*Two devils enter.*)

DEVILS: Where are you going?

GUO: I am the Duchess of Guo.

273

生前也忒受用了，如今且随我到枉死城中去。（贴哭介）哎哟，好苦呵，怨恨如山堆垛。只问你多大幽城，怕着不下这愁魂一个！

（杂拉贴叫苦下）（旦急上看科）呀，方才这个是我裴家姐姐，也被乱兵所害了。兀的不痛杀人也！

【北雁儿落带得胜令】想当日天边夺笑歌，今日里地下同零落。痛杀俺冤由一命招，更不想惨累全家祸。呀，空落得提起着泪滂沱，何处把恨消磨！怪不得四下愁云裹，都是俺千声怨气呵。（望科）那边又是一个鬼魂，满身鲜血，飞奔前来。好怕人也！悲么，泣孤魂独自无回和。惊么，只落得伴冥途野鬼多。（虚下）

【南侥侥令】（副净扮杨国忠鬼魂跑上）生前遭劫杀，死后见阎罗。（牛头执钢叉，夜叉执铁锤、索上拦介）（副净跑下）（牛头、夜叉复赶上）杨国忠那里走？（副净）呀，我是当朝宰相，方才被乱兵所害。你每做甚又来拦我？（牛头）奸贼，俺奉阎王之命，特来拿你，还不快走。（副净）那里去？（牛头、夜叉）向小小酆都城一座，教你去剑树与刀山寻快活。

DEVILS (*Laughing*): So it is you! You had too good a time in life; come with us now to the City of Avenging Spirits.

GUO (*Weeping*): Alas!

> *My sorrows are greater than a mountain;*
> *Will the city be able to hold them?*

(*As the devils drag her off,* Lady Yang *hurries in to watch them.*)

LADY: That was my sister; she too has been killed by the troops. Poor thing!

> *Once we vied for imperial favour with songs and smiles;*
> *But now we share the same fate in the nether regions—*
> *My entire family ruined because of me!*
> *The thought of it makes me weep;*
> *Can I ever forget my sorrow?*
> *No wonder this mist is filled with my sobs and sighs.*

(*She looks round.*) I see another ghost, dripping with blood, running this way. What a terrifying sight!

> *I cry, but no one joins me in my mourning;*
> *Trembling to meet so many wandering spirits.* (*Exit.*)

(Yang Guozhong's *ghost runs in.*)

YANG:

> *I died by the sword,*
> *And now I must appear*
> *Before the King of Hell.*

(*Enter the ox-headed devil with a steel trident and another monster from hell with an iron mace and chains. They block the prime minister's way, and catch him when he tries to run.*)

DEVILS: Where are you going, Yang Guozhong?

YANG: I am the prime minister. Just now I was killed in a mutiny of troops; why are you two blocking my way?

DEVILS: You traitor! We have come to arrest you by order of the King of Hell. Come with us.

YANG: Where to?

DEVILS:

> *To hell, to appreciate our tortures,*

（牛头拉副净，执叉叉背，夜叉锁副净下）

（旦急上看科）呵呀，那不是我的哥哥。好可怜人也！（作悲科）

【北收江南】呀，早则是五更短梦，瞥眼醒南柯。把荣华抛却，只留得罪殃多。唉，想我哥哥如此，奴家岂能无罪？怕形消骨化，忏不了旧情魔。且住，一望茫茫，前行无路，不如仍旧到马嵬驿中去罢。（转行科）待重转驿坡，心又早怯懦。听了这归林暮雀，犹错认乱军呵。

（虚下）（副净扮土地上）"地下常添枉死鬼，人间难觅返魂香。"小神马嵬坡土地是也。奉东岳帝君之命，道贵妃杨玉环原系蓬莱仙子，今死在吾神界内，特命将他肉身保护，魂魄安顿，以候玉旨，不免寻他去来。（行介）

【南园林好】只他在翠红乡欢娱事过，粉香丛冤孽债多，一霎做电光石火。将肉质护泉窝，教魂魄守坟窠。（虚下）

The forest of swords and the hill of knives.
(*The ox-headed devil beats* Yang *across the back with his trident, while the monster puts chains on him. As they drag him off,* Lady Yang *hurries in to watch them.*)
LADY: Ah, that was my cousin! Poor man! (*She weeps.*)
Life is nothing but a fleeting dream,
From which all too soon we wake
To find that our splendour is gone,
And only our sins are left.
If this is the case with my cousin, I must be guilty too.
But even if my bones are ground to dust,
I fear I can never atone for the sin of my love.
I can find no road to lead me on, so I may as well return to Mawei Station. (*She walks back.*)
I retrace my steps to Mawei Slope;
But my heart is full of fear,
And the twittering birds that fly to their nests at dusk
Remind me of the clamouring troops. (*Exit.*)
(*Enter a tutelary god.*)
TUTELARY GOD:
Many are the ghosts of the wrongly slain!
But no incense can restore the dead to life.
I am the tutelary god of Mawei. The God of the Eastern Mountain has ordered me to watch over the body and spirit of Yang Yuhunan, who was a fairy in the fairy mountain in a former life and has now died in my territory. After that I must wait for further orders from Heaven.
So now I shall look for her. (*He walks on.*)
Leading a life of luxury and pleasure,
Scented and powdered, her sins were surely many;
But now she is no more—
Gone out like a spark from a flint
Or a flash o lightning,
Her body under the earth,
While her watchful spirit hovers above her grave.

【北沽美酒带太平令】(旦行上)度寒烟蔓草坡,行一步一延俄。(看介)呀,这树上写的有字,待我看来(作念科)贵妃杨娘娘葬此。(作悲科)原来把我就埋在此处了。唉,玉环,玉环!(泣科)只这冷土荒堆树半棵,便是娉婷袅娜,落来的好巢窝。我临死之时,曾分付高力士,将金钗、钿盒与我殉葬,不知曾埋下否?怕旧物向尘埃抛堕,则俺这真情肯为生死差讹?就是果然埋下呵,还只怕这残尸败蜕,抱不牢同心并朵。不免叫唤一声,(叫科)杨玉环,你的魂灵在此。我呵,悄临风叫他、唤他。(泣科)可知道伊原是我,呀,直恁地推眠妆卧!

(副净上唤科)兀那啼哭的,可是贵妃杨玉环鬼魂么?(旦)奴家正是。是何尊神?乞恕冒犯。(副净)吾神乃马嵬坡土地。(旦)望尊神与奴做主咱。(副净)贵妃听吾道来:"你本是蓬莱仙子,因微过谪落凡尘。今虽是浮生限满,旧仙山隔断红云。"(代旦解白练科)吾神奉岳帝敕旨,解冤结免汝沉沦。(旦福科)多谢尊神,只不知奴与皇上,还有相见之日么?(副净)此事非吾

(*Exit.*)

(*Enter* Lady Yang.)

LADY:

> *Passing the misty reeds,*
> *I linger at every step.*

(*She looks round.*) Ah, there is some writing on that tree; let me have a look at it. (*She reads.*) Lady Yang lies here. (*She weeps.*) So I was buried here! (*She weeps again.*)

> *This lonely mound of clay and this withered tree*
> *Are the final resting place of such a beauty!*

When I was about to die, I told Gao Lishi to bury the hairpin and the jewel box with my body. I wonder if he did as I asked.

> *But even if he threw them away,*
> *My love will remain unchanged in death;*
> *And if they were buried beneath the ground,*
> *When my body decays it cannot hold them together.*

Let me call my body. (*She calls.*) Yang Yuhuan! Your spirit is here now, calling in the wind. (*She weeps.*)

> *She and I were one; why should she pretend to sleep*
> *And refuse to answer me?*

(*Enter the tutelary god.*)

TUTELARY GOD: Is that the ghost of Lady Yang crying there?

LADY: Yes. What god are you? Please pardon me for being here.

TUTELARY GOD: I am the tutelary god of Mawei.

.LADY: I beg you to help me!

TUTELARY GOD: Listen! Formerly a fairy in the fairy mountain, you were sent to earth to expiate some fault; and now, though you have ended your span of life on earth, your former abode is hidden by dusty clouds. (*He unfastens the white belt around her neck.*) By the order of the God of the Eastern Mountain, I am delivering you from your sins to save you from hell.

LADY (*Curtseys*): I thank you. May I ask whether I shall ever meet the emperor again?

TUTELARY GOD: That I cannot tell you.

(Lady Yang *weeps.*)

神所晓。(旦作悲科)(副净)贵妃,且在马嵬
驿暂住幽魂,吾神去也。(下)(旦)苦呵,不
免到驿中佛堂里,暂且栖托则个。(行科)
【南尾声】重来绝命庭中过,看树底泪痕犹
渍。怎能够飞去蓬山寻旧果!

土埋冤骨草离离, 储嗣宗

回首人间总祸机。 薛能

云雨马嵬分散后, 韦绚

何年何路得同归。 韦庄

TUTELARY GOD: You may stay for the time being at the station; I shall be leaving you now. (*Exit.*)

LADY (*Sighing*): I had better stay in the sacrificial hall.
(*She walks on.*)

> As I pass the courtyard where I hanged myself,
> I can see the tear stains under the pear tree.
> When shall I soar back to my fairy mountain?

(***Exit.***)

第二十七出　骂贼

（外扮雷海青抱琵琶上）"武将文官总旧僚，恨他反面事新朝。纲常留在梨园内，那惜伶工命一条。"自家雷海青是也。蒙天宝皇帝隆恩，在梨园部内做一个供奉。不料禄山作乱，破了长安，皇帝驾幸西川去了。那满朝文武，平日里高官厚禄，荫子封妻，享荣华，受富贵，那一件不是朝廷恩典！如今却一个个贪生怕死，背义忘恩，争去投降不迭。只图安乐一时，那顾骂名千古。唉，岂不可羞，岂不可恨！我雷海青虽是一个乐工，那些没廉耻的勾当，委实做不出来。今日禄山与这一班逆党，大宴凝碧池头，传集梨园奏乐。俺不免乘此，到那厮跟前，痛骂一场，出了这口愤气。便粉骨碎身，也说不得了。且抱着琵琶，去走一遭也呵！

【仙吕村里迓鼓】虽则俺乐工卑滥，硁硁愚暗，也不曾读书献策，登科及第，向鹓班高站。只这血性中，胸脯内，倒有些忠肝义胆。今日个睹了丧亡，遭了危难，值了变

SCENE 27

The Patriot and the Rebel

(*Enter the lute-player* Lei Haiqing, *carrying his lute.*)
LEI:

> *Still the same old generals and ministers,*
> *But they become turncoats and serve the new regime;*
> *We musicians, at least, have stuck to our principles,*
> *And are not afraid to sacrifice our lives.*

I am Lei Haiqing, by the grace of the emperor appointed a musician in the imperial Pear Garden Academy. Who could have thought that An Lushan would rebel and take the capital, forcing the emperor to go to Chengdu! The court officials had high positions and huge salaries, and their sons and wives were given titles. They owed all their dignity and wealth to the government; but now, forgetting gratitude in their fear of death, they have all surrendered to the rebels, thinking only of their present comfort and not caring for the verdict of history. This is shameful and disgusting! Though I am only a musician, I could not do the shameless things that they do. Today An Lushan is feasting with those traitors at the Frozen Azure Pool, and they have ordered music. I shall take this opportunity to give him a good cursing to vent my indignation. Even if I am torn limb from limb, it will be worth it. I am going there now with my lute.

> *I am only a humble, unlettered musician*
> *I have never studied or sent memorials to the throne,*
> *Never passed the civil service examination*
> *Or won high official rank;*
> *But I have blood in my veins,*
> *Loyalty in my heart, and a sense of justice;*
> *And in face of this calamity and crisis,*
> *I cannot help gnashing my teeth in anger and sorrow.*

惨,不由人痛切齿,声吞恨衔。

【元和令】恨子恨泼腥膻莽将龙座淹,癞蛤
蟆妄想天鹅啖,生克擦直逼的个官家下殿
走天南。你道恁胡行堪不堪?纵将他寝皮
食肉也恨难劖。谁想那一班儿没掂三,歹
心肠,贼狗男,

【上马娇】平日价张着口将忠孝谈,到临危
翻着脸把富贵贪。早一齐儿摇尾受新衔,
把一个君亲仇敌当作恩人感。咱,只问你
蒙面可羞惭?

【胜葫芦】眼见的去做忠臣没个敢。雷海青
呵,若不把一肩担,可不枉了戴发含牙人是
俺。但得纲常无缺,须眉无愧,便九死也心
甘。(下)

【中吕引子】【绕红楼】(净引二军士上)抢占
山河号大燕,袍染赭,冠戴冲天。凝碧清
秋,梨园小部,歌舞列琼筵。

孤家安禄山。自从范阳起兵,所向无
敌。长驱西入,直抵长安。唐家皇帝,逃入
蜀中去了,锦绣江山归吾掌握。(笑介)好
不快活。今日聚集百官,在凝碧池上做个
太平筵宴,洒乐一回。内侍每,众官可曾齐
到?(杂)都在外殿伺候。(净)宣过来。
(军)领旨。(宣介)主上宣百官进见。(四伪

284

I hate the barbarian who has polluted the throne,
Like the toad in the proverb who tried to eat the swan,
And who has forced our emperor to fly.
His treason is so disgusting
That even if I eat his flesh and sleep on his hide,
I shall never forget my hatred!
Yet those rotten courtiers, those good-for-nothing curs,
Who talked so much of loyalty and piety,
As soon as disaster came just turned their coats
To grab at wealth and position.
They fawn and cringe when they accept new titles,
Taking their deadly foe as their benefactor.
Have they no sense of shame?
Not one has the courage to be a patriot!
Ah! Lei Haiqing,
Unless you shoulder this task, you are no true man!
If I can stick to principles, and acquit myself like a man,
I am willing to die several deaths. (*Exit.*)

(*Enter* An Lushan *with two guards.*)

AN:

I have seized the empire and renamed it Yan!
In purple robes and an imperial headdress
By the Frozen Azure Pool this fine autumn day,
I will have the imperial musicians to play at my feast.

Since I, An Lushan, started the rebellion at Fanyang, I encountered virtually no resistance; so I advanced west until I reached the capital. The Tang emperor has fled to Chengdu, and this magnificent empire is in my hands. (*He laughs.*) Wonderful! Today I have summoned all the officials to feast and make merry by the pool. Attedants! Have all the ministers arrived?

GUARDS: They are waiting outside.

AN: Tell them to come in.

GUARDS: Yes, Your Majesty. (*Calling out.*) The emperor orders his ministers to enter.

(*Enter four puppet officials.*)

285

官上)"今日新天子,当时旧宰臣。同为识时者,不是负恩人。"(见介)臣等朝见。愿主上万岁,万万岁!(净)众卿平身。孤家今日政务稍闲,特设宴在凝碧池上,与卿等共乐太平。(四伪官)万岁。(军)筵宴完备,请主上升宴。(内奏乐,四伪官跪送酒介)(净)

【中吕过曲】【尾犯序】龙戏碧池边,正五色云开,秋气澄鲜。紫殿逍遥,暂停吾玉鞭。开宴,走绯衣鸾刀细割,揎锦袖,犀盘满献。(四伪官献酒再拜介)瑶池下,熊罴鹓鹭,拜送酒如泉。

(净)内侍每,传旨唤梨园子弟奏乐。(军)领旨。(向内介)主上有旨,着梨园子弟奏乐。(内应奏乐介)(军送净酒介)(合)

【前腔】【换头】当筵,众乐奏钧天。旧日霓裳,重按歌遍。半入云中,半吹落风前。稀

OFFICIALS:

>*We are old colleagues,*
>*And now we have a new master;*
>*You cannot call us disloyal;*
>*But we know how to change with the times.*

(*They kowtow to An.*) Long live the emperor!

AN: You may rise. Today I have a little leisure, so I have invited you to feast at the Frozen Azure Pool to celebrate the pacification of the empire.

OFFICIALS: Long live the emperor!

GUARDS: May it please Your Majesty, the feast is ready. (*Music sounds offstage, and the four puppet officials kneel to offer wine to An Lushan.*)

AN:

>*Now the dragon is at play beside the azure pool,*
>*Through bright-hued clouds gleams the limpid autumn sky;*
>*I take my pleasure here in the purple palace;*
>*My jade-adorned whip cast aside, the feast begins:*
>*Red-coated attendants are busy carving meat,*
>*And roll up their silken sleeves to present it on plates.*

(*The puppet officials offer wine and knwtow.*)

>*Like bears and pelicans,*
>*They bow as they offer me wine.*

Attendants, order the musicians of the Pear Garden Academy to play.

GUARDS: Yes, Your Majesty. (*They pass the order on.*)

The emperor orders the musicians of the Pear Garden Acaddemy to start playing.

(*A response is heard offstage, music sounds and more wine is poured.*)

ALL:

>*Here at the feast the heavenly music is played,*
>*The strains of the Rainbow Dance*
>*Soar high above to mingle with the clouds,*
>*Borne off at last by the breeze.*

见，除却了清虚洞府，只有那沉香亭院。今日个仙音法曲，不数大唐年。

（净）奏得好。（四伪官）臣想天宝皇帝，不知费了多少心力，教成此曲，今日却留与主上受用，真乃齐天之福也。（净笑介）众卿言之有理，再上酒来。（军送酒介）（外在内泣唱介）

【前腔】【换头】幽州鼙鼓喧，万户蓬蒿，四野烽烟。叶堕空宫，忽惊闻歌弦奇变，真个是天翻地覆，真个是人愁鬼怨。（大哭介）我那天宝皇帝呵，金銮上百官拜舞，何日再朝天？

（净）呀，什么人啼哭？好奇怪！（军）是乐工雷海青。（净）拿上来。（军拉外上见介）（净）雷海青，孤家在此饮太平筵宴，你敢擅自啼哭，好生可恶！（外骂介）唉，安禄山，你本是失机边将，罪应斩首。幸蒙圣恩不杀，拜将封王。你不思报效朝廷，反敢称兵作乱，秽污神京，逼迁圣驾。这罪恶贯盈，指日天兵到来诛戮，还说什么太平筵

They is rare music, only played before
In the palace of the moon
Or at Aloes Pavilion;
But here today
We hear this heavenly music once again,
Though the calendar of Tang has been annulled.

AN: Bravo! Well played!

OFFICIALS: The Tang emperor went to great pains to have this dance rehearsed; but now it is Your Majesty who enjoys it. Your Majesty is indeed favoured by Heaven!

AN (*Laughs*): True. More wine!

(*More wine is poured. Lei Haiqing heard weeping and singing offstage.*)

Lei (*Offstage*):
While the drums of war are rolling
And thousand of homesteads lie waste,
While beacon fires are gleaming
And leaves fall in the empty palace,
One is startled to hear this beautiful melody played!
For ruin has seized the empire,
And both men and ghosts lament.

(*He cries aloud.*) Ah, my emperor!
When will you sit on your golden throne again?

AN: Who is that crying out there? This is very strange.

GUARDS: It is the musician Lei Haiqing.

AN: Bring him in. (*The guards bring Lei in.*) Lei Haiqing, we are drinking here to celebrate victory. How dare you moan like that out there?

LEI: An Lushan, you were an officer who was defeated in battle, and you should have been sentenced to death; yet the emperor was merciful and spared your life. He even made you a prince! But instead of trying to serve the government well, you rebelled with your army. You have befouled the capital and forced the emperor to fly. You are an arch criminal, who will soon be put to the sword when the imperial army comes back. Who are you to talk of

289

宴！（净大怒介）咦，有这等事。孤家入登大位，臣下无不顺从，量你这一个乐工，怎敢如此无礼！军士看刀伺候。（二军作应，拔刀介）（外一面指净骂介）

【扑灯蛾】怪伊忒负恩，兽心假人面，怒发上冲冠。我虽是伶工微贱也，不似他朝臣觍觍。安禄山，你窃神器，上逆皇天，少不得顷刻间尸横血溅。（将琵琶掷净介）我掷琵琶，将贼臣碎首报开元。

（军夺琵琶介）（净）快把这厮拿去砍了。（军应拿外砍下）（净）好恼，好恼！（四伪官）主上息怒。无知乐工，何足介意。（净）孤家心上不快，众卿且退。（四伪官）领旨。臣等恭送主上回宫。（跪送介）（净）酒逢知己千盅少，话不投机半句多。（怒下）（四伪官起介）杀得好，杀得好。一个乐工，思量做起忠臣来，难道我每吃太平宴的，倒差了不成！

feasts and victory?

AN (*Furious*): What insolence! Since I ascended the throne, no one has disobeyed me. How dare you, a common musician, defy me? Men, draw your swords!

(*The guards draw their swords.*)

LEI (*Cursing and pointing at* An):

> *My blood boils at the sight of this heartless monster,*
> *This beast with a human face!*
> *Though I am only a common musician,*
> *I am not so shameless as these turncoat officials.*
> *An Lushan! For defying the will of Heaven.*
> *You soon will fall, a corpse bespattered with blood!*

(*He throws his lute at* An.)

> *Here comes my lute!*
> *May it break your head,*
> *And avenge my former master!*

(*The guards seize the lute.*)

AN: Take him quickly and kill him! (*The guards drag* Lei *off.*) May he be accursed!

OFFICIALS: Do not be angry, Your Majesty. Why pay any attention to a foolish musician?

AN: My pleasure is spoiled. You may leave me.

OFFICIALS: Your Majesty's orders shall be obeyed. Let us see the emperor back to the palace. (*They kneel.*)

AN:

> *A thousand cups with good friends are not enough;*
> *But when insults are hurled, one sentence is too much!*

(*An leaves in towering rage.*)

OFFICIALS (*Rising*) It served that musician right—he deserved to be killed. Fancy a musician posing as a patriot! He positively tried to put us in the wrong!

> *We are all of us simply acting a part;*

【尾声】大家都是花花面，一个忠臣值甚钱。
（笑介）雷海青，雷海青，毕竟你未戴乌纱识
见浅！

三秦流血已成川，　罗隐
为虏为王事偶然。　李山甫
世上何人怜苦节，　陆希声
直须行乐不言旋。　薛稷

For how much, after all, is a loyalty minister worth?
And where did your loyalty land you, Lei Haiqing?
You were foolish because you had never been an official!

(***Exeunt***.)

第二十八出　闻铃

（丑内叫介）军士每趱行，前面伺侯。
（内鸣锣，应介）万岁爷，请上马。（生骑马，丑随行上）

【双调近词】【武陵花】万里巡行，多少悲凉途路情。看云山重叠处，似我乱愁交并。无边落木响秋声，长空孤雁添悲哽。寡人自离马嵬，饱尝辛苦。前日遣使臣赍奉玺册，传位太子去了。行了一月，将近蜀中。且喜贼兵渐远，可以缓程而进。只是对此鸟啼花落，水绿山青，无非助朕悲怀。如何是好！（丑）万岁爷，途路风霜，十分劳顿。请自排遣，勿致过伤。（生）唉，高力士，朕与妃子，坐则并几，行则随肩。今日仓卒西巡，断送他这般结果，教寡人如何撇得下也！（泪介）提起伤心事，泪如倾。回望马嵬坡下，不觉恨填膺。（丑）前面就是栈道

294

SCENE 28
Hearing the Bells

(*Offstage*, Gao Lishi *shouts to the soldiers.*)

GAO: Forward, men! Wait for the emperor ahead.

(*Gongs sound offstage.*)

GAO (*Off*): Will you mount your horse, sire?

(*Enter the emperor on horseback, followed by* Gao Lishi.)

EMPEROR:

> *Sorrow has dogged my steps throughout my travels;*
> *The far-off clouds that merge with the distant mountains*
> *Are like the tangle of my grief and cares;*
> *In the autumn woods, that stretch to the horizon,*
> *The leaves are falling, falling;*
> *And in the sky a lone wild goose laments.*

Since I left Mawei I have suffered all manner of hardships. The other day I sent an envoy with the imperial seal to cede my throne to the crown prince. Now, after travelling for a month, we are nearing Chengdu. We are far from the rebels, and can travel more slowly; but the birds and flowers, the rivers and hills, only add to my sorrow.

GAO: Your Majesty, you are tired after the journey. You must not grieve, but keep up your spirits.

EMPEROR: Ah, Gao Lishi, in the past I always had Lady Yang at my side. I can never forgive myself for the death she met on this journey west. (*He sheds tears.*)

> *Thinking of her tragic end,*
> *My tears keep falling;*
> *And I look back towards Mawei*
> *With a broken heart.*

GAO: The path ahead is steep. Keep a firm grip on your reins, sire, and ride slowly.

295

了,请万岁爷挽定丝缰,缓缓前进。(生)袅
袅旗旌,背残日,风摇影。匹马崎岖怎暂
停,怎暂停!只见阴云黯淡天昏暝,哀猿断
肠,子规叫血,好教人怕听。兀的不惨杀人
也么哥,兀的不苦杀人也么哥!萧条凄生,
峨眉山下少人经,冷雨斜风扑面迎。

(丑)雨来了,请万岁爷暂登剑阁避雨。
(生作下马、登阁坐介)(丑作向内介)军士每,
且暂驻扎,雨住再行。(内应介)(生)"独自
登临意转伤,蜀山蜀水恨茫茫。不知何处
风吹雨,点点声声迸断肠。"(内作铃响介)
(生)你听那壁厢,不住的声响,聒的人好不
耐烦。高力士,看是什么东西?(丑)是树
林中雨声,和着檐前铃铎,随风而响。(生)
呀,这铃声好不做美也!

【前腔】淅淅零零,一片凄然心暗惊。遥听
隔山隔树,战合风雨,高响低鸣。一点一滴
又一声,一点一滴又一声,和愁人血泪交相
迸。对这伤情处,转自忆荒茔。白杨萧瑟

EMPEROR:

Our pennants, fluttering in the setting sun,
Cast long, weird shadows:
Our horses doggedly plod on and on,
Over the mountain path.
The sky is dark with rain clouds,
Monkeys wail fbitterly,
And the nightingale's song, so lonely and anguished,
Is sad to hear.
Few men have skirted this high mountain,
And a cold wind blows the rain into our faces.

GAO: It is raining, sire. Will you go into the pavilion to take shelter?

(*The emperor dismounts and walks up to the pavilion.*)

GAO: (*Calling to the guards offstage*): We are resting for a while, men. We shall go on when the rain stops.

(*The guards give an answering shout.*)

EMPEROR:

I walk here alone in grief,
My sorrow endless as the hills and streams:
The wind has driven storm clouds over;
Rain falling endlessly makes me sick at heart.

(*Bells are heard offstage.*)

Listen! What is that uncanny, tinkling sound? Find out what it is, Gao Lishi.

GAO: It is the rain in the forest and the bells hanging from the eaves, which sound in the wind.

EMPEROR: What a dismal note!

Tinkling and jangling of bells
And the dismal drip of rain
Make me sick at heart.
These melancholy sounds
Carry across the hills and woods,
Now high, now low, according to the wind,
To mingle with my tears of bitter anguish.

297

雨纵横，此际孤魂凄冷。鬼火光寒，草间湿
乱萤。只悔仓皇负了卿，负了卿！我独在
人间，委实的不愿生。语娉婷，相将早晚伴
幽冥。一恸空山寂，铃声相应，阁道崚嶒，
似我回肠恨怎平！

（丑）万岁爷且免愁烦。雨止了，请下
阁去罢。（生作下阁、上马介，丑向内介）军士
每，前面起驾。（众内应介）（丑随生行介）
（生）

【尾声】迢迢前路愁难罄，招魂去国两关情。
（合）望不尽雨后尖山万点青。

（生）剑阁连山千里色，　骆宾王

　　　离人到此倍堪伤。　罗　邺

　　　空劳翠辇冲泥雨，　秦韬玉

　　　一曲淋铃泪数行。　杜牧

In this sad atmosphere,
I think of the deserted grave
Where the poplars rustle in the rain
And her ghost is lonely now,
With only the will-o'-the-wisp for company,
And the glowworms in the wet grass.
I am filled with remorse because in panic
I did her a fearful wrong.
Alone in the world, I have no desire to live on,
But long to join her soon in the nether world.
I cry, but the hills are silent;
Only the bells chime in tune with my sorrow:
And the path is rugged and twisting,
Like my tortured feelings.

GAO: Do not grieve, sire. The rain has stopped. Will you go down now?

(*The emperor leaves the pavilion, and mounts his horse again.*)

GAO (*Addressing the men offstage*): Guards! To horse!

(*An answering shout is heard, and they set off again.*)

EMPEROR:
The road ahead is long, and my sorrow is endless,
As I grieve for the dead and long for my native place.

TOGETHER:
Ahead stretch endless mountains,
Green after the rain.

(***Exeunt.***)

299

第二十九出　情悔

【仙吕入双调】【普贤歌】(副净上)马嵬坡下太荒凉,土地公公也气不扬。祠庙倒了墙,没人烧炷香,福礼三牲谁祭享!

小神马嵬坡土地是也,向来香火颇盛。只因安禄山造反,本境人民尽皆逃散,弄得庙宇荒凉,香烟断绝。目今野鬼甚多,恐怕出来生事,且往四下里巡看一回。正是"只因神倒运,常恐鬼胡行"。(虚下)(魂旦上)

【双调引子】【捣练子】冤叠叠,恨层层,长眠泉下几时醒?魂断苍烟寒月里,随风窣窣度空庭。

"一曲霓裳逐晓风,天香国色总成空。可怜只有心难死,脉脉常留恨不穷。"奴家杨玉环鬼魂是也。自从马嵬被难,荷蒙岳帝传敕,得以栖魂驿舍,免堕冥司。(悲介)我想生前与皇上在西宫行乐,何等荣宠!今一旦红颜断送,白骨冤沉,冷驿荒垣,孤

SCENE 29
Lady Yang's Spirit Repents

(*Enter the tutelary god.*)
TUTELARY GOD:

>*Mawei is such a desolate place,*
>*Even I, the local god, am in low spirits.*
>*The wall of my temple has fallen down,*
>*And no one comes to burn incense,*
>*Much less to sacrifice meat offerings.*

I am the tutelary god of Mawei. Many pilgrims used to come here, but since An Lushan's rebellion everybody has run away; so the temple is deserted and no more incense is burned. Recently, too, there have been many wandering spirits about, who are liable to cause trouble. I had better make a tour of inspection.

>*Since the god is out of luck,*
>*I fear the ghosts may run wild.* (*Exit.*)

(*Enter* Lady Yang's *ghost.*)
LADY:

>*Grief and regret overwhelm me;*
>*When will the dead awaken?*
>*Sadly, in the grey mist and pale moonlight,*
>*I drift through the empty courtyard with the wind.*
>*The Rainbow Dance has gone with morning wind,*
>*The peerless beauty has vanished into nothing;*
>*But the heart does not die;*
>*Its endless sorrow remains.*

I am Lady Yang's ghost. Since I died at Mawei, the God of the Eastern Mountain had allowed me to stay here instead of going to hell. (*She weeps.*) In my life I enjoyed great favour and honour, taking pleasure with the emperor in the palace. But now my beauty is gone, my corpse is buried in the earth, and my lonely sapirit

301

魂淹滞。你看月淡星寒,又早黄昏时分,好不凄惨也!

【过曲】【三仙桥】古驿无人夜静,趁微云,移月暝,潜潜趱趱,暂时偷现影。魆地间心耿耿,猛想起我旧丰标,教我一想一泪零。想、想当日那态娉婷,想、想当日那妆艳靓,端得是赛丹青描成、画成。那晓得不留停,早则肌寒肉冷。(悲介)苦变做了鬼胡由,谁认得是杨玉环的行径!

(泪介)(袖出钗盒介)这金钗、钿盒,乃皇上定情之物,已从墓中取得。不免向月下把玩一回。(副净潜上,指介)这是杨贵妃鬼魂,且听他说些什么。(背立听介)(旦看钗盒介)

【前腔】看了这金钗儿双头比并,更钿盒同心相映。只指望两情坚如金似钿,又怎知翻做断绠。若知为断绠,枉自去将他留下了这伤心把柄。记得盒底夜香清,钗边晓镜明,有多少欢承爱领。(悲介)但提起那恩情,怎教我重泉目瞑!(哭介)苦只为钗和盒,那夕的绸缪,翻成做杨玉环这些时的

302

lingers on here in this cold and desolate station. The moon is gleaming faintly in the sky, and the stars are glittering coldly. What a mournful evening it is!

This old station is silent and deserted,
And for a time, while clouds obscure the moon,
I can steal out of hiding.
When I think of my former beauty my tears start falling;
For with my charms and splendid robes
I was lovelier than a painting.
Who could tell that so soon I would be dead and cold?
(*She weeps.*)
Who would recognize this ghost
As the former Lady Yang?

(*She takes out the hairpin and the box.*) These are the pledges of love given me by the emperor, which I have taken from the grave. Let me have another look at them under the moonlight.

(*The tutelary god enters.*)

TUTELARY GOD: That is Lady Yang's spirit. I wonder what she is saying. (*He listens.*)

LADY (*Looking at the hairpin and the box*):

I look at the double-headed golden pin
And the jewel box carved with a love-knot;
I thought that our love would remain as firm as these,
But it has been shattered just as a thread is snapped.
If I had known that our love would end like this,
I would never have entered into this pledge
Which has caused me so much sorrow.
I remember all the joy and love we had,
When the jewel box gave off its fragrance at night
And the hairpin glittered in the morning mirror.

(*Sadly.*)

When I think of our past love,
How can I bear to close my eyes in death?

(*She weeps.*)

For the sake of our pledge that night,

303

悲哽。

（副净背听，作点头介）（旦）咳，我杨玉环，生遭惨毒，死抱沉冤。或者能悔前愆，得有超拔之日，也未可知。且住，（悲介）只想我在生所为，那一桩不是罪案。况且弟兄姊妹，挟势弄权，罪恶滔天，总皆由我，如何忏悔得尽！不免趁此星月之下，对天哀祷一番。（对天拜介）

【前腔】对星月发心至诚，拜天地低头细省。皇天，皇天！念杨玉环呵，重重罪孽，折罚来遭祸横。今夜呵，忏愆尤，陈罪眚，望天天高鉴宥我垂证明。只有一点那痴情，爱河沉未醒。说到此悔不来，惟天表证。纵冷骨不重生，拼向九泉待等。那土地说，我原是蓬莱仙子，谪谪人间。天呵，只是奴家恁般业重，敢仍望做蓬莱座的仙班，只愿还杨玉环旧日的匹聘！

（副净）贵妃，吾神在此。（旦）原来是土地尊神。（副净）

【越调过曲】【忆多娇】我趁月明，独夜行。见你拜祷深深仔细听，这一悔能教万孽清。管感动天庭，感动天庭，有日重圆旧盟。

（旦）多蒙尊神鉴悯。只怕奴家呵，

【前腔】业障萦，凤慧轻。今夕徒然愧悔生，泉路茫茫隔上清。（悲介）说起伤情，说起

What sorrow have I brought on myself!
(*The tutelary god listens and nods.*)
How unhappy I am! Coming to a sad end in life, I am restless in
death. Perhaps if I repent my past sins I may be able to return to
paradise. But all that I did my life was bad, and the crimes that
my cousin and sisters committed in their greed for power will all be
laid at my door; so how can I be forgiven? Let me pray earnestly
to heaven under the moon and stars. (*She bows to heaven.*)

Before heaven and earth, the moon and the stars,
In all sincerity I review my past;
For all my sins I deserved this punishment;
But tonight, repentant, I confess my crimes;
May heaven pardon me and be my witness!
Olny my love I can never repent,
For I am still drowning in a sea of love;
And even if I cannot be reborn,
I will go on loving the emperor in hell.

The tutelary god said that I was once a fairy in the fairy mountain
who was sent down to earth; but since I am so sinful,

I dare not hope to rejoin the fairies.
All I ask is to return to my former love.

TUTELARY GOD: Lady Yang!
LADY: So the tutelary god is here.
TUTELARY GOD:

Walking alone at night under the moon,
I overheard your earnest prayer;
Since true remorse can wash away great sins,
Your penitence will move the gods on high
To pardon you and restore you to your love.

LADY: Thank you for your sympathy.

But I fear my faults were too many,
My virtues too few,
And that I am repenting in vain;
For the nether regions
Are far removed from heaven. (*She weeps.*)

伤情,只落得千秋恨成。

（副净）贵妃不必悲伤,我今给发路引一纸。千里之内,任你魂游便了。（作付路引介）听我道来,

【斗黑麻】你本是蓬莱籍中有名,为堕落皇宫,痴魔顿增。欢娱过,痛苦经,虽谢尘缘,难返仙庭。喜今宵梦醒,教你逍遥择路行。莫恋迷途,莫恋迷途,早归旧程。

【前腔】（旦接路引谢介）深谢尊神,与奴指明。怨鬼愁魂,敢望仙灵!（背介）今后呵,随风去,信路行。荡荡悠悠,日隐宵征。依月傍星,重寻钗盒盟。还怕相逢,还怕相逢,两心痛增。

　　（副净）吾神去也。

　　（旦）晓风残月正潸然, 韩琮
　　（副净）对影闻声已可怜。李商隐
　　（旦）昔日繁华今日恨, 司空图
　　（副净）只应寻访是因缘。方干

The thought of this makes me sad;
I am fated to grieve for ever.

TUTELARY GOD: Do not be so sad. I will give you a travel permit, with which you can wander at will for a hundred miles around. (*He gives her the permit.*)

Listen—

You were once an immortal,
But when you went to the palace
You were led astray by love;
Now you have tasted pleasure and pain,
And though you have left the world of men
You are not permitted yet to return to heaven.
It is good that tonight you have woken from your dream,
And I shall allow you to wander wherever you please
If you forsake your old ways;
And I hope that you may soon return to heaven.

LADY (*Curtseying*):

I thank you with all my heart for pointing me out a way;
For how dare an unhappy ghost aspire to heaven?

(*To herself.*)

From now on I shall drift as I please with the wind,
Travelling at night and vanishing by day,
Guiding myself by the moon and stars,
To find my former love.
And yet, if we meet again,
I fear it can only add to our pain.

TUTELARY GOD: I must leave you now.

(*Exeunt.*)

第三十出　剿寇

【中吕引子】【菊花新】(外戎装,领四军上)谬
承新命陟崇阶,挂印催登上将台。惭愧出
群才,敢自许安危全赖。

　　"建牙吹角不闻喧,三十登坛众所尊。
家散万金酬士死,身留一剑答君恩。"下官
郭子仪,叨蒙圣恩,特拜朔方节度使,领兵
讨贼。现今上皇巡幸西川,今上即位灵武。
当此国家多事之秋,正我臣子建功之日。
誓当扫清群寇,收复两京,再造唐家社稷,
重睹汉官威仪,方不负平生志愿也。众将
官,今乃黄道吉日,就此起兵前去。(众应、
呐喊、发号启行介)(合)
【中吕过曲】【驮环着】拥鸾旌羽盖,蹴起尘
埃。马挂征鞍,将披重铠,画戟雕弓耀彩。
军令分明,争看取奋鹰扬堂堂元帅。端的
是孙吴无赛,管净扫妖氛毒害。机谋运,阵
势排,一战收京,万方宁泰。(齐下)

SCENE 30
Suppressing the Rebellion

(*Enter* Guo Ziyi *in military dress with four soldiers.*)
GUO ZIYI:

> *I have taken a new command by His Majesty's order,*
> *And am hurrying now to my post;*
> *It is not that I have outstanding ability,*
> *But the fate of the realm is in my hands today.*
> *The bugle blows and all the ranks are hushed;*
> *I take command and all the troops respect me.*
> *I spend my private fortune on my men;*
> *And serve the emperor with my sword.*

The emperor has appointed me military governor of the Northern
Circuit, and odered my troops to suppress the rebels. The old
emperor has gone to Chengdu, and his son, the new emperor, has
ascended the throne at Lingwu. These troubled times give us the
opportunity to serve our country well. I swear to wipe out the
rebels, retake the capital, and restore the Tang empire. This is the
wish of my life. Today is an auspicious day, generals. Let us set
off.

(*With an answering shout, they start marching.*)
ALL:

> *With feathery canopies and banners,*
> *We gallop in a cloud of dust;*
> *Our horses are well saddled, our generals clad in heavy*
>   *armour,*
> *And our halberds and bows gleam in the sun.*
> *With strict discipline and superb leadership,*
> *We shall certainly stamp out the revolt,*
> *We apply our strategy and form our lines;*
> *One battle will win back the capital*

【前腔】(丑末扮番将、引军卒行上)倚兵强将
勇,倚兵强将勇,一鼓前来。陈似推山,势
如倒海。不断征云皑皑,鬼哭神号,到处里
染腥风,杀人如芥。自家大燕皇帝麾下大
将史思明、何千年是也。唐家立了新皇帝,
遣郭子仪杀奔前来。奉令着我二人迎敌。
(末)闻得郭子仪兵势颇盛,我等二人分作
两队,待一人与他交战,一人横冲出来,必
获大胜。(丑)言之有理。大小三军,就此
分队杀上前去。(四杂应,做分行介)向两下
分兵迎待,先一合拖刀佯败。磨旗惨,战鼓
哀。奋勇先登,振威夺帅。

　　(末领众先下)(外领军上,与丑对战一合
介)(丑)来将何名?(外)吾乃大唐朔方节
度使郭。天兵到此,还不下马受缚,更待何
时?(丑)不必多讲,放马过来。(战介,丑败
介,走下)(末领卒上,截外战介)(外)来的贼

And bring peace again to the people. (Exeunt.)
(Enter the Tartar generals, Shi Siming *and* Ho Qiannian, *with their troops.)*

GENERALS:

> *Relying on superior strength and courage,*
> *We rush ahead like an avalanche or storm;*
> *The clouds of war loom dark*
> *As gods and devils howl,*
> *And we mow the people down like grass,*
> *Until even the air reeks of blood.*

We are the generals Shi Siming and Ho Qiannian of Emperor An Lushan of the great Yan empire. The Tangs have set up a new emperor and sent Guo Ziyi to attack us, and our orders are to resist him.

HO: I hear that Guo has a strong army. Let us divide forces, so that one of us engages him first, and the other attacks from the flank. In this way we shall certainly beat him.

SHI: You are right. Form into two groups, men, for the attack.

(The soldiers divide into two groups.)

ALL:

> *In two groups we await the enemy;*
> *In our first encounter we shall pretend defeat;*
> *But then with beating drums and flags*
> *We shall advance to fight for victory.*

*(*Ho *and his troops march off.* Guo *leads in his troops to fight* Shi.)*

SHI: Who are you?

GUO ZIYI: I am Guo Ziyi, military governor of the Northern Circuit of the great Tang empire. Since our army has arrived here, you should get down from your horse and surrender. What are you waiting for?

SHI: Stop bluffing. Come and fight it out.

(They fight, and Shi *is defeated and flies. Then* Ho *enters with his troops and engages* Guo *again.)*

GUO ZIYI: Surrender, you rebel!

311

将,快早投降。(末)郭子仪,你可赢我么?
(外)休得饶舌。(战介,丑复上混战介)(丑、末
大败逃下)(外)且喜贼将大败而逃,此去长
安不远,连夜杀奔前去便了。(众)得令。
(行介)(合)

【添字红绣鞋】三军笑口齐开,齐开,旌旗满
路争排,争排。拥大将,气雄哉,合图画上
云台。把军书忙裁,忙裁,捷奏报金阶,捷
奏报金阶。

【尾声】两都早慰云霓待,九庙重瞻日月开,
复立皇唐亿万载。

悲风杀气满山河, 白居易
师克由来在协和。胡曾
行望凤京旋凯捷, 贺朝
千山明月静干戈。杜荀鹤

HO: Do you think you can beat me?

GUO ZIYI: Stop wagging your tongue, and come on.

(*They fight. Shi re-enters and joins in the fight; but both* Ho *and* Shi *are defeated and fly.*)

GUO ZIYI: Now the rebels have been routed, and the capital is not far off. Let us advance towards it without delay.

SOLDIERS: We will carry out your orders! (*They march forward.*)

All our men are smiling broadly,
As we advance with banners flying;
We have a heroic commander,
Whose portrait will hang with those of famous generals;
Let us send a quick dispatch
To announce our victory to the government.
They are waiting for us now in the capital
As people wait in time of drought for rain.
Soon we shall see our ancestral temples again,
And re-establish our empire to last for ever.

(**Exeunt.**)

第三十一出 哭像

(生上)"蜀江水碧蜀山青,赢得朝朝暮
暮情。但恨佳人难再得,岂知倾国与倾
城。"寡人自幸成都,传位太子,改称上皇。
喜的郭子仪兵威大振,指日荡平。只念妃
子为国捐躯,无可表白,特敕成都府建庙一
座。又选高手匠人,将旃檀香雕成妃子生
像。命高力士迎进宫来,待寡人亲自送入
庙中供养。敢待到也。(叹科)咳,想起我
妃子呵,

【正宫端正好】是寡人昧了他誓盟深,负了
他恩情广,生拆开比翼鸾凰。说什么生生
世世无抛漾,早不道半路里遭魔障。

【滚绣球】恨寇逼的慌,促驾起的忙。点三
千羽林兵将,出延秋,便沸沸扬扬。甫伤心
第一程,到马嵬驿舍傍,猛地里爆雷般齐呐
起一声的喊响,早子见铁桶似密围住四下
里刀枪。恶歆歆单施逞着他领军元帅威能
大,眼睁睁只逼拶的俺失势官家气不长,落
可便手脚慌张。

恨子恨陈元礼呵,

【叨叨令】不催他车儿马儿,一谜家延延挨

314

SCENE 31
Mourning Before the Image

(*Enter the emperor.*)
EMPEROR:

> *Green the hills and streams of this western land,*
> *Where day and night I mourn;*
> *I should never have given up my love,*
> *Not though she cost me my empire.*

Since coming to Chengdu I have abdicated and made the crown prince emperor. Fortunately Guo Ziyi has been victorious, and soon the rebellion will be supressed. I feel that something should be done in memory of Lady Yang, who sacrificed her life for the state; so I have ordered the authorities to build a temple in Chengdu, and skilled artisans have been chosen to make a life-size image of her out of sandalwood. Gao Lishi has been told to bring it to the palace, and I shall escort it to the temple myself. It should be here soon. (*He sighs.*) Ah, my love—

> *I broke my pledge and did you a great wrong;*
> *So the love birds were torn apart.*
> *Though we swore we would never give each other up,*
> *Yet all too soon misfortune overtook us.*
> *The rebels were pressing us hard as we travelled in haste,*
> *And there was a mutiny of the imperial guards;*
> *At our first stop, at Mawei Station,*
> *Like a bolt from the blue the guards set up an outcry;*
> *We were closely hemmed in, as if by an iron barrel,*
> *And swords and spears were drawn.*
> *Then Commander Chen was all-powerful,*
> *For in such straits I had no authority,*
> *And I lost my head. Confound that Commander Chen!*
> *Instead of urging the carriage and horses on,*

挨的望;硬执着言儿语儿,一会里喧喧腾腾
的谤;更排些戈儿戟儿,一哄中重重叠叠的
上;生逼个身儿命儿,一霎时惊惊惶惶的
丧。(哭科)兀的不痛杀人也么哥,兀的不
痛杀人也么哥!闪的我形儿影儿,这一个
孤孤凄凄的样。

　　寡人如今好不悔恨也!

【脱布衫】羞杀咱掩面悲伤,救不得月貌花
庞。是寡人全无主张,不合呵将他轻放。

【小梁州】我当时若肯将身去抵搪,未必他
直犯君王;纵然犯了又何妨,泉台上,倒博
得永成双。

【玄篇】如今独自虽无恙,问余生有甚风光!
只落得泪万行,愁千状!(哭科)我那妃子
呵,人间天上,此恨怎能偿!

　　(丑同二宫女、二内监捧香炉、花幡,引杂抬
杨妃像,鼓乐行上)(丑见生科)启万岁爷,杨娘
娘宝像迎到了。(生)快迎进来波。(丑)领
旨。(出科)奉旨:宣杨娘娘像进。(宫女)领
旨。(做抬像进、对生,宫女跪,扶像略俯科)杨
娘娘见驾。(丑)平身。(宫女起科)(生起立
对像哭科)我那妃子呵,

【上小楼】别离一向,忽看娇样。待与你叙
我冤情,说我惊魂,话我愁肠……(近前叫

316

He kept delaying, protesting, and making things worse,
To come forward at last with all his lances and halberds,
Forcing us in our panic to give her up.
(*He weeps.*) Ah, what a tragedy! Now I am left all alone; I could die of remorse.

I cover my face in shame and sorrow.
Because of my folly my beautiful darling was killed.
I should never have let her go;
For had I been willing to shield her with my body,
They might not have dared to attack the emperor;
Or suppose they had struck me down,
What would it have mattered?
We should be together at least in the world of shades.
Now I live on alone, but my life has no meaning;
Nothing but endless tears and endless sorrow.

(*He weeps.*) Ah, my darling,
Whether in earth or heaven,
This sorrow will never end!

(*Enter* Gao Lishi *with two maids and two eunuchs carrying a censer and pennants, and attendants carrying* Lady Yang's *image. Music is heard.*)

GAO: May it please Your Majesty, Lady Yang's image has arrived.

EMPEROR: Bring it in.

GAO: Yes, sire. (*He steps out and announces.*) The emperor orders the image of Lady Yang to be brought in.

MAIDS: The emperor's orders shall be obeyed. (*They carry in the image, kneel before the emperor, and cause the image to bow before him.*) Lady Yang is here, Your Majesty.

GAO: You may rise.
(*The maids stand up.*)

EMPEROR (*Rising from his seat and weeping*): Ah, my love—
We have been separated so long!
Now that I see your beloved face again,
I shall tell you of my unhappiness and fears.

(*He draws nearer.*) Ah, my darling,

科)妃子,妃子,怎不见你回笑庞,答应响,移身前傍。(细看像,大哭科)呀,原来是刻香檀做成的神像!

(丑)銮舆已备,请万岁爷上马,送娘娘入庙。(杂扮校尉,瓜、旗、伞、扇、銮驾队子上)(生)高力士传旨,马儿在左,车儿在右,朕与娘娘并行者。(丑)领旨。(生上马,校尉抬像,排队引行科)(生)

【玄篇】谷碌碌凤车呵紧贴着行,象亭亭龙鞭呵相对着扬。依旧的辇儿厮并,肩儿齐亚,影儿成双。情暗伤,心自想。想当时联镳游赏,怎到头来刚做了恁般随倡!

(到科)(丑)到庙中了,请万岁爷下马。(生下马科)内侍每,送娘娘进庙去者。(銮驾队子下)(内侍抬像,同宫女、丑随生进,生做入庙看科)

【满庭芳】我向这庙里抬头觑望,问何如西宫南苑,金屋辉光?那里有鸳帏绣幔芙蓉帐!空则儿颤巍巍神幔高张,泥塑的宫娥两两,帛装的阿监双双。剪簇簇幡旌飏,招不得香魂再转,却与我摇曳吊心肠。

Why don't you smile or answer me, or draw near?
(*He looks at the image closely, and gives a cry.*)
   It is only an image made of sandalwood!

GAO: The carriage is ready, Your Majesty, for you to escort Her Ladyship to the temple.

(*Attendants come in carrying pennants and canopies.*)

EMPEROR: Give the order, Gao Lishi, that my horse and the carriage carrying the image are to proceed side by side, so that I can be with her.

GAO: Yes, sire.

(*The emperor mounts his horse, the atendants pick up the image, and the procession moves forward.*)

EMPEROR:

   Her carriage rumbles along beside me;
   Her coachman raises his whip as I raise mine;
   We are riding together again now, shoulder to shoulder;
   But I sigh to think of our pleasure trips in the past,
   For who could have thought that today
   We would accompany each other
   In such a sorrowful procession?

GAO: We have reached the temple. Will Your Majesty alight?

(*The emperor dismounts.*)

EMPEROR: Attendants, escort Her Ladyship into the temple.

(*The procession moves off, the eunuchs and maids carrying the image, while* Gao *and the emperor enter the temple. The emperor looks around.*)

   I look around the temple,
   So unlike the palace with its gilded dome;
   There are no embroidered hangings,
   Only the sacred curtain before the altar
   With earthen palace maids and eunuchs in pairs;
   Yet though the pennants flutter,
   They cannot summon back my loved one's spirit,
   But only serve to make me sadder still.

(*He sits down.*)

319

（生前坐科）（丑）吉时已届，候旨请娘娘升座。（生）宫人每，伏侍娘娘升座者。（宫女应科）领旨。（内细乐，宫女扶像对生，如前略俯科）杨娘娘谢恩。（丑）平身。（生起立，内鼓乐，众扶像上座科）（生）

【快活三】俺只见宫娥每簇拥将，把团扇护新妆。犹错认定情初，夜入兰房。（悲科）可怎生冷清清独坐在这彩画生绡帐！

（丑）启万岁爷，杨娘娘升座毕。（生）看香过来。（丑跪奉香，生拈香科）

【朝天子】熏腾腾宝香，映荧荧烛光，猛逗着往事来心上。记当日长生殿里御炉傍，对牛女把深盟讲。又谁知信誓荒唐，存殁参商！空忆前盟不暂忘。今日呵，我在这厢，你在那厢，把着这断头香在手添凄怆。

高力士看酒过来，朕与娘娘亲奠一杯者。（丑奉酒科）初赐爵。（生捧酒哭科）

【四边静】把杯来擎掌，怎能够檀口还从我手内尝。按不住凄惶，叫一声妃子也亲陈上。泪珠儿溶溶满觞，怕添不下半滴葡萄

GAO: The auspicious hour has come. We are waiting for Your Majesty's order to carry Her Ladyship to her throne.

EMPEROR: Maids, help Lady Yang to the throne.

MAIDS: The emperor's orders shall be obeyed.

(*Music sounds offstage as they carry forward the image to the emperor.*) Lady Yang thanks Your Majesty.

GAO: You may rise.

(*The maids rise.*)

EMPEROR: (*Stands up, and music sounds again offstage as they bear the image to the throne*):

Seeing the maids gathered around her,
Screening the newly dressed beauty with their fans,
I am carried back in thought to that night of love
When first I entered her chamber. (*He weeps.*)
But now she sits alone
Within these painted silk curtains.

GAO: Your Majesty, Lady Yang has ascended the throne.

EMPEROR: Bring me the incense.

(Gao Lishi *kneels to present the incense to the emperor, who burns it before the image.*)

Incense against the gleaming candlelight
Reminds me of the past,
When at the Palace of Eternal Youth beside the tripod,
We pledged our love before the stars in heaven;
But our pledge proved all in vain;
Its unfading memory alone remains.
I am here today, but where are you?
This broken incense-stick increases my grief.

Gao Lishi, bring the wine, and I shall pour the libation myself.

GAO (*Handing him the wine*): The first libation.

ENPEROR (*Weeping as he takes the cup*):

Holding the goblet in my hand,
I would that her lips could still drink from this cup.
I cannot suppress my grief.
Calling her name I offer this libation,

321

酿。

（丑接杯献座科）（生）我那妃子呵，

【耍孩儿】一杯望汝遥来享，痛煞煞古驿身亡。乱军中抔土便埋藏，并不曾洒半碗凉浆。今日呵，恨不诛他肆逆三军众，祭汝含酸一国殇。对着这云帏像，空落得仪容如在，越痛你魂魄飞扬。

（丑又奉酒科）亚赐爵。（生捧酒哭科）

【五煞】碧盈盈酒再陈，黑漫漫恨未央，天昏地暗入痴望。今朝庙宇留西蜀，何日山陵改北邙！（丑又接杯献座科）（生哭科）寡人呵，与你同穴葬，做一株冢边连理，化一对墓顶鸳鸯。

（丑又奉酒科）终赐爵。（生捧酒科）

【四煞】奠灵筵礼已终，诉衷情话正长。你娇波不动，可见我愁模样？只为我金钗钿盒情辜负，致使你白练黄泉恨渺茫。（丑接杯献科）（生哭科）向此际捶胸想，好一似刀裁了肺腑，火烙了肝肠。

The goblet so full of my tears
That I fear not another drop of wine could be added.
(Gao Lishi *places the cup on the shrine.*)
Ah, my darling—
May your spirit come to the libation!
Dying at the old post station,
You were buried in haste and confusion,
And no sacrifice was offered at your grave.
Today I wish I could slay the whole rebel army
To sacrifice to your sad martyrdom.
Facing this image which looks like your living self,
I grieve the more that your spirit is gone.
GAO (*Handing him another cup*): The second libation.
EMPEROR (*Weeping as he takes the cup*):
Again I offer the brimming wine;
But my grief is dark and fathomless,
And standing dazed I feel the whole world turn dark.
In far-off Chengdu we dedicate your temple;
But when shall we move your grave back to Chang'an?
(Gao *again places the cup on the shrine, and the emperor weeps.*)
Shall we ever be buried together,
To turn into two love birds on twin boughs
Mourning above the grave?
GAO (*Handing him wine again*): The third libation.
EMPEROR (*Taking the cup*):
Now the libation is over,
But there is no end to my lament;
Your charming eyes remain fixed;
Do you see my unhappy face?
It is because I broke my pledge of love,
That now you are mourning in the nether regions.
(Gao *puts the cup on the shrine. The emperor weeps.*)
I beat my breast; my heart seems slashed with a knife,
My entrails burnt with fire.

（丑、宫女、内侍俱哭科）（生看像惊科）呀，高力士，你看娘娘的脸上，兀的不流出泪来了。（丑同宫女看科）呀，神像之上，果然满面泪痕。奇怪，奇怪！（生哭科）哎呀，我那妃子呵，

【三煞】只见他垂垂的湿满颐，汪汪的含在眶，纷纷的点滴神台上。分明是牵衣请死愁容貌，回顾吞声惨面庞。这伤心真无两，休说是泥人堕泪，便教那铁汉也肠荒！

（丑）万岁爷请免悲伤，待奴婢每叩见娘娘。（同宫女、内侍哭拜科）（生）

【二煞】只见老常侍双膝脆，旧宫娥伏地伤。叫不出娘娘千岁，一个个含悲向。（哭科）妃子呵，只为你当日在昭阳殿里施恩遍，今日个锦水祠中遗爱长。悲风荡，肠断杀数声杜宇，半壁斜阳。

（丑）请万岁爷与娘娘焚帛。（生）再看酒来。（丑奉酒焚帛，生酹酒科）

【一煞】叠金银山百座，化幽冥帛万张。纸铜钱怎买得天仙降？空着我衣沾残泪鹃留怨，不能勾魂逐飞灰蝶化双，蓦地里增悲怆。甚时见鸾骖碧汉，鹤返辽阳？

(Gao Lishi, *the maids and the eunuchs shed tears. The emperor looks at the image and gives a start.*)

Look, Gao Lishi! Are those not tears on her face?

(*They all stare at the image.*)

GAO: Yes, the image is crying! This is a miracle!

EMPEROR (*Weeping*):

Tears are falling on her cheeks,
Brimming over in her eyes,
And dropping on the altar.
She looks the same as on that day
When she offered to sacrifice herself,
And clung to my robes, yet turned her head to sob.
Has there ever been grief like this?
The earthen images are weeping too,
And even a man of iron would pity our sorrow.

GAO: Do not be so sad, Your Majesty. Let us all pay homage to Her Ladyship. (*He bows with the maids.*)

EMPEROR:

I see the old eunuch kneeling there,
While her former maids are sobbing on the ground,
Unable to utter her name. (*He weeps.*)
It is because you were kind to all in the palace
That they remember your love today in the temple.
My heart is broken, the nightingale is crying,
And the evening sun is sinking below the wall.

GAO: Will it please Your Majesty to burn the sacrificial paper money?

EMPEROR: Bring more wine. (*Gao brings wine again, and burns the paper, while the emperor pours the final libation.*)

Hundreds of stacks of gilded paper,
Millions of sacrificial coins,
Cannot buy back my darling.
I weep in vain like the nightingale,
And long in vain to become a butterfly
To follow her spirit.

（丑）天色已晚，请万岁爷回宫。（生）宫娥，可将娘娘神帐放下者。（宫娥）领旨。（做下神幔，内暗抬像下科）（生）起驾。（丑应科）（生作上马，銮驾队子复上，引行科）（生）

【煞尾】出新祠泪未收，转行宫痛怎忘？对残霞落日空凝望！寡人今夜呵，把哭不尽的衷情，和你梦儿里再细讲。

　　　　数点香烟出庙门，曹邺

　　　　巫山云雨洛川神。权德舆

　　　　翠蛾仿佛平生貌，白居易

　　　　日暮偏伤去住人。对彦冲

When, oh when, will her ghost return to me?

GAO: It is growing late, Your Majesty. Will you return to your palace?

EMPEROR: Lower the sacred curtain.

MAIDS: We will, Your Majesty. (*They lower the curtain and secretly remove the image.*)

EMPEROR: Let us go.

(Gao Lishi *passes on the order. The emperor mounts his horse, and the procession forms and begins to march.*)

Leaving the temple in tears, I return to my palace
Sunk in undying sorrow.
I gaze forlorn at the clouds in the setting sun;
Tonight in sleep I shall tell her my sorrow again.

(*Exeunt.*)

第三十二出　神诉

【仙吕入双调】【柳摇金】(贴引二仙女、二仙官队子行上)工成玉杼,机丝巧殊,锦过天除。摇珮还星渚,云中引凤舆。却望着银河一缕,碧落映空虚。俯视尘寰,山川米聚。吾乃天孙织女是也。织成天锦,进呈上帝。行路中间,只见一道怨气,直冲霄汉。不知下界是何地方?(叫介)仙宫,(官应介)(贴)你看这非烟非雾,怨气模糊,试问下方何处?

(官应,作看介)启娘娘,下界是马嵬坡地方。(贴)分付暂驻云车,即宣马嵬坡土地来者。(官应,众拥贴高处坐介)(官向内唤介)马嵬坡土地何在?(副净应上)来也。
【越调斗鹌鹑】则俺在庙里安身,忽听得空中换取。则他那天上宣差,有俺甚地头事

SCENE 32
The God's Report

(*Enter the* Weaving Maid *with two fairy maids and two angels.*)
WEAVING MAID:

I have finished weaving on my jasper loom,
And presented my silk before the Heavenly Palace;
And now with pendants tinkling
I return to the Milky Way,
My phoenix carriage gliding through the clouds.
In front the Milky Way hangs in the azure deep,
And below I see the earth,
Whose mountains and rivers look like specks of sand.

I am the Weaving Maid, and I have just finished making celestial silk to present to the Heavenly Emperor. On my way here I noticed an air of gloom rising to the sky; I wonder what part of the earth it comes from? (*She calls out.*) Angels! (*The angels answer her.*) Do you see that sad, foggy atmosphere? What place is that down below?

ANGELS (*Looking down*): That is Mawei Slope, my lady.

WEAVING MAID: Tell the carriage to stop, and summon the tutelary god of Mawei.

(*The angels assent, and the* Weaving Maid *ascends a high throne.*)

ANGELS (*Calling*): Where is the tutelary god of Mawei?

(*Enter the tutelary god.*)

TUTELARY GOD: Here I am!

I was resting in my temple
When some one called me from above.
What can those heavenly envoys want with us on earth?

ANGELS: Come quickly, god of Mawei!

TUTELARY GOD: There they are, shouting again. It makes me

329

务？(官唤科)土地快来。(副)他不住的唱叫扬疾，唬的我慌忙急遽。只索把急张拘诸的袍袖来拂，乞留屈碌的腰带来束。整顿了这破丢不答的平顶头巾，扶定了那滴羞扑速的齐眉拐拄。

(见官科)仙官呼唤，有何使令？(官)织女娘娘呼唤你哩。(副净)

【紫花儿序】听说道唤俺的是天孙织女，我又不曾在河边去掌渡司桥，可因甚到坡前来觅路寻途？(背科)哦，是了波，敢只为云中驾过，道俺这里接待全疏，(哭科)待将咱这卑职来勾除。(回向官科)仙官可怜见波，小神官卑地苦，接待不周，特带得一陌黄钱在此，送上仙官，望在娘娘前方便咱。则看俺庙宇荒凉鬼判无，常只是尘蒙了神案，土塞在台基，草长在香炉。

(官笑科)谁要你的黄钱。娘娘有话问你哩，快去，快去。(引副净见介)(副净)马嵬坡土地叩见。愿娘娘圣寿无疆。(仙女)平身。(副净起科)(贴)土地，我在此经过，见你界上有怨气一道，直冲霄汉。是何缘故？(副净)娘娘听启，

330

quite nervous; I had better hurry.

I hastily dust myself with my sleeves,
Hastily tighten my belt,
Hastily straighten my cap,
And hastily take my stick.

(*He greets the angels.*) What orders have you for me, my lords?

ANGELS: The Weaving Maid wants to see you.

TUTELARY GOD: So the Weaving Maid wants to see me!

I have never had charge of the bridge across the Milky Way;
So why should she ask for me? (*To himself.*)
Ah, yes, she must be angry
Because when she passes overhead in the clouds
I have never welcomed her. (*He weeps.*)
Now she will dismiss me from this humble post.

(*To the angels.*) Have pity on me, my lords. This is a poor place, so I have not been able to welcome her properly here. I have some paper coins for you, my lords. Please put in a good word for me.

Look how deserted my temple is:
Not even spirits come here.
The table is covered with dust,
The shrine is clogged with earth,
And the incense tripod is overgrown with grass.

ANGELS (*Laughing*): Who wants your money? Her Ladyship has a question to ask you. Come along. (*They lead him to the* Weaving Maid.)

TUTELARY GOD: The tutelary god of Mawei greets you, my lady. May you be blessed for ever.

FAIRIES: You may rise.

(*The god rises.*)

WEAVING MAID: God of Mawei, as I passed here I noticed a sad atmosphere from your territory penetrating to the sky. What caused it?

TUTELARY GOD: I will tell you, my lady—

【天净沙】这的是艳晶晶霓裳曲里娇姝,袅亭亭翠盘掌上轻躯。(贴)是那一个?(副净)是唐天子的贵妃杨玉环,磣磕磕黄土坡前怨屈,因此上痛咽咽幽魂不去,霭腾腾黑风在空际吹嘘。

(贴)原来就是杨玉环。记得天宝十载渡河之夕,见他与唐天子在长生殿上,誓愿世为夫妇。如今已成怨鬼,甚是可怜。土地,你将死时光景说与我听着。(副净)

【调笑令】子为着往蜀、侍銮舆,鼎沸般军声四下里呼。痛红颜不敢将恩负,哭哀哀拜辞了君主。一霎时如花命悬三尺组,生擦擦为国捐躯。

(贴)怎生为国捐躯,你再细细说来。(副净)

【小桃红】当日个闹镬铎激变羽林徒,把驿庭四面来围住。若不是慷慨佳人将难轻赴,怎能够保无虞,扈君王直向西川路,使普天下人心悦服。今日里中兴重睹,兀的不是再造了这皇图。

(贴)虽如此说,只是以天下之主,不能庇一妇人,长生殿中之誓安在?李三郎畅

332

There is a beautiful woman here,
Who was famed for the Rainbow Garment Dance,
And who used to dance lightly
On the emerald disk.

WEAVING MAID: Who is she?

TUTELARY GOD: Yang Yuhuan, the concubine of the Tang emperor.

She died a tragic death at Mawei Slope,
So her unhappy spirit hovers there,
Causing a cheerless wind to whirl in the air.

WEAVING MAID: So it is she. I remember that evening in the tenth year of the Tianbao period, when I crossed the Milky Way, I saw her and the Tang emperor at the Palace of Eternal Youth swearing to be husband and wife in all their future lives. But now, poor thing, she is an unhappy spirit. Tell me how she died.

TUTELARY GOD:

She was accompanying the emperor to Chendgdu
When the discontented soldiers mutinied;
Then, to repay his kindness,
With bitter tears she bade him farewell for ever
And in a flash had hanged herself,
Dying to save the state.

WEAVING MAID: What do you mean by saying that she died for the state?

TUTELARY GOD:

The imperial guards had mutinied
And besieged the posting station;
So if she had not sacrificed herself so bravely
There would surely have been trouble:
The emperor would never have reached Chengdu unscathed,
Nor would the people have been appeased.
But now the state is recovering,
So am I not right to say she died to save it?

WEAVING MAID: Do you mean to say that the ruler of the whole empire could not protect one woman? What of his pledge at the

好薄情也。（副净）娘娘，那杨妃呵，

【秃厮儿】并不怨九重上情违义忤，单则捱九泉中恨债冤逋。痛只痛情缘两断不再续，常则是悲此日，忆当初，欷虚。

（贴）他可说些什么来？（副净）

【圣药王】他道是恩已虚，爱已虚，则那长生殿里的誓非虚。就是情可辜，意可辜，则那金钗、钿盒的信难辜。拼抱恨守冥途。

（贴）他原是蓬莱仙子，只因凤孽，迷失本真。今到此地位，还记得长生殿中之誓。有此真情，殊堪鉴悯。（副净）再启娘娘，杨妃近来，更自痛悔前愆。（贴）怎见得？（副净）

【麻郎儿】他夜夜向星前扪心泣诉，对月明叩首悲吁。切自悔愆尤积聚，要祈求罪业消除。

【幺篇】因此上怨呼，恨吐，意苦。虽不能贯白虹上达天都，早则是结紫孛冲开地府。不堤防透青霄横当仙路。

（贴）原来如此。既悔前非，诸愆可释。吾当保奏天庭，令他复归仙位便了。（副净）娘娘呵，

【络丝娘】虽则保奏他仙班再居，他却还有痴情几许。只恐到仙宫，但孤处，愿永证前盟夫妇。

Palace Eternal Youth? How heartless the emperor is!

TUTELARY GOD: Ah, my lady—

Lady Yang does not blame the emperor for heartlessness;
She is willing to suffer among the shades;
She grieves only because they are parted,
And thinking of him and of the past she weeps.

WEAVING MAID: What does she say?

TUTELARY GOD: She says,

Though his love and kindness came to nothing,
The pledge they made in the palace still holds good;
Other vows may be broken,
But that pledged with the hairpin and the box will not be
*   forgotten;*
And she will rest true to him, grieving, among the shades.

WEAVING MAID: She was a fairy in paradise, who was fated to become a mortal; but still she remembers the pledge in the Palace of Eternal Youth. I find this very touching.

TUTELARY GOD: She has repented her former sins too, my lady.

WEAVING MAID: How do you know that?

TUTELARY GOD:

Each night she opens her heart to the stars and the moon,
And with tears and sighs repents of all her sins,
And prays to make amends.
Her sighs cannot reach heaven, yet they have made
A dismal atmosphere in the nether regions
Which now has soared to the sky
And drifted into your path.

WEAVING MAID: So that is it. Well, if she repents, all her sins can be forgiven. I shall speak for her in heaven and have her restored to the position among the fairies.

TUTELARY GOD: My lady,

Even if you restore her to her old position,
She will not renounce her love;
Even when she returns to the fairy palace,
She will grieve as long as her pledge is unfulfilled.

335

（贴）是儿好情痴也。你且回本境，吾自有道理。（副净）领法旨。

【尾声】代将情事分明诉，幸娘娘与他做主。早则看马嵬坡少一个苦游魂，稳情取蓬莱山添一员旧仙侣。

（下）（贴）分付起驾，回璇玑宫去。（众应引行介）

【仙吕入双调过曲】【金字段】【金字令】红颜薄命，听说真冤苦。黄泉长恨，听说多酸楚。更抱贞心，妆盟不负。【三段子】悔深顿令真元露，情坚炼出金丹固，只合登仙把人天恨补。

往来朝谒蕊珠宫，赵嘏
乌鹊桥成上界通。刘威
纵目下看浮世事，方干
君恩已断尽成空。卢弼

WEAVING MAID: Yes, she is very steadfast in her love. You may
go back to your post now. I shall see to this.

TUTELARY GOD: Your orders shall be obeyed.

I have told the whole story,
And the Weaving Maid will see to it;
There will be one sad, wandering spirit the less here,
And one fairy restored to the fairy mountain. (Exit.)

WEAVING MAID: Let us go back now to my palace.

(*They walk on.*)

Yang Yuhuan's story is a sad one,
And her sorrow in the world of shades is bitter;
But she is loyal to her love,
And will not break her pledge;
Repentance has made her see the light,
And unchanging love has given her immortality;
So she shall go back to heaven and be happy again.

(***Exeunt.***)

第三十三出　刺逆

（丑扮李猪儿太监帽、毡笠、箭衣上）"小小身材短短衣，高檐能走壁能飞。怀中匕首无人见，一皱眉头起杀机。"自家李猪儿便是，从小在安禄山帐下。见俺人材俊俏，性格聪明，就与儿子一般看待。一日禄山醉后，忽然现出猪首龙身，自道是个猪龙，必有天子之分。因此把俺名字，就顺口唤做猪儿。不想他如今果然做了皇帝，却宠爱着段夫人，要立他儿子庆恩为太子。眼见这顶平天冠，不要说俺李猪儿没福戴他，就是他长子大将军庆绪，也轮不到头上了。因此大将军心怀怨恨，与俺商量，要俺今夜入宫行刺。唉，安禄山，安禄山，你受了唐天子那样大恩，尚且兴兵反叛，休怪俺李猪儿今日反面无情也。（内打二更介）你听，谯楼已打二鼓，不免乘此夜静，沿着宫墙前去走一遭也呵。（行介）

【双调二犯江儿水】阴森夹道，行不尽阴森夹道，更深人静悄。（内作鸟声介）怕惊飞宿鸟，（内作犬吠介）犬吠哗哗，祸机儿包贮好。

SCENE 33

Assassination of the Rebel

(*Enter* Pigsy Li, *wearing a broad-brimmed hat and tight-fitting costume.*)

PIGSY:

> *I'm short and wear a short jacket,*
> *But I can walk on roofs and vault over walls,*
> *Carrying a hidden dagger.*
> *And if I frown it means that someone will die.*

I am Pigsyg Li. I have served An Lushan since I was a boy, and because I am clever and smart-looking, he has treated me as his own son. One day when he was drunk he imagined he was transformed into a monster with a dragon's body and pig's head, and decided this meant he would some day become an emperor. After that he gave me the name Pigsy. Now he really has become emperor; but he is so fond of his new concubine Duan that he wants to make her son his heir. That means I no hope of wearing the crown, and even his eldest, An Qingxu, won't have a chance. An Qingxu, who is high marshal, is angry and has arranged with me to go tonight to the palace to assasinate the emperor. Ah, An Lushan, you were kindly treated by the Tang emperor, yet you rebelled against him; so you can't blame me for turning against you. (*The second watch is sounded.*) Listen! Up there on the tower the second watch has sounded. I will skirt the palace wall now, while the night grows quiet. (*He walks on.*)

> *The dark avenue seems endless,*
> *And everything is silent late at night.*

(*A bird cries.*)

> *A bird flies past and I tremble.*

(*A dog barks.*)

> *A dog is barking; I must beware!*

339

（内打更介）那边巡军来了，俺且闪在大树边，躲避一回。（躲介）（小生、末、中净、老旦扮四军，巡更上）"百万军中人四个，九重门外月三更。"（末）大哥每，你看那御河桥树枝，为何这般乱动？（老）莫不有甚奸细在内。（中净）这所在那得有奸细，想是柳树成精了。（小生）呸，你每不听得风起么？（众）不要管，一路巡去就是了。（绕场走下）（丑出行介）好唬人也。只见刁斗暗中敲，巡军过御桥。星影云飘，月影花摇，险些儿漏风声难自保。一路行来，此处已近后殿，不免跳过墙去。苑墙恁高，那怕他苑墙恁高，翻身一跳，（作跳过介）已被俺翻身一跳。（内作乐介）你听，恁般时候，还有笙歌之声。喜得宫中都是熟路，且自慢慢而去。等待他醉模糊把锦席抛。

（虚下）（净作醉态，老旦、中净、二宫女扶侍，二杂扮内侍、提灯上）（净）孤家醉了，到便殿中安息去罢。（杂引净到介）（净坐介）（二杂先下）（净）宫娥，段夫人可曾回宫？（老旦、中净）回宫去了。（净）看茶来吃。（老旦、

(*Watchmen are heard approaching.*) The watchmen are coming.
I will hide behind a tree. (*He hides himself.*)
(*Enter four watchmen.*)

WATCHMEN:

> *Here four of us are guarding a million troops;*
> *At midnight the moon shines high above the palace.*

FIRST WATCHMAN: Look, you fellows! Why are the branches of
that tree by the bridge shaking?

SECOND WATCHMAN: Could it be a spy?

THIRD WATCHMAN: How could a spy get in here? There must be
a fairy in that willow tree.

FOURTH WATCHMAN: Nonsense. Can't you hear that the wind
has risen?

ALL: All right. Let's go on. (*Exeunt.*)

PIGSY (*Coming out of hiding*): That was a near thing!

> *Sounding their watch in the dark they have crossed the*
> *bridge;*
> *Stars twinkle through the floating clouds,*
> *And flowers that sway in the moonlight cast shifting*
> *shadows.*
> *That was a narrow escape!*

Now I am near the back court, I will jump over this wall.

> *Though the wall is high,*
> *I can clear it at a bound.* (*He leaps.*)
> *And here I am inside the palace grounds.*

(*Music sounds offstage.*) It is late, yet I can hear music. Luckily
I know my way about here. I'll take it easy

> *And wait till An staggers drunkenly to bed.* (*Exit.*)

(*Enter An Lushan, pretending to be drunk, helped by two palace
maids and two eunuchs carrying lanterns.*)

AN: I'm drunk. I'll take a rest in the pavilion.

(*He enters and sits down. The two eunuchs withdraw.*)

Maids, has Lady Duan gone back to the palace?

MAIDS: Yes, Your Majesty.

AN: Then bring me some tea. (*The maids assent and go off. An*

341

中净应下）（净作醒叹介）唉，孤家原不曾醉。只为打破长安之后，便想席卷中原。不料各路诸将，连被郭子仪杀得大败，心中好生着急。又因爱恋段夫人，酒色过度，不但弄得孤家身子疲软，连双目都不见了。因此今夜假装酒醉，令他回宫，孤家自在便殿安寝，暂且将息一宵。（老旦、中净捧茶上）皇爷，茶在此。（净作饮介）（内打三更介）（中净）夜已三更，请皇爷安寝罢。（净）宫娥每，把殿门紧闭了。（老旦、中净应作闭门介）（净睡介）（老旦、中净坐地盹介）（净作惊介）为何今夜睡卧不宁，只管肉飞眼跳？（叫介）宫娥！（中净惊醒介）想是皇爷独眠不惯，在那里唤人哩。姐姐你去。（老旦）姐姐，还是你去。（推，浑介）（净又叫介）宫娥，是什么人惊醒孤家？（老旦、副净）没有人。（净）传令外面军士，小心巡逻。（老旦、副净）领旨。（作开门出，向内传介）（内应介）（老旦、副净进，忘闭门、复坐地盹介）（净做睡不着介）又记起一事来，段夫人要孤家立他的儿子庆恩为太子，这事明日也要定了。（做睡着介）（丑潜上）俺李猪儿在黑影里，等了多时。才听得笙歌散后，段夫人回宫，说禄山醉了在便殿安息。是好机会也呵。（行介）

sits up soberly and sighs.) I'm not drunk in the least. After taking
the capital I meant to conquer the whole empire; but my generals
are all being defeated by Guo Ziyi, and I am very uneasy. At the
same time I have been indulging too heavily in wine and women,
fondling Lady Duan until I have no strength left and even my eyes
are growing dim. So tonight I pretended to be drunk and sent her
back to the palace; and now I shall stay here to rest.

(*Enter the maids with tea.*)

MAIDS: Here is the tea, sire.

(*An drinks. The third watch sounds offstage.*)

MAIDS: It is midnight now. Your Majesty had better rest.

AN: Bar the door well.

(*The maids assent and close the door. An goes to sleep, and the
maids doze on the ground.*)

AN (*Startled from his sleep*): How is it that I cannot rest tonight,
and feel so nervous? (*Calling.*) Maids!

FIRST MAID (*Waking*): His Majesty seems restless sleeping alone;
he's calling. You go, sister.

SECOND MAID: No, you go.

(*Each pushes the other.*)

AN (*Calling*): Who was it that woke me up?

MAIDS: There is no one, sire.

AN: Order the guards outside to keep a close watch.

MAIDS: Yes, Your Majesty.

(*The maids open the door to pass on the order, and an answer is
heard; then the maids come in again but forget to close the door.
Sitting on the ground they doze off once more.*)

AN: (*Sleepless*): I remember another thing. Lady Duan wants her
son to be made crown prince. I must see to that tomorrow. (*He
sleeps.*)

(Pigsy Li *creeps in.*)

PIGSY: I've been waiting in the dark for a long time. When the
music ended I heard that Lady Duan was returning to her palace
and that An Lushan was drunk and staying in this rest chamber.
My chance has come!

【前腔】潜身行到,悄不觉潜身行到。(内喊小心巡逻介)巡更的空闹吵,怎知俺宫闱暗绕,苑路斜抄,凑昏君沉醉倒。这里已是便殿了。且喜门儿半开在此,不免捱身而入。(进介)莫把兽环摇,(作听介)听鼾声殿角高。你看守宿的宫女,都是睡着。(作剔灯介)咱剔醒兰膏,(揭帐介)揭起鲛绡,(出刀介)管教他泼残生登时了。(净作梦语,丑惊,伏地,徐起细听介)梦中絮叨,原来是梦中絮叨。(内打四更介)残更频报,趁着这残更频报,赤紧的向心窝刺一刀。

(刺净急下)(净作大叫一声跌地,连跳作死介)(老旦、中净惊醒介)那里这般响动?(看介)阿呀,不好了!(向外叫介)外厢值宿军士快来。(四杂军上)为何大惊小怪?(老旦、中净)皇爷忽然梦中大叫,急起看时,只见鲜血满身,倒在地下。(四杂)有这等事!(作进看介)呀,原来被人刺中心窝而死。好奇怪,我每紧守外厢,还有许多巡军拦路,这贼从哪里进来?毕竟是你每做出来的。(老旦、副净)好胡说,你每在外厢护卫,放了

I have stolen in, unknown to all!
(*The watchmen shout offstage.*)
The watchmen are shouting for nothing;
They don't know that I have passed them,
And entered the palace to surprise the drunken despot.
Here is the rest chamber. Luckily the door is ajar, so I can just slip in. (*He enters the room.*)
I do not even touch the door handle. (*He listens.*)
I can hear some people snoring in the corner.
Ha, the palace maids who should be keeping watch are asleep. (*He trims the lamp.*)
I will trim the lamp a little.
(*He raises the curtain.*)
And lift the curtain.
(*He takes out a dagger.*)
This will dispatch the despot!
(*An says a few words in his sleep. Pigsy, startled, crouches down, then slowly gets up to listen carefully.*)
He is only talking in his sleep.
(*The fourth watch sounds offstage.*)
While the fourth watch sounds,
I will stab him to the heart.
(*He stabs An and runs off. An Lushan cries out, falls to the ground, rolls over and dies.*)
MAIDS (*Waking up*): What was that noise? (*They look round.*) Help! Murder! (*They call out.*) Come quickly, guards!
(*Enter four guards.*)
GUARDS: What's the trouble?
MAIDS: His Majesty suddenly gave a cry in his sleep. When we got up to look, we found him on the ground covered with blood.
GUARDS: What! (*They enter and look.*) Ah, he has been stabbed in the heart. That's strange. We were on guard outside and there are many watchmen making the rounds; how could an assassin have got in? You must have done it.
MAIDS: How dare you! You guards outside must have let the

贼进来。明日大将军查问，少不得一个个
都是死。（军）难道你每就推得干净？（诨
介）（杂扮将官上）"凶音来紫殿，令旨出青
宫。"大将军有令：主上被唐朝郭子仪遣人
刺死，即着军士抬往段夫人宫中收殓，候大
将军即位发丧。（四杂）得令。（抬净尸、随杂
下）（老旦、副净向内介）

　　　　鱼文匕首犯车茵，刘禹锡
　　　　当值巡更近五云。王建
　　　　胸陷锋芒脑涂地，陆龟蒙
　　　　已无足迹在人群。赵嘏

assassin in. When the high marshal investigates this tomorrow, none of you will escape alive.

GUARDS: So you hope to escape punishment, eh?

(*They quarrel*)

(*Enter a lieutenant.*)

LIEUTENANT:

Now sad news has been heard,
His Highness gives an order.

Since the emperor has been murdered by assassins sent by Guo Ziyi of the house of Tang, the high marshal orders the guards to carry the body to Lady Duan's palace, to be buried after His Highness has ascended the throne.

GUARDS: Yes, sir. (*They carry the body off.*)

(***Exeunt.***)

第三十四出　收京

【仙吕过曲】【甘州歌】【八声甘州】(外金盔、袍服,生、小生、净、末扮四将,各骑马,二卒执旗行上)宣威进讨,喜日明帝里,风静皇郊。欃枪涤尽,看把乾坤重造。扬鞭漫将金镫敲,整顿中兴事正饶。(外)下官郭子仪,奉命统兵讨贼。且喜禄山授首,庆绪奔逃,大小三军就此振旅进城去。(众应,行介)【排歌】收驰辔,近吊桥,只见长安父老拜前旄。欢声动,笑语高,卖将珠串奉香醪。

(到介)(众)启元帅,已进京城。请在龙虎卫衙门,权时驻扎。(外、众下马,作进,外正坐,四将傍坐介)(外)忆昔长安全盛时,(生、小生)今朝重到不胜悲。(净、末)漫挥满目河山泪,(外)始悟新丰壁上诗。(四

SCENE 34
Recovering the Capital

(Guo Ziyi *rides in, wearing a gilded helmet and robe, accompanied by four generals on horseback and two soldiers carrying flags.*)

GUO ZIYI:

We have come in all our might and conquered;
Peace reigns again in the capital,
For the rebel arms have been subdued,
And the time has come to build the world anew.
Raising my whip, I set spurs to my steed;
We have much to do to set our house in order.

I, Guo Ziyi, fought the rebels at His Majesty's command. Now An Lushan is dead, and his son An Qingxu has fled. Let us march into the city.

(*With an answering shout they march forward.*)

We pull on our reins as we approach the drawbridge,
Where the citizens of the capital welcome us
With joy and heartfelt laughter.
They have sold their possessions to buy us wine.

GENERALS: Commander, we have entered the capital. Please make the office of the imperial guards your temporary headquarters.

(*They dismount and enter the office. Guo Ziyi sits down in the middle, and the four generals sit around him.*)

GUO ZIYI:

Remembering the capital at the height of its glory,

LEFT and RIGHT GENERALS:

On our return we cannot but feel sad.

VANGUARD and REARGUARD GENERALS:

We weep at the sight of the old familiar landmarks.

349

将)请问元帅,什么新丰壁上诗?(外)诸将不知,本镇当年初到西京,偶见酒楼壁上,有术士李遐周题诗一首。(四将)题的是何诗句?(外)那诗上说:"燕市人皆去,函关马不归。若逢山下鬼,环上系罗衣。"(四将)这却怎么解?(外)当时也详解不出。如今看来,却句句验了。(将)请道其详。(外)禄山统燕、蓟军马,入犯两京,可不是"燕市人皆去"么?后来哥舒兵败潼关,正是"函关马不归"了。(四将)是,果然不差。后面两句,却又何解?(外)"山下鬼"者,嵬字也。"环"乃贵妃之名,恰应马嵬赐死之事。(四将)原来如此,可见事皆前定。今仗元帅洪威,重收宫阙,真乃不世之勋也。(外叹介)唉,西京虽复,只是天子暂居灵武,上皇远狩成都;千官尚窜草莱,百姓未归田里。必先肃清宫禁,洒扫园陵;务使钟虡不移,庙貌如故;上皇西返,大驾东回;才完得我郭子仪身上的事也。(四将打恭介)

GUO ZIYI:

> *Now I understand the writing on the wall.*

GENERALS: What writing on the wall, commander?

GUO ZIYI: I will tell you. When I first came to the capital, I saw on the wall of an inn some lines written by the fortune-teller Li Xiazhou.

GENERALS: What were they?

GUO ZIYI: He had written:

> *When the northern town is deserted,*
> *And no horses return from the Pass,*
> *He comes to the ghost beneath the hill,*
> *And there hangs a silken dress on the ring.*

GENERALS: What does that mean?

GUO ZIYI: At that time I couldn't understand it either; but I realize now that all his prophecies have come true.

GENERALS: Please explain it to us.

GUO ZIYI: An Lushan led all the troops of the north against the capital; that is what is meant by "When the northen town is deserted." Then General Geshu Han was defeated at the Pass; that is what is meant by "And no horses return from the Pass."

GENERALS: Quite right. But what do the last two lines mean?

GUO ZIYI: The third line referred to Mawei Slope, while the fourth predicted how Lady Yang would die.

GENERALS: So that's it. This shows how all things are predestined by fate. Now thanks to your might the capital has been recovered; that was a wonderful achievement.

GUO ZIYI (*Sighs*): Though the capital has been recovered, the reigning emperor is still at Lingwu, while the old emperor is far away in Chengdu; the ministers have fled and citizens have not yet dared return to their homes. We must first clean up the palace and sweep the imperial tombs, so that sacrifices can be resumed and the ancestral temples restored. Then the former emperor will return from Chengdu and His Majesty will come back from Lingwu. Only then will my work be finished.

全仗元帅。"双手重扶唐社稷,一肩独荷李乾坤。"(外)说便这般说,这中兴事,大费安排。诸公何以教我?(四将)不敢。(外)

【商调过曲】【高阳台】九庙灰飞,诸陵尘暗,腥膻满目狼籍。久阙宫悬,伤心血泪时滴。(合)今日、妖氛幸喜消尽也,索早自扫除修葺。(外)左营将官过来。(生)有。(外)你将这令箭一枝,前去星夜雇募人夫扫除陵寝,修葺宗庙,候圣驾回来致祭。(合)待春园,樱桃熟绽,荐陈时食。

　　(外付令箭,生收介)领钧旨。(末)元帅在上,帝京初复,十室九空。为今要务,先当招集流移,使安故业。(外)言之然也。

【前腔】【换头】堪惜,征调千家,流离百室,哀鸿满路悲戚,须早招徕,闾阎重见盈宝。(合)安辑,春深四野农事早,恰趁取甲兵初释。(外)右营将官过来。(小生)有。(外)你将这令箭一枝,前去出榜安民,复归旧

GENERALS (*Bowing*): The whole burden of restoring the Tang empire rests on your shoulders, commander.

GUO ZIYI: You may say so. The task of reconstruction will be a hard one. What advice have you for me?

GENERALS: How dare we presume to advise you?

GUO ZIYI:
> *Ashes are flying in the ancestral temples,*
> *And the tombs are darkened by dust;*
> *The dirt and disorder make one shed tears of anguish.*

ALL:
> *But now that the monster has been destroyed,*
> *We can clean and repair the palace.*

GUO ZIYI: Left general!

LEFT GENERAL: Here, commander!

GOU ZIYI: Take this arrow of authority, and hire workers to sweep clean the tombs and repair the temples immediately, so that the emperor can sacrifice when he returns.

ALL:
> *By then cherries will be ripe,*
> *And will be offered in sacrifice.*

(Guo Ziyi *gives the arrow to the left general.*)

LEFT GENERAL: Your orders shall be carried out.

REARGUARD GENERAL: The imperial city has been recovered, commander, but nine out of ten houses are empty. It is important to order the refugees to return home and take up their former tasks.

GUO ZIYI: You are right.
> *Cruel conscription has broken up thousands of homes,*
> *And the lot of the refugees on the roads is bitter;*
> *They should be recalled at once,*
> *So that our country may prosper once again.*

ALL:
> *First bring peace.*
> *Now it is spring there is work to do in the fields,*
> *And arms should be laid aside.*

GUO ZIYI: Right general!

业。(合)遍郊圻,安宁妇子,勉修耕织。

(外付令箭,小生接介)领钧旨。(净)元帅在上,国家新造,纲纪宜张,还须招致旧臣,共图更始。(外)此言正合我意。

【前腔】【换头】虽则、暂总纲维,独肩弘巨,同心早晚协力。百尔臣工,安危须仗奇策。(合)欣得、南阳已自佳气满,好共把旧章重节。(外)后营将官过来。(末)有。(外)你将这令箭一枝,榜示百官,限三日内,齐赴军前,共襄国事,(合)佐中兴升平泰运,景从云集。

(外付令箭,末接介)领钧旨。(生、小生)元帅在上,长安久无天日,士民渴仰圣颜。庶政以渐举行,銮舆必先反正。(外)二位所言,乃中兴大本也。本镇早已修下迎驾表文在此。

RIGHT GENERAL: Here, commander!

GUO ZIYI: Take this arrow of authority, and issue a proclamation to reassure the people, bidding them come back to their former work.

ALL:
Let there be peace in all the villages;
Men should till their land, and women weave cloth.

(Guo Ziyi *gives him the arrow.*)

RIGHT GENERAL: Your orders shall be carried out.

VANGUARD GENERAL: Now that the state is newly established, commander, we must have law and order. We should recall the former officials, and work together for reconstruction.

GUO ZIYI: I agree with you.
Though we now hold the reins of government
And shoulder all responsibilities,
We must rely on the help of all the officials
To keep the empire safe.

ALL:
Now order is restored,
We must renew our forebears' best traditions.

GUO ZIYI: Rearguard general!

REARGUARD GENERAL: Here, commander!

GUO ZIYI: Take this arrow of authority, and summon all former officials to report to our headquarters within three days to discuss affairs of state.

ALL:
Let them all come like gathering clouds
To assist in the work of reconstruction and peace.

(Guo Ziyi *gives him the arrow.*)

REARDGUARD GENERAL: Your orders shall be carried out.

LEFT and RIGHT GENERALS: Commander, the sun has not shone on the capital for a long time; the citizens are waiting eagerly for the emperor's return. Order can only be restored gradually; but first we must invite His Majesty back.

GUO ZIYI: Yes, this is the crux of the matter; and I have already written a memorial requesting the emperor to return.

355

【前腔】【换头】目极，云蔽行宫，尘蒙西蜀，臣心夙夜难释。反正銮舆，群情方自归一。（众共泣介）（合）凄恻，无君久切人痛愤，愿早把圣颜重识。（外）前营将官过来。（净）有。（外）你将这令箭一枝，带领龙虎军士五千，备齐法驾，赍我表文，前往灵武，奉迎今上皇帝告庙。并候圣旨，遣官前往成都，迎请上皇回銮。（净接令箭介）领钧旨。（外）左右看香案过来，就此拜发表文。（杂应、设香案，丑扮礼生上，赞礼）（外同四将拜表介）（合）就军前瞻天仰圣，共尊明辟。

（丑下）（净捧表文介）（四将）小将等就此前去。

削平妖孽在斯须，　方千
（外）依旧山河捧帝居。　皮日休
（合）听取满城歌舞曲，　杜牧
风云长为护储胥。　李商隐

Clouds hid the former emperor from sight
For he rode through dust into the far horizon;
His subjects have been concerned for him night and day.
But only on both emperors' return,
Will all our hearts become as one.
(*They shed tears.*)

ALL:

We are sad and indignant when our sovereign is absent,
And we long to see him soon.

GUO ZIYI: Vanguard general!

VANGUARD GENERAL: Here, commander!

GUO ZIYI: Take this arrow of authority, and lead five thousand imperial guards with full equipage to carry my memorial to Lingwu and escort His Majesty back to sacrifice at the ancestral temples. Then wait for His Majesty's order to dispatch an envoy to Chengdu to invite our former emperor to return also.

VANGUARD GENERAL: Your orders shall be carried out.

GUO ZIYI: Attendants, bring the table for sacrifice. We shall pay homage to the emperor as we send off the memorial.

(*A table is brought, and they bow before the memorial.*)

ALL:

Before our troops we pay homage to the emperor.
(*The vanguard general takes the memorial.*)
Now we shall set about our tasks.

(*Exeunt.*)

第三十五出　看袜

【商调过曲】【吴小四】(老旦扮酒家妪上)驿坡头,门巷幽,拾得娘娘锦袜收。开着店儿重卖酒,往来客人尽见投。聊度日,不用愁。

老身王嬷嬷,一向在这马嵬坡下,开个冷酒铺儿度日。自从安禄山作乱,人户奔逃。那时老身躲入驿内佛堂,只见梨树之下有锦袜一只,是杨娘娘遗下的。老身收藏到今,谁想是件至宝。如今郭元帅破贼收京,太平重见,老身仍旧开张酒铺在此。但是远近人家,闻得有锦袜的,都来铺中饮酒,兼求看袜。酒钱之外,另有看钱,生意十分热闹。(笑介)也算是老身交运了。今早铺设下店儿,想必有人来也。(虚下)(小生巾、服行上)

【中吕过曲】【驻马听】翠辇西临,古驿千秋遗恨深。叹红颜断送,一似青冢荒凉,紫玉销沉。小生李谟,向因兵戈阻路,不能出京。如今渐喜太平,闻得马嵬坡下王嬷嬷酒店中,藏有贵妃锦袜一只,因此前往借观。呀,那边一个道姑来了。(丑扮道姑上)

358

SCENE 35
Lady Yang's Stocking

(*Enter* Mistress Wang, *an inn-keeper.*)

WANG:

> *I live in a lonely spot on Mawei Slope;*
> *But since I picked up Lady Yang's silk stocking*
> *All the passers-by stop here for wine,*
> *And I need not worry how to make ends meet.*

I am Mistress Wang, and I've alwsys kept a wineshop here by Mawei Slope; but when An Lushan rebelled and many people fled, I hid myself in the Buddhist shrine in the post station, and there under the pear tree I found a silk stocking belonging to Lady Yang. I've kept it ever since, and it has proved a real treasure; because now that Commander Guo has defeated the rebels, won back the capital and restored peace, I've opened shop again; and people from far and wide who have heard about the stocking come here to drink and to look at it; and I charge them extra for that. So business has been very good. (*Laughs.*) It's my good luck! Now I've just opened shop. Soon customers should be coming. (*Exit.*)

(*Enter the young scholar* Li Mo.)

LI MO:

> *The imperial carriage rumbled west,*
> *Leaving eternal sorrow in this old station;*
> *For here the beauty was sacrificed,*
> *Like the unlucky beauties of old.*

I am Li Mo. I could not leave the capital before because there was fighting on the road; but things are quieter now, and I've heard that in Mistress Wang's shop at the foot of Mawei Slope there is a silk stocking that once belonged to Lady Yang. So I am going to see it. Ah, there is a nun coming.

(*Enter the abbess of a southern nunnery.*)

"满目沧桑都换泪,空留锦袜与人看。"(见介)(小生)姑姑何来?(丑)贫道乃金陵女贞观主,来京请藏,兵阻未归。今闻王嬷嬷店中,有杨娘娘锦袜,特来求看。(小生)原来也是看袜的,就请同行。(同行介)(合)玉人一去杳难寻,伤心野店留残锦。且买酒徐斟,暂时把玩端详审。

(小生)此间已是,不免径入。(同作进介)(老旦迎上)里面请坐。(小生、丑作坐介)(外上)老汉郭从谨,喜得兵戈宁息,要往华山进香。经过这马嵬坡下,走的乏了。有座酒店在此,且吃三杯前去。(进介)店主人取酒来。(老旦)有酒。(外与小生、丑见介)请了。(小生向老旦介)王嬷嬷,我等到此,一则饮酒,二则闻有太真娘娘的锦袜,要借一观。(老旦笑介)锦袜果有一只。只是老身呵,

【前腔】宝护深深,什袭收藏直至今。要使他香痕不减,粉泽常留,尘涴无侵。果然堪爱又堪钦,行人欲见争投饮。客官,只要不惜囊金,愿与君把玩端详审。

(小生)这个自然。我每酒钱之外,另

ABBESS:

>*The transience of human life brings tears to my eyes;*
>*Nothing is left of the beauty but her stocking.*

LI MO: Where are you from, mother?

ABBESS: I am the abbess of Jinling Nunnery. I came to the capital to fetch some sacred canons, and the war prevented my returning south. I have heard that Mistress Wang has a silk stocking that was worn by Lady Yang; so I have come out of my way to see it.

LI MO: Then we are both here for the same purpose. Let us go there together.

BOTH(*Walking on*)

>*The beauty lost and gone, it is sad to think*
>*Of her silk stocking kept in a country inn.*
>*Let us buy wine and sip it slowly,*
>*While we look well at the relic.*

LI MO: Here we are. Let's go straight in. (*They enter together, and* Mistress Wang *welcomes them.*)

WANG: Take a seat inside. (*They sit down.*)

(*Enter the old peasant* Guo Congjin)

PEASANT: My name is Guo Congjin. Now that the war is over I am going on a pilgrimage to Huashan. Passing Mawei Slope I feel tired; and since there is a wineshop here, I will stop for a while. (*He enters.*) Inn-keeper, bring me wine!

WANG: Yes, sir.

PEASANT (*Greeting* Li Mo *and the abbess*): Good day to you.

LI MO (*To the inn-keeper*): Mistress Wang, we have come her not only for wine but because we hear that you have a silk stocking of Lady Yang's. We would like to have a look at it, if we may.

WANG (*Laughs*): Yes, I have such a silk stocking;

>*Which I have been keeping carefully as a treasure,*
>*That it may not lose its scent or grow dusty and soiled;*
>*For it really is a wonderful sight;*
>*But if passers-by wanting to see it consent to pay extra,*
>*I am willing to let them have a look.*

LI MO: Of course, we shall pay extra for the sight.

有青蚨便了。(老旦)如此待老身去取来。
(虚下)(持袜上)"玉趾罢穿还带腻、罗巾深
裹便闻香。"客官,锦袜在此。请看。(小生
作接,展开同丑看介)呀,你看锦文缜缴、制度
精工。光艳犹存,异香未散。真非人间之
物也。(丑)果然好香!(外作饮酒不顾介)
(小生作持袜起,看介)

【驻云飞】你看薄衬香绵,似一朵仙云轻又
软。昔在黄金殿,小步无人见。怜,今日酒
垆边,等闲携展。只见线迹针痕,都砌就伤
心怨。可惜了绝代佳人绝代冤,空留得千
古芳踪千古传。

(外作恼介)唉,官人,看他则甚! 我想
天宝皇帝,只为宠爱了贵妃娘娘,朝欢暮
乐,弄坏朝纲。致使干戈四起,生民涂炭。
老汉残年向尽,遭此乱离。今日见了这锦
袜,好不痛恨也。

【前腔】想当日一捻新裁,紧贴红莲着地开,
六幅湘裙盖,行动君先爱。唉,乐极惹非
灾,万民遭害。今日里事去人亡,一物空留
在。我蓦睹香袜重痛哀,回想颠危还泪揩。

(老旦)呀,这客官见了锦袜,为何着
恼?敢是不肯出看钱么!(外)什么看钱?

WANG: I'll go and fetch it then. (*She goes out, to return presently with the stocking.*) This silk stocking once encased her foot. Before it is unwrapped one smells her perfume. Here you are. Take a look at it.

LI MO (*Taking the stocking and looking at it with the abbess*): Look how fine the embroidered designs on it are, and how exquisitely it is made! It is still glossy and beautiful and rarely fragrant. This is certainly no ordinary thing.

ABBESS: Yes, it does smell sweet.

(*The old peasant goes on drinking, paying no attention.*)

LI MO (*Standing up to examine the stocking*): Look!

> Thinly-lined with scented cotton,
> Light and soft as a fairy cloud,
> In the golden court it was never seen,
> But here in the wineshop whoever wishes can touch it.
> Each stitch seems to speak of sorrow.
> Unhappy beauty! What an unhappy end!
> Now she is nothing but a romantic tradition.

PEASANT (*Annoyed*): Confound it, sir! Why do you keep staring at that? Just because he doted on Lady Yang, our former emperor spent all his time in pleasure and neglected affairs of state, with the result that there was a rebellion and the people suffered unspeakably. I am nearing the end of my life, and I had a hard time of it during the revolt; so today the sight of this thing makes my blood boil.

> I think of the days when the stocking was newly made,
> And she slipped it on, beneath her wide silk skirts,
> To capture the heart of the emperor.
> But at the height of their joy, revolt broke out,
> And the whole people suffered.
> It is all past history now, and this only remains;
> But the sight of it reminds me of my sorrow,
> And the thought of our empire's downfall makes me weep.

WANG: Why does this silk stocking make you so angry, sir? You don't want to pay extra, I suppose.

（老旦）原来是个村老儿，看钱也不晓得。
（小生）些须小事，不必斗口。（向丑介）姑姑
也请细观。（向老旦介）待小生一并送钱便
了。（递袜介）（丑接起看介）唉，我想太真娘
娘，绝代红颜，风流顿歇。今日此袜虽存，
佳人难再。真可叹也。

【前腔】你看琐翠钩红，叶子花儿犹自工。
不见双跌莹，一只留孤凤。空，流落恨何
穷，马嵬残梦。倾国倾城，幻影成何用！莫
对残丝忆旧踪，须信繁华逐晓风。

　　（递袜与老旦介）嬷嬷，我想太真娘娘，
原是神仙转世。欲求喜舍此袜，带到金陵
女贞观中，供养仙真。未知许否？（老旦笑
介）老身无儿无女，下半世的过活都在这袜
儿上，实难从命。（小生）小生愿出重价买
去。如何？（外）这样遗臭之物，要他何用。
（老旦）老身也不卖的。（外作交钱介）拿酒钱
去。（小生作交钱介）我每看袜的钱，一总在
此。（老旦收介）多谢了。

　　一醉风光莫厌频，　鲍溶
　　（丑）几多珠翠落香尘。　卢纶
　　（小生）惟留坡畔弯环月，　李益
　　（外）郊外喧喧引看人。　宋之问

PEASANT: Pay what extra?

WANG: What an old country bumpkin! He doesn't even understand that.

LI MO: Let us not quarrel over such a trifle. (*To the abbess.*) Wouldn't you like to see it? (*To the inn-keeper.*) I shall pay for us all. (*He passes the stocking on.*)

ABBESS (*Taking the stocking*): Ah, Lady Yang was such a beauty, yet now she is no more. Though today we see this stocking, its unhappy wearer will never come here again!

> *We can see the green and red designs*
> *Of leaves and flowers finely embroidered;*
> *But where is the wearer now?*
> *Only a stocking is left, and endless sorrow;*
> *The tragedy of Mawei is a fleeting dream,*
> *And the beauty that ruined a kingdom is but an illusion.*
> *We should not think of past splendour looking at this,*
> *But should know that pomp and glory are gone like the wind.*
> (*She gives the stocking back to the inn-keeper.*)

I believe, ma'am, Lady Yang was no ordinary mortal; she must surely have been a fairy in her last life. So I would like you to give this stocking to my nunnery where we can dedicate it to the gods. Would you agree to this?

WANG (*Laughing*): I have no children, only this stocking to support me in my declining years. I can't afford to give it away.

LI MO: Would you sell it, if I paid you a good price for it?

PEASANT; Why pay for this stinking thing?

WANG: No, sir, it is not for sale.

PEASANT (*Paying for his wine*): Here is the wine money.

LI MO (*Paying her too*): And this is for all of us, for looking at the stocking.

WANG: Thank you, sir.

(***Exeunt.***)

第三十六出　尸解

【正宫引子】【梁州令】(魂旦上)风前荡漾影难留，叹前路谁投。死生离别两悠悠，人不见，情未了，恨无休。

【如梦令】"绝代风流已尽，薄命不须重恨。情字怎消磨？一点嵌牢方寸。闲趁，闲趁，残月晓风谁问！"我杨玉环鬼魂，自蒙土地给与路引，任我随风来往。且喜天不收，地不管，无拘无系，煞甚逍遥。只是再寻不到皇上跟前，重逢一面。(悲介)好不悲伤！今日且顺着风儿，看到那一处也。(行介)

【正宫过曲】【雁鱼锦】【雁过声全】悄魂灵御风似梦游，路沉沉不辨昏和昼。经野树片时权栖宿，猛听冷烟中鸟啾啾，唬得咱早难自停留。青磷荒草浮，倩他照着我向前冥冥走。是何处殿角几重云影覆？(看介)呀，原来就是西宫门首了。不免进去一看。(作欲进，二门神黑白面、金甲，执鞭、简上)(立高处介)"生前英勇安天下，死后威灵护殿

SCENE 36
The Resurrection

(*Enter* Lady Yang's *spirit.*)

LADY:

> *I fly like a shadow before the wind,*
> *Not knowing where to go.*
> *Though cut of from the world of men,*
> *My love remains and my everlasting sorrow.*
> *I need not regret the loss of my peerless beauty,*
> *But how can I forget my undying love?*
> *In the morning breeze and under the waning moon,*
> *I walk alone, for there is no one near!*

I am Lady Yang's spirit. Since the tutelary god gave me a travel permit and allowed me to travel freely, unchecked by heaven or earth, I have been wandering about as I pleased. I cannot reach the emperor or see him again. (*She weeps.*) Alas! Today I shall drift wherever the wind takes me.

(*She moves on.*)

> *As if in a dream I travel on the wind;*
> *The road is dark, it is neither night nor day;*
> *When I rest for a while in the lonely woods,*
> *Birds calling through the cold mist frighten me*
> *And drive me on; and the twinkling will-o'-the-wisps*
> *In the wild grass light my way. Where am I now?*
> *I see some buildings looming through the clouds.*

(*She looks.*) Ah, this is the west palace. I will go in to have a look. (*She is about to enter, when two door gods appear, one white-faced, one black-faced. Wearing golden armour and holding maces, they stand on a high place.*)

DOOR GODS:

> *In our life we were brave and fought to defend our land;*

门。"（举鞭、简拦旦介）何方女鬼，不得擅入。
（旦出路引介）奴家杨玉环，有路引在此。
（门神）原来是杨娘娘。目今禄山被刺，庆
绪奔逃，郭元帅扫清宫禁，只太上皇远在蜀
中，新天子尚留灵武，因此大内，寂无一人，
宫门尽扃锁钥。娘娘请自进去，吾神回避。
（下）（旦作进介）你看"宫花都是断肠枝，帘
幕无人窣地垂。行到画屏回合处，分明钗
盒奉恩时。"（泪介）（场上先设宫中旧床帷、器
物介）【二犯渔家傲】【雁过声换头】踌躇，往
日风流。【普天乐】（作坐床介）记盒钗初赐，
种下这恩深厚。痴情共守，（起介）又谁知
惨祸分离骤！唉，你看沉香亭、华萼楼都这
般荒凉冷落也。（作登楼介）并没有人登画
楼，并没有花开并头，【雁过声】并没有奏新
讴—端的有、荒凉满目生愁！凄然，不由人
泪流！呀，这里是长生殿了。我想起来，
（泪介）（场上先设长生殿乞巧香案介）这壁厢是
咱那日陈瓜果夜香来乞巧，那壁厢是他恁
时
向牛女凭肩私拜求。（哭介）我那皇上呵，

Dead, our bold spirits still protect the palace.
(*Barring her way.*) What ghost are you? No one may pass through here.

LADY(*Taking out her travel permit*): I am Lady Yang. Here is my permit.

DOOR GODS: So it is Your Ladyship. An Lushan has been assassinated, his son has fled, and Commander Guo has just cleaned up the palace; but the old emperor is still at Chengdu and the new emperor at Lingwu, so the palace is empty and all the doors are locked. We will let you in, however. (*Exeunt.*)

LADY(*Entering*):
How sad the flowers in the palace look!
All the curtains are drawn and there is no one here.
When I come to the painted screen,
I remember how I was given the pledge of love.?
(*She sheds tears as she looks at the couch and curtains.*)
I falter as I think of the past.
(*She sits on the couch.*)
When the hairpin and the box were given me,
I thought that his love and favour would last for ever.
(*She rises.*)
Who could have foreseen our agony
And our sudden separation?

Ah, Aloes Pavilion and Blooming Flower Pavilion look quite deserted now. (*She goes up to one pavilion.*)
Now no one comes to the painted pavilion,
No flowers bloom here,
No songs are sung here;
And this decay and neglect
Move me to tears.

And here is the Palace of Eternal Youth.
I remember that evening here
When I offered fruit to pray for happiness;
And standing shoulder to shoulder,
We prayed to the stars in heaven. (*She weeps.*)

怎能够霎时一见也！方才门神说，上皇犹
在蜀中。不免闪出宫门，到渭桥之上，一望
西川则个。（行介）【二犯倾杯序】【雁过声
换头】凝眸，一片清秋，（登桥介）【渔家傲】
望不见寒云远树峨眉秀。【倾杯序】苦忆蒙
尘，影孤体倦。病马严霜，万里桥头，知他
健否？纵然无恙，料也为咱消瘦。待我飞
将过去。（作飞，被风吹转介）（哭介）哎哟，天
呵！【雁过声】我只道轻魂弱魄飞能去，又
谁知千水万山途转修。（作看介）呀，你看
佛堂虚掩，梨树欹斜。怎么被风一吹，仍在
马嵬驿内了！（场上先设佛堂梨树介）【喜渔
灯犯】【喜渔灯】驿垣夜冷，一灯微漏。佛堂
外，阴风四起。看月暗空厩，【朱奴儿】猛伤
心泪垂。【玉芙蓉】对着这一株靠檐梨树
幽，（坐地泣介）【渔家傲】这是我断香零玉沉
埋处。好结果一场厮耨，空落得薄命名留。
【雁过声】当日个红颜艳冶千金笑，今日里
白骨抛残土半丘。我想生受深恩，死亦何
悔。只是一段情缘，未能终始，此心耿耿，
万劫难忘耳。【锦缠道犯】【锦缠道】谩回
首，梦中缘、花飞水流，只一点故情留。似

Ah, my emperor, how I long to see you again, if only for one moment! The door gods said that he is still in Chengdu; so I will leave the palace and walk up the bridge to look westwards. (*She walks on.*)

I gaze at the clear autumn scenery
(*She walks up the bridge.*)
Through the cold clouds and distant forests;
I cannot see the western mountains,
But I think of him travelling lonely and tired
On a weary horse in bitter frosty weather,
And I wonder if he is well.
But even if well, he must be pining for me.

Let me fly west. (*She tries to take flight, but is blown back by the wind.*) Ah! (*She weeps.*)

I thought my airy spirit could fly there;
But the way is long through rivers and mountains.

(*She looks.*) Here are the Buddhist shrine and the pear tree! The wind must have blown me back to Mawei Station.

The station is cold at night,
A single lamp gleams in the hall,
A cold wind sighs,
And dim moonlight falls into the empty stable.
I shed sad tears as I look at the pear tree
Growing beside the eaves.

(*She sits on the ground.*)

Here I took my own life and was buried;
And all that is left of me now is a sad story.
I had such beauty that one smile of mine
Was worth a thousand golden coins;
But now my white bones lie rotting in the earth.

I was loved so much in my life, I should have nothing to regret now that I am dead; but I cannot forget that, whatever trials I may meet, I shall never be able to see him again.

The past seems like a dream;
Water flows on and on, and flowers have withered,

春蚕到死,尚把丝抽。剑门关离宫自愁,马
嵬坡夜台空守,想一样恨悠悠。【雁过声】
几时得金钗钿盒完前好,七夕盟香续断头!

(副净上)"天边传敕使,泉下报幽魂。"
(见介)贵妃,有天孙娘娘赍捧玉旨到来,须
索准备迎接。吾神先去也。(旦)多谢尊
神。(分下)(杂扮四仙女,执水盂、幡节,引贴捧
敕上)

【南吕引子】【生查子】玉敕降天庭,鸾鹤飞
前后。只为有情真,召取还蓬岫。

(副净上,跪接介)马嵬坡土地迎接娘
娘。(贴)土地,杨妃魂灵何在?速召前来,
听宣玉敕。(副)领法旨。(下)(引旦去魂帕
上,跪介)(贴宣敕介)玉旨已到,跪听宣读。
玉帝敕曰:咨尔玉环杨氏,原系太真玉妃,
偶因微过,暂谪人间。不合迷恋尘缘,致遭

But my love remains the same;
I am like the silkworm
That in death still wraps itself in threads of silk.
In the mountain passes the emperor mourns alone,
And here in the station I keep watch in vain,
Longing alike for each other.
But shall we ever renew our love,
Fulfilling our pledge
And the vow made that night to the stars?
   (*Enter the tutelary god.*)
TUTELARY GOD:
   From the far horizon an emissary comes,
   To announce good tidings to the lonely spirit.
My lady, the divine Weaving Maid is coming with an order from the Heavenly Emperor. You had better prepare to greet her, while I will go ahead to welcome her.
LADY: Thank you, my lord. (*Exeunt.*)
   (*Enter the* Weaving Maid *with four fairies carrying holy water and pennants.*)
WEAVING MAID:
   I bring an order down from Heaven,
   And phoenixes and storks follow in my train;
   Because she is true to her love,
   I have come to summon her back to paradise.
   (*The tutelary god comes in and kneels to the goddess.*)
TUTELARY GOD: The tutelary god of Mawei is here to welcome Your Ladyship.
WEAVING MAID: Where is Lady Yang's spirit? Quickly bring her to me to hear the Heavenly Emperor's order.
TUTELARY GOD: I will, Your Ladyship. (*He goes out and comes back leading* Lady Yang, *who kneels fearfully before the goddess.*)
WEAVING MAID: Here is the order from Heaven. Listen well! "Yang Yuhuan, once a fairy in heaven, was sent for some slight fault for a time to earth. Because she loved earthly splendour, she

373

劫难。今据天孙奏尔吁天悔过,凤业已消,真情可悯。准授太阴炼形之术,复籍仙班,仍居蓬莱仙院。钦哉谢恩。(旦叩头介)圣寿无疆。(见贴介)天孙娘娘叩首。(贴)太真请起。前天宝十载七夕,我正渡河之际,见你与唐天子在长生殿上,密誓情深。昨又闻马嵬土地诉你悔过真诚,因而奏闻上帝,有此玉音。(旦)多谢娘娘提拔。(贴取水盂,付副净介)此乃玉液金浆。你可将去,同玉妃到坟前,沃彼原身,即得炼形度地,尸解上升了。炼毕之时,即备音乐、幡幢,送归蓬莱仙院。我先缴玉敕去也。(副净)领法旨。(贴)"驾回双凤阙,云拥七襄衣。"(引仙女下)(副净)玉妃恭喜,就请同到冢上去。(副净捧水盂,引旦行介)

【南吕过曲】【香柳娘】往郊西道北,往郊西道北,只见一拳培塿,(副净)到了。(旦作悲介)这便是我前生宿艳藏香数。(副净)小神向奉西岳帝君勅旨,将仙体保护在此。

suffered a heavy punishment; but now, according to the report of the Weaving Maid, she has repented and prayed to Heaven for forgiveness, so her past faults are pardoned. To relieve her from her misery, we grant her resurrection. Let her be restored to her place among the fairies, and return to the fairy mountain." Now thank His Divine Majesty.

LADY (*Kowtowing*): I thank the Heavenly Emperor. (*To the* Weaving Maid.) And I thank Your Ladyship.

WEAVING MAID: You may rise. In the tenth year of the Tianbao period, I was crossing the Milky Way on the seventh of the seventh moon, when I saw you and the Tang emperor in the Palace of Eternal Youth making a vow of love. Not long ago I heard from the tutelary god of Mawei that you had repented truly; so I reported it to the Heavenly Emperor, who issued this order.

LADY: I thank Your Ladyship from the bottom of my heart.

WEAVING MAID (*Giving the flask of holy water to the tutelary god*): This is holy water. Take this and go with Lady Yang to her grave. When you pour this water on her body, she will be resurrected and become a fairy. When this is done, prepare music and canopies to escort her to the fairy mountain. I am going back now to report that my task is done.

TUTELARY GOD: Yes, Your Ladyship.

WEAVING MAID:

I shall return now to the phoenix arches,
My carriage sailing over the white clouds.

(*Exit the* Weaving Maid *with her train.*)

TUTELARY GOD (*To Lady Yang*): Congratulations, my lady! Please come with me to the grave. (*Carrying the flask of water, he leads her on.*)

Going to the western suburb, then bearing to the north,
We come to a low mound.

This is it.

LADY (*Weeping*):

So this is where I was buried in my last life!

TUTELARY GOD: By order of the God of the Western Mountain, I

待我去扶将出来。(作向古门扶杂,照旦妆饰,
扮旦尸锦褥包裹上)(副净解去锦褥,扶尸立介)
(旦见作惊介)看原身宛然,看原身宛然,紧
紧合双眸,无言闭檀口。(副净将水沃尸介)
把金浆点透,把金浆点透,神光面浮,(尸作
开眼介)(旦)秋波忽溜。

　　(尸作手足动,立起向旦走一二步介)(旦惊
介)呀,

【前腔】果霎时再活,果霎时再活,向前移
走,觑形模与我无妍丑。(作迟疑介)且住,
这个杨玉环已活,我这杨玉环却归何处去?
(尸作忽走向旦,旦作呆状,与尸对立介)(副净拍
手高叫介)玉妃休迷,他就是你,你就是他。
(指尸向旦介)这躯壳是伊,(指旦向尸介)这
魂魄是伊,真性假骷髅,当前自分剖。(尸
逐旦绕场急奔一转,旦扑尸身作跌倒,尸隐下)
(副净)看元神入彀,看元神入彀,似灵胎再
投,双环合凑。

【前腔】(旦作起,立定徐唱介)乍沉沉梦醒,乍
沉沉梦醒,故吾失久,形神忽地重圆就。猛

have been watching over your body. Let me carry it out now. (*He goes out and returns carrying* Lady Yang's *body wrapped in a silk quilt. Taking off the quilt he supports the corpse.*)

LADY (*Startled*):
> *She looks the same as ever;*
> *Only her eyes and lips are closed!*

(*The tutelary god sprinkles holy water on the body.*)

TUTELARY GOD:
> *I sprinkle her with holy water;*
> *Till her face shines with a heavenly light.*

(*The corpse opens her eyes.*)

LADY: Ah! Her eyes are open!

(*The corpse stirs, then takes a few steps towards* Lady Yang.)
> *She is really alive,*
> *And moving forward, the image of myself!*

(*She hesitates.*) One moment, though! If that Lady Yang is alive, what is to become of me?

(*The corpse suddenly walks towards* Lady Yang's *spirit, who stares at her without moving.*)

TUTELARY GOD (*Clapping his hands and shouting*): Don't hesitate! You and she are one.

(*He points at the corpse.*)
> *This is your body!* (*He points at her.*)
> *And you are her spirit!*
> *Now let true nature reassert itself,*
> *And the spirit clothe itself in flesh again!*

(*The corpse pursues* Lady Yang, *and they run round the stage. Then* Lady Yang's *spirit turns and falls on the body, which is removed.*)
> *Now I see the spirit entering the body,*
> *Like a child re-entering its mother's womb,*
> *Or like two rings that join in one.*

LADY (*Rising from the ground*):
> *I have woken up from a deep, deep sleep,*
> *After losing myself so long;*

回思惘然,猛回思惘然,现在自庄周,蝴蝶复何有。我杨玉环,不意今日冷骨重生,离魂再合。真谢天也。似亡家客游,似亡家客游,归来故丘,室庐依旧。

土地请上,待吾拜谢。(副净)小神不敢。(旦拜,副净答拜介)(旦)

【前腔】谢经年护持,谢经年护持,保全枯朽,更断魂落魄蒙骈覆。(副净)音乐、幡幢已备,候送玉妃归院。(旦欲行又止介)且住,我如今尸解去了,日后皇上回銮,毕竟要来改葬。须留下一物在此,做个记验才好。土地,你可将我裹身的锦褥,依旧埋在冢中,不可损坏。(副净)领仙旨。(作取褥,褥作飞下介)(副净看介)呀,奇哉,奇哉!那锦褥化作一片彩云,竟自腾空飞去了。(旦看介)哦,是了。方才炼形之时,那锦褥也沾着金浆,故此得了仙气。化飞空彩云,化飞空彩云,也似学仙游,将何更留后?我想金钗、钿盒,是要随身紧守的,此外并无他物……(想介)哦,也罢,我胸前有锦香囊一个,乃翠盘试舞之时,皇上所赐,不免解来留下便了。(作解香囊看介)解香囊在手,解香囊在手,(悲介)他日君王见收,索强似人

But now my body and spirit are one again.
I wonder in a daze
Where is the spirit that flew like a butterfly?
I never thought my body would be restored to me. I feel so thankful.

Like a traveller who has been on a distant journey,
I have come back to find my home unchanged.

(*To the tutelary god.*) I must thank you too, sir.

TUTELARY GOD: There is no need for thanks, my lady. (Lady Yang *curtseys to him, and he bows in return.*)

LADY:

Thank you for guarding me for over a year,
Watching over both my body and wandering spirit.

TUTELARY GOD: The music and canopies are ready to escort you back to paradise.

LADY (*Starts to leave, but stops again*): Wait a minute. Now I am resurrected; but when the emperor returns, he will want to move my body. I must leave something here as a token. Will you put the silk quilt that was wrapped round me back into the grave? Please don't let it get damaged.

TUTELARY GOD: Yes, Your Ladyship. (*He stoops to pick up the quilt, but it flies away.*) How extraordinary! That silk quilt has changed into a cloud and flown off!

LADY (*Looking after it*): Ah! Just now when my body was resurrected, the silk quilt had some holy water sprinkled over it too, giving it divine power.

So it was able to change into a cloud.
But in that case what shall I leave behind?

The hairpin and the box I must keep with me, and I have nothing else. (*She thinks.*) I know! I have the scented pouch which was given me after I danced on the emerald disk. I will leave that here. (*She unfastens the pouch and looks at it.*)

I take off the pouch and feel it for the last time.

(*She sheds tears.*)

The emperor is luckier than I,

379

难重觏。

（将香囊付副净介）土地，你可将此香囊，放在冢内。（副净接介）领仙旨。（虚下，即上）启娘娘，香囊已放下了。（杂扮四仙女，音乐、幡幢上）（见旦介）蓬莱山太真院中仙姬叩见。请娘娘更衣归院。（内作乐，旦作更仙衣介）（副净）小神候送。（旦）请回。（副下，仙女、旦行介）

【单调风云会】【一江风】指瀛洲，云气空濛覆，金碧开群岫。【驻云飞】嗏，仙家岁月悠，与情同久。情到真时，万劫还难朽。牢把金钗钿盒收，直到蓬山顶上头。（从高处行下）

销耗胸前结旧香，张祜
多情多感自难忘。陆龟蒙
蓬山此去无多路，李商隐
天上人间两渺茫。曹唐

For he at least will see something of mine again.
(*She gives the pouch to the tutelary god.*) Please put this in the grave.

TUTELARY GOD: I will, my lady. (*He goes out, then enters again.*) I have done as you asked.

(*Enter four fairies with music and equipage.*)

FAIRIES: We are fairies from the fairy mountain. Please change your dress and come with us.

(*Music sounds offstage, and* Lady Yang *puts on a fairy dress.*

TUTELARY GOD: Farewell, my lady.

LADY: Farewell.

(*Exit the tutelary god.* Lady Yang *walks on with the fairies.*)

We are going to the fairy mountain,
Where mist hangs close and peaks rise golden and green;
Time stands still with the fairies, like eternal love;
For true love will never die,
In spite of ten thousand trials.
I shall keep the golden hairpin and the box safe,
And take them with me to the airy mountain.

(***Exeunt.***)

第三十七出　弹词

（末白须，旧衣帽抱琵琶上）"一从鼙鼓起渔阳，宫禁俄看蔓草荒。留得白头遗老在，谱将残恨说兴亡。"老汉李龟年，昔为内苑伶工，供奉梨园，蒙万岁爷十分恩宠。自从朝元阁教演"霓裳"，曲成奏上，龙颜大悦。与贵妃娘娘，各赐缠头，不下数万。谁想禄山造反，破了长安，圣驾西巡，万民逃窜。俺每梨园部中，也都七零八落，各自奔逃。老汉来到江南地方，盘缠都使尽了。只得抱着这面琵琶，唱个曲儿糊口。今日乃青溪鹫峰寺大会，游人甚多，不免到彼卖唱。（叹科）哎，想起当日天上清歌，今日沿门鼓板，好不颒气人也。（行科）

【南吕一枝花】不堤防余年值乱离，逼拶得岐路遭穷败。受奔波风尘颜面黑，叹衰残霜雪鬓须白。今日个流落天涯，只留得琵琶在。揣羞脸上长街，又过短街。那里是高渐离击筑悲歌，倒做了伍子胥吹箫也那乞丐。

SCENE 37
The Rhapsody

(*Enter the white-bearded orchestra leadar* Li Guinian, *in tattered clothes, carrying a lute.*)

LI:

>*Since the drums of war began to roll,*
>*The palace has been overgrown with weeds;*
>*And only the white-haired musician is left*
>*To sing of the empire's fall and of our sorrow.*

I, Li Guinian, was a musician in the imperial conservatory, much favoured by the emperor. When I taught my colleagues the Rainbow Dance His Majesty was very pleased, and he and Lady Yang gave me tens of thousands of cash as a reward. Then An Lushan rebelled and took the capital by storm; the emperor went westwards and many people fled in confusion, the members of my orchestra among them. I went south to the Yangzi Valley, and when all my money was spent I started wandering about with my lute to sing for a living. Today there is a big fair at Vulture Peak Monastery at Qingxi, and there will be great crowds there; so I had better go there to sing. (*He sighs.*)

>*I used to sing before the emperor,*
>*But now I play the clapper from door to door.*
>*What a come-down!* (*He walks on.*)
>*To think that in my old age I should come to this!*
>*Wretched and poor, wandering up and down,*
>*Braving the wind and dust which have darkened my face,*
>*A decrepit old man with snow-white beard and hair,*
>*I have only my lute to befriend me*
>*As I trudge shame-faced from street to street;*
>*Not an avenging hero chanting a dirge,*
>*Only a beggar playing his instrument.*

【梁州第七】想当日奏清歌趋承金殿,度新声供应瑶阶。说不尽九重天上恩如海:幸温泉骊山雪霁,泛仙舟兴庆莲开,玩婵娟华清宫殿,赏芳菲花萼楼台。正担承雨露深泽,蓦遭逢天地奇灾:剑门关尘蒙了凤辇鸾舆,马嵬坡血污了天姿国色。江南路哭杀了瘦骨穷骸。可哀落魄,只得把霓裳御谱沿门卖,有谁人喝声采!空对着六代园陵草树埋,满目兴衰。

(虚下)(小生巾服上)"花动游人眼,春伤故国心。霓裳人去后,无复有知音。"小生李谟,向在西京留滞,乱后方回。自从宫墙之外,偷按"霓裳"数叠,未能得其全谱。昨闻有一老者,抱着琵琶卖唱。人人都说手法不同,像个梨园旧人。今日鹫峰寺大会,想他必在那里,不免前去寻访一番。一路行来,你看游人好不盛也。(外巾服,净长帽、帕子包首,扮山西客,携丑扮妓上)(外)"闲步寻芳惜好春",(副净)"且看胜会逐游人"。

I think of the past when I served in the golden court,
Playing sweet melodies at the marble steps,
And the emperor's bounty and kindness were like the sea.
I followed him when he went to the warm springs,
And to Lishan after the spring snow;
On fairy boats we enjoyed the lotus in bloom,
The moon in Huaqing Palace and all the flowers.
I was sunned in his kindness when the catastrophe came,
Then in the mountain pass the imperial carriage
Drove through the dust, and the unearthly beauty
Was killd at Mawei Station. Ragged and lean,
I have cried till my eyes are dim here, south of the river.
From door to door I sing the emperor's songs;
But no one ever encourages me with applause.
Here by the ancient tombs sunk deep in weeds,
I mourn the vicissitudes of human fortune. (*Exit.*)

(*Enter the scholar* Li Mo.)

LI MO:

The flowers here still dazzle all who see them,
And in spring I cannot but think of the old regime;
Since the dancers of the Rainbow Dance are gone,
There is none left to appreciate true music.

I, Li Mo, stayed at the capital during the rebellion, and have only returned south recently. Once, outside the palace wall, stealthily noted down several parts of the Rainbow Dance; but I did not get the whole. The other day I heard of an old man who makes his living by singing rhapsodies, who does not play like an ordinary musican but was probably a member of the imperial conservatory. Today there is a big fair at Vulture Peak Monastery, and I shall probably find him there. The road is thronged with people.

(*Enter three Shanxi merchants with a sing-song girl.*)

FIRST MERCHANT:

We stroll along in spring to enjoy the sights,

SECOND MERCHANT:

And watch the people going to the fair.

385

（净）大姐，咱和你"及时行乐休空过"。
（丑）客官，"好听琵琶一曲新"。（小生向副
净科）老兄请了。动问这位大姐，说什么
"琵琶一曲新"？（副净）老兄不知，这里新
到一个老者，弹得一手好琵琶。今日在鹫
峰寺赶会，因此大家同去一听。（小生）小
生正要去寻他，同行何如？（众）如此极好。
（同行科）行行去去，去去行行，已到鹫峰寺
了。就此进去。（同进科）（副净）那边一个
圈子，四围板凳，想必是波。我每一齐捱进
去，坐下听者。（众作坐科）（末上见科）列位
请了，想都是听曲的。请坐了，待在下唱来
请教波。（众）正要领教。（末弹琵琶唱科）

【转调货郎儿】唱不尽兴亡梦幻，弹不尽悲
伤感叹，大古里凄凉满眼对江山。我只待
拨繁弦传幽怨，翻别调写愁烦，慢慢的把天
宝当年遗事弹。

　　（外）"天宝遗事"，好题目波。（净）大
姐，他唱的是什么曲儿，可就是咱家的西调
么？（丑）也差不多儿。（小生）老丈，天宝
年间遗事，一时那里唱得尽者。请先把杨
贵妃娘娘，当时怎生进宫，唱来听波。（末

THIRD MERCHANT:

Yes, lass, we must enjoy ourselves while we can.

SING-SONG GIRL:

Let us go and listen to the lute-player.

LI MO (*To the merchants*): Excuse me, did I hear the young lady
mention a lute-player?

SECOND MERCHANT: Yes. There has been an old man here
recently who plays the lute very well; today there is a fair at
Vulture Peak Monastery, so we are all going to listen to him.

LI MO: I am looking for the same man; may I go with you?

ALL: You are welcome. (*They walk on together.*) Here we are at
the monastery; let's go in. (*They enter.*)

SECOND MERCHANT: There are benches set in a circle; that must
be the place. Let us all go inside, and sit down to listen. (*They
take seats.*)

(*Enter* Li Guinian, *who bows to the audience.*)

LI: Good day, gentlemen. I suppose you have come to hear me
play. Please be seated; then I shall start singing and hope for your
instruction and criticism.

ALL: Please begin.

Li (*Playing his lute*):

I sing of kingdoms which rise and fall,
To vanish away like dreams;
And I play of sorrow and sighs.
I have seen such tragedy, I pluck the strings
To express my sorrow in the melodies.
And today I will tell you slowly
Of the former splendour of the Tianbao period.

FIRST MERCHANT: Ah, the Tianbao period! A good subject,
that.

THIRD MERCHANT: What tune is that, lass? Is that a Shanxi air?

SING-SONG GIRL: It is something like it.

LI MO: Excuse me, sir, you will never finish singing about the
whole Tianbao period. Will you first sing to us about Lady Yang,
and how she entered the palace.

弹唱科)

【二转】想当初庆皇唐太平天下,访丽色把蛾眉选刷。有佳人生长在弘农杨氏家,深闺内端的玉无瑕。那君王一见了欢无那,把钿盒金钗亲纳,评跋做昭阳第一花。

(丑)那贵妃娘娘,怎生模样波?(净)可有咱家大姐这样标致么?(副净)且听唱出来者。(末弹唱科)

【三转】那娘娘生得来仙姿佚貌,说不尽幽闲窈窕。真个是花输双颊柳输腰,比昭君增妍丽,较西子倍风标,似观音飞来海峤,恍嫦娥偷离碧霄。更春情韵饶,春酣态娇,春眠梦悄。总有好丹青,那百样娉婷难画描。

(副净笑科)听这老翁说的杨娘娘标致,恁般活现,倒像是亲眼见的,敢则谎也。(净)只唱得好听,管他谎不谎。那时皇帝怎么样看待他来,快唱下去者。(末弹唱科)

【四转】那君王看承得似明珠没两,镇日里高擎在掌。赛过那汉宫飞燕倚新妆,可正是玉楼中巢翡翠,金殿上锁着鸳鸯,宵假昼傍。直弄得个伶俐的官家颠不剌、懵不剌,

LI (*Playing on his lute*):

> *In the good old days there was peace throughout the land,*
> *And the emperor chose himself beautiful concubines.*
> *There was a lovely girl named Yang,*
> *Like flawless jade in her maiden bower;*
> *As soon as the emperor saw her she won his heart,*
> *He gave her a hairpin and a jewel box as gifts,*
> *And raised her to be the first of the ladies at court.*

SING-SONG GIRL: What did she look like?

THIRD MERCHANT: Was she as pretty as our young lady here?

SECOND MERCHANT: Hush, let him go on.

Li (*Plucking his lute*):

> *She was more like a fairy than a mortal;*
> *I can give no true picture of her charms.*
> *Flowers are not as fair as her cheeks,*
> *Nor willows more slender than her waist;*
> *She was lovelier than the famous beauties of old,*
> *Like the goddess Guanyin who rises from the waves,*
> *Or the moon goddess stealing from the deep blue sky.*
> *I remember her springtime passion,*
> *Her springtime drowsiness snd tipsiness;*
> *But not even the finest painter*
> *Could paint her infinite charms.*

SECOND MERCHANT (*Laughing*): Listen to the old man! He seems to be painting a portrait to the life, as if he had seen Lady Yang. What a liar!

THIRD MERCHANT: If he sings well, who cares whether he is lying or not? Go on. How did the emperor treat her?

LI (*Plucking his lute*):

> *Our sovereign treasured her as a matchless pearl,*
> *Caressing her all day long,*
> *Outdoing the Han emperor's love for his Lady Swallow;*
> *They were like two halcyons in a marble tower,*
> *Or a pair of love birds in a golden palace,*
> *Together day and night; for our noble lord*

撇不下心儿上。弛了朝纲,占了情场,百支
支写不了风流帐。行厮并,坐厮当。双,赤
紧的倚了御床,博得个月夜花朝同受享。

（净倒科）哎呀,好快活,听的咱似雪狮
子向火哩。（丑扶科）怎么说?（净）化了。
（众笑科）（小生）当日宫中有"霓裳羽衣"一
曲,闻说出自御制,又说是贵妃娘娘所作,
老丈可知其详? 请唱与小生听咱。（末弹
唱科）

【五转】当日呵,那娘娘在荷庭把宫商细按,
谱新声将霓裳调翻。昼长时亲自教双环。
舒素手,拍香檀,一字字都吐自朱唇皓齿
间。恰便似一串骊珠声和韵闲,恰便似莺
与燕弄关关,恰便似鸣泉花底流溪涧,恰便
似明月下泠泠清梵,恰便似嗕岭上鹤唳高
寒,恰便似步虚仙珮夜珊珊。传集了梨园
部、教坊班,向翠盘中高簇拥着个娘娘,引
得那君王带笑看。

（小生）一派仙音,宛然在耳,好形容
波。（外叹科）哎,只可惜当日天子宠爱了
贵妃,朝欢暮乐,致使渔阳兵起。说起来令
人痛心也!（小生）老丈,休只埋怨贵妃娘

Could not for one moment forget her.
He neglected affairs of state
In his eagerness for tournaments of love,
And their romance was always new
As they walked or sat together,
Or reclined on the imperial couch,
Taking their pleasure together day and night,
Before the flowers or under the bright moon.

THIRD MERCHANT (*Falling backwards*): Ah, this is fine! I feel like a snow lion before a fire.

SING-SONG GIRL (*Helping him up*): What do you mean?

THIRD MERCHANT: I've melted! (*They laugh.*)

LI MO: In those days they played a Rainbow Garment Dance in the palace. Some people said it was composed by the emperor; but others said it was composed by Lady Yang. Do you know the story? Please sing it for us.

LI (*Plucking his lute*):

Lady Yang worked in Lotus Pavilion
On the musical score, and composed the new dance;
In those long summer days she taught her two maids herself,
The scented sandalwood castanets in her soft hands,
The words falling like pearls from her red lips and dazzling
*   teeth.*
Her voice was pure and clear,
Like the song of orioles or swallows,
Like a rippling stream that flows beneath the flowers,
Like the sound of distant chanting beneath the moonlight,
Like the cry of storks above sheer mountain peaks,
Like the tinkle of jade pendants worn by fairies
As they fly through the sky by night.
Then all the emperor's musicians gathered,
And she danced among them all on the emerald disk,
While the emperor watched with a smile.

LI MO: One seems to hear the divine music from this wonderful description.

娘。当日只为误任边将,委政权奸,以致庙
谟颠倒,四海动摇。若使姚、宋犹存,那见
得有此。(外)这也说的是波。(末)嗨,若
说起渔阳兵起一事,真是天翻地覆,惨目伤
心。列位不嫌絮烦,待老汉再慢慢弹唱出
来者。(众)愿闻。(末弹唱科)

【六转】恰正好呕呕哑哑霓裳歌舞,不堤防
扑扑突突渔阳战鼓。划地里出出律律纷纷
攘攘奏边书,急得个上上下下都无措。早
则是喧喧嗾嗾、惊惊遽遽、仓仓卒卒、挨挨
拶拶出延秋西路,銮舆后携着个娇娇滴滴
贵妃同去。又只见密密匝匝的兵,恶恶狠
狠的语,闹闹炒炒、轰轰割割四下喳呼,生
逼散恩恩爱爱、疼疼热热帝王夫妇。霎时
间画就了这一幅惨惨凄凄绝代佳人绝命
图。

　　(外、副净同叹科)(小生泪科)哎,天生丽
质,遭此惨毒。真可怜也!(净笑科)这是
说唱,老兄怎么认真掉下泪来!(丑)那贵
妃娘娘死后,葬在何处?(末弹唱科)

【七转】破不剌马嵬驿舍,冷清清佛堂倒斜。
一代红颜为君绝,千秋遗恨滴罗巾血。半

392

FIRST MERCHANT: It's a pity, though, that because the emperor was so infatuated with Lady Yang and spent all his time in her company, the rebellion broke out at Yuyang. It's a sad story.

LI MO: You can't put all the blame on Lady Yang, sir. The catastrophe happened and the whole empire was shaken because the emperor appointed disloyal subjects as frontier generals and let a traitor run the government. If the good ministers Yao and Song had been alive, this would never have happened.

FIRST MERCHANT: Yes, there's something in what you say.

LI: Ah, that rebellion was a real catastrophe. It makes me sad to think about it; but if you gentlemen are not bored, I will sing slowly of what happened.

ALL: We would like to hear.

LI (*Plucking his lute*):

> *They were singing and dancing the Rainbow Dance,*
> *When drums rolled and alarm of war was spread from the*
> *frontier;*
> *Then terror seized them all, and in confusion*
> *With cries of alarm the imperial court fled westwards,*
> *The gentle lady following the emperor's carriage.*
> *But the soldiers mutinied and hemmed them in,*
> *Shouting in anger and threatening to revolt,*
> *Till they forced the lovers to part.*
> *And so the beauty came to a pitiful end.*

(*The first and second merchants sigh.*)

LI MO: How sad that such a beautiful woman should end so tragically! (*He sheds tears.*)

THIRD MERCHANT (*Laughing*): This is only a story; why take it to heart?

SING-SONG GIRL: Where was Lady Yang buried after she died?

LI (*Plucking his lute*):

> *In that desolate Mawei Station,*
> *By the lonely, broken-down shrine of Buddha,*
> *The peerless beauty died for the emperor,*
> *Hanging herself with her silken belt.*

棵树是薄命碑碣，一抔土是断肠墓穴。再
无人过荒凉野，莽天涯谁吊梨花谢！可怜
那抱幽怨的孤魂，只伴着呜咽咽的望帝悲
声啼夜月。

（外）长安兵火之后，不知光景如何？
（末）哎呀，列位，好端端一座锦绣长安，自
被禄山破陷，光景十分不堪了。听我再弹
一波。（弹唱科）

【八转】自銮舆西巡蜀道，长安内兵戈肆扰。
千官无复紫宸朝，把繁华顿消，顿消。六宫
中朱户挂蟏蛸，御榻傍白日狐狸啸。叫鸱
鸮也么哥，长蓬蒿也么哥。野鹿儿乱跑，苑
柳宫花一半儿凋。有谁人去扫，去扫！玳
瑁空梁燕泥儿抛，只留得缺月黄昏照。叹
萧条也么哥，染腥臊也么哥！染腥臊，玉砌
空堆马粪高。

（净）呸，听了半日，饿得慌了。大姐，
咱和你喝烧刀子，吃蒜包儿去。（做腰边解
钱与末，同丑诨下）（外）天色将晚，我每也去
罢。（送银科）酒资在此。（末）多谢了。

Ah, the pity of it!
There is only a broken bough to mark the place,
And a low mound of earth where she was buried;
But no one ever passes that lonely spot;
And in all that desolation who will mourn
The withering of the pear blossom?
There her sad, lonely spirit cries to the moon,
With the dirge of the nightingale.

FIRST MERCHANT: What was it like after the sack of the capital and the fire?

LI: Ah, gentlemen, Chang'an used to be a magnificent city; but after it was taken by the rebels terrible things happened there. Let me sing on.

(*Plucking his lute.*)

After the emperor's carriage drove westwards,
The capital was sacked by the rebels,
And the ministers ceased to pay homage at court.
The old pomp and splendour vanished,
Cobwebs hung on the crimson palace lintels,
Hyenas howled in broad daylight by the throne,
Owls hooted and rank weeds and brambles spread;
The stags ran wild and the fllowers and trees were neglected,
While the courtyards went unswept.
Swallow droppings fell from the lonely beams,
There was only a crescent moon in the gathering dusk;
The whole palace was left to go to ruck and ruin,
With horse dung thick on the marble steps.

THIRD MERCHANT: Confound it! After listening all this time I feel famished! Let's go to get a drink, sister, and eat some dumplings with garlic.

(*He takes some money from his purse and gives it to* Li, *then walks off with the sing-song girl.*)

FIRST MERCHANT: It is growing late. We had better be going too.

(*He gives* Li *money.*) Here's something to buy a drink with.

LI: Thank you.

（外）无端唱出兴亡恨，（副净）引得傍人也泪流。（同外下）（小生）老丈，我听你这琵琶，非同凡手。得自何人传授？乞道其详。（末）

【九转】这琵琶曾供奉开元皇帝，重提起心伤泪滴。（小生）这等说起来，定是梨园部内人了。（末）我也曾在梨园籍上姓名题，亲向那沉香亭花里去承值，华清宫宴上去追随。（小生）莫不是贺老？（末）俺不是贺家的怀智。（小生）敢是黄幡绰？（末）黄幡绰同咱皆老辈。（小生）这等想必是雷海青？（末）我虽是弄琵琶却不姓雷。他呵，骂逆贼久已身死名垂。（小生）这等，想必是马仙期了。（末）我也不是擅场方响马仙期，那些旧相识都休话起。（小生）因何来到这里？（末）我只为家亡国破兵戈沸，因此上孤身流落在江南地。（小生）毕竟老丈

FIRST MERCHANT: He sang of good fortune which ended in disaster,

SECOND MERCHANT: And we, who heard his song, were moved to tears.

(*The first and second merchants leave.*)

LI MO: Excuse me, sir but your lute-playing is so brilliant, may I ask who your teacher was?

LI:

> *This lute of mine has served the emperor;*
> *The thought of it makes me sad.*

LI MO: In that case, you must have been a member of the imperial conservatory.

LI:

> *My name was once on the register of musicians;*
> *I have played among the flowers of Aloes Pavilion,*
> *And attended imperial feasts at Huaqing Palace.*

LI MO: Are you He then?

LI:

> *No, I am not He Huaizhi.*

LI MO: Are you Huang Fanchuo?

LI:

> *We were colleagues.*

LI MO: Then you must be Lei Haiqing.

LI:

> *Though I play the lute too, I am not;*
> *For he died a glorious death after cursing the rebel.*

LI MO: Then you must be Ma Xianqi.

LI:

> *No, I am not Ma Xianqi, the stone-chime player.*
> *But please do not speak to me of those old friends.*

LI MO: Why have you come here?

LI:

> *When the capital fell and there was so much fighting,*
> *I fled to the south, a helpless refugee.*

LI MO: But who are you?

是谁波？（末）您官人絮叨叨苦问俺为谁，则俺老伶工名唤做龟年身姓李。

（小生揖科）呀，原来却是李教师。失瞻了。（末）官人尊姓大名，为何知道老汉？（小生）小生姓李，名谟。（末）莫不是吹铁笛的李官人么？（小生）然也。（末）幸会，幸会。（揖科）（小生）请问老丈，那"霓裳"全谱可还记得波？（末）也还记得，官人为何问他？（小生）不瞒老丈说，小生性好音律，向客西京。老丈在朝元阁演习"霓裳"之时，小生曾傍着宫墙，细细窃听，已将铁笛偷写数段。只是未得全谱，各处访求，无有知者。今日幸遇老丈，不识肯赐教否？（末）既遇知音，何惜末技。（小生）如此多感，请问尊寓何处？（末）穷途流落，尚乏居停。（小生）屈到舍下暂住，细细请教何如？（末）如此甚好。

【煞尾】俺一似惊乌绕树向空枝外，谁承望做旧燕寻巢入画栋来。今日个知音喜遇知音在，这相逢，异哉！恁相投，快哉！李官

LI:

> *Why do you insist on knowing my name, sir?*
> *I am an old musician—Li Guinian.*

LI MO (*Bowing*): So you are the orchestra leader! It is a privilege to meet you.

LI: What is your honourable name, sir? And how did you come to hear of me?

LI MO: My name is Li Mo.

LI: Are you the gentleman who plays the iron flute?

LI MO: Yes, I am.

LI: I am delighted to make your acquaintance. (*He bows.*)

LI MO: May I ask, sir, if you still remember the entire score of the Rainbow Dance?

LI: I think so. But why do you ask?

LI MO: Frankly, I have always been fond of music. When I was staying in the capital you were rehearsing the dance at the pavilion, and I listened outside the palace wall and noted down several parts for my flute. But I did not get the entire score; and though I have searched everywhere I have never found anyone who knows it. Today I am lucky to have met you; and I wonder if you will teach it to me?

LI: To a true music-lover, I would not begrudge parting with my little knowledge.

LI MO: I am most grateful to you. May I ask where you are staying?

LI: Ah, I have fallen on hard times and at present have nowhere to stay.

LI MO: Would you condescend to stay at my humble house for a while, so that I can have the advantage of your instruction?

LI: Thank you.

> *I have flown like a frightened crow from bough to bough,*
> *But now like a swallow return to a well-known nest.*
> *What a joy to have met a genuine lover of music!*

人呵,待我慢慢的与你这一曲霓裳播千载。

(末)桃蹊柳陌好经过,张籍
(小生)聊复回车访薜萝。白居易
(末)今日知音一留听,刘禹锡
(小生)江南无处不闻歌。顾况

I shall teach you the Rainbow Dance, sir;
And you shall hand it down to posterity!

(***Exeunt***.)

第三十八出　私祭

【南吕引子】【小女冠子】(老旦、贴道扮同上)
(老旦)旧时云髻抛宫样,(贴)依古观共焚
香。(合)叹夜来风雨催花葬,洗心好细翻
经藏。

(老旦)"寂寂云房掩竹扃,(贴)春泉漱
玉响泠泠。(老旦)舞衣施尽余香在,(贴)
日向花前学诵经。"(老旦)吾乃天宝旧宫人
永新是也。与念奴妹子,逃难出宫,直至金
陵,在女贞观中做了女道士。且喜十分幽
静,尽可修持。此间观主,昨自西京,购请
道藏回来。今日天气晴和,着我二人检晒
经函。且索细细翻阅则个。(场上先设经
桌,老旦、贴同作翻介)

【双调过曲】【孝南枝】【孝顺歌】金函启,玉
案张,临风细翻春昼长。只见尘影弄晴光,

SCENE 38

Sacrifice at the Nunnery

(*Enter the former palace maids* Yongxin *and* Niannu, *dressed as nuns.*)

YONGXIN:

In the old days we dressed our hair in the palace fashion;

NIANNU:

Now in this nunnery we burn incense together.

BOTH:

We sigh because a night of wind and rain
Has made the flowers fall;
And pure at heart we study the sacred canons.

YOUGXIN:

I close the bamboo gate in the quiet court.

NIANNU:

The mountain spring makes a sound like tinkling jade,

YONGXIN:

The scent remains on a skirt once worn for dancing,

NIANNU:

But now we chant sutras by the flowers each day.

YONGXIN: I am Yongxin, who used to be a palace maid. I fled with my sister Niannu from the palace during the rebellion, and we came straight to Jinling to become nuns. It is very quiet here, and we can study in peace. The abbess has just brought back some Taoist canons from the capital, and since the weather is fine we have been told to sun them. We shall go through them carefully.

(*They start sunning the books on the table.*)

BOTH:

Opening the gilded volumes on the marble table,
We turn the books in the breeeze of this long spring day;
And as we shake off the dust in the sunlight,

403

灵花满空降。(老旦)想当日在宫中,听娘娘教白鹦哥念诵心经。若是早能学道,倒也免了马嵬之难。(贴)那热闹之时,那个肯想到此。(老旦)便是昨日听得观主说,马嵬坡酒家拾得娘娘锦袜一只,还有游人出钱求看哩,何况生前!(合)枉了雪衣提唱。是色非空,谁观法相?【琐南枝】赢得锦袜香残,犹动行人想。(杂扮道姑捧茶上)"玉经日下晒,香茗雨前烹。"二位仙姑,检经困乏了,观主教我送茶在此。(老旦、贴)劳动了。(作饮茶介)(杂)呵呀,一片黑云起来,要下雨哩。(老旦、贴)快把经函收拾罢。(作收拾介)(杂)你看莺乱飞,草正芳,恰好应清明,雨漂荡。

(下)(场上收经桌介)(老旦)不是小道姑说起,倒忘了今日是清明佳节哩。此时家家扫墓,户户烧钱。妹子,我与你向受娘娘

We fancy that heavenly flowers have dropped from the sky.

YONGXIN: I remenber how Lady Yang used to teach the white parrot in the palace to recite the Buddhist sutras. If she had studied the Truth early, she would not have died at Mawei.

NIANNU: But in all that bustle and excitement, who would think of such things?

YONGXIN: That's true. Yesterday I heard our abbess say that some inn-keeper has picked up one of Lady Yang's silk stockings, and people are paying money to look at it. So, of course, in her lifetime.

BOTH:

In vain she taught her parrot to chant the sutra:
"All earthly existence is but vanity."
For she failed to understand the Truth,
And now her silk stocking with its lingering perfume
Serves only to draw a sigh from passers-by.

(*A nun comes in carrying tea.*)

NUN:

They are sunning the canons,
I bring them fragrant tea.

You must be tired, sisters. The abbess told me to bring you some tea.

BOTH: Thank you, sister. (*They drink the tea.*)

NUN: Look at that black cloud coming. It's going to rain.

BOTH: Yes, let's put the canons away quickly. (*They clear away the books.*)

NUN:

Orioles are darting about
And the grass is lush,
During this spring festival,
The time for showers of rain. (*Exit.*)

(*The table is cleared.*)

YONGXIN: If that little nun hadn't mentioned it, I would have forgotten that it's the Qingming Festival today. Now people everywhere are remembering their dead and visiting their ancestral

之恩，无从报答。就把一陌纸钱，一杯清茗，遥望长安哭奠一番。多少是好。（贴）姐姐，这是当得的，待我写个牌位儿供养。（作写位供介）娘娘呵，

【前腔】想着你恩难罄，恨怎忘，风流陡然没下场。那里是西子送吴亡，错冤做宗周为褒丧。（贴）呀，庭下牡丹，雨中开了一朵。此花最是娘娘所爱，不免折来供在位前。（合）名花无恙，倾国佳人，先归黄壤。总有麦饭香醪，浇不到孤坟上。（哭叫介）我那娘娘嗄，只落得望断眸，叫断肠，泪如泉，哭声放！（暗下）

【锁南枝】（末行上）江南路，偶踏芳，花间雨过沾客裳。老汉李龟年，幸遇李谟官人，相留在家。今日清明佳节，出门闲步一回。却好撞着风雨。懊恨故国云迷，白首低难望。且喜一所道院在此，不免进去避雨片时。（作进介）松影间，鹤唳长，且自暂徘徊，石坛上。

tombs to burn paper coins. We have never been able to repay Lady Yang's kindness to us. Suppose we face th capital to dedicate some paper coins and a bowl of tea to her?

NIANNU: That would be a very fitting thing to do. Just wait till I've written her name on a tablet. (*She writes on a tablet and places it in the table. They bow before it and shed tears.*)

BOTH:

Ah, Lady Yang, we can never repay your kindness.
We are sorry you came to such a sudden end,
And are now accused of causing the empire's ruin.

NIANNU: There's a peony blossoming in the court in the rain. That was her favourite flower. Let's pick it and dedicate it to her.

BOTH:

The beautiful flower remains,
But the beautiful woman has returned to dust;
And even though we sacrifice oatmeal and wine,
We cannot pour a libation
Over her distant tomb.

(*They weep.*) Ah, dear mistress!

We may cry our eyes out, but in vain!
Our tears fall like a fountain, but in vain! (*Exeunt.*)

(*Enter Li Guinian.*)

LI:

Wandering aimlessly down these southern roads,
My clothes are soaked with rain among the flowers.

I was lucky to meet Li Mo, who has put me up in his house. Today is the Qingming Festival, and I came out for a stroll; but it has started to rain.

My native place is far beyond the clouds,
And a white-haired man looks vainly towards the horizon.

How fortunate! I see a nunnery here. I'll go in to take shelter from the rain. (*He walks through the gate.*)

Here pine trees cast their long and leisured shadows,
And storks cry clear and loud;
I shall stroll beside the shrine.

你看座列群真,经藏万卷,好不庄严
也。(作看牌念介)皇唐贵妃杨娘娘灵位。
(哭介)哎哟,杨娘娘,不想这里颠倒有人供
养!(拜介)

【前腔】【换头】一朝把身丧,千秋抱恨长。
(老旦、贴一面上)那个啼哭?(作看惊介)这人
好似李师父的模样,怎生到此?(末)恨杀
六军跋扈,生逼得君后分离,奇变惊天壤。
可怜小人李龟年,(老旦、贴)原来果是李师
父,(末)不能够逢令节,奠一觞,没揣的过
仙宫,拜灵爽。

（老旦、贴出见介)李师父,弟子每稽首。
(末)姑姑是谁?(作惊认介)呀,莫非永、念
二娘子么?(老旦、贴)正是。(各泪介)(末)
你两个几时到此?(老旦、贴)师父请坐。我
每去年逃难南来,出家在此。师父因何也
到这里?(末)我也因逃难,流落江南。前
在鹫峰寺中,遇着李谟官人,承他款留到
家,不想又遇你二人。(老旦、贴)那个李谟
官人?(末)说起也奇。当日我与你每在朝
元阁上演习霓裳,不想这李官人,就在宫墙
外面窃听。把铁笛来偷记新声数段。如今
要我传授全谱,故此相留。(老旦、贴悲介)

Here are the shrines of saints and a library of thousands of sacred canons; what an impressive sight! (*He reads the tablet.*) "The shrine of Lady Yang of the Tang empire." (*He weeps.*) Alas, Lady Yang, to think that there is someone here who remembers you! (*He bows.*)

You died a sudden death,

Leaving us everlasting sorrow.

(*Enter the two nuns.*)

BOTH: Who is crying there? (*They look at* Li *and start.*) That man looks like the orchestra leader Li Guinian. How did he get here?

LI:

Ah, how I hate those mutinous guards,

Who forced the lovers to part.

What a tragedy!

And I, poor Li Guinain....

BOTH: Yes, it is!

LI:

Could not sacrifice at your grave in the festival,

But passing this holy place I have found your shrine.

(*The two nuns come forward to greet him.*)

BOTH: How are you, sir?

LI: Who are you? (*He recognizes them.*) Ah, aren't you Yougxin and Niannu?

BOTH: Yes. (*They shed tears.*)

LI: When did you two come here?

BOTH: Please sit down a while. We came south last year during the rebellion, and have joined this order. But what brings you here?

LI: I fled south at the same time. The other day at Vulture Peak Monastery I came across Li Mo, who invited me to stay in his house. I never thought to find you both here too.

BOTH: Who is Li Mo?

LI: That's a curious story. When we were rehearsing the Rainbow Dance in the pavilion, Li Mo was listening outside the palace wall, and he noted down several sections of the music with this iron flute. Now he wants me to teach him the whole thing. That is

409

唉,"霓裳"一曲倒得流传,不想制谱之人已归地下,连我每演曲的也都流落他乡。好伤感人也。(各悲介)(老旦、贴)

【供玉枝】【五供养】言之痛伤,记侍坐华清,同演霓裳。玉纤抄秘谱,檀口教新腔。【玉交枝】他今日青青墓头新草长,我飘飘陌路杨花荡。【五供养】(合)蓦地相逢处各沾裳,【月上海棠】白首红颜,对话兴亡。

(末)且喜天色晴霁,我告辞了。(老旦、贴)且自消停。请问师父,梨园旧人,都怎么样了?(末)贺老与我同行,途中病故;黄幡绰随驾去了;马仙期陷在城中,不知下落;只有雷海青骂贼而死。

【前腔】追思上皇,泽遍梨园,若个能偿!(泣介)那雷老呵,他忠魄昭白日,羞杀我遗老泣斜阳。(老旦、贴)师父,可晓得秦、虢二夫人都被乱兵杀死了?(末)便是朱门丽人都可伤,长安曲水谁游赏?(合)蓦地相逢处各沾裳。白首红颜,对话兴亡。

(老旦贴)不知万岁爷,何日回銮?(末)

why I am his guest.

BOTH (*Weeping*): Ah, the dance is remembered, but the lady who composed the music is dead and gone, while we who played it are wanderers far from home. (*They weep.*)

It makes us sad to speak of it.
In Huaqing Palace we played this music,
Which she had copied with her own delicate hands,
And with her own sweet lips she taught us the tune.
Now fresh grass grows on her grave,
While we have wandered the roads like willow seeds.

TOGETHER:

At this sudden meeting we shed tears,
A white-headed old man and two maids,
We lament the ups and downs of fortune.

LI: The sky has cleared now; I must be going.

BOTH: Stay a little longer. Can you tell us what happened to all the members of the conservatory?

LI: He Huaizhi left with me, but died of sickness on the road; Huang Fanchuo followed the emperor; Ma Xianqi remained in the capital and I don't know what has become of him; and Lei Haiqing died cursing the rebel leader.

When I think at the emperor's kindnss to us musicians,
I know we can never repay it. (*He weeps.*)
Lei's loyalty outshines the blazing sun,
And puts to shame the tears I shed in gloom.

BOTH: Did you know that the Duchess of Qin and the Duchess of Guo were both killed in the mutiny too?

LI: Yes, so I heard.

Those beauties who lived behind vermilion gates.
Can no longer enjoy the sights of the River Bend.

TOGETHER:

At this sudden meeting we shed tears,
A white-headed old man and two maids,
We lament the ups and downs of fortune.

BOTH: We wonder when the emperor will return to the capital.

李官人向在西京,近因郭元帅复了长安,兵
戈宁息,方始得归。想上皇不日也就回銮
了。(老旦、贴)如此,谢天地。(末)日晚途
遥,就此去了。(老旦、贴)待与娘娘焚了纸
钱,素斋少叙。

　　(末)南来今只一身存,　韩愈
　(老、贴)新换霓裳月色裙。　王建
　　(末)人世几回伤往事,　刘禹锡
　(老、贴)落花时节又逢君。　杜甫

LI: Li Mo was detained in the capital. It was only recently, when Commander Guo recovered Chang'an and restored peace, that he could come south. His Majesty should be returning soon.

BOTH: We must thank the gods!

LI: It is late now, and I have a long way to go; I must be leaving.

BOTH: Won't you stay to burn some paper coins to Lady Yang? And then we can have a simple meal together.

(*Exeunt.*)

第三十九出　仙忆

【南吕引子】【挂真儿】(旦仙扮、老旦扮仙女随上)驾鹤骖鸾去不返,空回首天上人间。端正楼头,长生殿里,往事关情无限。

　　【浣溪纱】"缥缈云深锁玉房,初归仙籍意茫茫。回头未免费思量。忽见瑶阶琪树里,彩鸾栖处影双双。几番抛却又牵肠。"我杨玉环,幸蒙玉旨,复位仙班,仍居蓬莱山太真院中。只是定情之物,身不暂离;七夕之盟,心难相负。提起来好不话长也!

【高平过曲】【九回肠】【解三酲】没奈何一时分散,那其间多少相关。死和生割不断情肠绊,空堆积恨如山。他那里思牵旧缘愁不了,俺这里泪滴残魂血未干,空嗟叹。

【三学士】不成比目先遭难,拆鸳鸯说甚仙班。(出钗盒看介)看了这金钗钿盒情犹在,早难道地久天长盟竟寒。【急三枪】何时得青鸾便,把缘重续,人重会,两下诉愁烦!

SCENE 39
A Fairy Visits

(*Enter* Lady Yang, *now a fairy, with her fairy maid.*)
LADY:

> *Though I ride the phoenix, I cannot return to earth,*
> *And so it is vain to look back at the world below;*
> *Yet I lose myself still in memories of the past,*
> *Of the Palace of Eternal Youth and Aloes Pavilion.*
> *Deep clouds have hidden my pavilion*
> *But I turn back to gaze at it with longing;*
> *Paired phoenixes among the jasper trees*
> *Remind me of my love though I try to forget him.*

I am Yang Yuhuan. By order of the Heavenly Emperor I have had
the good fortune to regain my place among the fairies, and have
come back to stay in the fairy mountain. But I will never part with
my pledge of love, and I cannot forget the vow we made that night
to the stars. Ah, it is a long story!

> *We were forced to part in haste,*
> *But death cannot end our love,*
> *And sorrow lies heavy on us as a mountain.*
> *On earth he thinks of the past with infinite grief,*
> *While here I shed tears and sigh in vain;*
> *For since disaster tore us apart,*
> *What use is it to be ranked among the immortals?*

(*She takes out the hairpin and the box.*)

> *At the sight of the hairpin and the box*
> *I know my love is unchanged;*
> *Through all eternity I shall never forget our vow;*
> *But will we ever have a blue bird as messenger,*
> *Or arrange to meet again*

（贴上）"试上蓬莱山顶望，海波清浅鹤飞来。"自家寒簧，奉月主娘娘之命，与太真玉妃索取霓裳新谱。来此已是，不免径入。（进见介）玉妃，稽首。（旦）仙子何来？（贴笑介）玉妃还认得我寒簧么？（旦想介）哦，莫非是月中仙子？（贴）然也。（旦）请坐了。（贴坐介）（旦）梦中一别，不觉数年。今日远临，乞道来意。（贴）玉妃听启，

【清商七犯】【簇御林】只为霓裳乐在广寒，羡灵心，将谱细翻。特奉月主娘娘之命，

【莺啼序】访知音远叩蓬山，借当年图谱亲看。（旦）原来为此。当日幸从梦里获听仙音，虽然摹入管弦，尚愧依稀错误。【高阳台】何烦、蟾宫谬把遗调拣，我寻思起转自潜潜。（泪介）（贴）呀，玉妃为何掉下泪来？

（旦）【降黄龙】痛我历劫遭磨，宫冷商残。

【二郎神】朱弦已断，羞将此调重弹。烦仙子转奏月主，说我尘凡旧谱，不堪应命。伏

416

And together share our sorrow?

(*Enter* Hanhuang *from the moon.*)

HANHUANG:

I gaze from the peak of the fairy mountain,
And see limpid waves and a single stork in flight.

I am the fairy maid Hanhuang, and I have been ordered by the goddess of the moon to ask Lady Yang for the score of the Rainbow Dance. This is the place; let me go in. (*She enters the door.*) Lady Yang!

LADY: Where have you come from, fairy maid?

HANHUANG (*Laughing*): Don't you remember me?

LADY (*Thinks*): Oh, aren't you a fairy from the moon?

HANHUANG: Yes.

LADY: Please sit down. (Hanhuang *sits down.*) Many years have passed since we parted in that dream; but today you have come again from a great distance. May I ask the purpose of this visit?

HANHUANG: I'll tell you.

You put our Rainbow Dance to music so well
That the goddess of the moon has ordered me
To come all this way to your fairy mountain
To ask to see your composition.

LADY: So that's it. When I put down the notations after hearing the divine music in my dream, I was afraid there might have been mistakes; so I am very flattered to know that the goddess wants to see it.

But thinking of it makes me want to cry.

(*She sheds tears.*)

HANHUANG: Why are you crying

LADY:

I am sad to think of the misfortune,
Which made me set music aside.
Now that my lute's vermilion strings are broken,
I am ashamed to play the old tune again.

Please tell your mistress that the score I wrote on earth is not good enough to present to her, and beg her to excuse me.

417

乞矜宥。(贴)玉妃休得固拒,我月主娘娘呵,慕你聪明绝世罕,【集贤宾】度新声占断人间。求观恨晚,休辜负云中青盼。(旦)既蒙月主下访,前到仙山,偶然追忆,写出一本在此。(贴)如此甚好。(旦)侍儿,可去取来。(老应下,取上)谱在此。(旦接介)仙子,谱虽取到,只是还须誊写才好。(贴)为何?(旦)你看呵,【黄莺儿】字阑珊,模糊断续,都染就泪痕斑。

(贴)这却不妨。(旦付谱介)如此,即烦呈上月主,说梦中窃记,音节多讹,还求改正。(贴)领命,就此告别。

(贴)从初直到曲成时, 王建
(旦)争得姮娥子细知。唐彦谦
(贴)莫怪殷勤悲此曲, 刘禹锡
(旦)月中流滟与谁期。李商隐

(贴持谱下)(旦)侍儿闭上洞门,随我进来。(老应随下)

HANHUANG: Please don't refuse.
Our mistress admires your outstanding talent
And is eager to listen to your new tune,
Which is said to be unsurpassed in the world of men;
Don't let her be disappointed.

LADY: You are doing me too great an honour. As a matter of fact, some time ago, when I had just arrived here, I wrote down the score from memory.

HANHUANG: Good.

LADY: Go and fetch it, my fairy.

(*The fairy maid assents, and presently brings in the score.*)

FAIRY: Here it is, madam.

LADY (*Taking it*): Here is the score; but it needs recopying.

HANHUANG: Why?

LADY: Don't you see?
The notes are blured and stained with tears.

HANHUANG: That doesn't matter.

LADY (*Giving her the music*): In that case, please tell your mistress that since I memorised this in my dream I must have made many mistakes, and I hope she will correct them.

HANHUANG: I shall give her your message. (*She goes out with the music.*)

LADY: Close the gate, fairy, and come with me. (*The fairy assents.*)

(***Exeunt.***)

第四十出　见月

【仙吕入双调过曲】【双玉供】【玉胞肚】(杂扮四将、二内侍,引生骑马、丑随行上)(合)重华迎待,促归程把回銮仗排。离南京不听鹃啼,怕西京尚有鸿哀。【五供养】喜山河未改,复睹这皇图风采。(众百姓上,跪接介)扶风百姓迎接老万岁爷。(生)生受你每,回去罢。(百姓叩头呼"万岁"下)(生众行介)【玉胞肚】纷纷父老竞拦街,叩首齐呼"万岁"来。

(丑)启万岁爷,天色已晚,请銮舆就在凤仪宫驻跸。(生下马介)众军士,外厢伺候。(军)领旨。(下)

(生进介)高力士,此去马嵬,还有多少路?(丑)只有一百多里了。(生)前已传旨,令该地方官建造妃子新坟,你可星夜前往,催督工程,候朕到时改葬。(丑)领旨。"暂辞

SCENE 40
Looking at the Moon

(*Four lieutenants and two eunuchs lead in the emperor, who is on horseback attended by* Gao Lishi.)

TOGETHER:

With a full cortege we escort the emperor back;
When we left Chengdu we heard no more
The dirge of the nightingale;
But we fear that Chang'an may yet resound
With the cries of affrighted swans.
We are glad that the mountains and rivers remain the same,
And that we can view our magnificent empire again.

(*Citizens come in and kneel by the roadside to welcome the old emperor.*)

CITIZENS: We citizens of Fufeng greet Your Majesty's return!

EMPEROR: We thank you all. Please go to your homes again.

(*The citizens bow and shout "Long live the emperor!" then walk off.*)

TOGETHER (*Walking on*):

See how the elders are barring the way,
To pay homage and wish long life to the emperor.

GAO: It is late, sire. Will you spend the night at Fengyi Palace?

EMPEROR (*Dismounting*): Soldiers and officers, wait for us outside.

LIEUTENANTS: Your Majesty's orders shall be obeyed.

(*Exeunt.*)

EMPEROR (*Entering*): How far is it to Mawei. Gao Lishi?

GAO: Only a few dozen miles.

EMPEROR: I have ordered the local authorities to build a new grave for Lady Yang. Go there as fast as you can and see that the work is quickly done. When I arrive, the reburial can take place.

凤仪去,先向马嵬行。"(下)(内侍暗下)(生)
"西川出狩乍东归,驻跸离宫对夕晖。记得
去年尝荔饭,一回追想一沾衣。"寡人自幸
蜀中,不觉一载有余。幸喜西京恢复,回到
此间,你看离宫寥寂,暮景苍凉。好伤感人
也!

【摊破金字令】黄昏近也,庭院凝微霭。清
宵静也,钟漏沉虚籁。一个愁人有谁偢睬?
已自难消难受,那堪墙外,又推这轮明月
来。寂寂照空阶,凄凄浸碧苔。独步增哀,
双泪频揩,千思万量没布摆。

　　寡人对着这轮明月,想起妃子冷骨荒
坟,愈觉伤心也!

【夜雨打梧桐】霜般白,雪样凯,照不到冷坟
台。好伤怀,独向婵娟陪待。蓦地回思当
日,与你偶尔离开,一时半刻也难打捱,何
况是今朝永隔幽明界。(泣介)我那妃子
呵,当初与你钗、盒定情,岂料遂为殉葬之
物。欢娱不再,只这盒钗,怎不向人间守,
翻教地下埋?

GAO: I will go at once, sire. (Gao Lishi *and the other eunuchs leave*)

EMPEROR:

> *Returning east from Chengdu*
> *And staying in this pleasure palace,*
> *As I gaze at the setting sun I remember*
> *The oatmeal I tasted here last year;*
> *And the thought of it makes me shed tears.*

Over a year has passed since I went to Chengdu, and now that Chang'an is in our hands again I am on my way back. But the pleasure palace is lonely and the evening is sad. How mournful it is!

> *As twilight falls and a light mist gathers,*
> *Through the still dusk the clear clepsydra sounds;*
> *But who can understand my unbearable anguish?*
> *Behind the wall rises the moon*
> *To shine in silence on the lonely steps*
> *Where green moss grows.*
> *I pace about in sadness and wipe my tears,*
> *Not knowing how to contain my grief.*

The sight of the moon makes me think of my darling lying cold in her lonely grave, and this makes me more sad.

> *The moonlight is white as frost or snow,*
> *But it cannot shine through the cold, cold clay;*
> *And sadly I watch it alone.*
> *In the past if I left you even for a moment,*
> *I found it hard to bear;*
> *But now cruel death has parted us for ever.*

(*He weeps.*) Ah, my darling, when we pledged our love with the hairpin and the jewel box, little did I think they would so soon be buried with you.

> *Our happiness is gone,*
> . *The tokens of love*
> *Are no more in the world of men*
> *But under the earth.*

(叹介)咳,妃子,妃子,想你生前音容如昨,教我怎生忘记也!

【摊破金字令】【换头】休说他娇鬓妍笑,风流不复偕,就是赪颜微怒,泪眼慵抬,便千金何处买。纵别有佳人,一般姿态,怎似伊情投意解,恰可人怀。思量到此呆打孩。我想妃子既殁,朕此一身虽生犹死,倘得死后重逢,可不强如独活。孤独愧形骸,余生死亦该。惟只愿速离尘埃,早赴泉台,和伊地中将连理栽。

记得当年七夕,与妃子同祝女牛,共成密誓,岂知今宵月下,单留朕一人在此也!

【夜雨打梧桐】长生殿,曾下阶,细语倚香腮。两情谐,愿结生生恩爱。谁想那夜双星同照,此夕孤月重来。时移境易人事改。月儿,月儿,我想密誓之时,你也一同听见的!记鹊桥河畔,也有你姮娥在,如何厮赖!索应该撺掇他牛和女,完成咱盒共钗。

(内侍上)夜色已深,请万岁爷进宫安息。

(生)银河漾漾月辉辉, 崔橹

万乘凄凉蜀路归。 崔道融

香散艳消如一梦, 王道

离魂渐逐杜鹃飞。 韦庄

(*He sighs.*) How shall I ever forget how you looked and spoke?

> *Her enchanting laughter is no more,*
> *Nor her adorable frowns;*
> *And not all the gold in the world can buy back*
> *Her blushes, her anger and her tears.*
> *Even if other beauties resemble her,*
> *No other understands and delights me so well.*
> *Thinking of her I am numb with sorrow;*
> *And since she is dead, I too am more dead than alive.*
> *If I could but meet her after death,*
> *I would rather die than continue living alone;*
> *I am tired of life and long to be in my grave,*
> *To leave this world and enter the nether regions,*
> *Rejoining her under the earth.*

I remember how we prayed to the stars on the seventh day of the seventh moon and made a secret vow; but now I am all alone under the moonlight.

> *In the Palace of Eternal Youth*
> *We came hand in hand down the steps,*
> *Whispering cheek to cheek*
> *And swearing to love for ever.*
> *Who could tell that, though the two stars shone on us both,*
> *Today the lonely moon would reappear*
> *To find so great a change in the world of men?*

Ah, Moon! When we made our vow, you must have heard it too; for you were there by the Milky Way. Can you deny it? *Will you not find the Weaving Maid and the Cowherd*

> *To help make our pledge of love come true?*

(*Enter an attendant.*)

ATTENDANT: It is after midnight. Will it please Your Majesty to go into the palace to rest?

(***Exeunt.***)

第四十一出　驿备

【越调过曲】【梨花儿】(副净扮驿丞上)我做驿丞没偏僱,缺供应付常吃打。今朝驾到不是耍,嗏,若有差迟便拿去杀。

自家马嵬驿丞,从小衙门办役。考了杂职行头,挨选马嵬大驿。虽然陆路冲繁,却喜津贴饶溢。送分例,落下些折头;造销算,开除些马匹。日支正项俸薪,还要月扣衙门工食。怕的是公吏承差,吓的是徒犯驿卒。求买免,设定常规;比月钱,百般威逼。及至摆站缺人,常把屁都急出。今更有大事临头,太上皇来此驻跸。连忙唤各色匠人,将驿舍周围收拾。又因改葬贵妃娘娘,重把坟茔建立。恐土工窥见玉体,要另选女工四百。报道高公公已到,催办工程紧急。若还误了些儿,(弹纱帽介)怕此头要短一尺。(末扮驿卒上)(见介)老爹,我已将各匠催齐,你放心,不须忧戚。(副净)还有女工呢?(末)现有四百女工,都在驿门齐集。(副净)快唤进来。(末唤介)女工每

426

SCENE 41

Preparations at the Station

(*Enter the station master of Mawei.*)
STATION MASTER:

A station master has a hard life,
When supplies are not enough, I get a beating;
And now the emperor is coming, it's no joke,
For if anything goes wrong I shall lose my head.

I am the station master of Mawei. As a young man I served as runner in the district government, and after passing the examination I was appointed to this big station. Many couriers pass this way and there is money in it for me, because I always take something from the tribute, and I get more by cutting the number of horses. Then, apart from my regular salary, I squeeze something out to the workers' food each month. The only thing I'm afraid of is these public duties; still, I can lord it over the conscripts and grooms. I've fixed rates for men who want to avoid conscription, and various means of extorting monthly dues. Only the shortage of hands sometimes leaves me in a fix. Now something big is coming: the old emperor will soon be here. I've ordered my men to tidy up the place at once, and a new grave is being built to rebury Lady Yang. In order that her body won't be seen by any men, I've had to get four hundred women workers. I hear His Lordship Gao has arrived and is urging them to work faster. If it isn't ready in time, (*He beats his official cap.*) I'm afraid I shall lose my head and grow one foot shorter.

(*Enter a station attdendant.*)

ATTENDANT: It's all right, sir; I've got all the workers ready.
STATION MASTER: What about the women workers?
ATTENDANT: There are four hundred women at the door.
STATION MASTER: Call them in.

427

走动。（贴、净、杂扮村妇，丑短须女扮，各携锹锄上）"本是村庄妇，来充埋筑人。"（见介）女工每叩头。（末）起来点名。（副净点介）周二妈。（净应）（副净）吴姥姥。（贴应）（副净）郑胖姑。（杂应）（副净）尤大姐。（丑掩口作娇声应介）（副净作细看介）咦，怎么这个女工掩着了嘴答应，一定有些蹊跷。驿子与我看来。（末应扯丑手开看介）老爹，是个胡子。（副净）是男，是女？（丑）是女。（副净）女人的胡子，那里有生在嘴上的，我不信。驿子，再把他裤裆里搜一搜。（末应作搜丑，诨介）老爹，这胡子是假充女工的。（副净）哎呀，了不得，这是上用钦工，非同小可。亏得我老爹精细，若待皇帝看见，险些把我这颗头，断送在你胡子嘴上了。好打，好打。（丑）只因老爹这里催得紧，本村凑得三百九十九名，单单少了一名，故此权来充数，明日另换便了。（副净）也罢，快打出去。（末应，打丑下）（副净看众笑介）如今我老爹疑

428

ATTENDANT (*Calling out*): Women, come on in.

(*Enter the women workers with hoes and picks, among them a man with a short beard disguised as a woman.*)

WOMEN: We are countrywomen conscripted to work as grave diggers. (*They greet the station master.*)

ATTENDANT: Get up. We're going to call the roll.

STATION MASTER (*Reading from a list*): Aunty Zhou. (*The first woman answers.*) Mistress Wu. (*The second woman answers.*) Stout Zheng. (*The third woman answers.*) Mistress You. (*The fourth woman puts her hand over her mouth and answers in a tiny voice.*)

STATION MASTER (*Looking at the fourth woman closely*): Why should you hide your mouth? There's something strange here. Attendant, have a look at her!

ATTENDANT (*Pulling the hand from the woman's mouth*): Sir, this fourth woman has a beard.

STATION MASTER: Is she a man or a woman?

ATTENDANT: A woman, sir.

STATION MASTER: How can a woman have a beard? I don't believe it. Make an investigation.

ATTENDANT (*Searching the woman*): Sir, this is a man disguised as a woman.

STATION MASTER: Hell and damnation! This work is for the emperor; it isn't an ordinary job. It's a good thing I'm so alert. If the emperor saw that beard, I would lose my head. Give the man a good beating.

FOURTH WOMAN: It's because your men insisted on four hundred women, sir, and there are only three hundred and ninety-nine in this village; so I had to come to make up the mumber. Tomorrow we shall try to find another woman somewhere.

STATION MASTER: All right. Throw him out.

(*The attendant drives him out.*)

(*Enter* Mistress Wang, the *inn-keeper.*)

WANG:

In order to present the silk stocking to the emperor,

心起来，只怕连你每也不是女人哩。（众笑介）我每都是女人。（副净）口说无凭，我老爹只要用手来大家摸一摸，才信哩。（作捞摸，众作躲避走笑介）（净）笑你老爹好长手，（杂）刚刚摸着一个繫别带。（副净）弄了一手白鋆香，（贴）拿去房中好下酒。（浑介）（老旦一面上）"欲将锦袜献天子，权把铧锹充女工。"老身王嬷嬷，自从拾得杨娘娘锦袜，过客争求一看，赚了许多钱钞。目今闻说老万岁爷回来，一则收藏禁物，恐有祸端，二则将此袜献上，或有重赏，也未可知。恰好驿中金报女工，要去撺上一名。葬完就好进献，来此已是驿前了。（末上见介）你这老婆子，那里来的？（老旦）来投充女工的。（末）住着。（进介）老爹，有一个投充女工的老婆子在外。（副净）唤进来。（末出，唤老旦进见介）（副净）你是投充女工的么？（老旦）正是。（副净）我看你年纪老了些，怕做不得工。只是现少一名，急切里没有人，就把你顶上罢。你叫甚名字？（老旦）叫做王嬷嬷。（副净）好，好！恰好周、吴、郑、王四人。你四人就做个工头，每一人管领女工九十九人。住在驿中操演，伺候驾到便了。（众）晓得。（做各见浑介）（副净）你每各拿了锹锄，待我老爹亲自教演一番。（众应各拿锹锄，副净作教演势，众学介）（副净）

【亭前柳】锹镢手中拿，挖掘要如法。莫教

430

I have brought a hoe and come here as a worker.
I am Mistress Wang. Since I picked up Lady Yang's silk stocking, many passers-by have wanted to see it and I've made a lot of money. Now I hear the old emperor has returned, and I'm afraid if I keep it I may get into trouble;
but if I present it to him I may be given a reward. It's lucky that the station is conscripting women workers. I'll join them, then after the reburial I can present this stocking. Here I am at the station.

(*Enter the attendant.*)

ATTENDANT: Where are you from, old woman?

WANG: I've come to join the women workers.

ATTENDANT: Wait here. (*He goes in.*) Sir, here's an old woman who wants to work with the others.

STATION MASTER: Bring her in. (*The attendant goes out and fetches* Mistress Wang *in.*) Do you want to join in this work?

WANG: Yes, sir.

STATION MASTER: You look rather old; I don't suppose you're fit for much. Still, we're one woman short, and we shan't be able to get anyone else right away; so you'll do. What's your name?

WANG: My name is Wang.

STATION MASTER: All right. You four—Zhou, Wu, Zheng and Wang can be the foremen. Each of you be responsible for ninety-nine workers. Stay in the station to practise what you are to do while we wait for His Majesty to arrive.

WOMEN: Yes, sir. (*They greet each other.*)

STATION MASTER: Take up your tools now, and I'll show you what to dio.

(*They pick up their tools and the station master makes movements which they imitate.*)

Hold your tools like this;
This is the way to dig;
You mustn't touch the lady's body,
But part the soil with care.

431

侵玉体,仔细拨黄沙。(合)大家、演习须熟
沉,此奉钦遵,切休得有争差。

　　(众)老爹,我每呵,
【前腔】田舍业桑麻,惯见弄泥沙。小心齐
用力,怎敢告消乏。(合)大家、演习须熟
滑,此奉钦遵,切休得有争差。

　　(副净)且到里边连夜操演去。(众应
介)

　　　　　　玉颜虚掩马嵬尘,　高骈
　　　　　　云雨虽亡日月新。　郑畋
　　　　　　晓向平原陈祭礼,　方干
　　　　　　共瞻銮驾重来巡。　僧广宣

TOGETHER:
> *We must practise till we're sure of what to do,*
> *And can carry out orders correctly.*

WOMEN: Sir,
> *We're all used to work on the land,*
> *And used to digging;*
> *We shall take great care and do our best,*
> *And not complain of feeling tired.*

TOGETHER:
> *We must practise till we're sure of what to do,*
> *And can carry out orders correctly.*

STATION MASTER: Go on in, then, and practise till you can do it right.

> (*They assent and troop off.*)

> (***Exeunt.***)

第四十二出　改葬

【商调引子】【忆秦娥】(生引二内侍上)伤心处,天旋日转回龙驭。回龙驭,踟蹰到此,不能归去。

　　寡人自蜀回銮,痛伤妃子仓卒捐生,未成礼葬。特传旨另备珠襦玉匣,改建坟茔,待朕亲临迁葬,因此驻跸马嵬驿中。(泪介)对着这佛堂梨树,好凄惨人也!

【商调过曲】【山坡羊】恨悠悠江山如故,痛生生游魂血污。冷清清佛堂半间,绿阴阴一本梨花树。空自吁,怕夜台人更苦。那里有珮环夜月归朱户,也慢想颜面春风识画图。(丑暗上).

(见介)奴婢奉旨,筑造贵妃娘娘新坟,俱已齐备。请万岁爷亲临启墓。(生)传旨起

434

SCENE 42
The Reburial

(*Enter the emperor with two eunuchs.*)
EMPEROR:

The heavens have revolved,
The sun has come out again,
And the emperor's carriage is on its way back to Chang'an;
But at Mawei I hesitate, loth to go on.

I am on my way back from Chengdu. Because of my distress over
Lady Yang's death in the mutiny and the fact that she had no
proper burial, I have ordered pearl-decked garments and a marble
casket to be prepared, and a new grave built. And in order to
attend the interment myself, I have come to stay at Mawei Station.
(*He sheds tears.*) The sight of the Buddhist shrine and the pear
tree only brings my loss home to me more keenly.

To me, in my endless sorrow,
These surroundings are unchanged;
But it tortures me to think of her wandering spirit.
By the lonely Buddhist shrine,
The pear tree casts a cool green shade;
All my sighs are useless,
Yet she in the nether world must be suffering more.
No more will her spirit return to the palace,
Her pendants tinkling under the moon;
Nor can I hope to see her face again,
Fresh as the sights of spring!

(*Enter Gao Lishi.*)
GAO: As Your Majesty directed, I have superintended the building
of a new grave for Lady Yang. Now everything is ready,
whenever it pleases you to begin the ceremony.
EMPEROR: Order my carriage.

435

驾。领旨。（传介）军士每，排驾。（杂扮军
士上，引行介）"马嵬坡下泥土中，不见玉容
空死处。"（到介）（丑）启万岁爷，这白杨树
下，就是娘娘埋葬之处了。（生）你看蔓草
春深，悲风日薄。妃子，妃子，兀的不痛杀
寡人也。（哭）号呼，叫声声魂在无？歊歔，
哭哀哀泪渐枯。

　　（老旦、杂、贴、净四女工带锄上）（老旦）老
万岁爷来了。我每快些前去，伺候开坟。
（丑）你每都是女工么？（众应介）（丑启生介）
女工每到齐了。（生）传旨，军士回避。高
力士，你去监督女工，小心开掘。（丑应传
介）（军士下）（众女工作掘介）（众）
【水红花】向高岗一谜下锹锄，认当初，白杨
一树。怕香销翠冷伴蚍蜉，粉肌枯，玉容难
睹。（众惊介）掘下三尺，只有一个空穴，并
不见娘娘玉体！早难道为云为雨，飞去影

GAO: Yes, sire, (*He passes on the order.*) Guards, prepare the carriage! (*Guards walk in.*)

GUARDS:

> *Under the slope, deep in the ground,*
> *We search for the buried beauty;*
> *But nothing remains of her save the burial place.*

GAO: Your Majesty, it was under this poplar tree that Lady Yang was buried.

EMPEROR: Ah, the weeds have grown rank in spring, and the wind is moaning. Take pity, my darling, on my wretchedness! (*He weeps.*)

> *I groan and call your name;*
> *Is your spirit here?*
> *I weep till my tears run dry.*

(*Enter* Mistress Wang *and three other women workers with hoes.*)

WANG: The old emperor is here. Let us hurry over, ready to open the grave.

GAO: Are you the women workers? (*They assent.*)

GAO (*To the emperor*): The women are here.

EMPEROR: Order the guards to withdraw for the time being. Inspect the women's work, Gao Lishi, and make sure that they take great care.

(Gao *passes on the order, and the guards march out. The women start to dig.*)

WOMEN:

> *With picks and hoes we level the mound*
> *Marked by the poplar;*
> *But we fear that her sweetness has gone,*
> *Like the mayfly that lives just one day;*
> *Her white skin must have withered,*
> *Her beauty must have vanished.*

(*Startled.*) We have dug three feet down; but there is only an empty hole, with no sign of Lady Yang's body.

> *How could she disappear,*
> *Leaving no trace behind?*

都无,但只有芳香四散袭人裾也罗。

(净)呀,是一个香囊。(丑)取来看。(净递囊,丑接看哭介)我那娘娘呵,你每且到那厢伺候去。(众应下)(丑启生介)启万岁爷,墓已启开,却是空穴。连裹身的锦褥和殉葬的金钗、钿盒都不见了。只有一个香囊在此。(生)有这等事!(接囊看大哭介)呀,这香囊乃当日妃子生辰,在长生殿上试舞"霓裳",赐与他的。我那妃子呵,你如今却在何处也!

【山坡羊】惨凄凄一匼空墓,杳冥冥玉人何去?便做虚飘飘锦褥儿化尘,怎那硬撑撑钗盒也无寻处。空剩取香囊犹在土,寻思不解缘何故,恨不得唤起山神责问渠。(想介)高力士,你敢记差了么?(丑)奴婢当日,曾削杨树半边,题字为记。如何得差!(生)敢是被人发掘了?(丑)若经发掘,怎得留下香囊?(生呆想不语介)(丑)奴婢想来,自古神仙多有尸解之事。或者娘娘尸解仙去,也未可知。即如桥山陆寝,止葬黄帝衣冠。这香囊原是娘娘临终所佩,将来葬入新坟之内,也是一般了。(生)说的有理。高力士,就将这香囊裹以珠襦,盛以玉匣,依礼安葬便了。(丑)领旨。(生哭介)

There is only a sweet smell
Which perfumes all around.

ONE WOMAN: Oh, look! Here is a scented pouch!

GAO: Bring it to me. (*The woman brings over the pouch, and* Gao *weeps when he sees it.*) Alas, my lady! You women wait over there. (*The women go out.*) Your Majesty, the grave has been opened, but it is empty. Even the silk quilt wrapped round the body and the gold hairpin and the jewel box that were buried with her have disappeaerd. There is nothing left but this scented pouch.

EMPEROR: How could that be? (*He takes the pouch from* Gao *and weeps.*) I gave her this pouch on her birthday, after she had danced the Rainbow Garment Dance at the Palace of Eternal Youth. Where are you now, my darling?

The grave is gone!
My fair one is gone!
But even if the silk quilt had turned to dust,
How can we account for the durable hairpin and the box?
Why is there only the scented pouch in her grave?
I wish I could summon the fountain god
To question him.

(*He thinks.*) Can you be mistaken, Gao Lishi?

GAO: That day I peeled off part of the bark of the poplar, and wrote on the tree to mark the place. How could I mistake it?

EMPEROR: Could her body have been exhumed?

GAO: But in that case, why should the scented pouch have been left? (*The emperor reflects in silence.*) There have been many cases, sire, of immortals who were raised from the dead. Perhaps Her Ladyship has attained immortality. In the sepulchre of the Yellow Emperor at Qiaoshan, only the emperor's clothes were buried; and since this pouch was worn by Her Ladyship when she died, if we bury it in the new grave it will serve the same purpose.

EMPEROR: You are right. Wrap this scented pouch in the pearl-decked garments, put them in the marble casket, and let the burial take place with due ceremony.

GAO: It shall be done, sire.

439

号呼,叫声声魂在无?欷歔,哭哀哀泪渐枯。

（丑持囊出介）（作盛囊入匣介）香囊盛放停当,女工每那里?（众上）（丑)你每把这玉匣,放在墓中,快些封起坟来。（众作筑坟介）

【水红花】当时花貌与香躯,化虚无,一抔空墓;今朝玉匣与珠襦,费工夫,重泉深锢。更立新碑一统,细把泪痕书。从今流恨满山隅也罗。

（丑)坟已封完,每人赏钱一贯。去罢。（众谢赏、叩头介)(净、贴、杂先下)(丑问老旦介)你这婆子,为何不去?(老旦)禀上公公,老妇人旧年在马嵬坡下,拾得杨娘娘锦袜一只,带来献上老万岁爷。（丑)待我与你启奏。（见生介)启万岁爷,有个女工,说拾得杨娘娘锦袜一只,带来献上。(生)快宣过来。（丑唤老旦进见介)婢子叩见老万岁爷。（献袜介)(生)取上来。（丑取送生介)(老旦起立介)(生看哭介)呀,果然是妃子的锦袜,你

440

EMPEROR:

> *I groan and call your name;*
> *Is your spirit here?*
> *I weep till my tears run dry.*

(Gao *puts the pouch in the casket.*)

GAO: Now the pouch is in its place. Where are the women workers?

(*The women enter.*)

GAO: Put the marble casket in the grave, and seal it quickly.

(*They build the grave.*)

WOMEN:

> *Her flowr-like beauty and sweetness have turned to nothing,*
> *And the grave is empty.*
> *In the marble casket, beside the pearl-decked garments,*
> *The scented pouch is buried again in the earth;*
> *A new inscription has been written with tears,*
> *And sorrow will haunt these lonely hills for ever.*

GAO: Now that you have sealed up the grave, I will give you a string of cash apiece as reward. You may go.

(*The women bow in thanks, and all but* Mistress Wang *go out.*)

GAO: (*To* Mistress Wang): Why are you still here, old woman?

WANG: My lord, last year I picked up one of Lady Yang's silk stocking at the foot of Mawei Slope, and I have brought it here to present to the old emperor.

GAO: Wait, while I report this. (*To the emperor.*) Your Majesty, there is a woman here who says she picked up a silk stocking belonging to Lady Yang and has brought it to present to Your Majesty.

EMPEROR: Bring her in at once.

(Gao Lishi *calls* Mistress Wang *to enter.*)

WANG: Long live the emperor! (*She kneels and holds out the stocking.*)

EMPEROR: Bring it here.

(Gao Lishi *takes the stocking and gives it to the emperor.* Mistress Wang *rises.*)

EMPEROR (*With tears*): Yes, this is her stocking. Her perfume

441

看芳香未散,莲印犹存。我那妃子呵,(哭
介)

【山坡羊】俊弯弯一钩重睹,暗濛濛余香犹
度。袅亭亭记当年翠盘,瘦尖尖稳逐红鸳
舞。还忆取、深宵残醉余,梦酣春透勾人
觑。今日里空伴香囊留恨俱。(哭介)号
呼,叫声声魂在无? 欷歔,哭哀哀泪渐枯。

高力士,赐他金钱五千贯,就着在此看守
贵妃坟墓。(老旦叩头介)多谢老万岁爷。
(起出看锄介)"无心再学持锄女,有钞甘为
守墓人。"(下)(外引四军上)"见辟乾坤新定
位,看题日月更高悬。"(见介)臣朔方节度
使郭子仪,钦奉上命,带领卤簿,恭迎太上
皇圣驾。(生)卿荡平逆寇,收复神京,宗庙
重新,乾坤再造,真不世之功也。(外)臣忝
为大帅,破贼已迟,负罪不遑,何功之有!
(生)卿说那里话来,高力士,分付起行。

still clings to it, and the imprint of her foot is still clear. Ah, my love—

> *I see your delicate stocking again,*
> *With some of your fragrance about it still.*
> *It recalls the sight of your shapely feet*
> *As they danced on the emerald disk,*
> *Or tempted me in my sleep*
> *After we had drunk deeply late into the night.*
> *But now the stocking and the fragrant pouch*
> *Bring only sorrow.* (*He weeps.*)
> *I groan and call your name;*
> *Is your spirit here?*
> *I weep till my tears run dry.*

Gao Lishi, give this woman five thousand strings of cash as a reward, and let her stay here to watch Lady Yang's grave.

WANG (*Kowtows*): I thank Your Majesty! (*She goes out looking at her hoe.*)

> *Now I shan't have to use this hoe any more.*
> *I've got money and the job of minding the grave!*

(*Exit.*)

(*Enter* Commander Guo Ziyi *with four soldiers.*)

GUO ZIYI:

> *Order is now restored in the world;*
> *The sun and moon are hanging on high.*

(*He greets the emperor.*) Your subject, Guo Ziyi, military governor of the Northern Circuit, has come by His Majesty's order with a cortege to welcome your return, sire.

EMPEROR: Yours was a truly remarkable achievement, my lord. You succeeded in wiping out the rebels and recovering the capital, so that the imperial sacrifice could be renewed and the empire rebuilt.

GUO ZIYI: I was late in crushing the rebels; therefore I deserve punishment and can claim no credit.

EMPEROR: No one can say that, my lord. Gao Lishi, order the

443

（丑）领旨。（传介）（生更吉服介）（众引生行
介）

【水红花】五云芝盖簇銮舆，返皇都，旌旗溢
路。黄童白叟共相扶，尽欢呼，天颜重睹。
从此新丰行乐，少帝奉兴居。千秋万载巩
皇图也罗。

　　　　肠断将军改葬归，徐夤
　　　　下山回马尚迟迟。杜牧
　　　　经过此地千年恨，刘沧
　　　　空有香囊和泪滋。郑嵎

carriage to proceed.

GAO: Yes, sire. (*He passes on the order.*)

(*The emperor changes into ceremonial dress, and they move on.*)

ALL:

> Under canopies with auspicious cloud designs,
> The imperial carriage returns;
> The road to the capital is lined with flags,
> Old and young cheer at the sight of his sacred face;
> Henceforth the aged emperor will rest in comfort,
> While his son reigns in his place;
> And the empire will be safe for ever and ever.

(***Exeunt.***)

第四十三出　怂合

【南吕引子】【阮郎归】(小生上)碧梧天上叶初飞,秋风又报期。云中遥望鹊桥齐,隔河影半迷。

　　"岂是仙家好别离,故教迢递作佳期。只缘碧落银河畔,好在金风玉露时。"吾乃牵牛是也。今当下界上元二年七月七夕,天孙将次渡河,因此先在河边伺候。记得天宝十载,吾与天孙相会之时,见唐天子与贵妃杨玉环,在长生殿上拜祷设誓,愿世世为夫妇。岂料转眼之间,把玉环生生断送,好不可怜人也。

【南吕过曲】【香偏满】佳人绝世,千秋第一冤祸奇。把无限绸缪轻抛弃,可怜非得已。死生无见期,空留万种悲,枉罚下多情誓。

【朝天懒】【朝天子】(贴引杂扮二仙女上)好会

446

SCENE 43

The Gods Pity the Lovers

(*Enter the* Heavenly Cowherd.)

COWHERD:

> *Green plane trees shed their leaves,*
> *As the autumn wind heralds our festival;*
> *In the clouds I see the magpies build our bridge,*
> *And I look across the stream for my Weaving Maid.*
> *The gods are not in favour of separation.*
> *Yet our meeting time is fixed;*
> *The Milky Way is our only trysting place,*
> *During the time of autumn wind and dew.*

I am the Cowherd. In the world of men today is the seventh day of the seventh moon in the second year of the Shangyuan period. Soon the Weaving Maid will be crossing the Milky Way, so I am waiting for her by the stream. I remember in the tenth year of the Tianbao period, when I met my love we saw the Tang emperor and Lady Yang praying and making a vow in the Palace of Eternal Youth, because they wanted to be lovers for ever. But soon after that the unhappy was sacrificed.

> *She was such a beautiful lady,*
> *Yet she suffered such a great wrong;*
> *For against her will she cast away*
> *A life of unbounded love and joy;*
> *And now separated by death,*
> *The unhappy couple will never meet again.*
> *Only sorrow is left to them,*
> *And their vow of love is vain.*

(*Enter the* Weaving Maid *with two fairies.*)

WEAVING MAID:

> *Every year in heaven the lovers meet,*

447

年年天上期,不似尘缘浅,有变移。【水红花】见仙郎河畔独徘徊,把驾频催。(杂报介)天孙到。(小生迎介)天孙来了。(同织女对拜介)(合)【懒画眉】相逢一笑深深拜,隔岁离情各自知。

(小生)天孙,请同到斗牛宫去。(携贴行介)携手步云中,(贴)仙裙飐好风。(合)河明乌鹊渚,星聚斗牛宫。(到介)(杂暗下)

(小生)天孙请坐。(坐介)

【二犯梧桐树】【金梧桐】琼花绕绣帷,霞锦摇珠珮。(贴合)斗府星宫,岁岁今宵会。【梧桐树】银河碧落神仙配,地久天长,岂但朝朝暮暮期。【五更转】愿教他人世上夫妻辈,都似我和伊,永远成双作对。

(小生)天孙,

【浣溪纱】你且慢提,人间世、有一处怎偏忘记?(贴)忘了何处?(小生)可记得长生殿里人一对,曾向我焚香密誓齐?(贴)此李

448

Unlike lovers on earth who are fickle;
I see the Cowherd waiting beyond the stream,
And hurry on in my carriage.

FAIRIES: (*Calling out*): The Heavenly Weaving Maid is here.

COWHERD (*Meeting her*): So you have come.

(*They greet each other.*)

TOGETHER:
Meeting again we smile and bow to each other,
And realize how much
Each has missed the other during the past year.

COWHERD;
Come now to the palace. (*They walk arm in arm.*)
Arm in arm we walk in the clouds.

WEAVING MAID:
The cool breeze rustles my fairy skirt.

TOGETHER:
The moon shines bright over the magpies' ford.
And the stars have clustered around the Milky Way.

(*The fairies leave.*)

COWHERD: Let us sit down. (*They take seats.*)
Here fairy blossoms grow by embroidered curtains,
And your pearly pendants quiver on cloud-coloured silk.

WEAVING MAID:
In this palace of the stars,
We meet every year on this night,
A fairy couple by the Milky Way
Whose love is not only for a few days and nights,
But lasts for ever. We wish all lovers on earth
Could remain together for ever like us.

COWHERD: One monent, though.
You have forgotten one couple on the earth.

WEAVING MAID: Whom have I forgotten?

COWHERD:
Do you remember those two in the Palace of Eternal Youth
Who burnt incense and made a vow before us?

449

三郎与杨玉环之事也,我怎不记得。(小生)天孙既然记得,须念彼、堕万古伤心地,他愿世世生生,忍教中路分离。

(贴)提记玉环之事,委实可伤。我前因马嵬土地之奏,

【刘泼帽】念他独抱情无际,死和生守定不移,含冤流落幽冥地。因此呵,为他奏玉墀,令再证蓬莱位。

(小生笑介)天孙虽则如此,只是他呵,

【秋夜月】做玉妃、不过群仙队,寡鹄孤鸾白云内,何如并翼鸳鸯美。念盟言在彼,与圆成仗你。

(贴)仙郎,我岂不欲为他重续断缘。只是李三郎呵,

【东瓯令】他情轻断,誓先隳,那玉环呵,一个钟情枉自痴。从来薄幸男儿辈,多负了佳人意。伯劳东去燕西飞,怎使做双栖!

(小生)天孙所言,李三郎自应知罪。但是当日马嵬之变呵,

【金莲子】国事危,君王有令也反抗逼,怎救的、佳人命摧。想今日也不知怎生般悔恨与伤悲。

(贴)仙郎恁般说,李三郎罪有可原。他若果有悔心,再为证完前誓便了。(二杂上)启娘娘,天鸡将唱,请娘娘渡河。(贴)

WEAVING MAID: You mean the Tang emperor and Lady Yang. Of course I remember.

COWHERD: If you remember, think how unhappy they must be now.

They wished to be lovers for ever;
How could we let them be parted?

WEAVING MAID: Her story is really a sad one. When the tutelary god of Mawei told me of it, I was touched by

Her love which remained unaltered even in death,
And by the way she was wronged and condemned to wander
In the nether world; so I reported the matter
To the Heavenly Emperor, and he restored her
To the fairy mountain.

COWHERD (*Laughing*): Even so , that isn't good enough.

She may be a fairy ranked among the angels,
But torn from her lover she pines alone.
Since she made the vow, you should help her to fulfil it.

WEAVING MAID: It's not that I don't want to help her find her lover again; but since the emperor gave her up lightly and broke his pledge, she is tormenting herself for nothing.

There have always been heartless men who forsake their love;
And when two birds fly in opposite directions,
How can we bring them together again?

COWHERD: Of course, there's something in what you say, and the emperor ought to be feeling remorse. Still, that day during the mutiny—

The empire's fate hung in the balance,
And even the Son of Heaven had no power
To save her from death.
Today, I think, his heart must be torn with regret.

WEAVING MAID: If you say so, there may be some excuse for him. And if we find that he is really repentant, we can help to make their pledge come true.

(*Enter the two fairies.*)

FAIRIES: Madam, the heavenly cock will soon be crowing; it's time

451

就此告辞。(小生)河边相送。(携手行介)

【尾声】没来由将他人情事闲评议,把这度
良宵虚废。唉,李三郎、杨玉环,可知俺破
一夜工夫都着你!

云阶月地一相过,　杜牧

争奈闲思往事何!　白居易

一自仙娥归碧落,　刘沧

千秋休恨马嵬坡。　徐夤

to be going back across the Milky Way.

WEAVING MAID: I must bid you goodbye.

COWHERD: Let me see you to the bank. (*They walk arm in arm.*)
   We have wasted our trysting time
   Discussing problems that don't concern us.

Ah, Emperor Ming Huang and Lady Yang, do you know that
We have wasted a whole night because of you.

(***Exeunt.***)

第四十四出　雨梦

【越调引子】【霜天晓角】(生上)愁深梦杳，白发添多少？最苦佳人逝早，伤独夜，恨闲宵。

"不堪闲夜雨声频，一念重泉一怆神。挑尽灯花眠不得，凄凉南内更何人？"朕自幸蜀还京，退居南内，每日只是思想妃子。前在马嵬改葬，指望一睹遗容，不想变为空穴，只剩香囊一个。不知果然尸解还是玉化香消？徒然展转寻思，怎得见他一面？今夜对着这一庭苦雨、半壁愁灯，好不凄凉人也！

【越调过曲】【小桃红】冷风掠雨战长宵，听点点都向那梧桐哨也。萧萧飒飒，一齐暗把乱愁敲，才住了又还飘。那堪是凤帏空，串烟销，人独坐，厮凑着孤灯照也，恨同听没个娇娆。(泪介)猛想着旧欢娱，止不住泪痕交。

(内打初更介)(小生内唱，生作听介)呀，何处歌声，凄凄入耳，得非梨园旧人乎？不

454

SCENE 44
A Rainy Night

(*Enter the emperor.*)

EMPEROR;

> *My grief is so great, I can find no comfort in dreams;*
> *And my hair is turning white*
> *As I mourn for my love who died so soon,*
> *Leaving me lonely at night.*
> *The sound of rain at night is hard to bear,*
> *Thinking of her, my heart is racked with pain;*
> *I trim the candle, for I cannot sleep:*
> *Who else within the palace is sad as I?*

Since my return to the capital I have taken no part in affairs of state, spending my days thinking of Lady Yang. At the reburial at Mawei I hoped to see her once again; but the grave was empty except for her scented pouch, and we could not tell whether she had been carried to heaven or whether her body had decayed. Though I long for her all night, I can never see her again. Tonight with this sad rain and this mournful lamp, I am overcome with grief.

> *Cold wind and rain contend in the endless night,*
> *Battering the creaking plane trees to make me grieve;*
> *The wind dies down only to howl again,*
> *A dreary sound, when here behind the curtain*
> *I am sitting alone by the lamp*
> *With no girl beside me to listen to the storm.*

(*He weeps.*)

> *As I think of past joys my cheeks are wet with tears.*

(*The first watch sounds offstage, and singing is heard in the distance. The emperor listens.*) Ah, where does this plaintive, far-off melody come from? Can it be one of my old musicians? I

455

免到帘前,凭阑一听。(作起立凭阑介)此张野狐之声也,且听他唱的是甚曲儿?(作一面听、一面欷歔掩泪介)(小生在场内立高处唱介)

【下山虎】万山蜀道,古栈岩峣。急雨催林杪,铎铃乱敲。似怨恨愁,碎聒不了,响应空山魂暗消。一声儿忽慢袅,一声儿忽紧摇。无限伤心事,被他逗挑,写入清商传恨遥。

(内二鼓介)(生悲介)呀,原来是朕所制"雨淋铃"之曲。记昔朕在栈道,雨中闻铃声相应,痛念妃子,因采其声,制成此曲。今夜闻之,想起蜀道悲凄,愈加肠断也。

【五韵美】听淋铃,伤怀抱。凄凉万种新旧绕,把愁人禁虐得十分恼。天荒地老,这种恨谁人知道。你听窗外雨声越发大了。疏还密,低复高,才合眼,又几阵窗前把人梦搅。

(丑上)"西宫南内多秋草,夜雨梧桐落叶时。"(见介)夜已深了,请万岁爷安寝罢。(内三鼓介)(生)呀,漏鼓三交,且自隐几而

456

will stand by the curtain in the corridor and listen. (*He rises and walks across to the balustrade.*) It is Zhang Yehu singing! Let me listen to his song. (*As he listens he sheds tears. The musician enters and stands on a step singing.*)

ZHANG:

> The steep path winds aross a thousand hills,
> And the way is rugged;
> When a squall of rain sweeps over the treetops,
> The bells on the pack-horses start ringing;
> And the sound is like a lament
> Which echoes on and on in the lonely hills,
> Now slow, now fast,
> To call forth all the anguish in men's hearts.
> And this I set down in music.

(*The second watch sounds offstage.*)

EMPEROR (*Sadly*): This is the tune I composed called "Bells in the Rain." When I was travelling through the mountains I heard bells ringing in the rain, and thought of her; so I expressed the sounds in music. Hearing this now reminds me of that sad journey, and I feel more broken-hearted than ever.

> The song of the bells in the rain tears at my heart,
> Old and new sorrows bind me in agony;
> And heaven and earth will come to an end,
> Before anyone can describe my misery.

Listen! The rain outside is falling faster, heavier and louder than ever. As soon as I close my eyes, it pours down again to waken me.

(*Enter* Gao Lishi.)

GAO:

> The autumn grass grows thick in the west palace;
> It is the time for leaves to fall,
> And rain beats on the plane trees in the night.

It is late, Your Majesty. Won't you rest?

(*The third watch sounds offstage.*)

EMPEROR: So it is midnight now. I will sleep here on the couch. I

457

卧。哎,今夜呵,知甚梦儿得到俺眼里来
也!(仰哭介)

【哭相思】悠悠生死别经年,魂魄不曾来入
梦。

　　(睡介)(丑)万岁爷睡了,咱家也去歇
息儿咱。(虚下)(小生、副净扮二内侍带剑上)
"幽情消未得,入梦感君王。"(向上跪介)万
岁爷请醒来。(生作醒看介)你二人是那里
来的?(小生、副净)奴婢奉杨娘娘之命,来
请万岁爷。

【五般宜】只为当日个乱军中祸殃惨遭,悄
地向人丛里换妆隐逃,因此上流落久蓬飘。
(生惊喜介)呀,原来杨娘娘不曾死,如今却
在那里?(小生、副净)为陛下朝想暮想,恨
紫愁绕,因此把驿庭静扫,(叩头介)望銮舆
幸早。说要把牛女会深盟,和君王续未了。

　　(生泪介)朕为妃子百般思想,那晓得
却在驿中。你二人快随朕前去,连夜迎回
便了。(小生、副净)领旨。(引生行介)

【山麻稽】【换头】喜听说如花貌,犹兀自现
在人间,当面堪邀。忙教、潜出了御苑内夹
城复道,顾不得夜深人静,露凉风冷,月黑

458

wonder what dreams will come to me tonight?

(*He weeps as he lies down.*)

> *Though death has parted us for over a year,*
> *Her spirit has never been near me even in dreams.*

(*He sleeps.*)

GAO: The emperor is asleep; I had better rest too. (*Exit.*)

(*Enter two attendants wearing swords.*)

ATTENDANTS (*Kneeling*): Wake up, Your Majesty!

EMPEROR (*Waking and seeing them*): Who are you?

ATTENDANTS: Lady Yang ordered us to come to invite Your Majesty to visit her.

> *The day that trouble broke out among the guards,*
> *She changed her dress and slipped away through the crowd,*
> *And she has been a wanderer ever since.*

EMPEROR (*Amazed and overjoyed*): What! So she did not die after all! Where is she now?

ATTENDANTS:

> *Her Ladyship has been longing for you, sire,*
> *Giving herself up to sorrow day and night;*
> *Now we have swept the station clean,*
> *We beg Your Majesty to come;*
> *For she longs to fulfil the pledge*
> *That you made that night before the stars.*

EMPEROR (*Shedding tears*): I have been longing for her all this time, little thinking that she was at the station still. Lead me there quickly. We will bring her back to the palace this very night.

ATTENDANTS: Your Majesty's orders shall be obeyed.

(*They lead the emperor on.*)

EMPEROR:

> *I hear with joy that her flower-like beauty*
> *Is still in the world of men;*
> *Hastily leaving the palace I slip through dark alleys,*
> *Though the night is late,*
> *The city is asleep,*
> *The dew and wind are cold,*

459

途遥。

（末上拦介）陛下久已安居南内，因何深夜微行，到那里去？（生惊介）

【恋牌令】何处泼官僚，拦驾语哓哓？（末）臣乃陈元礼，陛下快请回宫。（生怒介）咳，陈元礼，你当日在马嵬驿中，暗激军士逼死贵妃，罪不容诛。今日又待来犯驾么？君臣全不顾，辄敢肆狂骁。（末）陛下若不回宫，只怕六军又将生变。（生）咳，陈元礼，你欺朕无权柄，闲居退朝。只逞你有威风，卒悍兵骄。法难恕，罪怎饶。叫内侍，快把这乱臣贼子首级悬枭。

（小生、副净）领旨。（作拿末杀下，转介）启万岁爷已到驿前了。请万岁爷进去。（暗下）（生进介）

【黑麻令】只见没多半空寮、废寮，冷清清临着这荒郊、远郊。内侍，娘娘在那里？（回顾介）呀，怎一个也不见了。单则听飒刺刺风摇、树摇，啾唧唧四壁寒蛩，絮一片愁苗、

The moonlight is dim
And the way is far.

(Commander Chen Yuanli *enters and bars the way.*)

CHEN: Your Majesty should be inside the palace. Why are you wandering out incognito at night?

EMPEROR (*Startled*): Who is this rough officer who stops me so rudely?

CHEN: I am Commander Chen Yuanli. Will it please Your Majesty to return to the palace?

EMPEROR (*Angrily*): Curse you, Chen Yuanli! That day in Mawei Station you incited the guards and forced Lady Yang to commit suicide. Execution is too good for you. How dare you oppose me again,

Not recognizing my authority,
But behaving with such arrogance?

CHEN: If Your Majesty will not go back, the troops may mutiny again.

EMPEROR: Curse you again!

You think because I have given up the throne
That I have no more authority!
You rely on your troops to take such liberties.
This cannot be forgiven. Here!
Cut off this rebel's head!

ATTENDANTS: It shall be done, sire. (*They seize* Chen *and drag him off to kill him, then return.*) Your Majesty, we have reached the station. Will it please you to enter?

(*Exeunt.*)

EMPEROR (*Entering*):

I see the empty stables,
Lonely in the desolate wilderness.

Attendants, lead me to my lady! (*He looks round.*) Where have they gone?

I hear only the wind as it sighs through the trees,
And the shrill notes of insects all around.
My heart is breaking with sorrow. (*He weeps.*)

461

怨苗。（哭介）哎哟，我那妃子呵，叫不出花娇、月娇，料多应形消、影消。（内鸣锣，生惊介）呀，好奇怪，一霎时连驿亭也都不见，倒来曲江池上了。好一片大水也。不堤防断砌颓坦，翻做了惊涛、沸涛。

（望介）你看大水中间，又涌出一个怪物。猪首龙身，舞爪张牙，奔突而来。好怕人也！（内鸣锣，扮猪龙、项带铁索、跳上扑生，生惊奔，赶至原处睡介）（二金甲神执锤上，击猪龙喝介）咄，孽畜，好无礼！怎又逃出，到此惊犯圣驾，还不快去。（作牵猪龙、打下）（生作惊叫介）哎哟，唬杀我也。（丑急上、扶介）万岁爷，为何梦中大叫？（生作呆坐、定神介）高力士，外边什么响？（丑）是梧桐上的雨声？（内打四更介）（生）

【江神子】【别体】我只道谁惊残梦飘，原来是乱雨萧萧。恨杀他枕边不肯相饶，声声点点到寒梢，只待把泼梧桐锯倒。

高力士，朕方才梦见两个内侍，说杨娘娘在马嵬驿中来请朕去。多应芳魂未散。朕想昔时汉武帝思念李夫人，有李少君为之召魂相见，今日岂无其人！你待天明，可即传旨，遍觅方士来与杨娘娘召魂。（丑）

Ah, my darling,

   Though I call my beauty she will not appear to me;
   She must have vanished again.

(*Gongs sound offstage, and the emperor gives a start.*)

That is strange. The station has vanished, and I have come to the
River Bend. What a great flood!

   The ruins have changed
   Into angry, seething waves.

(*He looks round.*) See, a monster is coming out of the water! It
has the head of a pig and the body of a dragon; and it is rushing
towards me with threatening tusks and claws.

(*Gongs sound offstage, and a monster with iron chains on its neck*
rushes forward to attack the emperor, who runs in fright back to
the couch. Two gods in gold armour, carrying maces, enter and
beat off the monster.)

GODS: How dare you, monster! How dare you escape and frighten
His Majesty? Go back now, quickly? (*They beat the monster and*
drag it off.)

EMPEROR (*Startled*): Ah, I have had the fright of my life.

(Gao Lishi *hurries in.*)

GAO: Did you call out in your sleep, sire?

EMPEROR (*Dazed, sitting up on the couch*): What is that noise
outside, Gao Lishi?

GAO: It is only rain on the plane trees.

(*The fourth watch sounds offstage.*)

EMPEROR:

   I wondered what had woken me from my dream;
   It was only the rain beating down on the frozen treetops.
   I shall have these wretched trees cut down!

Just now I dreamed, Gao Lishi, that two attendants came to tell
me Lady Yang was in Mawei Station and wanted me to go there. It
must have been her spirit that caused this dream. In ancient times,
when Emperor Wu of the Han Dynasty mourned for Lady Li, a
necromancer summoned her spirit for him. There must still be such
necromancers today. As soon as dawn breaks, order one to be

领旨。（内五鼓介）（生）

【尾声】纷纷泪点如珠掉，梧桐上雨声厮闹。

只隔着一个牕儿直滴到晓。

半壁残灯闪闪明，吴融

雨中因想雨淋铃。罗隐

伤心一觉兴亡梦，方壶居士

直欲裁书问杳冥。魏朴

found to summon Lady Yang's spirit.

GAO: It shall be done, sire.

(*The fifth watch sounds offstage.*)

EMPEROR:

> *My tears fall like pearls,*
> *While the rain pours down on the plane trees,*
> *Echoing each other through my window till dawn.*

(***Exeunt.***)

第四十五出　觅魂

（净扮道士，小生、贴扮道童，执幡引上）"临邛道士鸿都客，能以精诚致魂魄。为感君王展转思，便教遍处殷勤觅。"贫道杨通幽是也。籍隶丹台，名登紫篆。呼风掣电，御气天门。摄鬼招魂，游神地府。只为太上皇帝思念杨妃，遍访异人召魂相见，俺因此应诏而来。太上皇十分欢喜，诏于东华门内，依科行法。已曾结就法坛，今晚登坛宣召。童儿，随我到坛上去来。（童捧剑、水同行科）（净）

【仙吕点绛唇】俺为他一点情缘，死生衔怨。思重见，凭着咱道力无边，特地把神通显。

（场上建高坛科）（小生、贴）已到坛了。（净）是好一座法坛也。

【混江龙】这坛本在虚空辟建，象涵太极法先天。无中有阴阳攒聚，有中无水火陶甄。（童）基址从何而立？（净）基址呵，遣五丁，差六甲，运戊己中央当下立。（童）用何工夫而成？（净）用工夫，养婴儿，调姹女，配

466

SCENE 45
The Search for Lady Yang's Spirit

(*Enter the necromancer,*) Yang Tongyou, *followed by a page carrying a sacred banner.*)
NECROMANCER:

A necromancer of Linqiong,
I can summon spirits at will,
And since my sovereign longs for his lady,
I shall search high and low for her spirit.

I am Yang Tongyou, the necromancer. Registered in the list of immortals, I can command the wind and lightning and ascend to heaven, or summon spirits and ghosts and wander in hell. In his longing for Lady Yang, the old emperor asked for a magician to call her spirit, and I was sent for. He is pleased now, and has ordered me to work my magic inside Donghua Gate. The altar is prepared, and this evening I shall mount it to call her spirit. Come with me, boy, to the altar.

(*The page, carrying the necromancer's sword and holy water, follows him.*)

Divided by death,
His great love makes him long to see her again;
So I must practise sorcery,
And display my magic power over spirits.

(*They reach a high altar.*)

BOY: Here we are at the altar.
NECROMANCER: This is a wonderful altar.

This altar, built in mid-air,
Is a symbol of Primary Truth;
From nothingness came the male and female principles,
And all existence is but the interplay
Of the elements of fire and water.

乙庚金木刹那全。(童)坛上可有户牖?
(净)户牖呵,对金鸡,朝玉兔,坎离卯酉。
(童)方向呢?(净)方向呵,镇黄庭,通紫
极,子午坤乾。(童)这坛可有多少大?
(净)虽只是倚方隅,占基阶,坛场咫尺,却
可也纳须弥,藏世界,道里由延。(童)原来
包罗恁宽!(净)上包着一周天三百六十躔
度,内星辰日月。(童)想那分统处量也不
小。(净)中分统四大洲,忆万百千阎浮界,
岳渎山川。(童)坛上谁听号令?(净)听号
令,则那些无稽滞,司风,司火,司雷,司电。
(童)谁供驱遣?(净)供驱遣,无非这有职
掌,值时、值日、值月、值年。(童)绕坛有何
景象?(净)半空中绕嗺嗺鸾吟凤啸,两壁

BOY: Where is the foundation of the altar?
NECROMANCER: I summoned giants,
> *Who erected it in the centre of the universe.*

BOY: How was it built?
NECROMANCER:
> *It was built with inner force,*
> *And completed in no time.*

BOY: Are there doors leading to it?
NECROMANCER:
> *Yes, facing the sun and the moon.*

BOY: In what directions?
NECROMANCER:
> *In the direction of the Court of Heaven*
> *And the polar star.*

BOY: How big is the altar?
NECROMANCER:
> *Though it seems to occupy a small piece of ground,*
> *You could put the whole universe into it.*

BOY: It must be huge!
NECROMANCER:
> *On top is the whole heavenly sphere,*
> *With all the planets and stars.*

BOY: I suppose it is quite big inside too.
NECROMANCER:
> *Inside are the four continents*
> *With their hundreds of millions of people,*
> *And all their rivers and mountains.*

BOY: Who will obey your commands at the altar?
NECROMANCER:
> *The genii of the winds, fire, thunder and lightning.*

BOY: Who will run your errands?
NECROMANCER:
> *The genii of the hours, days, months and years.*

BOY: What surrounds the altar?

厢列森森虎伏龙眠。端的是一尘不染,众妄都蠲。(童)若非吾师无边道力,安能建此无上法坛?(净)这全托赖着大唐朝君王分福,敢夸俺小鸿都道力精虔。(童)请吾师上坛去者。(内细乐,二童引净上坛科)(净)趁天风,随仙乐,双引着鸾旌高步斗。(内钟鼓科)(净)响金钟,鸣法鼓,恭擎象简向朝元。(童献香科)请吾师拈香。(净拈香科)这香呵,不数他西天竺旃柱林青狮窟,根蟠鸷鹫,东洋海波斯国瑞龙脑形似蚕蝉。结祥云,腾宝雾,直冲霄汉;透清微,萦碧落,普供真玄。第一炷,祝当今皇帝、享无疆圣寿,保洪图社稷,巩国祚延绵。第二炷,愿疆场静,烽燧销;普天下各道、各州、各境里,民安盗息无征战;禾黍登,蚕桑茂,百姓每若老、若幼、若壮者,家封户给乐田园。

470

NECROMANCER:

In mid-air phoenixes chirp,
And on all sides dragons and tigers couch.
There is not a speck of earthly dust or dross.

BOY: Only you with your infinite magic power could build such a wonderful altar.

NECROMANCER:

No, it is due to the good fortune of the emperor,
Not to any power of mine.

BOY: Now, sir, will you please ascend the altar.

(*Music sounds offstage as they ascend the altar.*)

NECROMANCER:

With fairy music carried on the breeze,
We follow the sacred banner and the censer.

(*Bells and drums sound offstage.*)

Bronze bells ring and magic drums are played,
As I raise the ivory sceptre with due respect towards heaven.

BOY (*Handing him the incense*): Master, please present the incense.

NECROMANCER (*Holding the incense*):

This incense is not inferior
To the sandalwood of western India
Which grows from phoenix-shaped roots in the caves of lions;
Nor does it fall short
Of the ambergris of Persia,
Which congeals in the eastern ocean in cicada form;
Its precious smoke soars like a cloud to heaven
And hangs in the azure deep to the glory of Buddha.
Herewith I offer the first stick of incense
To wish the emperor boundless happiness;
May his empire rest secure, and long may he reign.
And now I offer the second stick of incense
With a wish for all wars to cease;
May the whole world be at peace,
With no rebellion or fighting
In any single province, district or village;

471

第三炷,单只为死生分,情不灭,待凭这香头一点,温热了夜台魂;幽明隔,情难了,思情此香烟百转,吹现出春风面。(童献花介)散花。(净散花科)这花呵,不学他老瞿叠对迦叶糊涂笑捻,谩劳他诸天女访维摩撒漫飞旋。俺特地采蘅芜,踏穿阆苑,几度价寻怀梦摘遍琼田。显神奇,要将他残英再接相思树,施伎俩,管教他落花重放并头莲。(童献灯科)献灯。(净捧灯科)这灯呵,烂辉辉灵光常向千秋照,灿荧荧心灯只为一情传。抵多少衡遥石怀中秘授,还形烛帐里高燃。他则要续痴情,接上这残灯焰,俺可待点神灯,照彻那旧冤愆。(童献法盏科)请吾师咒水。(净捧水科)这水呵,曾游比目,曾泛双鸳。你漫道当日个如鱼也那得水,可知道到头来,水、米也没有半点交缠。数不尽情河爱海波终竭,似那等幻泡浮沤浪

472

May the harvest of wheat and mulberries be good,
May old and young lead a happy life at home.
And now I offer the third stick of incense
For the love that endures though the lovers are parted by
    death;
May the spark of fire in my censer
Kindle the ghost in the shades who remembers her love,
And cause her fair form to reappear.

BOY (*Handing him flowers*): Now for the flower-scattering ceremony.

NECROMANCER (*Scattering the flowers*):
This is no imitation of old Gautama
Who held a flower before his smiling disciple Kasyapa,
Nor of the angels who called on Vimalakirtti
And scattered flowers around the saint.
No, I have made a trip to paradise,
To pluck asphodels from the immortal fields,
And with my magic art
Put back the fallen petals on the tree of love,
And make it blossom again.

BOY (*Presenting the lamp*): Here is the lamp.

NECROMANCER (*Holding the lamp*):
This sacred lamp shines bright through eternity,
And glows in true lovers' hearts;
It is better than magic candles
Which can cause the beloved to reappear;
For it can rekindle the dying embers of love,
And make an end of all sorrows of the past.

BOY (*Presenting the cup*): Please utter an incantation over the water.

NECROMANCER (*Holding the cup*)
In this water the love birds used to sport,
Like fish that frisk in the waves;
But now they are torn apart,
The ocean of love has run dry

易掀。他只道曾经沧海难为水，怎如俺这一滴杨枝彻九泉。（童）供养已毕，请问吾师如何行法召魂咱？（净）你与我把招魂衣摄，遗照图悬，龙墀净扫，凤幄高褰。等到那二更以后，三鼓之前，眠猧不吠，宿鸟无喧，叶宁树杪，虫息阶沿，露明星黯，月漏风穿，潜潜隐隐，冉冉翩翩，看步珊珊是耶非一个佳人现，才折证人间幽恨，地下残缘。

　　（内奏法音科）（丑捧青词上）"九天青鸟使，一幅紫鸾书。"（进跪科）高力士奉太上皇之命，谨送青词到此。（童接词进上科）（净向丑拱科）中官，且请坛外少候片时。（丑应下）（净）

【油葫芦】俺子见御笔青词写凤笺，漫从头仔细展。单子为死离生别那婵娟，牢守定真情一点无更变，待想他芳魂两下重相见，俺索召李夫人来帐中。煞强如西王母临殿

And vanished like bubbles of foam;
For the thirsty spirit who longs for the sea of love,
This drop of water from my willow twig
Will penetrate to the heart of the nether regions.

BOY: Now the offerings have been made; how are you going to call up the spirit, master?

NECROMANCER:

Bring me the garment for calling up the spirit,
Hang up the portrait,
Sweep the court,
And fasten the curtains.
After the second watch and before the third,
When dogs and birds are hushed in sleep,
When even leaves cease to rustle on the trees,
When insects stop their shrilling,
When the stars grow dim and the dew gleams bright,
When the moon peeps out and the wind is still,
Then, shadowy and nebulous,
Her lovely form will hover near;
And they shall resume their interrupted love.

(*Trumpets sound offstage.*)

(*Enter* Gao Lishi holding *a petition from the emperor.*)

GAO:

A messenger from the Son of Heaven,
I come with a petition.

(*He kneels.*) I, Gao Lishi, by His Majesty's command, have brought you a petition.

(*The page takes the petition and hands it to the necromancer.*)

NECROMANCER (*Greeting* Gao): My lord, will you please wait outside? (*Exit* Gao.)

Here I see a message in the emperor's hand,
And open the scroll to read from the beginning;
He declares that his love is unchanged though the lady is dead,
And he wishes to meet her spirit again.
When I call up her much loved spirit to the curtain,

前,稳情取汉刘郎遂却心头愿,向今宵同款款话因缘。

（动法器科）（净作法、焚符念科）此道符章,鹤翥鸾翔,功曹符使,速莅坛场。（杂扮符官骑马舞上,见科）仙师,有何法旨?（净付符科）有烦使者,将此符命,速召贵妃杨氏阴魂到坛者。（杂接符科）领法旨。（做上马绕场下）（净）

【天下乐】俺只见力士黄巾去召宣,扬也波鞭不暂延。管教他闪阴风一灵儿勾向前,俺这里静悄悄坛上躬身等,他那里急煎煎宫中望眼穿,呀,怎多半日云头不见转?

为何此时还不到来,好疑惑也!

【那吒令】阔迢迢山前水前,望香魂渺然。黯沉沉星前月前,盼芳容杳然。冷清清阶前砌前,听灵踪悄然。不免再烧一道催符去者。（焚符科）蠢硃符不住烧,歹剑诀空掐遍,枉念杀波没准的真言。

（杂上见科）覆仙师:小圣人间遍觅杨氏阴魂,无从召取。（净）符使且退。（杂）领法旨。（舞下）（净下坛科）童儿,请高公公相

It will please him more than the sight of a goddess from
heaven.
May his wish be granted:
Tonight they shall speak of their love.
(*He bows with the censer, makes passes and burns a charm.*)
May this charm fly away like a bird,
To summon a genie now to the altar.
(*A genie rides in, dancing.*)

GENIE: What are your sacred commands, greatest of magicians?

NECROMANCER (*Giving him the petition*): I must trouble you to take this to summon the spirit of Lady Yang to the altar immediately.

GENIE (*Taking the petition*): I go , my lord. *He rides round the stage, and leaves.*

NECROMANCER:
The genie has gone to summon Lady Yang,
Cracking his whip, without a moment's delay,
And her spirit will soon appear with the chilly wind;
I wait here quietly, bowing before the altar,
While the emperor waits in anxious suspense in the palace.
Why is he not back yet? This delay is very strange.
I scan the distant hills and streams,
But her spirit has not appeared;
Nor is she there beneath the dim stars and moon,
Nor before the lonely steps of the court.
I had better send another message. (*He burns another charm.*)
I burn these vermilion incantations in vain,
And make passes with my magic sword in vain;
My arts prove unavailing.
(*The genie returns.*)

GENIE: Oh, great magician, I have searched the whole earth for Lady Yang's spirit; but she is not to be found.

NECROMANCER: In that case, you may go.

GENIE: Very good, my lord. (*He dances and makes off.*)

NECROMANCER (*Descending from the altar*): Boy, ask His

见者。（童向内请科）高公公有请。（丑上）
"玉漏听长短，芳魂问有无？"（见科）仙师，
杨娘娘可曾召到么？（净）方才符使到来，
说娘娘无从召取。（丑）呀，如此怎生是好？
（净）公公且去覆旨，待贫道就在坛中，飞出
元神，不论上天入地，好歹寻着娘娘。不出
三日，定有消息回报。（丑）太上皇思念甚
切，仙师是必用意者。"且传方士语，去慰
上皇情。"（下）（内细乐，净更鹤氅科）童儿在
坛小心祇候，俺自打坐出神去也。（童）领
法旨。（内鸣钟、鼓各二十四声，净上坛端坐，叩
齿作闭目出神科）（童）你看我师出神去了。
不免放下云帏，坛下伺候则个。（作放坛上
帐幔，净暗下）（童）"坛上钟声静，天边云影
闲。"（同下）（末扮道士元神从坛后转行上）

【鹊踏枝】暝子里出真元，抵多少梦游仙。
俺则待踏破虚空，去访婵娟。贫道杨通幽，
为许上皇寻觅杨妃魂魄，特出元神，到处遍
求。如今先到那里去者？（思科）嗄，有了，

478

Lordship to come in.

BOY (*Calling*): Lord Gao Lishi, my master asks you to come in.

(*Enter* Gao Lishi.)

GAO:

> Listening to the sound of the clepsydra,
> I come to inquire if they have found her spirit.

Have you called up Lady Yang's spirit?

NECROMANCER: Just now my genie came back to report that Lady Yang cannot be found.

GAO: Oh! What are we to do then?

NECROMANCER: You had better report this to His Majesty, while I go into a trance at the altar. My spirit will fly to heaven and hell, and will certainly end by finding her. Within three days I shall bring you good news.

GAO: The emperor is very anxious; I hope you will do all you can. I will go back to tell him what has happened and try to comfort him. (*Exit.*)

(*Music sounds, and the necromancer puts on his cape.*)

NECROMANCER: Attend the altar well, boy; I am going into a trance.

BOY: Yes, master.

(*Bells and drums sound twenty-four times, the necromancer sits up straight, clenches his teeth, closes his eyes and goes into a trance.*)

BOY: Now my master has gone into a trance, I will put down the curtain and wait by the altar.

(*He lowers the curtain.*)

> The bells are hushed on the altar;
> Clouds sail across the sky. (*Exeunt.*)

(*Enter the necromancer's spirit from behind the curtain.*)

NECROMANCER:

> My spirit wanders in a trance like a genie,
> To tread the void and find the lady's ghost.

I have promised the emperor to search for the spirit of Lady Yang, and have gone into a trance; but where shall I look first? (*He*

479

且慢自叫阊阖，轻干玉殿，索先去赴幽冥，大索黄泉。

　　来此已是酆都城了。（向内科）森罗殿上判官何在？（判跳上，小鬼随上）"善恶细分铁算子，古今不出大轮回。"仙师何事降临？（末）贫道特来寻觅大唐贵妃杨玉环鬼魂。（判）凡是宫嫔妃后，地府另有文册。仙师请坐，且待呈簿查看。（末坐科，鬼送册，判递册科）（末看科）

【寄生草】这是一本宫嫔册，历朝妃后编。有一个厌弧箕服把周宗殄，有一个牝鸡野雉把刘宗煽，有一个蛾眉狐媚把唐宗变。好奇怪，看古今来椒房金屋尽标题，怎没有杨太真名字其中现。

　　地府既无，贫道去了。不免向天上寻觅一遭也。（虚下）（判跳舞下，鬼随下）（二仙女旌幢，引贴朝服、执拂上）"高引霓旌朝绛阙，缓移凤舄踏红云。"吾乃天孙织女，因向玉

480

thinks.)

I must not trespass too lightly in paradise
And the palace of jade; I will first search the nether regions,
To look for her in hell.

Here I am before hell. (*Calling.*) Where is the judge of hell?

(*Enter the judge, dancing, followed by a ghostly attendant.*)

JUDGE:

With my iron abacus I reckon men's virtues and sins;
For all shall receive their deserts in a future life.

What do you want here, master?

NECROMANCER: I have come to search for Lady Yang's spirit.

JUDGE: We have a special book for the registration of queens and
court ladies. Have a seat while I fetch it for you.

(*The necromancer sits down, and the ghostly attendant passes him
the book.*)

NECROMANCER (*Reading*):

This is the list of court ladies and queens of all reigns.
Here is she who overthrew the house of Zhou
With the omens of bow and winnowing fan.
Here is Lady Pheasant, who nearly ruined the Han empire.
Here is the one called the Fox,
Who tried to change the ruling house of Tang.
How strange that though all the court ladies since ancient
*   times*
Are mentioned here,
The name of Lady Yang is not to be found.

Since she is not in hell, I must search for her in heaven.

(*Exeunt.*)

(*Enter two fairy maids holding standards, who lead in the*
Weaving Maid *in ceremonial dress.*)

WEAVING MAID:

With rainbow pennants raised high,
I now approach the crimson court of heaven,
Treading in phoenix shoes

宸朝见,来到天门。前面一个道士来了,看是谁也?(末上)

【幺篇】拔足才离地,飞神直上天。(见贴科)原来是织女娘娘,小道杨通幽叩首。(贴)通幽免礼,到此何事?(末)小道奉大唐太上皇之命,寻访玉环杨氏之魂。适从地府求之不得,特来天上找寻。谁知天上亦无,因此一逴出来。若不是伴嫦娥共把蟾宫恋,多敢是趁双成同向瑶池现。(贴)通幽,那玉环之魂,原不在地下,不在天上也。(末)呀,早难道逐梁清又受天曹谴,要寻那霓裳善舞的俊杨妃,到做了留仙不住的乔飞燕。

(贴)通幽,杨妃既无觅处,你索自去覆旨便了。(末)娘娘,覆旨不难。不争小道呵,

【后庭花滚】没来由向金銮出大言,运元神排空如电转。一口气许了他上下里寻花貌,莽担承向虚无中觅丽娟。(贴)谁教你弄嘴来?(末)非是俺没干缠、自寻驱遣,单

482

Upon the rosy clouds.

I am the Weaving Maid, on my way to pay homage to the Heavenly Emperor, and I have just reached the gate of paradise. I see a necromancer coming; I wonder who he is. (*Enter the necromancer's spirit.*)

NECROMANCER:

My feet had hardly left the ground
When my spirit arrived in heaven.

(*He greets the* Weaving Maid.) Madam, my respects.

WEAVING MAID: Good day. What brings you here?

NECROMANCER: At the order of the old Tang emperor, I am searching for Lady Yang's spirit. Having failed to find her in hell, I came to look in heaven; but she is not there either, so I am leaving. I wonder if she is with the goddess of the moon or by the Jade Pool with the Queen Mother of the West?

WEAVING MAID: I can tell you, her spirit is neither in heaven nor hell.

NECROMANCER:

Can she have been punished by Heaven again?
Has the beauty who danced the Rainbw Dance disappeared?

WEAVING MAID: Since you cannot find her, you had better go back to report your failiure.

NECROMANCER: Yes, my lady. Only—

I was foolish enough to boast at court
That my spirit, advancing as swiftly as lightning,
Would certainly find the fair one in the void.

WEAVING MAID: Who told you to boast?

NECROMANCER:

It is not that I wanted to look for trouble;
But the emperor is so firm in his love,
He will never forget their former pledge.

WEAVING MAID: He let her die at Mawei; what love can he have for her?

NECROMANCER:

No, my lady, you are wronging him.

483

则为俺君王钟情生死坚,旧盟不弃捐。
(贴)马嵬坡下既已碎玉揉香,还讨甚情来?
(末)娘娘,休屈了人也。想当日乱纷纷乘
舆值播迁,翻滚滚羽林生闹喧,恶狠狠兵骄
将又专,焰腾腾威行虐肆煽,闹炒炒不由天
子宣,昏惨惨结成妃后冤。扑刺刺生分开
交颈鸳,格支支轻捋扯并蒂莲,致使得娇怯
怯游魂逐杜鹃,空落得哭哀哀悲啼咽楚猿。
恨茫茫高和太华连,泪漫漫平将沧海填。
(贴)如今死生久隔,岁月频更,只怕此情也
渐淡了。(末)那上皇呵,精诚积岁年,说不
尽相思累万千。镇日家把娇容心坎镌,每
日里将芳名口上编。听残铃剑阁悬,感衰
梧秋雨传。暗伤心肺腑煎,漫销魂形影怜。
对香囊呵惹恨绵,抱锦袜呵空泪涟,弄玉笛
呵怀旧怨,拨琵琶呵忆断弦。坐凄凉,思乱
缠,睡迷离,梦倒颠。一心儿痴不变,十分
家病怎痊! 痛娇花不再鲜,盼芳魂重至前。
(贴)前夜牛郎曾为李三郎辩白,今听他说
来,果如此情真。煞亦可怜人也! (末)小

As they fled in confusion, a mutiny broke out;
The guards were insolent, their commander presumptuous,
So their disaffection spread like wild fire,
And they would not carry out the emperor's orders.
Thus the lady was hounded to death, and the lovers were
*   parted.*
In life they were like two flowers on a single bough,
Or a pair of love birds;
But when they were torn apart she pined for her love,
And he moaned in his loneliness;
His sorrows were great as a mountain,
And his tears would fill an ocean.

WEAVING MAID: Now that they have been separated so long, I suppose the emperor feels her loss less keenly.

NECROMANCER:

The emperor has been faithful all these years,
And longs for her day and night;
Her image is carved on his heart,
And every day her name is on his lips;
The sound of bells on the mountain road,
Or the autumn rain on the plane trees,
Nearly breaks his heart with grief.
The sight of her scented pouch renews his sorrow,
And caressing her silk stocking he sheds tears.
When he strums the lute he mourns their separation;
By day he is plunged in despair,
And by night he dreams of the past.
If this continues, the emperor must soon die
Of a broken heart, tormented as he is,
By grief for this flower which can blossom no more,
And longing for her spirit to return.

WEANVING MAID: Some time ago the cowherd pleaded for him too. Judging by what you say, it seems he is really true to his love. In that case, he is to be pitied.

道呵,生怜他意中人缘未全,打动俺闲中客情慢牵,因此上不辞他往返蹟,甘将这辛苦肩。猛可把泉台踏的穿,早又将穹苍磨的圆。谁知他做长风吹断鸢,似晴曦散晓烟。莽桃源寻不出花一片,冷巫山找不着云半边。好教俺向空中难将袖手展,伫云头惟有睁目延。百忙里幻不出春风图画面,捏不就名花倾国妍。若不得红颜重出现,怎教俺黄冠独自还!娘娘呵,则问他那精灵何处也天?

(贴)通幽,你若必要见他,待我指一个所在,与你去寻访者。(末稽首科)请问娘娘,玉环见在何处?

【青哥儿】谢娘娘与咱、与咱方便,把玉人消息、消息亲传,得多少花有根芽水有源。则他落在谁边,望赐明言。我便疾到跟前,不敢留连。(贴)通幽,你不闻世界之外,别有世界,山川之内,另有山川么?(末)听说道世外山川,另有周旋,只不知洞府何天,问渡何缘?(贴)那东极巨海之外,有一仙山,名曰蓬莱。你到那里,便有杨妃消息了。(末)多谢娘娘指引。枉了上下俄延,都做

NECROMANCER:

I pity him, madam, parted like this from his love,
For not even a stranger could fail to be moved by his grief;
So I counted no trouble too great, and accepted this task.
But though I have searched through heaven and hell,
She has flown away like a kite with a broken string,
Or a morning mist that vanishes in the sunlight;
And, powerless to exercise my art,
I can only stare at the cloudy sky,
Unable to make the beauty reappear
In her flower-like loveliness.
But if she cannot be found,
How dare I go back alone?
Ah, my lady,
Where can her spirit be?

WEAVING MAID: Well, if you are determined to find her, I can tell you where to look.

NECROMANCER (*Bowing*):

I beg you to tell me.
I thank Your Ladyship for your help,
And beg you for news of her;
Flowers have their roots, water its source,
And if you will tell me where she is,
I will go there without delay.

WEAVING MAID: Have you never heard of other worlds outside this one?

NECROMANCER:

I have. But which do you mean?
And how can I reach it?

WEAVING MAID: Beyond the Eastern Ocean there is a fairy mountain named Penglai. If you go there, you will hear news of her.

NECROMANCER: Thank you for your directions.

I have travelled up and down on the wrong track!
So she is beyond the impassable ocean,

了北辙南辕。元来只隔着弱水三千,溟渤风烟,在那麟凤洲偏,蓬阆山巅。那里有蕙圃芝田,白鹿玄猿。琪树翩翩,瑶草芊芊。碧瓦雕楹,月馆云轩。楼阁蜿蜒,门闼勾连。隔断尘喧,合住神仙。(贴)虽这般说,只怕那里绝天涯,跨海角,途路遥远,你去不得。(末)哎,娘娘他那里情深无底更绵绵,谅着这蓬山路何为远。

(贴)既如此,你自前去。咱"又闻人世无穷恨,待绾机丝补断缘"。(引仙女下)(末)不免御着天风,到海外仙山,找寻一遭去也。(作御风行科)

【煞尾】稳踏着白云轻,巧趁取罡风便,把碗大沧溟跨展。回望齐州何处显,淡濛濛九点飞烟。说话之间,早来到海东边万仞峰巅。这的是三岛十洲别洞天,俺只索绕清虚阆苑,到玲珑宫殿。是必破工夫找着那玉天仙。

> 与招魂魄上苍苍, 黄滔
> 谁识蓬山不死乡? 越嘏
> 此去人寰知远近, 秦系
> 五云遥指海中央。 韦庄

Beyond the wind and mist in the fairy mountain,
Where phoenix and unicorn are,
With magic orchids and sacred herbs,
White stags, black apes, strange trees and plants of jasper.
There the carved eaves and emerald tiles
Of moon and cloud pavilions
Entwine and intermingle,
Far from all bustling crowds in the land of fairies.

WEAVING MAID: That fairyland lies beyond the farthest horizon; it
may prove too far for you to go.

NECROMANCER: Ah, lady,

For him with his deep and lasting love,
I would count no place too far.

WEAVING MAID: In that case, go.

The silk upon my loom will join together
The broken threads of love and end their sorrow.

(*Exit with fairies.*)

NECROMANCER:

Now let me fly with the wind,
To search the fairy mountain beyond the ocean.

(*He floats on the wind.*)

Firmly treading the soft white clouds,
I cross the ocean which looks like a bowl beneath me;
And gazing at the earth below
Can see only nine faint wisps of smoke.
In a flash I have reached the eastern side of the ocean,
And from a high peak survey the other world.
I shall cross the heavenly fields to the fairy palace,
And spare no effort to find the fairy maid.

(***Exit.***)

第四十六出　补恨

【正宫引子】【燕归梁】(贴扮织女上)怜取君王情意切,魂遍觅,费周折。好和蓬岛那人说,邀云珮,赴星阙。

前夕渡河之时,牛郎说起杨玉环与李三郎长生殿中之誓,要我与彼重续前缘。今适在天门外,遇见人间道士杨通幽,说上皇思念贵妃一意不衰,令他遍觅幽魂。此情实为可悯。已指引通幽到蓬山去了,又令侍儿召取太真到此,说与他知。再细探其衷曲,敢待来也。(仙女引旦上)

【锦堂春】说璇宫有命,云中忙驾香车。强驱愁绪来天上,怕眉黛恨难遮。

(仙女报,旦进见介)娘娘在上,杨玉环叩见。(贴)太真免礼,请坐了。(旦坐介)适蒙娘娘呼唤,不知有何法旨?(贴)一向不曾问你,可把生前与唐天子两下恩情,细说一

SCENE 46
Making Amends

(*Enter the* Weaving Maid.)
WEAVING MAID:

> *The emperor longs so deeply for his love,*
> *That he spares no pains to summon up her spirit;*
> *His sincerity has touched me,*
> *And I have bid her come from her fairy mountain.*

A few nights ago when I crossed the Milky Way, the Cowherd reminded me of the pledge Lady Yang and the Tang emperor made in the Palace of Eternal Youth, and asked me to help them to meet again. And just now, outside the gate of paradise, I happened to see a necromancer who told me that the emperor is still as much in love with her as ever and has ordered him to find her spirit. It is a sad story. So I directed the necromancer to the fairy mountain. Now I have told my attendant to fetch Lady Yang to tell her of this, in order to learn how she feels. She should be here soon.

(*A fairy leads in* Lady Yang.)
LADY:

> *Receiving a summons from the Weaving Maid,*
> *I have come quickly through the clouds in my carriage,*
> *Trying to disguise my sorrow,*
> *Though I cannot banish it completely.*

(*The fairy announces her and she enters.*) I am here, Your Ladyship.

WEAVING MAID: Don't stand on ceremony. Please be seated.

LADY (*Sitting down*): You sent for me, my lady. What are your instructions?

WEAVING MAID: I have never asked you for your story; but now I would like to hear all about your love for the Tang emperor during your life on earth.

遍与我知道。(旦)娘娘听启，

【正宫过曲】【普天乐】欢生前，冤和业。(悲介)才提起，声先咽。单则为一点情根，种出那欢苗爱叶。他怜我慕，两下无分别。誓世世生生休抛撇，不提防惨凄凄月坠花折，悄冥冥云收雨歇，恨茫茫只落得死断生绝。

【雁过声】【换头】(贴)听说、旧情那些。似荷丝劈开未绝，生前死后无休歇。万重深，万重结。你共他两边既恁疼热，况盟言曾共设，怎生他陡地心如铁，马嵬坡便忍将伊负也？

【倾杯序】【换头】(旦泪介)伤嗟，岂是他顿薄劣！想那日遭磨劫，兵刃纵横，社稷阽危，蒙难君王怎护臣妾？妾甘就死，死而无怨，与君何涉！(哭介)怎忘得定情钗盒那根节。

(出钗盒与贴看介)这金钗、钿盒，就是君王定情日所赐。妾被难之时，带在身边。携入蓬莱，朝夕佩玩，思量再续前缘。只不知可能够也？(贴)

【玉芙蓉】你初心誓不赊，旧物怀难撇。太

LADY: Yes, madam.
>   *It makes me sad to speak of my sins during life;*
>   *And at mention of them I choke with tears.*
>   *Our love for each other took root and blossomed,*
>   *Until we felt our hearts were one,*
>   *And pledged to remain together*
>   *In all our future lives.*
>   *But then, alas! The moon fell,*
>   *The flower withered and our joy was shattered,*
>   *We were torn apart by death.*

WEAVING MAID:
>   *Such then is your love—*
>   *Though sundered it still endures*
>   *Like the filaments in the lotus root*
>   *Not severed even in death.*
>   *But if you loved each other so much*
>   *That you made a pledge together,*
>   *How could he be so hard-hearted*
>   *As to give you up at the station?*

LADY (*Shedding tears*):
>   *It wasn't because the emperor was heartless;*
>   *But that day, in the mutiny,*
>   *Swords were unsheathed and the empire was in peril;*
>   *In such a crisis how could he protect me?*
>   *I was willing to die and do not regret my death;*
>   *It was nothing to do with him.* (*She sheds tears.*)
>   *But our pledge of love I never can forget!*

(*She shows the* Weaving Maid *the hairpin and the jewel box.*)
He gave me these when we pledged our love, and I had them with
me when I died; so I took them to the fairy mountain to keep with
me for all time. I long so much to resume our love; but how can
that be possible?

WEAVING MAID:
>   *So you have remained true to your pledge.*
>   *You bear no grudge against him for your death*

493

真,我想你马嵬一事,是千秋惨痛,此恨独绝。谁道你不将殒骨留微憾,只思断头香再蒸。蓬莱阙,化愁城万叠。(还旦钗盒介)只是你如今已登仙班,情缘宜断。若一念牵缠呵,怕无端又令从此堕尘劫。

(旦)念玉环呵,

【小桃红】位纵在神仙列,梦不离唐宫阙。千回万转情难灭。(起介)娘娘在上,倘得情丝再续,情愿谪下仙班。双飞若注鸳鸯牒,三生旧好缘重结。(跪介)又何惜人间再受罚折!

(贴扶介)太真,坐了。我久思为你重续前缘。只因马嵬之事,恨唐帝情薄负盟,难为作合。方才见道士杨通幽,说你遭难之后,唐帝痛念不衰,特令通幽升天入地,各处寻觅芳魂。我念他如此钟情,已指引通幽到蓬莱山了。还怕你不无遗憾,故此召问。今知两下真情,合是一对。我当上奏天庭,使你两人世居忉利天中,永远成双,以补从前离别之恨。

【催拍】那壁厢人间痛绝,这壁厢仙家念热:两下痴情怎奢,痴情怎奢。我把彼此精诚,

Or the tragedy of Mawei Station,
And only long to be together again,
Transforming your fairy mountain
Into a city of sorrow.
(*Returning her the hairpin and the box.*) But now that you rank
as an immortal you should free yourself of earthly desires; because
if you allow them to entangle you,
You may be banished to the world of men.

LADY:

Alas! Though I am ranked with the immortals,
I dream all the time of an earthly palace;
And, come what may, my love can never die.
(*She rises.*) If only we could love again, madam, I would gladly
be banished from heaven.
For if our names were on the list of lovers
And we could be together again, (*She kneels.*)
No punishment on earth could frighten me.

WEAVING MAID (*Helping her up*): Be seated. I have wanted for a
long time to help you; but after what happened at Mawei I felt
Emperor Ming Huang must be quite heartless and since he had
broken his pledge it was impossible to bring you together again.
Just now, however, I met a necromancer who said that since you
died the emperor has never stopped longing for you, and has sent
him in search of your spirit to heaven and hell. Since the emperor
is still true to you, I instructed the necromancer to go to your fairy
mountain; but thinking you might bear some grudge against the
emperor, I called you here to sound you out. Now that I know you
are both true to your love, I shall bring your case to the Heavenly
Emperor and ask him to make amends for your past unhappiness by
sending you both to the highest heaven, to live together for ever.
For there in the world of men he is grieving,
While here among the immortals you long for him too;
Your love is so firm, I shall plead with the Heavenly Emperor
To let your grief be atoned for
And your love remain whole for ever.

495

上请天阙。补恨填愁，万古无缺。（旦背泪介）还只怕孽障周遮，缘尚蹇，会犹赊。

（转向贴介）多蒙娘娘怜念，只求与上皇一见，于愿足矣。（贴）也罢。闻得中秋之夕，月中奏你新谱"霓裳"，必然邀你。恰好此夕正是唐帝飞升之候。你可回去，令通幽届期径引上皇，到月宫一见。何如？（旦）只恐月宫之内，不便私会。（贴）不妨。待我先与姮娥说明。你等相见之时，我就奏请玉音到来，使你情缘永证便了。（旦）多谢娘娘，就此告辞。（贴）

【尾声】团圆等待中秋节，管教你情偿意惬。

（旦）只我这万种伤心，见他时怎地说！

　　（旦）身前身后事茫茫，　天竺牧童
　　　　　却厌仙家日月长。曹唐
　　（贴）今日与君除万恨，　薛逢
　　　　　月宫琼树是仙乡。薛能

LADY (*Turning away and shedding tears*):
I am only afraid that our sins may prove a barrier,
To keep us from each other.
(*She turns to the* Weaving Maid.) I thank you with all my heart
for your sympathy. All I ask is to see him once more.

WEAVING MAID: Very well. I hear that at the Mid-Autumn
Festival they will be playing the new score of the Rainbow Garment
Dance, and you will certainly be invited. That night is also the
night for the emperor to leave the world of men. When you go
back, tell the necromancer to lead the emperor to the moon on that
day to meet you there.

LADY: Are lovers' meetings allowed in the palace of the moon?

WEAVING MAID: It can be arranged. I shall tell the mistress of the
moon beforehand. By the time you meet, I shall have procured an
imperial decree to make you lovers for ever.

LADY: I thank Your Ladyship. Now I must go.

WEAVING MAID:
You will meet your lover again at the Mid-Autumn Festival,
When all your wishes will be fulfilled.

LADY:
But how can I tell him of my countless sorrows
When we meet again?

(***Exeunt.***)

第四十七出　寄情

【南吕过曲】【懒画眉】(末扮道士元神上)海外曾闻有仙山，山在虚无缥缈间。贫道杨通幽，适见织女娘娘，说杨妃在蓬莱山上。即便飞过海上诸山，一迳到此。见参差宫殿彩云寒。前面洞门深闭，不免上前看来。(看介)试将银榜端详觑，(念介)"玉妃太真之院。"呀，是这里了。(做抽簪叩门介)不免抽取琼簪轻叩关。

【前腔】(贴扮仙女上)云海沉沉洞天寒，深锁云房鹤径闲。(末又叩介)(贴)谁来花下叩铜环？(开门介)是那个？(末见介)贫道杨通幽稽首。(贴)到此何事？(末)大唐太上皇帝，特遣贫道问候玉妃。(贴)娘娘到璇

SCENE 47
A Message of Love

(*Enter the necromancer's spirit.*)

NECROMANCER:

> *I have heard of a fairy mountain beyond the ocean,*
> *In far-off, unknown regions.*

I have just met the Heavenly Weaving Maid, who tells me that Lady Yang is in the fairy mountain; so I have flown over mountains and seas to come here.

> *I see a towering palace*
> *In clouds of many colours,*
> *But the gate is closed.*

Let me go closer to see if this is the right place.

(*He looks.*)

> *I look with care at the silver door place.*

(*He reads.*) "The house of Lády Yang." Ah, this is it. (*He knocks at the gate.*)

> *Now I knock lightly at the gate.*

(*Enter a fairy attendant.*)

ATTENDANT:

> *Our frozen palace is deep in a sea of clouds,*
> *Visited only by storks that fly through the mist.*

(*The necromancer knocks again.*)

> *Then who knocks at the door amid the flowers?*

(*She opens the door.*)

NECROMANCER (*Bowing*): I am Yang Tongyou, the necromancer.

ATTENDANT: What do you want here?

NECROMANCER: The Tang emperor asked me to send his regards to your mistress.

ATTENDANT: Her Ladyship has gone to the palace of the stars.

玑宫去了，请仙师少待。（末）原来如此。我且从容伫立瑶阶上。（贴）远远望见娘娘来了。（末）遥听仙风吹珮环。

【前腔】（旦引仙女上）归自云中步珊珊，闻有青鸾信远颁。（见末介）呀，果然仙客候重关。（贴迎介）（旦）道士何来？（贴）正要禀知娘娘，他是唐家天子人间使，衔命迢遥来此山。

　　（旦进介）即是上皇使者，快请相见。（仙女请末进介）（末见科）贫道杨通幽稽首。（旦）仙师请坐。（末坐介）（旦）请问仙师何来？（末）贫道奉上皇之命，特来问候娘娘。（旦）上皇安否？（末）上皇朝夕思念娘娘，因而成疾。

【宜春令】自回銮后，日夜思，镇昏朝潜潜泪滋。春风秋雨，无非即景伤心事。映芙蓉人面俱非，对杨柳新眉谁试？特地将他一点旧情，倩咱传示。

Please wait a moment.

NECROMANCER: Very well.

> *I will wait here by the jasper steps.*

ATTENDANT: There far away Her Ladyship is coming.

NECROMANCER:

> *And the fairy wind*
> *Carries the echo of her pendants here.*

(*Enter* Lady Yang *with a fairy maid.*)

LADY:

> *Returning through the clouds,*
> *I hear a messenger has come from far away.*

(*She sees the necromancer.*)

> *Yes, here is a stranger waiting at the gate.*

(*The fairy attendant approaches her.*) Where does this necromancer come from?

ATTENDANT: I was just going to report to you, madam.

> *He brings a message from Emperor Ming Huang,*
> *And has come from far away.*

LADY (*Advancing*): Since he comes from the emperor, let him approach. (*The attendant leads the necromancer to her.*)

NECROMANCER (*Bowing*): The necromancer Yang Tongyou greets Your Ladyship.

LADY: Please be seated. (*The necromancer sits down.*) May I ask the purpose of your visit?

NECROMANCER: By Emperor Ming Huang's order, I have come to bring you his regards.

LADY: How is he?

NECROMANCER:

> *Thinking of you day and night,*
> *The emperor has fallen ill;*
> *For, shedding tears, he longs for you all the time.*
> *Spring wind and autumn rain awaken his grief,*
> *Flowers remind him of your face, and willows of your*
>   *eyebrows;*
> *So now he has ordered me to send you his love.*

【前腔】（旦泪介）肠千断，泪万丝。谢君王
钟情似兹。音容一别，仙山隔断违亲侍。
蓬莱院月悴花憔，昭阳殿人非物是。漫自
将咱一点旧情，倩伊回示。

　　（末）贫道领命。只求娘娘再将一物，
寄去为信。（旦）也罢。当年承宠之时，上
皇赐有金钗、钿盒，如今就分钗一股，劈盒
一扇，烦仙师代奏上皇。只要两意能坚，自
可前盟不负。（作分钗盒，泪介）侍儿，将这
钗盒送与仙师。（贴递钗盒与末介）（旦）仙师
请上，待妾拜烦。（末）不敢。（拜介）

【三学士】旧物亲传全仗尔，深情略表孜孜。
半边钿盒伤孤另，一股金钗寄远思。幸达
上皇，只此心坚似始，终还有相见时。

　　（末）贫道还有一说，钗盒乃人间所有之物，
献与上皇，恐未深信。须得当年一事，他人
不知者，传去取验，才见贫道所言不谬。

　　（旦）这也说得有理。（旦低头沉吟介）

【前腔】临别殷勤重寄词，词中无限情思。
哦，有了。记得天宝十载，七月七夕长生
殿，夜半无人私语时。那时上皇与妾并肩

LADY (*Shedding tears*):

> *Broken-hearted and in tars,*
> *I thank the emperor for his love;*
> *Since our separation I cannot attend him in person,*
> *But broken-hearted in the fairy mountain*
> *Am like a wilting flower or waning moon;*
> *While he in his palace longs for me too.*
> *I would like you to send him my love.*

NECROMANCER: I will, Your Ladyship. But I beg you to give me some token.

LADY: Very well. When we pledged our love, the emperor gave me a double hairpin and a jewel box. I will give you half of the hairpin and half of the box to send to him. Tell him that if we remain true, we shall be able to fulfil our pledge. (*She takes out the hairpin and the box and divides them into two, shedding tears.*) Girl, give these to the master. (*Her maid passes the hairpin and the box to the necromancer.*) Let me thank you, master.

NECROMANCER: You need not thank me. (*They bow to each other.*)

LADY:

> *I depend on you to send him these tokens of love;*
> *Two separate halves, they convey my sadness.*
> *And tell him that if our love remains unchanged,*
> *Sooner or later we shall meet again.*

NECROMANCER: Excuse me, madam, but these tokens were made on earth, and if I give them to the emperor, how can be sure that I received them from you? Can you tell me of something which none but yourselves knew of?

LADY: Yes, you are right. (*She lowers her head in thought.*)

> *Before the necromancer leaves, let me add a message*
> *To show my infinite love.*

Ah! I have it!

> *At midnight in the seventh day of the seventh moon*
> *In the tenth year of the Tianbao period,*

而立，因感牛女之事，密相誓心：愿世世生生，永为夫妇。（泣介）谁知道比翼分飞连理死，绵绵恨无尽止。

（末）有此一事，贫道可覆上皇了。就此告辞。（旦）且住，还有一言。今年八月十五日夜，月中大会，奏演"霓裳"，恰好此夕，正是上皇飞升之候。我在那里专等一会，敢烦仙师届期指引上皇到彼。失此机会，便永无再见之期了。（末）贫道领命。（旦）仙师，说我

含情凝睇谢君王，白居易

尘梦何如鹤梦长。曹唐

（末）密奏君王知入月，王建

众仙同日听霓裳。李商隐

When everyone else was sleeping,
The emperor and I were in the Palace of Eternal Youth.
And as we stood shoulder to shoulder, thinking of the Weaving Maid and the Cowherd in heaven, we vowed to love each other through all future lives.

(*She weeps.*)

We had no inkling then of this separation,
And our everlasting sorrow!

NECROMANCER: With this, I can report back to the emperor. Now I must leave you.

LADY: Wait, one word more! On the fifteenth of this eighth moon, there will be a big celebration in the moon when the Rainbow Garment Dance will be performed; and that night the emperor will leave the earth. I shall wait for him in the moon. Will you please guide him there that day? If he misses that opprtunity, he will never see me again

NECROMANCER: I shall do as you wish, madam.

LADY: Thank you, master.

(***Exeunt.***)

第四十八出　得信

【仙吕引子】【醉落魄】(生病装,宫女扶上)相思透骨沉疴久,越添消瘦。蘼芜烧尽魂来否？望断仙音,一片晚云秋。

"黯黯愁难释,绵绵病转成。哀蝉将落叶,一种为伤情。"寡人梦想妃子,染成一病。因令方士杨通幽摄召芳魂,谁料无从寻觅。通幽又为我出神访求去了。唉,不知是方士妄言,还不知果能寻着？寡人转展萦怀,病体越重。已遣高力士到坛打听,还不见来。对着这一庭秋景,好生悬望人也！

【仙吕过曲】【二犯桂枝香】【桂枝香】叶枯红藕,条疏青柳,渐刺刺满处西风,都送与愁人消受。【四时花】悠悠、欲眠不眠欹枕头。非耶是耶睁望眸。问巫阳,浑未剖。【皂罗袍】活时难救,死时怎求？他生未就此生顿休。【桂枝香】可怜他渺渺魂无见,量我这恹恹病怎瘳。

506

SCENE 48
The Message Is Received

(*Enter the emperor, now ill, supported by maids.*)
EMPEROR:

> *I have wasted away with longing,*
> *For in spite of all my prayers*
> *Her spirit has not appeared;*
> *And waiting for news of my love,*
> *I see nothing but evening clouds in the autumn sky.*
> *Wasting away, I cannot shake off my sorrow;*
> *The fall of leaves and cicada's chirp in autumn*
> *Only increase my grief.*

Sick with longing for Lady Yang, I asked the necromancer, Yang Tongyou, to call up her spirit; but unable to find her he has gone into a trance. (*He sighs.*)I do not know whether the necromancer is lying or whether she can be found, and the suspense is making my illness worse. I have sent Gao Lishi to find out what is happening at the altar, but he has not returned yet. The autumn fills me with longing.

> *The leaves of the red lotus have withered,*
> *And the once green willows are left with empty boughs;*
> *The blustering west wind only adds to my grief.*
> *Sleepless on my pillow,*
> *Suspecting that she is near I open my eyes;*
> *But the necromancer is helpless.*
> *And since I was powerless to save her life,*
> *What chance have I of finding her after death?*
> *No, we shall never meet again in this life,*
> *The necromancer will not be able to find her,*
> *And my sickness will soon prove mortal.*

(*Enter* Gao Lishi *with the hairpin and the jewel box.*)

【不是路】(丑持钗盒上)鹤转瀛洲,信物携将
远寄投。忙回奏,(见生叩介)仙坛传语慰离
忧。(生)高力士,你来了么?问音由,佳人
果有佳音否?莫为我淹煎把浪语诌。(丑)
万岁爷听启,那仙师呵,追寻久,遍黄泉碧
落俱无有。(生惊哭介)呀,这等说来,妃子
永无再见之期了。兀的不痛杀寡人也!
(丑)万岁爷,请休屡愁。

　　那仙师呵,

【前腔】御气遨游,遇织女传知在海上洲。
(生)可曾得见?(丑)蓬莱岫,见太真仙院
榜高头。(生)元来妃子果然成仙了。可有
什么说话?(丑)说来由,含情只谢君恩厚,
下望尘寰两泪流。

(生)果然有这等事?(丑)非虚谬,有当年
钗盒亲分授,寄来呈奏。

　　(进钗盒介)这钿盒、金钗,就是娘娘临
终时,付奴婢殉葬的。不想娘娘携到仙山
去了。(生执钗盒大哭介)我那妃子嗄,

GAO:

> The fairy stork has returned with these tokens,
> And I hurry in to make my report.

(*He kowtows to the emperor*)

> May the message from the altar
> Comfort his lonely heart.

EMPEROR: Ah, Gao Lishi, you have come back. Is there any news? Don't make up a story just to comfort me.

GAO: May it please Your Majesty,

> The necromancer searched high and low,
> But failed to find her either in heaven or hell.

EMPEROR (*With a cry of despair*): Then I shall never see her again! (*He groans.*)

GAO: Don't grieve, sire.

> The holy man in his wanderings
> Learned from the Weaving Maid that Lady Yang
> Is in the fairy mountain beyond the ocean.

EMPEROR: Did he see her then?

GAO: Yes,

> In Penglai Mountain he found a mansion
> Marked with her name.

EMPEROR: So she has really become an immortal! What did she say?

GAO:

> She thanked Your Majesty for your kindness,
> And looking down to earth she shed tears.

EMPEROR: Is this true?

GAO:

> It must be true, for she gave him these tokens,
> And asked him to bring them to Your Majesty.

(*He presents the half hairpin and the box.*) Her Ladyship told me to bury this hairpin and the jewel box with her when she died; and she must have taken them to the fairy mountain.

EMPEROR (*Holding the hairpin and the box and sheding tears*): Alas, my love!

509

【长拍】钿盒分开，钿盒分开，金钗拆对，都似玉人别后，单形只影，两载寡侣，一般儿做成离愁。还忆付伊收，助晓妆云鬟，晚香罗袖。此际轻分远寄与，无限恨，个中留，见了怎生释手。枉自想同心再合，双股重俦。

且住。这钗盒乃人间之物，怎到得天上？前日墓中不见，朕正疑心，今日如何却在他手内？

（丑）万岁爷休疑，那仙师早已虑及，向娘娘问得当年一件密事在此。（生）是那一事，你可说来。（丑）娘娘呵，把

【短拍】天宝年间，天宝年间，长生殿里，恨茫茫说起从头。七夕对牵牛，正夜半凭肩私咒。（生）此事果然有之。谁料钗分盒剖！（泣介）只今日呵，翻做了孤雁汉宫秋。

（丑）万岁爷，且省愁烦。娘娘还有话说。（生）还说什么？（丑）娘娘说，今年中秋之夕，月宫奏演"霓裳"，娘娘也在那里。教仙师引着万岁爷，到月宫里相会。（生喜介）既有此话，你何不早说。如今是几时

The two halves of the box are divided,
And the double hairpin is single now;
These symbolize our separation and sadness
For the last two years.
I remember when I gave her these two tokens:
The one to put in her hair in the morning,
The other to scent her silken sleeve at dusk;
And now she has taken one half of each
And sent them to me to express her infinite sadness.
It is vain to hope for reunion.

One minute, though. These are earthly things; how could they be taken to heaven? Their disappearance from her grave that day seemed rather suspicious. How did the necromancer come by them ?

GAO: Your Majesty need not doubt him. The holy man realized that these tokens would not be conclusive evidence, so he asked Lady Yang to give him some further proof that he had seen her.

EMPEROR: What did she tell him?

GAO: Lady Yang told him in great distress—

Of a scene that took place in the Palace of Eternal Youth,
In the Tianbao period, on the seventh day of the seventh moon,
When you made a vow at midnight under the stars.

EMPEROR: Yes, that is so.

Who could have foreseen that these tokens would now be divided! (He weeps.)
I am like a lonely swan in the palace.

GAO: Take comfort, sire, for Lady Yang has another message for you.

EMPEROR: What is it?

GAO: She says that at the Mid-Autumn Festival the Rainbow Garment Dance will be performed in the moon, and she will be present. She asked the necromancer to lead Your Majesty to the moon to meet her.

EMPEROR (*Overjoyed*): Why did you not say that earlier! What is

511

了？（丑）如今七月将尽，中秋之期只有半
月了。请万岁爷将息龙体。（生）妃子既许
重逢，我病体一些也没有了。

【尾声】广寒宫，容相就。十分愁病一时休。
倒挽不过人间半月秋！

　　　　　海外传书怪鹤迟，卢纶
　　　　　词中有誓两心知。白居易
　　　　　更期十五团圆夜，徐夤
　　　　　纵有清光知对谁！戴叔伦

the date today?

GAO: It is the end of the seventh moon; there is only half a month till the Mid-Autume Festval. Please rest well now, sire.

EMPEROR:

Now that she consents to see me again, I no longer feel ill.
With this permission to join her in the moon,
My sickness has gone;
But I can hardly endure another half month in the world of men.

(***Exeunt.***)

第四十九出　重圆

【双调引子】【谒金门】(净扮道士上)情一片，幻出人天姻眷。但使有情终不变，定能偿夙愿。

贫道杨通幽，前出元神在于蓬莱。蒙玉妃面嘱，中秋之夕引上皇到月宫相会。上皇原是孔升真人，今夜八月十五数合飞升。此时黄昏以后，你看碧天如水，银汉无尘，正好引上皇前去。道犹未了，上皇出宫来也。(生上)

【仙吕入双调】【忒忒令】碧澄澄云开远天，光皎皎月明瑶殿。(净见介)上皇，贫道稽首。(生)仙师少礼。今夜呵，只因你传信约蟾宫相见，急得我盼黄昏眼儿穿。这青霄际，全托赖引步展。

(净)夜色已深，就请同行。(行介)(净)明月在何许？挥手上青天。(生)不知天上宫阙，今夕是何年？(净)我欲乘风归去，只

SCENE 49
The Lovers' Reunion

(*Enter the necromancer.*)

NECROMANCER:

> *Now love will cause a reunion in heaven;*
> *For when love is constant, all wishes will come true.*

Going into a trance, I went to the fairy mountain, and there Lady Yang told me to lead the emperor to the moon to meet her on the Mid-Autumn Festival; for the emperor in his last life was an angel too, and this is the day for him to go back to heaven. It is after dusk now and the azure sky is as limpid as water, without a spot of dust in the air. The time has come to take him there. Now His Majesty is leaving the palace.

(*Enter the emperor.*)

EMPEROR:

> *Deep and clear the azure sky,*
> *All clouds have sunk to the far horizon*
> *And the moon shines bright above the palace.*

NECROMANCER (*Bowing*): Long live the emperor!

EMPEROR: Don't stand on ceremony, master.

> *Since you told me that she would see me tonight in the moon,*
> *I have anxiously waited all evening.*
> *I depend on you now to lead me up to the sky.*

NECROMANCER: Yes, it is dark enough now. Let us go. (*They walk forward.*)

> *The moon is high; let us go up the sky.*

EMPEROR:

> *What year can it be in the palace above?*

NECROMANCER:

> *I ride on the wind, but fear the cold in the moon;*

恐琼楼玉宇,高处不胜寒。(合)起舞弄清影,何似在人间。(生)仙师,天路迢遥,怎生飞渡?(净)上皇,不必忧心。待贫道将手中拂子,掷作仙桥,引到月宫便了。(掷拂子化桥下)(生)你看,一道仙桥从空现出。仙师忽然不见,只得独自上桥而行。

【嘉庆子】看彩虹一道随步显,直与银河霄汉连,香雾濛濛不辨。(内作乐介)听何处奏钧天,想近着桂丛边。

(虚下)(老旦引仙女,执扇随上)

【沉醉东风】助秋光玉轮正圆,奏霓裳约开清宴。吾乃月主嫦娥是也。月中向有"霓裳"天乐一部,昔为唐皇贵妃杨太真于梦中闻得,遂谱出人间。其音反胜天上。近贵妃已证仙班。吾向蓬山觅取其谱,补入钧天,拟于今夕奏演。不想天孙怜彼情深,欲为重续良缘。要借我月府,与二人相会。太真已令道士杨通幽引唐皇今夜到此,真千秋一段佳话也。只为他情儿久,意儿坚,合天人重见。因此上感天孙为他方便。仙女每,候着太真到时,教他在桂阴下少待。

TOGETHER:

With dancing shadows we leave the world of men.

EMPEROR: It is a long way to heaven, master. Are we to fly there?

NECROMANCER: Set your heart at rest, sir. I shall change the wand in my hand into a fairy bridge to the moon.

(*He throws his wand, and a bridge appears. The necromancer vanishes.*)

EMPEROR: Now a fairy bridge has appeared in the sky, and the necromancer has vanished. I had better go on alone.

The brilliant rainbow bridge
Extends with every step I take,
Until it reaches the Milky Way,
And all ahead is in a fragrant mist. (*Music sounds.*)
Heavenly music is being played;
I must be near the cassia bush in the moon. (*Exit.*)

(*Enter* Chang'e, *the goddess of the moon, with fairy attendants holding fans.*)

CHANG'E:

The roundness of our brilliant orb,
Adds splendour to the autumn;
Now we shall play the Rainbow Dance and feast.

I am Chang'e, the mistress of the moon. We used to have a Rainbow Garment Dance, which was learned by Lady Yang of the Tang court in a dream; and the score she wrote for the world of men is even better than ours. After she joined the immortals in the fairy mountain, I asked her for her version to add to our heavenly repertoire; and this evening we shall perform it. Moved by the love of the Tang emperor and Lady Yang, the Weaving Maid has arranged to have them reunited, and means them to meet here in the moon; so Lady Yang has asked the necromancer Yang Tongyou to lead the emperor here tonight. This is a marvellous story!

They have love so long, and proved so true,
That the stars have helped them to meet again.

Fairies, when Lady Yang arrives, tell her to wait under the cassia

等上皇到来见过,然后与我相会。(仙女)
领旨。(合)桂华正妍,露华正鲜。撮成好
会,在清虚府洞天。

(老旦下)(场上设月宫,仙女立宫门候介)
(旦引仙女行上)

【尹令】离却玉山仙院,行到彩蟾月殿,盻着
紫宸人面。三生愿偿,今夕相逢胜昔年。

(到介)(仙女)玉妃请进。(旦进介)月主
娘娘在那里?(仙女)娘娘分付,请玉妃少
待。等上皇来见过,然后相会。请少坐。

(旦坐介)(仙女立月宫傍候介)(生行上)

【品令】行行度桥,桥尽漫俄延。身如梦里,
飘飘御风旋。清辉正显,入来翻不见。只
见楼台隐隐,暗送天香扑面。(看介)“广寒
清虚之府”,呀,这不是月府么? 早约定此
地佳期,怎不见蓬莱别院仙!

(仙女迎介)来的莫非上皇么?(生)正
是。(仙女)玉妃到此久矣,请进相见。

518

tree. I will join her after she has seen the emperor.

MAIDS: Yes, madam.

TOGETHER:

The cassia tree is in flower,
The dew is fresh;
Now is the time in this limpid sphere
For lovers to meet again. (*Exit* Chang'e.)

(*The fairy maids wait by the gate of the moon palace. Enter* Lady Yang *with her attendant.*)

LADY:

Leaving the fairy mountain,
I come to the palace of the moon,
Longing to see the emperor again;
And if this wish is granted,
Our reunion will prove sweeter than any past joys.

MAID: Please enter, Your Ladyship.

LADY (*Entering the gate*): Where is the goddess of the moon?

MAID: Her Ladyship left word for you to wait here, madam. After you have met the emperor, she will join you both. Please sit down. (Lady Yang *sits down, the fairy maids standing beside her. Enter the emperor.*)

EMPEROR:

Walking on and on across the bridge,
At last I reach its end;
As if in a dream, I am soaring on the wind,
There is moonlight all around, but I cannot see the moon,
Only indistinct pavilions,
From which wafts a sweet perfume.

(*He looks ahead.*) The Palace of Boundless Cold. Ah, this is the moon.

We arranged to meet here, but where is my fairy maid
Of the fairy mountain?

MAID (*Greeting him*): Are you Emperor Ming Huang?

EMPEROR: I am.

MAID: Lady Yang is waiting for you. Please come in to meet her.

(生)妃子那里？(旦)上皇那里？(生见旦哭介)我那妃子呵！(旦)我那上皇呵！(对抱哭介)(生)

【豆叶黄】乍相逢执手,痛咽难言。想当日玉折香摧,都只为时衰力软,累伊冤惨,尽咱罪愆。到今日满心惭愧,到今日满心惭愧,诉不出相思万万千千。

(旦)陛下,说那里话来！

【姐姐带五马】【好姐姐】是妾孽深命蹇,遭磨障,累君几不免。梨花玉殒,断魂随杜鹃。【五马江儿水】只为前盟未了,苦忆残缘,惟将旧盟痴抱坚。荷君王不弃,念切思专,碧落黄泉为奴寻遍。

(生)寡人回驾马嵬,将妃子改葬。谁知玉骨全无,只剩香囊一个。后来朝夕思想,特令方士遍觅芳魂。

【玉交枝】才到仙山寻见,与卿卿把衷肠代传。(出钗盒介)钗分一股盒一扇,又提起乞巧盟言。(旦出钗、盒介)妾的钗盒也带在此。(合)同心钿盒今再联,双飞重对钗头

EMPEROR: Where are you, my darling?

LADY: Where is the emperor?

EMPEROR (*Catching sight of her*): Ah, my love!

LADY : My love! (*They caress each other and shed tears.*)

EMPEROR:

> *Meeting her, I clasp her hands and sob,*
> *Hardly able to utter my grief,*
> *As I think of that day when she died;*
> *Because I proved weak in a crisis,*
> *She came to a tragic end;*
> *It was all my fault, and my heart is filled with shame.*
> *Shame fills my heart, and I cannot express all my longing.*

LADY: You mustn't say that.

> *It was my unhappy fate, my heavy sins,*
> *That caused the riot and endangered your life;*
> *And when I had died on the pear tree,*
> *I followed you in spirit to the west.*
> *But our pledge was unfulfilled,*
> *And in longing for your love I was true to our vow.*
> *I am glad that you did not forget me, but still remained*
>   *constant,*
> *And searched through heaven and hell for my spirit.*

EMPEROR: When I returned to Mawei for your reburial and could not find your body, but only the scented pouch, I could not stop longing for you. I sent the necromancer to search high and low for your spirit,

> *And at last he found you in the fairy mountain,*
> *And gave you my message.*

(*He takes out the hairpin and the jewel box.*)

> *Here is one half of the hairpin,*
> *One half of the box;*
> *And he mentioned the vow we made that night.*

LADY (*Taking out the two other halves*): I have kept my halves too.

燕。漫回思不胜黯然，再相看不禁泪涟。

（旦）幸荷天孙鉴怜，许令断缘重续。今夕之会，诚非偶然也。

【五供养】仙家美眷，比翼连枝，好合依然。天将离恨补，海把怨愁填，（生合）谢苍苍可怜，泼情肠翻新重建。添注个鸳鸯牒，紫霄边，千秋万古证奇缘。

（仙女）月主娘娘来也。（老旦上）"白榆历历月中影，丹桂飘飘云外香。"（生见介）月姐拜揖。（老旦）上皇稽首。（旦见介）娘娘稽首。（老旦）玉妃少礼，请坐了。（各坐介）（老旦）上皇，玉妃，恭喜仙果重成，情缘永证。往事休提了。

【江儿水】只怕无情种，何愁有断缘。你两人呵，把别离生死同磨炼，打破情关开真面，前因后果随缘现。觉会合寻常犹浅，偏您相逢，在这团圆宫殿。

（仙女）玉旨降。（贴捧玉旨上）"织成天

TOGETHER:

> *Now the box is complete again,*
> *The divided hairpin is whole;*
> *But past memories wring our hearts,*
> *And we gaze at each other through tears.*

LADY: How fortunate it was for us that the Weaving Maids took pity on us and brought us together again.

> *This meeting tonight exceeds my wildest hopes;*
> *Now, as two lovers among the immortals,*
> *We have come together again.*
> *The broken heaven has been repaired,*
> *The unfathomable sea has been filled.*
> *We thank the gods*

TOGETHER:

> *For taking pity on us and restoring our love;*
> *As lovers we are enrolled in the purple heavens,*
> *And our strange romance will outlast eternity.*

MAID: The mistress of the moon is here.

(*Enter* Chang'e, *goddess of the moon.*)

CHANG'E:

> *The white elm in the moon has cast its shadow;*
> *The cassia wafts its fragrance to the clouds.*

EMPEROR (*Greeting her*): Good evening, my lady.

CHANG'E: Good evening, emperor.

LADY (*Greeting her*): Good evening, my lady.

CHANG'E: Good evening, madam. Please be seated. (*They sit down.*) I congratulate you both on attaining godhead, so that you can love for ever. But say no more of the past.

> *All we need fear is the lack of love,*
> *For if there is love there can be no separation*
> *You two have been tempered by separation and death,*
> *Breaking all that fetters love to win true freedom.*
> *There is cause and effect in all in heaven and earth;*
> *And that is why you meet tonight in our orb.*

MAID: An edit from the Heavenly Emperor!

上千丝巧，绾就人间百世缘。"(生、旦跪介)
(贴)"玉帝勅谕唐皇李隆基、贵妃杨玉环：
咨尔二人，本系元始孔升真人、蓬莱仙子。
偶因小谴，暂住人间。今谪限已满，准天孙
所奏，鉴尔情深，命居忉利天宫，永为夫妇。
如敕奉行。"(生、旦拜介)愿上帝圣寿无疆。
(起介)(贴相见，坐介)(贴)上皇，太真，你两
下心坚，情缘双证。如今已成天上夫妻，不
比人世了。

【三月海棠】忉利天，看红尘碧海须臾变。
永成双作对，总没牵缠。游衍，抹月批风随
过遣，痴云腻雨无留恋。收拾钗和盒旧情
缘，生生世世消前愿。

　　(老旦)群真既集，桂宴宜张。聊奉一
觞，为上皇、玉妃称贺。看酒过来。(仙女
捧酒上)酒到。(老旦送酒介)

【川发棹】清虚殿，集群真，列绮筵。桂花中

(*Enter the* Weaving Maid *holding the* Heavenly Emperor's edict.*)

WEAVING MAID:

> *I weave a web in the sky*
> *To join mortal lovers together.*

(*The emperor and* Lady Yang *kneel.*)

This is His August Majesty's decree: Emperor Ming Huang and Lady Yang Yuhuan were formerly angels in heaven; but owing to certain faults they were sent to live awhile on earth. Now the time for their banishment is over, and since they love each other dearly we agree to the Weaving Maid's request; let them remain as lovers in Tridiva, the highest heaven.

EMPEROR and LADY YANG (*Bowing*): Long live the Heavenly Emperor! (*They rise.*)

(*The goddess of the moon congratulates them, and they all sit down.*)

WEAVING MAID: Emperor Ming Huang and Lady Yang, because you remained faithful each other you have now become lovers in heaven.

> *You will see how the dusty earth and azure seas*
> *Change in the twinkling of an eye;*
> *But you will remain for ever without a care.*
> *You can freely roam with the wind beneath the moon,*
> *For you have cast aside all earthly passions;*
> *You need think no more of the past,*
> *Of the hairpin and the jewel box;*
> *You shall have your hearts' desire—*
> *Never again to be parted.*

CHANG'E: As we are all here, let the feast begin. Bring me wine, and I shall toast the emperor and Lady Yang.

(*A fairy maid brings wine.*)

MAID: Here is the wine, madam.

CHANG'E: (*Offering a toast*):

> *Here in the Palace of Clear Limpidity,*
> *Angels assemble and a feast is spread;*

一对神仙,桂花中一对神仙,占风流千秋万年。(合)会良宵,人并圆;照良宵,月也圆。

【前腔】【换头】(贴向旦介)羡你死抱痴情犹太坚,(向生介)笑你生守前盟几变迁。总空花幻影当前,总空花幻影当前,扫凡尘一齐上天。(合)会良宵,人并圆;照良宵,月也圆。

【前腔】【换头】(生、旦)敬谢嫦娥把衷曲怜;敬谢天孙把长恨填。历愁城苦海无边,历愁城苦海无边,猛回头痴情笑捐。(合)会良宵,人并圆;照良宵,月也圆。

【尾声】死生仙鬼都经遍,直作天宫并蒂莲,才证却长生殿里盟言。

(贴)今夕之会,原为玉妃新谱"霓裳"。天女每那里?(众天女各执乐器上)"夜月歌

Among the cassia flowers is a fairy couple
Whose romance will last for ever.

TOGETHER:

Here on this wonderful night,
The lovers are reunited,
And the moon shines full upon them.

WEAVING MAID (*To Lady Yang*):

I admire your love and your constancy after death.
(*To the emperor.*)
And you, after faltering, kept your vow in the end.
But all things are like the reflection of flowers in a mirror,
You must shake off earthly dust to ascend to heaven together.

TOGETHER:

Here on this wonderful night,
The lovers are reunited,
And the moon shines full upon them.

EMPEROR and LADY YANG:

We thank the goddess of the moon
For her sympathy with our story;
And we thank the Weaving Maid
For this happy end to our sorrow.
We have passed through cities of woe and seas of grief,
But now we can smile at the past and discard our earthly
    love.

TOGETHER:

Here on this wonderful night,
The lovers are reunited,
And the moon shines full upon them.
They have passed through life and death
And existed as spirit and fairy,
To be united at last in paradise,
Like two lotus flowers on a single stem,
Their former pledge fulfilled.

WEAVING MAID: We arranged the feast this evening in order to
play the new score of Lady Yang's Rainbow Garment Dance.

残鸣凤曲,天风吹落步虚声。"天女每稽首。
(贴)把"霓裳羽衣"之曲,歌舞一番。(众舞
介)

【高平调】【羽衣第三叠】【锦缠道】桂轮芳,
按新声,分排舞行。仙珮互趋跄,趁天风,
惟闻遥送叮当。【玉芙蓉】宛如龙起游千
状,翩若鸾回色五章。霞裙荡,对琼丝袖
张。【四块玉】撒团团翠云,堆一溜秋光。
【锦渔灯】袅亭亭现猴岭笙边鹤氅,艳晶晶
会瑶池筵畔虹幢,香馥馥蕊殿群姝散玉芳。
【锦上花】呈独立,鹄步昂;偷低度,凤影藏。
敛衣调扇恰相当,【一撮棹】一字一回翔。
【普天乐】伴洛妃,凌波样;动巫娥,行云想。
音和态,宛转悠扬。【舞霓裳】珊珊步蹴高
霞唱,更泠泠节奏应宫商。【千秋岁】映红
蕊,含风放;逐银汉,流云漾。不似人间赏,
要铺莲慢踏,比燕轻飏。【麻婆子】步虚、步
虚瑶台上,飞琼引兴狂。弄玉、弄玉秦台
上,吹箫也自忙。凡情、仙意两参详。【滚
绣球】把钧天换腔,巧翻成余弄儿盘旋未

Angels!

(*Enter angels carrying musical instruments.*)

    Now from the moon come strains of heavenly music;
    A high wind bears to earth the sound of dancing.

ANGELS: We angels salute you.

WEAVING MAID: Now start the Rainbow Garment Dance.

(*The dance begins.*)

ALL:

    In the bright moon, beside the fragrant cassia,
    We dance together to this new melody;
    Our tinkling pendants echo in the breeze,
    Our sinuous motions vie with coiling dragons,
    Our varied hues seem phoenixes in flight.
    Rosy skirts swirl clouds,
    Sleeves of white silk flutter,
    Then round and round like emerald clouds in autumn,
    Stately as storks erect on mountain summits,
    Bright as the rainbow in the western sky,
    Sweet as the blossoms scented damsels scatter;
    Poising like swans or drawing back like phoenixes,
    Our fans and garments move in unison,
    Whirling at every note;
    Like the nymph that glided across the waves,
    Or the mountain goddess that wandered in the clouds,
    We suit our gestures to the melody;
    Then the angels step it daintily and sing.
    Beating the rhythm on their instruments.
    Like crimson blossoms in the breeze
    Or floating clouds beside the Milky Way,
    No earthly dancing can compare with this:
    We dance on in the void before the Heavenly Palace,
    Enraptured like the fairy maid of old,
    Or the fair princess who played the flute with her lover,
    Combining heavenly bliss with earthly joy.
    To add fresh charms to this celestial music,

央。【红绣鞋】银蟾亮,玉漏长,千秋一曲舞
霓裳。

（贴）妙哉此曲,真个擅绝千秋也。就
借此乐,送孔升真人同玉妃,到忉利天宫
去。（老旦）天女每,奏乐引道。（天女鼓乐引
生、旦介）

【黄钟过曲】【永团圆】神仙本是多情种,蓬
山远,有情通。情根历劫无生死,看到底终
相共。尘缘倥偬,忉利有天情更永。不比
凡间梦,悲欢和哄,恩与爱总成空。跳出痴
迷洞,割断相想鞚;金枷脱,玉锁松。笑骑
双飞凤,潇洒到天宫。

【尾声】旧霓裳,新翻弄。唱与知音心自懂,
要使情留万古无穷。

谁令醉舞拂宾筵, 张说
上界群仙待谪仙。 方干
一曲霓裳听不尽, 吴融
香风引到大罗天。 韦绚
看修水殿号长生, 王建
天路悠悠接上清。 曹唐
从此玉皇须破例, 司空图
神仙有分不关情。 李商隐

Now round and round they whirl in the final movement;
The silvery moon is bright,
The jade clepsydra echoes deep,
And the Rainbow Garment Dance is surely immortal.

WEAVING MAID: Wonderful! This is really superb! Let the emperor and Lady Yang be escorted to the highest heaven with this music.

CHANG'E: Play on, angels, as you escort them. (*The angels play as they lead the emperor and* Lady Yang *forward.*)

True lovers are immortal;
Thus, though the fairy mountain is far away,
True love can reach it.
Love transcends life and death,
And lovers will meet at last;
Though life on earth is brief,
Love reigns eternal in the highest heaven;
There mortal joys and sorrows are no more,
And human love and kindness all seem vain;
For immortals escape from the snares of earthly delusion,
They shatter the yoke of human lust and longing,
And freed from all worldly fetters,
Laughing and riding on two phoenixes,
Soar joyously to heaven.

Epilogue

Here is the story of the Rainbow Dance
Made new, and lovers of music will understand
Its real meaning: true lovers who are constant
Will enjoy their love throughout eternity.